The MasterChef Cookbook

250 of the **best recipes** from the **MasterChef** series

CONTENTS

JOHN TORODE

To eat is to live and to eat well is to live better. This is my mantra and has never been far from my mind over the last few years whilst on the incredible MasterChef journey. To be involved in MasterChef and all its offshoots has been an extraordinary experience for me personally as a judge, and I think I can say it has been pretty amazing for all the contestants and everyone who works so hard behind the scenes putting the show together. The name MasterChef seems to evoke all sorts of memories through a generation. We had big boots to fill and I'm not sure any of us knew how it would pan out but we all knew we wanted to discover culinary greatness and we really have, time and time again.

I have always believed that good cooks are born – nature over nurture – that they have something special, something natural, a natural ability to feel their way. It is as though there is something innate that allows them to follow instinct rather than instruction, the ability to smell, taste, imagine, to listen to the way food cooks, to see a finished dish in their mind's eye and more importantly taste a combination of ingredients or a plate of food without it being cooked. A great cook will wander through a shop or a market and be able to assemble, taste and finish a dish in their head even by just seeing a few ingredients. These were the cooks that I hoped we could discover through MasterChef and I am extremely proud to say that we have, and many of them! What I don't think I expected however, was that we would discover so much raw potential that has literally blossomed on the screen in front of all our eyes.

This book is an incredible collection of dishes, inspirations, combinations and recipes that have been assembled over the past few years both in and out of the MasterChef kitchen. As we all know, cooking does not get tougher than in that kitchen (!) and whilst I have not sampled all of the dishes (I do not judge MasterChef: The Professionals) my great mate Gregg has and between us we know that each and every one of these in the book have made it for a reason. Simply that regardless of how good the finished dish might look every single one of the recipes makes bloody delicious food and that's what it's all about.

The winners of MasterChef all have the same thing in common, they can truly cook, to the point where amateurs become professionals and celebrities become truly great cooks who could make a career out of it if they so wish. Having said that, each of the winners has had their own little "thing" that for me makes them unique. Thomasina Miers loved the food of Mexico and when someone falls in love with food from a country, and indeed that country, it shines through. She now has restaurants, not one but many and is forging ahead following her passion. Peter Bayless, a classic French cook, knew that provincial and unpretentious was his style and it made him a winner. Steven Wallis, a man who could take few ingredients and make them sing and dance in my mouth and take the ordinary to the sublime. James Nathan, the man who loves fish and has a palate that allows his food to be seasoned and cooked to the point of danger, what he can do with a fish is truly fabulous, he has a real lightness of touch. Mat Follas, our forager, taking inspiration from the land and the sea and the seasons and bringing it all together on a plate where you can even taste the wind.

"To be a great cook you need to find your cooking heart and you need to practise, practise, practise."

The celebrities – well we have had them all from big personalities to international sportsmen. Matt Dawson was so competitive, a true sportsman and a true winner. Nadia Sawalha, a great family cook who knew what she knew but didn't know how – a true natural. Liz McClarnon, a gifted cook who could simply eat something and just recreate it, what a gift. And finally Jayne Middlemiss, someone who understands exactly what people want to eat and executes it just so, a real perfectionist. As with everything in life it takes all types and we all like something different, but how exciting to find such a wide range of talent.

It wouldn't be half as much fun without my old mate Gregg but that doesn't mean we always see eye to eye. I like to think it's healthy! As with all relationships, without the odd disagreement, the relationship cannot mature and grow nor the understanding of each other develop. There are few people in the world who have the understanding of food that Gregg does because few people have the love for food that Gregg does, just writing those words makes me chuckle, yes he loves to eat. We all know that and can I say about those puddings – he truly is the pudding man – BUT he also really gets food, cares about how produce is grown, how food is sourced, where it comes from, what is in season and what is not. Fury is not a word that I associate with Gregg but cook asparagus out of season and beware his wrath, cook thoughtfully and appropriately and beware his kisses and cuddles!

This is a great book but to be a great cook you need to find your cooking heart and you need to practise, practise, practise. Don't just cook a recipe and flick to the next page; stick with it and cook the same recipe over and over, add your own personality to the dish. I have never understood why if a concert pianist would never expect to play a new piece of music perfectly first time they play that we as cooks, be it amateurs or professionals, feel that the first time we cook a recipe that it should be perfect. Food is a variable and needs to be understood, maybe a little like the human race, one day it's your friend and the next day it can annoy you, but that is good, emotion and food go hand in hand, as does this book and a good cook in the making.

Be warned, whoever reads this book it could change YOUR life!

GREGG WALLACE

The question I am most frequently asked is: "What's the worst dish you've ever tried?" It's strange that people want to know my worst dish and not my favourite dish. Because over the last five years I have been lucky enough to eat – I would like to say "taste" but I have to confess "eagerly consumed" is more like it – some truly outstanding, memorable dishes. This book is a celebration of the best dishes from all three MasterChef competitions over the years. A truly mouth-watering collection. The worst dish ever served up? I couldn't say. It's bound to have been something raw. Cooking things is always a good first step. But I can assure you that you won't find it in this book!

It doesn't seem that long ago that I first met Karen Ross, the absolute boss of MasterChef. What a life changing moment that coffee meeting turned out to be. I had no idea then, I don't suppose any of us did quite know, what MasterChef would turn into. It has been one of the most exciting things that I've ever been involved in. Most certainly it's the greatest job I've ever had; I can't think of anyone who's got a better job.

Working with John is a treat. I've known John for almost 20 years, he hasn't changed. He still works stupidly hard and he is every bit as passionate about food as ever. I see more of John than I do my family. We do argue, we do fall out, but we laugh a lot and I wouldn't change a bit of him.

I've know Michel nearly as long as I've known John. Everybody knows what a class act he is; everybody in the industry has the utmost respect for him. Until you get to know the man, away from the chef whites, you don't realise what an absolute gentleman he is. What you don't see is Michel bent double crying with laughter at my attempts at French pronunciation. He claims I can't say "bouillabaisse" without looking like a bullfrog.

I'm very proud of what we've achieved with MasterChef. I believe we have set up the UK's premier cooking competitions and it is an honour to be able to spot and then nurture such amazing talent. We have had so many wonderful and gifted contestants coming to our kitchen. I think it's obvious that the judges want the contestants to succeed nearly as much as the contestants do.

I wasn't brought up with good food; it wasn't until I started my own veg supply company at the age of 24 that I began eating out. I instantly fell in love with the world of restaurants. I had never seen food prepared like that. I had never sampled most of the stuff on the menu. From my first proper gourmet lunch, I was off on a mission. A mission of gastronomic exploration. From that point on I started eating out once a week, then twice a week, and within a year I was dining out five or six times a week. I would make a point of ordering anything on a menu I hadn't yet tried. Sometimes after a particularly good lunch I flirt with the idea of abandoning myself completely to good food and wine. A life of gluttony! As I get older I've had to tone it down a bit, but I still eat out at least three times a week. This love of dining has never left me and I hope it never will.

We have a MasterChef for the professionals now and I love it every bit as much as the other two competitions. But remember, all the past winners from the other competitions were complete amateurs, just like you. They loved to

"Great things can be achieved by people cooking in their kitchens at home, if they dare to dream."

cook, they knew they had talent and they were keen to compare their skills with others, under pressure in the MasterChef kitchen. And all professionals were once amateurs, for that matter. Anyone with talent in the kitchen can learn to cook like a professional. Great things can be achieved by people cooking in their kitchens at home, if they dare to dream.

If you are thinking of entering MasterChef please do. It is a fantastic experience and for a very talented handful it is a life changing experience. The events and venues our finalists get to work in are incredible. Every finalist comes out of the competition completely inspired, and many go on to have very successful careers in the industry.

Before entering MasterChef be prepared, make sure you put plenty of kitchen time in. The invention test, the first test, is probably the hardest. It's the first time you will meet the judges, and with mystery ingredients you have no time to practise. The best cooks are the ones that cook all the time. These cooks have a large repertoire: ingredients don't faze them because their knowledge of dishes is so great, they can easily adapt whatever is in front of them into something tasty. Those contestants who enter MasterChef with only three or four well practised dishes up their sleeve are quickly found out. You can make it on MasterChef but you've got to put the time in first.

And even if you don't want to make it on MasterChef, time spent in your own kitchen at home trying out these recipes, let me tell you, that time will never ever be wasted. Once you start using this book, not only will you be cooking up some of the best dishes created in this country over the past five years, you will be teaching yourself new skills, skills that perhaps you may pass on to somebody else who will love you for it.

Good food – that's what we love on MasterChef.

Gregg

MICHEL ROUX JR

I often get asked, "What does it take to become a chef?" Well for me, I suppose the fact that I was almost born in a kitchen and into a family that takes any food matters rather seriously has had a great influence on me and on my career path.

I do firmly believe in natural talent when it comes to cooking, but even that has to be nurtured and certain skills and techniques must be mastered to become a true professional chef.

Passion, dedication, and a steely determination to succeed undoubtedly play a part, but a true chef also needs to possess a deep respect for nature and its larder. A chef must be attuned to the changing seasons and be able to make the humblest of ingredients into magical, ethereal food.

The Roux family has always helped and encouraged budding young chefs to achieve their full potential, and I see my involvement in MasterChef: The Professionals as another way to achieve this. The programme showcases all the necessary attributes needed to become a top chef and really puts the contestants through tough, realistic challenges for the judges to see if they have what it takes to make it as a top professional.

The programme does throw up a few surprises, good and bad, but that is life. Disasters happen and crestfallen chefs react differently. If they cannot take criticism then how will they react to a bad review or a customer sending his food back! This is where we see the true colours and temperament of the chef and find out if they are a prima donna or prepared to learn and go forward.

One thing that I love about being a chef is that, even at my age, I am still learning new tricks and tastes. A new method of cooking, another taste combination or way to present a dish, these are the things that excite me and keep my passion ignited.

The level of homegrown British chefs is now up there with the best, to the point where there are now very few French chefs in the top Michelin-starred restaurants in Britain. And in my experience, I see more of what is required to become a great chef in young British chefs, than in their French counterparts. This, I think, reflects a shift in British food culture that has also seen a mini revolution in the kitchen at home. People are reconnecting with food, with the pleasures of cooking a meal from scratch using fresh, seasonal ingredients. And if MasterChef has demonstrated anything over the years, it is that anyone with a passion for cooking can create truly great food, no matter what their day job might be.

If you do want to make cooking into your day job, one thing is for certain: becoming a chef is far from easy, it's a labour of love, hard and arduous, but it has to be one of the most fulfilling and rewarding of professions.

Michel

> "The level of homegrown British chefs is now up there with the best."

MONICA GALETTI

I was born on the Pacific Islands of Western Samoa, raised in New Zealand from the age of seven, with my sister and four brothers. Naturally with such a large family, and blessed with a Samoan appetite, food was always an issue for us! Being the eldest of the girls I had to learn to cook from a very young age as this is the norm in our culture. My siblings still taunt me with stories of how, at the age of 10, I used to serve them blackened pancakes and burnt boiled spuds.

After college, I went on to study for a Hospitality Management diploma. It was compulsory in the course to work in the kitchen as well. When I walked into that kitchen for the first time I knew I had found my calling. I remember watching with awe as the chef spun sugar and piped chocolate decorations. I wanted to be able to do that! From the beginning it was the creative and artistic side that attracted me to cooking, it was the magic.

Working for Michel at Le Gavroche has been the hardest training of my life but it has also been the most rewarding. His kitchen is a fountain of knowledge and even to this day I am still learning. To cook at the highest level means showing the utmost commitment to your chosen craft; having the dedication and self-sacrifice to follow your passion for food at the expense of almost everything else in your life. Being a woman in the kitchen means having all of the above plus the physical stamina to keep up with the boys, to be as good if not better!

MasterChef has been a fantastic experience and I've enjoyed every minute. Playing a part in finding Britain's culinary stars of the future has been a privilege and I wish them all the best for their wonderful careers ahead! It was clear from the beginning who were the really skilled chefs with the greatest potential, and who simply weren't ready to cook for Michel. If there's one piece of advice I would give to all young chefs it's that they need to remember their basic skills, whether it's filleting fish or making classic base sauces. And these skills should be perfected as they gain experience over time, not forgotten.

What's true of a restaurant chef is also true of the home cook. Learn the basics, keep those skills fresh, and you will have the confidence to try ever more adventurous dishes and create some magic of your own in the kitchen.

For me, cooking is all about expressing my creativity but I think it's also good to remember that eating a meal is about getting together with people. My homeland has never been famed for any great contributions to the culinary world. What it does have is a tradition of family gatherings based around great meals, usually a Sunday Feast. Sunday lunches are all about family, and Samoan families are not just big, they are massive: you'll find aunties, uncles, cousins, friends and even the odd neighbour all getting together over a meal. What I remember most is great island food and lots of laughter – and no one minding much if you blackened the pancakes!

Monica

> "If there's one piece of advice I would give to all young chefs it's that they need to remember their basic skills."

STARTERS
VEGETABLES & FISH
POULTRY
MEAT
GAME
DESSERTS

FRESH PEA SOUP WITH WHITE TRUFFLE OIL AND PARMESAN CRISPS

Jonny Stevenson single father of two, now head chef and 2008 finalist

PREPARATION TIME
15 minutes

COOKING TIME
20 minutes

SERVES 4

2 tbsp sea salt
2 tbsp sugar
1.8kg (4lb) freshly shelled garden
  peas, kept chilled (see MasterTip, left)
salt and white pepper
8 rounded tsp freshly grated
  Parmesan cheese
4 tsp white truffle oil (see MasterTip, p.22)

MASTER TIP
FRESH PEAS

Peas begin to lose their sweetness as soon as they are picked, which is why it is so important to buy the freshest you can find, still in their shells. Keeping them chilled helps to retain their sweetness. Bringing the water back to the boil as quickly as possible after dropping them into the pan allows you to time the cooking perfectly. If fresh peas are not in season, use frozen peas.

1 Bring 1 litre (1¾ pints) water to the boil in a large saucepan and add the salt and sugar. When the water is at a rapid boil, add the chilled peas. Cover immediately – it is important that you raise the water temperature as quickly as possible. Cook the peas until tender, about 6–9 minutes.

2 Drain the peas, reserving the cooking water. Place the cooked peas in a blender or food processor and pulse for 1–2 minutes, adding a little of the cooking water.

3 Pass the pea purée through a sieve, discarding the solids and remembering to scrape the bottom of the sieve. Adjust the consistency by adding enough cooking water to the sieved pea purée to give a smooth, silky soup. Season with salt and pepper.

4 Preheat the oven to 180°C (350°F/Gas 4). To make the crisps, put the 8 rounded tsp of grated Parmesan cheese onto a baking sheet lined with baking parchment. Flatten them out into rounds and bake for about 5–10 minutes. Remove them from the oven then, while they are still warm, lift them with a palette knife and drape them over a rolling pin so that they set in a rounded shape.

5 If necessary, reheat the soup in a pan. Add the truffle oil. Ladle the soup into 4 white cups or bowls and gently place the Parmesan crisps alongside.

JOHN TORODE "The truffle is heady and slightly sexy, the peas are sweet, and the Parmesan is crisp and salty. It's very clever – a great pea soup."

POTATO SOUP WITH PARSLEY PESTO

Julia Paterson client service advisor and 2007 quarter-finalist

PREPARATION TIME
15 minutes

COOKING TIME
30 minutes

SERVES 4

½ tbsp olive oil
2 rashers smoked back bacon, chopped
225g (8oz) onions, chopped
225g (8oz) floury potatoes such
  as Maris Piper or King Edwards
  (see MasterTip, p.197)
300ml (10fl oz) chicken stock
  (see MasterTip, p.21)
300ml (10fl oz) milk
25g (scant 1oz) conchigliette pasta

FOR THE PESTO
75g (2½oz) flat-leaf parsley
2 garlic cloves

60g (2oz) pine nuts
60g (2oz) Parmesan cheese,
  freshly grated
white pepper
2 tbsp olive oil

TO SERVE
300ml (10fl oz) double cream
chopped flat-leaf parsley
Parmesan cheese shavings

1 Heat the oil in a large saucepan. Sauté the bacon for about 5 minutes, stirring occasionally, until starting to brown. Add the onion and cook for a further 5 minutes until softened and translucent.

2 Meanwhile, peel and dice the potatoes. Add to the pan with the stock and milk and simmer for 8 minutes. Add the pasta and simmer for a further 10 minutes until soft.

3 Put all the pesto ingredients into a blender or food processor and blitz until a smooth consistency is reached.

4 To serve, add the cream to the soup, bring it back to the boil and ladle into bowls. Serve hot with a sprinkling of parsley, a swirl of pesto and a few Parmesan shavings.

SORREL SOUP WITH EGG
inspired by **Marta Perepeczko-Foley** Polish PA and 2007 quarter-finalist

60g (2oz) butter
1 onion, chopped
1 large potato, peeled and diced
300g (10oz) sorrel (see MasterTip, right)
1 litre (1¾ pints) chicken stock (see
  MasterTip, p.21)
salt and freshly ground black pepper
4 tbsp double cream
2 tbsp white wine vinegar
4 eggs

PREPARATION TIME
20 minutes

COOKING TIME
25 minutes

SERVES 4

1 Melt the butter in a saucepan and gently fry the onion for about 10 minutes until softened but not browned. Add the potato and half of the sorrel leaves to the pan and stir well, then cook for a further 2–3 minutes, covered.

2 Pour in the chicken stock and bring to the boil, then simmer for about 10–15 minutes or until the potato is tender. Remove from the heat, stir in the remaining sorrel leaves and process until smooth using a hand blender. Season well with salt and pepper and stir in 3 tbsp of the cream. Cook over a gentle heat for about 2 minutes, until steaming but not bubbling – do not allow to boil or the bright green colour will be lost.

3 In a separate pan, bring some water to the boil and add the vinegar. Crack each egg into a cup. Swirl the water round, then carefully tip each egg into the water and poach for 2–3 minutes. Remove with a slotted spoon to drain on kitchen paper.

4 Serve the soup in warmed bowls. Place a poached egg in the centre of each and garnish with the remaining drizzle of cream.

MASTER TIP
SORREL

It can sometimes be hard to find sorrel in the shops, but it is very easy to grow in a pot or garden bed. The young tender leaves, which have a less acidic tang than older ones, are an excellent addition to salads. Older sorrel makes fabulous soups and sauces, the latter being a classic accompaniment to fish, especially salmon. If sorrel is unavailable, Swiss chard and spinach are the best substitutes, adding a squeeze of lemon for that distinctive sorrel tang.

DORSET APPLE SOUP WITH WALNUT SCONES
Natasha Shergold IT manager and 2007 quarter-finalist

PREPARATION TIME
30 minutes

COOKING TIME
1 hour

SERVES 4

25g (scant 1oz) unsalted butter
500g (1lb 2oz) onions, roughly chopped
1 large Bramley apple, peeled, cored,
   roughly chopped and tossed in cider
   to prevent discoloration
250ml (8fl oz) medium-dry Dorset cider
2 tsp cider vinegar
750ml (1¼ pints) chicken stock (see
   MasterTip, opposite)
150g (5½oz) potato, peeled and diced
pinch of dried thyme
½ bay leaf
salt and freshly ground black pepper

FOR THE WALNUT SCONES
175g (6oz) self-raising flour, plus
   extra for dusting
pinch of salt
½ tsp baking powder
45g (1½oz) cold salted butter, diced
50g (1¾oz) walnuts, roughly chopped
75g (2½oz) natural full-fat yogurt at
   room temperature
2 tbsp whole milk

TO SERVE
½ red onion, thinly sliced
sprinkling of light soft brown sugar
20g (¾oz) Dorset Blue Vinney cheese

1 Melt 15g (½oz) of the butter in a large, heavy saucepan. Add the onions and sauté gently for about 10 minutes until lightly browned, stirring occasionally.

2 Meanwhile, make the scones. Preheat the oven to 220°C (425°F/Gas 7) and place a baking sheet inside to warm. Put the flour, salt and baking powder into a bowl and mix. Add the butter and rub in until the mixture resembles breadcrumbs. Add the chopped walnuts. Make a well in the middle and add the yogurt and milk. Quickly work in the liquid with a table knife until blended.

3 Knead the mixture on a floured surface a couple of times to ensure a fairly smooth dough. Using the palm of your hand, press it out until it is 2cm (¾in) thick. Use a 6cm (2½in) pastry cutter dipped in flour to cut 4 rounds. Dust the scones with flour and place on the baking sheet. Put in the oven to bake for 12 minutes until risen and golden.

4 Add the apple, cider, and vinegar to the onions in the pan, bring to the boil then reduce the heat and simmer until the cider is reduced by half (approximately 10 minutes). Add the stock, potato, thyme, and bay leaf to the pan. Simmer for 10–15 minutes until the potato is tender, stirring occasionally. Remove the bay leaf and purée the soup with a hand blender or in a food processor, then season to taste.

5 To serve, heat the remaining butter in a frying pan and gently fry the red onion until it is softened and starting to caramelize. Sprinkle with the brown sugar and cook for 2 minutes. Ladle the soup into warm bowls, topping with a crumbling of cheese and some caramelized onion slices. Serve with the walnut scones on the side.

1 Roast the bones in the oven for 20 minutes at 200°C (400°F/Gas 6).

2 Pour the fat from the pan, add 500ml (16fl oz) water and bring to the boil.

3 Pour over the bones in a large pan and add 2 litres (3½ pints) water.

4 Skim off foam, add the vegetables and simmer for 3 hours, uncovered.

5 Strain into a bowl; you will find an extra ladleful at the bottom of the pan.

6 When the stock has cooled, skim off any fat from the surface.

MASTER TIP

MAKING FRESH CHICKEN STOCK

Fresh stock is key to a great soup. Ask your butcher for chicken bones or make your stock from roast dinner leftovers. Roasting the chicken bones intensifies the colour and flavour of a stock; if you prefer a lighter stock, omit the roasting process. You will also need 1 onion, quartered, 1 leek and 1 carrot, both roughly chopped. You may need to top up the water to keep the ingredients covered during cooking. The stock can be frozen – a good trick is to reduce it, freeze it in an ice-cube tray, then transfer the cubes to a freezer bag.

JERUSALEM ARTICHOKE SOUP

Patrick Zahara property manager and 2006 quarter-finalist

PREPARATION TIME
30 minutes

COOKING TIME
25 minutes

SERVES 4

400g (14oz) Jerusalem artichokes
85g (3oz) lightly salted butter
1 onion, finely chopped
sea salt and white pepper
600ml (1 pint) full cream milk,
  plus extra if needed
3 tbsp double cream

1 tbsp white truffle oil
50g (1¾oz) wild mushrooms,
  such as ceps, chanterelles or
  boletus, or 15g (½oz) dried porcini,
  rehydrated (see MasterTip, p.54)

MASTER TIP

TRUFFLE OIL

Truffle oil is a great product for home chefs, and increasingly popular with restaurant chefs, too, as it imparts some of the flavour and aroma of truffles to a dish at a fraction of the price of truffles themselves. It contains some of the same chemicals as real truffles, but synthetically produced.

1 Peel the Jerusalem artichokes and put them in a bowl of water acidulated with lemon juice or white wine vinegar to prevent them from discolouring.

2 Melt 60g (2oz) of the butter in a large pan and slowly fry the onion with a pinch of salt for about 10 minutes, stirring occasionally, until translucent but not browned.

3 Drain the artichokes from the acidulated water and add them to the pan. Add the milk and simmer the artichokes for 25 minutes or until they are completely soft and collapse when crushed with a spoon. By the end of the simmering stage the milk will have reduced and may have become slightly curdy, but because the soup is to be blended this will not make any difference to the texture.

4 Meanwhile, fry the mushrooms in the remaining butter, seasoning them with salt and pepper.

5 Process the soup, using a hand blender or food processor, until the texture is smooth and, if you wish, pass it through a fine sieve to give it an extra-luxurious, velvety finish. Add the cream, the truffle oil and, if necessary, extra milk to bring the soup to the consistency that you require. Season to taste and whizz with a hand blender for 5 minutes so that it becomes frothy. Serve immediately in warm bowls with some of the mushrooms sprinkled on top, an extra drizzle of truffle oil and some good crusty sourdough bread.

GAZPACHO WITH MEDITERRANEAN SCONES

Peter Gerald personal trainer and 2005 quarter-finalist

4 large sweet red tomatoes, chopped
½ large cucumber, peeled and chopped
1 green pepper, deseeded and chopped
150g (5oz) Spanish onion, chopped
1 long mild red chilli, chopped
1 garlic clove, finely chopped
2 tbsp good-quality white wine vinegar
75g (2½oz) fresh white bread,
  crusts removed
500ml (16fl oz) tomato juice
1 tsp sugar
  salt and freshly ground black pepper

FOR THE SAVOURY SCONES
225g (8oz) self-raising flour,
  plus extra for dusting

1 tsp baking powder
pinch of salt
45g (1½oz) butter
50g (1¾oz) Gruyère cheese, grated
50g (1¾oz) sun-blush tomatoes
  in oil, drained and chopped
1 egg
100ml (3½fl oz) ice-cold milk
butter, to serve

TO GARNISH
4–6 tbsp crushed ice
4 tbsp extra virgin olive oil
8 large basil leaves, shredded
dash of Tabasco sauce (optional)

PREPARATION TIME
25 minutes

COOKING TIME
20 minutes

SERVES 4

1 Purée all the vegetables together in a food processor. Add the vinegar, bread, tomato juice, and sugar. Process again until thick and smooth. Season to taste. Refrigerate until very cold. Pass the soup through a fine sieve, pushing the mixture through with the back of a large spoon and discarding any remaining pulp. Chill again.

2 To make the scones, preheat the oven to 190ºC (375ºF/Gas 5). Sift the flour, baking powder, and salt together into a large bowl. Rub in the butter until the mixture resembles fine breadcrumbs, or blend together in a food processor. Stir in the grated cheese and tomatoes.

3 Whisk the egg and milk together briefly in a separate bowl. Pour about three-quarters of the egg mixture into the flour mixture. Quickly and lightly bind the ingredients together with a knife, adding extra egg mixture if necessary to give a soft, but not sticky, dough.

4 Dust a working surface with flour and tip the dough onto it. Working lightly and quickly, shape into a round measuring about 2.5cm (1in) deep. Cut about 8 rounds using a 5cm (2in) fluted or plain cutter. Brush the tops with a little of the leftover egg mixture.

5 Put the scones onto a baking tray lined with greaseproof paper. Bake in the oven for 15–18 minutes until well risen and golden brown.

6 Taste the gazpacho and adjust the seasoning as necessary. Serve in large bowls with a little crushed ice stirred through, depending on how thick you like gazpacho to be. Garnish with the olive oil and basil. If liked, sprinkle on a couple of drops of Tabasco sauce. Split and butter the scones and serve with the soup while they are still warm.

SPICED SQUASH SOUP WITH PARMESAN CROUTONS

Caroline Brewester banker turned food writer and 2005 finalist

PREPARATION TIME
45 minutes

COOKING TIME
30 minutes

SERVES 4

1 medium butternut squash, peeled, deseeded and cut into slices 1cm (½in) thick
2 tbsp sunflower oil, plus extra for greasing
15g (½oz) salted butter
1 onion, finely chopped
1 medium potato, peeled and diced
1 tsp ground coriander
1 tsp ground cumin

½ fresh red chilli, or more to taste, finely chopped
600ml (1 pint) hot vegetable stock, plus extra if needed
60ml (2fl oz) double cream
salt and freshly ground black pepper

FOR THE PARMESAN CROUTONS
2 thick slices slightly stale white bread, crusts removed
15g (½oz) Parmesan cheese, freshly grated

1 Preheat the oven to 200°C (400°F/Gas 6). Grease a large baking sheet with oil. Brush the squash slices with 1 tbsp of the sunflower oil. Lay the slices on the baking sheet and roast for about 10 minutes, until lightly browned on the bottom. Turn the slices over and roast for a further 10–15 minutes, until soft.

2 While the squash is roasting, melt the butter in a large saucepan over a low heat. Add the onion and potato and cook gently, stirring occasionally, until the onion is translucent and the potato has softened. Add the coriander, cumin and chilli and cook for 2 minutes.

3 Scrape or cut the roasted squash flesh from the skin, cut into chunks and add to the saucepan. Pour in the vegetable stock, adding a little extra if needed to just cover the vegetables. Bring to the boil then simmer for 15 minutes. Cool slightly then whizz with a hand blender until smooth. Return the soup to the saucepan and add the cream plus a little extra stock if the soup is very thick. Season to taste with salt and pepper and reheat the soup gently.

4 Preheat the grill to high. Cut the bread into 1cm (½in) cubes. Put the bread in a bowl, trickle over the remaining 1 tbsp of oil and stir to coat the bread with the oil. Put the bread cubes on a baking sheet and grill for about 1 minute, until golden brown. Turn over and grill for another minute, then sprinkle the Parmesan over the croutons and grill again until golden brown. Serve the soup in bowls with the croutons floating on top.

CURRIED BUTTERNUT SQUASH SOUP

Michelle Peters university researcher and 2009 semi-finalist

15g (½oz) unsalted butter
1 onion, chopped
1cm (½in) piece of fresh root ginger, finely chopped
4 garlic cloves, finely chopped
2 tsp ground coriander
1 tsp ground cumin
2 tsp garam masala

½ tsp hot chilli powder
1 butternut squash, peeled, deseeded and cut into large chunks
500ml (16fl oz) vegetable stock
salt and freshly ground black pepper
200ml (7fl oz) coconut milk
2 tbsp coconut cream
2 tbsp chopped fresh coriander

PREPARATION TIME
15 minutes

COOKING TIME
30 minutes

SERVES 4

1 Melt the butter in a large pan and sauté the onion for about 3 minutes with the ginger and garlic.
2 Add the spices to the onion mixture and fry for 5–7 minutes to develop their flavour.
3 Add the butternut squash to the pan with the stock. Season. Bring to the boil then simmer for about 20 minutes until the squash is tender. Add the coconut milk and stir.
4 Blitz with a hand blender or transfer to a food processor and blend until a smooth consistency is reached.
5 Ladle the soup into 4 bowls. Serve with a dash of coconut cream, fresh coriander and a sprinkle of freshly ground black pepper.

MASTER TIP

COCONUT MILK

Many supermarkets sell coconut milk in cans, but if you cannot obtain it you can make your own by combining equal parts of unsweetened desiccated coconut and boiling water in a blender for 30 seconds. Sieve through cheesecloth, squeezing the liquid out. It will keep in the fridge for 2 days.

GARLIC SOUP WITH SCALLOP TARTARE, CROUTES, AND PANCETTA

Gillian Wylie property developer turned chef and 2007 quarter-finalist

PREPARATION TIME
10 minutes

COOKING TIME
30 minutes

SERVES 4

10 garlic cloves
1 medium potato, peeled and cubed
1 litre (1¾ pints) chicken stock
  (see MasterTip, p.21) or
  vegetable stock
about 4 tbsp double cream
salt and white pepper

FOR THE CROUTES
1 short, skinny baguette
4 slices of pancetta

FOR THE TARTARE
4 scallops, without coral, diced
a few chives, finely snipped
drizzle of extra virgin olive oil

1 In a large pan, cover the garlic cloves with water and bring to the boil; drain and discard the water. Repeat this sequence 3 times to mellow the flavour of the garlic.

2 Add the potato and stock to the garlic and simmer for about 20 minutes until the potato is very soft. Blitz with a hand-held stick blender or transfer to a food processor and blend until smooth. Add a little of the cream to taste – too much will start to dilute the flavour rather than enhance it. Season with salt and pepper.

3 Preheat the grill to its highest setting. Cut 2 thin slices on the diagonal from the baguette. Toast on both sides, then carefully cut each slice through the middle into 2 slices and toast the cut sides.

4 Grill the pancetta on both sides until crispy.

5 To serve, ladle the soup into 4 bowls. Place diced scallop in the centre of each bowl – the heat of the soup will cook it. Lay a toasted croute and a slice of pancetta on top, sprinkle with chives and dress with a few drops of the olive oil.

INDONESIAN NOODLE SOUP
Simon Spindley service manager and 2006 quarter-finalist

1 litre (1¾ pints) clear chicken stock
   (see MasterTip, p.21, but omit the
   roasting stage)
2 tbsp mirin (Japanese rice wine)
2 tbsp nam pla (Thai fish sauce)
1 garlic clove, finely chopped
2 tbsp white wine vinegar
1 small fresh red chilli, deseeded
   and finely diced
grated zest and juice of 1 lime
1 small chicken breast fillet,
   finely diced

2 tbsp white sugar
2 tbsp dark soy sauce
2 tbsp Worcestershire sauce
3 spring onions, finely diced
1 head of pak choi, finely diced
1 red pepper, deseeded and finely diced
30g (1oz) fine dried rice noodles
50g (1¾oz) fine green beans, diced
300g (10oz) chestnut mushrooms, diced
sprigs of coriander

PREPARATION TIME
30 minutes

COOKING TIME
10 minutes

SERVES 4

1 Put the stock, mirin, nam pla, garlic, vinegar, chilli, and lime juice and zest in a large pan. Bring to the boil then turn down the heat and simmer for 10 minutes.

2 Add the chicken and return to the boil, then simmer for 10 minutes. After checking the taste, add the sugar, dark soy sauce, and Worcestershire sauce.

3 Add the spring onions, pak choi, and red pepper to the pan. Add the noodles to the pan with the remaining diced ingredients and cook for 3 minutes before serving. Garnish with coriander leaves and serve with boiled rice as an accompaniment.

MASTER TIP
HANDLING CHILLIES

Chillies can burn your hands as well as your mouth, so wear gloves to handle them or cover your fingers with a little oil to act as a barrier. Never touch the area near your eyes until you have washed your hands as the skin there is very sensitive.

THAI PRAWN SOUP WITH LEMONGRASS

Iwan Thomas Olympic sprinter and 2009 Celebrity finalist

16 large raw tiger prawns, shells on
1 litre (1¾ pints) chicken stock (see MasterTip, p.21)
2 stalks fresh lemongrass, lightly pounded, cut into 2.5cm (1in) lengths
50g (1¾oz) sliced fresh galangal
10 kaffir lime leaves, shredded
500g (1lb 2oz) straw mushrooms, halved or whole

4 tbsp nam pla (Thai fish sauce)
3 tbsp nam prik pao (chilli paste in oil)
4 tbsp lime juice
5 crushed fresh Thai (bird's eye) chillies

TO GARNISH
10g (¼oz) coriander, torn
1 small red pepper, deseeded and cut into fine ribbons

PREPARATION TIME
10 minutes

COOKING TIME
15 minutes

SERVES 4

1 Wash the prawns and shell them without removing the tails.
2 Bring the chicken stock to the boil in a large saucepan. Add the lemongrass, galangal, and lime leaves.
3 Bring back to the boil then add the straw mushrooms, nam pla, nam prik pao, and lime juice. Add the prawns and fresh chillies.
4 As soon as the prawns turn pink (about 2 minutes), serve the soup garnished with the coriander and strips of red pepper.

MASTER TIP

GALANGAL

Fresh galangal resembles root ginger, but is not so commonly found. If it is unavailable use dried or minced galangal, available in bottles or jars from Asian food shops or supermarkets.

JOHN TORODE "This is what good Asian food is all about – sourness, saltiness, and a good amount of chilli to make your lips tingle. There's the wonderful flavour of the prawns and the wonderful, wonderful broth. It's a joy."

EMERALD AND WHITE JADE SOUP AND BARBECUED SPARE RIBS IN HONEY SAUCE

Mark Moraghan actor and 2008 Celebrity finalist

PREPARATION TIME
30 minutes, plus marinating time

COOKING TIME
45 minutes

SERVES 4

FOR THE SPARE RIBS
2 tsp five-spice powder
225g (8oz) hoisin sauce
4–5 tbsp rice wine
500g (1lb 2oz) pork spare ribs,
   fat trimmed off
2 tbsp clear honey
2 tbsp soy sauce

FOR THE SOUP
250g (9oz) firm tofu,
   cut into 1cm (½in) cubes
salt
1 tbsp groundnut oil
225g (8oz) spinach, chopped
   into small pieces
600ml (1 pint) chicken stock
   (see MasterTip, p.21)
1 tsp sesame oil, to garnish

1 Mix the five-spice powder, hoisin sauce, and rice wine together and use to marinate the spare ribs for 1 hour.

2 Preheat the grill to medium-hot and the oven to 230°C (450°F/ Gas 8). Remove the ribs from the marinade and grill for 15 minutes until cooked, turning and basting with the marinade. Transfer to a baking dish and cook in the oven for 30 minutes. Reduce the heat to 200°C (400°F/Gas 6), baste the ribs with the honey and cook for a further 15 minutes.

3 To make the soup, blanch the tofu in boiling salted water for 2–3 minutes. Drain and set aside.

4 Heat the oil in a wok or large pan and stir-fry the spinach for 1 minute. Add ¼ tsp salt, stir for 10–15 seconds, then add the stock and bring to the boil. Add the tofu and 1 tsp salt and mix well. Drizzle with sesame oil. Drizzle the spare ribs with soy sauce and serve with the soup.

MOZZARELLA AND ROASTED VEGETABLES WITH SWEET BASIL DRESSING

Mark Todd ad man and 2005 finalist

1 red Romero pepper, deseeded and
   cut into 2.5cm (1in) strips
1 yellow Romero pepper, deseeded
   and cut into 2.5cm (1in) strips
2 courgettes, sliced
1 small aubergine, cut into 2.5cm
   (1in) cubes
1 red onion, cut into about 12 wedges
3 tbsp olive oil
sea salt and freshly ground
   black pepper
200g (7oz) Puy lentils
450ml (15fl oz) vegetable stock

85g (3oz) rocket leaves
60g (2oz) pitted black olives
1 ball of buffalo mozzarella
60g (2oz) pine nuts, toasted (see
   MasterTip, p.40)

FOR THE DRESSING
2 tbsp lemon juice
1 tsp Dijon mustard
1 tbsp clear honey
½ small garlic clove, crushed
about 20 basil leaves
6 tbsp olive oil

PREPARATION TIME
10 minutes

COOKING TIME
40 minutes

SERVES 4

1   Preheat the oven to 200°C (400°F/Gas 6). Scatter the vegetables in a roasting tin. Drizzle over the oil and season well, giving it all a good mix with your hands to ensure that everything is coated well with the oil. Roast for 35–40 minutes, turning a couple of times during cooking to brown all over.

2   Meanwhile, place the lentils in a saucepan with the stock and bring to the boil. Simmer for 15–20 minutes until the lentils are cooked but still retain some bite, and drain.

3   For the dressing, place the lemon juice, mustard, and honey in a spice grinder or small food processor and pulse to combine. Add the garlic and basil leaves, then gradually add the oil while the motor is running. Season.

4   Combine the roasted vegetables, cooked lentils, rocket leaves, and olives in the roasting tin, tossing everything together to combine. Serve with the mozzarella torn up on top, and scatter over the toasted pine nuts. Finally, drizzle over the sweet basil dressing.

ROAST FIGS WITH GORGONZOLA AND HONEY VINEGAR SAUCE

Alison Reynolds student and 2006 quarter-finalist

PREPARATION TIME
5 minutes

COOKING TIME
5 minutes

SERVES 4

8 ripe figs
salt and freshly ground black pepper
100g (3½oz) Gorgonzola cheese, cut
  into equal-sized cubes
4 tsp red wine vinegar
2 tbsp clear honey
85g (3oz) rocket, to garnish

MASTER TIP
GORGONZOLA CHEESE

Gorgonzola is an Italian blue-veined cheese originating from the eponymous town in Lombardy. This versatile cheese is made from unskimmed cow's and/or goat's milk and is eaten on its own or in creams and sauces. Gorgonzola has a pungent, rich flavour. When buying, try to avoid cheese with a brown appearance. Try to taste before buying and avoid a cheese that is overly bitter and sour.

1 Preheat the grill to hot and grease a baking tray. Place the figs in the baking tray, cut a cross in the top of each, season with salt and pepper and grill for 2 minutes or until warm through.
2 Place a cube of cheese on the top of each fig and grill for a further 2–3 minutes, or until the cheese starts to melt and colour.
3 Meanwhile, make the honey sauce by whisking together the vinegar and honey in a bowl.
4 To serve, place two figs on each plate, drizzle over the sauce and garnish with the rocket.

ROSEWATER BLINIS
WITH CREAMY LEMON SAUCE

Belinda Fife investment banker and 2009 quarter-finalist

PREPARATION TIME
30 minutes

COOKING TIME
12 minutes

SERVES 4

1 egg white
1 tbsp soy milk
2 tsp rosewater
2 tsp icing sugar
pinch of salt
2 tbsp plus 1 tsp rice flour
1 tsp tapioca flour
1 tsp potato flour
2 tsp sesame oil (plus additional
  oil for frying)
¼ tsp baking powder
1 tsp dark red rose petals
pinch of ground nutmeg

FOR THE LEMON SAUCE
60ml (2fl oz) Limoncello liqueur
100g (3½oz) vanilla caster sugar
¼ tsp lemon oil
1 tbsp lemon juice
1 tsp finely grated lemon zest
1 tbsp orange blossom honey
3–4 medium eggs
250ml (8fl oz) vegetable oil

TO GARNISH
25g (scant 1oz) flaked almonds
1 tbsp sesame seeds
1 tbsp linseeds

1 Preheat the oven to 180°C (350°/Gas 4). Spread the almonds and seeds for the garnish onto a baking sheet and bake for 3–5 minutes or until golden. Set aside to cool.

2 To make the blinis, combine all the ingredients in a bowl and whisk until the mixture is very smooth. In a little sesame oil, fry spoonfuls in batches, turning the blinis gently when bubbles appear on the surface (usually after about 30 seconds) and cooking for a further 20–30 seconds

MAKING BLINIS

Blinis have a classic status in Slavic cooking. Originally baked in the oven, they are usually now pan-fried like pancakes. They may be made with almost any variety of flour, buckwheat being the most common in the Russian version.

1 Fold the sifted flours, sugar, salt, and baking powder together with the wet ingredients then whisk until smooth.

2 Cook the blinis in batches, turning them over when bubbles appear on the surface and the edges are firm.

on the other side until lightly golden. Remove to kitchen paper prior to serving.

3   For the lemon sauce, combine the Limoncello, sugar, lemon oil, lemon juice and zest, and honey and heat until bubbling. Set the syrup aside to cool.

4   In a bowl, whisk the eggs and add the vegetable oil gradually until all is incorporated. Whisk in 4 tbsp of the cooled lemon syrup, to taste.

5   To serve, arrange the blinis on a plate. Top with creamy lemon sauce and garnish with almonds and seeds.

Please note: This recipe contains raw eggs so is not suitable for pregnant women or those with a vulnerable immune system.

BAKED ASPARAGUS WRAPPED IN PARMA HAM

Mark Moraghan actor and 2008 Celebrity finalist

16 asparagus spears
25g (scant 1oz) butter, melted
freshly ground black pepper
8 slices Parma ham
3 tbsp olive oil
juice of 1 lemon
green leaves, to serve

PREPARATION TIME
15 minutes

COOKING TIME
10 minutes

SERVES 4

1   Preheat the oven to 200°C (400°F/Gas 6). Prepare the asparagus (see MasterTip, p.221) and coat the spears with a little melted butter and a good grind of black pepper.

2   Halve the slices of Parma ham and use to wrap up each asparagus, rolling on a diagonal. Place on a baking sheet and cook in the oven for 5–6 minutes.

3   Meanwhile, whisk together the oil and lemon juice and season well.

4   Serve the asparagus with a selection of green leaves dressed with the olive oil and lemon dressing.

MASTER TIP

PARMA HAM

Parma ham is a specific type of Italian prosciutto produced in a designated area in the province of Parma. The hind leg of a pig is seasoned with brine and air-dried for many months. Parma ham is carved into paper-thin slices with a creamy white skirt of fat that is a crucial element in its complex sweet, salty, moist, and succulent taste.

SEASONAL SALAD OF BROAD BEANS, COURGETTES, FETA, AND MINT

Helen Gilmour 2007 quarter-finalist

PREPARATION TIME
30 minutes

COOKING TIME
5 minutes

SERVES 4

20g (¾oz) mint leaves
150ml (5fl oz) olive oil
pinch of caster sugar
3 courgettes
sea salt and freshly ground
   black pepper

250g (9oz) shelled broad beans
juice of 1 lemon
100g (3½oz) rocket leaves
100g (3½oz) barrel-aged feta cheese

1 Put half of the mint leaves, 100ml (3½fl oz) of the olive oil, and the sugar in a blender and whizz to mix together. Transfer to a bowl, refrigerate, and leave to infuse.
2 With a wide vegetable peeler, shave the courgettes into strips, place in a colander and sprinkle with sea salt and leave to drain.
3 Cook the broad beans in boiling water for 5 minutes until tender, drain and refresh in iced water.
4 In a small bowl, mix together the lemon juice and remaining olive oil to make a dressing. Season with salt and pepper.
5 Strain the mint oil dressing through a fine sieve, if you wish.
6 To assemble the salad, drain the broad beans and transfer to a salad bowl. Rinse the courgettes, drain them on kitchen paper and add to the broad beans. Then add the rocket leaves and crumble in the feta. Finely slice the remaining mint leaves and stir through the salad and dress with the lemon oil dressing, adding seasoning.
7 Serve drizzled with the mint oil dressing.

SALAD OF MARINATED BEETROOT WITH TRUFFLE HONEY AND GOAT'S CHEESE MASH

Daniel Graham sous chef and 2009 Professionals finalist

PREPARATION TIME
30 minutes

COOKING TIME
10 minutes

SERVES 4

2 large beetroots, thinly sliced widthways
 (you need 16 slices in total)
salt and freshly ground black pepper
60ml (2fl oz) red wine vinegar
1 tsp caster sugar
120ml (4fl oz) rapeseed oil
bunch of thyme, leaves removed
 and chopped

25g (scant 1oz) pine nuts, toasted
 (see MasterTip, p.40)
150g tub soft goat's cheese
4 tbsp double cream
25g (scant 1oz) truffle honey
 (see MasterTip, left) or clear honey
red vein sorrel or rocket,
 to garnish

MASTER TIPS

BEETROOT SLICES AND TRUFFLE HONEY

Small beetroot about the size of a walnut are far sweeter than older beetroot whose texture can be rather woody. For neat slices, top and tail each beetroot, then cut in half widthways. Stamp out the centre with a circular cutter and slice thinly. For a truly professional finish, use a mandolin for this.

Truffle honey is honey that has been infused with the flavour of black or white truffles. It has an irresistible blend of sweet and earthy flavours.

1 Place the slices of beetroot in a pan of salted boiling water for 6–8 minutes or until the beetroot is al dente. Drain thoroughly.
2 For the dressing, place the vinegar and caster sugar into a mixing bowl and mix well. Then slowly whisk in all of the oil (this dressing is a split dressing so don't worry when it does not come together). Add half of the chopped thyme, all the toasted pine nuts, and seasoning and stir to mix.
3 Put the cooked beetroot slices into the dressing when they are still warm and leave to infuse for 10 minutes.
4 For the goat's cheese mash, break down the goat's cheese in a mixing bowl and incorporate the cream, remaining chopped thyme, and salt and pepper, and finish with a little of the truffle honey (or clear honey), to taste.
5 To serve, remove three slices of beetroot from the marinade and place in the centre of each plate and then top with a spoonful of the goat's cheese. Add another slice of beetroot to the goat's cheese and then spoon the dressing over the top and around the plates. Finish with a sprinkle of the red vein sorrel or rocket.

GOAT'S CHEESE FRITTERS
WITH SPINACH AND APPLE SALAD
inspired by **Midge Ure** musician and 2007 Celebrity finalist

FOR THE FRITTERS
300g (10oz) goat's cheese
2 tbsp chopped basil
2 tbsp chopped
  flat-leaf parsley
1 tbsp chopped thyme leaves
sea salt and freshly ground
  black pepper
60g (2oz) plain flour
1 egg, beaten
40g (1½oz) Panko breadcrumbs
  (see MasterTip, right)
vegetable oil for deep frying

FOR THE SALAD
2 tbsp white wine vinegar
1 tsp Dijon mustard
1 tbsp clear honey
6 tbsp walnut oil or olive oil
125g (4½oz) baby spinach leaves
1 eating apple
60g (2oz) walnut halves, toasted
  (see MasterTip, p.40)

PREPARATION TIME
10 minutes

COOKING TIME
10 minutes

SERVES 4

1 For the fritters, take the goat's cheese, chop roughly and place in a bowl along with the herbs and seasoning, and mash together well.
2 Place the flour, egg, and breadcrumbs in three shallow dishes, and take a quarter of the goat's cheese mixture and roll it into a ball in your hands. Flatten slightly, then roll in the flour, dip in the egg and finally cover in the breadcrumbs.
3 Heat about 2.5cm (1in) of the oil in a wok, and fry the fritters in batches of 2, for about 1–2 minutes on each side or until golden brown and crispy.
4 Whisk together the vinegar, mustard, and honey in a small bowl, then gradually add the oil, whisking continuously. Season well.
5 Place the spinach leaves in another bowl. Core the apple and cut into matchsticks, then toss in with the spinach and quickly dress with the vinaigrette to prevent browning.
6 Serve the fritters on the dressed salad, and scatter the toasted walnuts over the top.

MASTER TIP
PANKO BREADCRUMBS

Panko breadcrumbs are used in Japanese cuisine and are made from bread without crusts, so they have a crisp, airy texture. They are increasingly available in supermarkets, but if you can't locate them, then replace with an equal measure of ordinary breadcrumbs.

WATERCRESS, PEAR, AND GOAT'S CHEESE SALAD WITH HONEY AND MUSTARD DRESSING

inspired by **Jayne Middlemiss** presenter and 2009 Celebrity champion

PREPARATION TIME
10 minutes

COOKING TIME
10 minutes

SERVES 4

25g (scant 1oz) butter
2 ripe but firm pears, cored and cut
  into long wedges
2 tbsp clear honey
large pinch of sea salt flakes
4 x 1.5cm (⅝in) thick slices from
  a goat's cheese log
4 handfuls watercress leaves,
  stems trimmed
25g (scant 1oz) pine nuts, toasted
  (see MasterTip, left)

FOR THE DRESSING
1 tsp wholegrain mustard
1 tsp Dijon mustard
1 tbsp white wine vinegar
1 tbsp clear honey
4 tbsp olive oil
salt and freshly ground black pepper

MASTER TIP

TOASTING NUTS

Oven-roasting or dry-frying nuts improves their flavour and texture. Toss frequently to prevent burning. Pine nuts will toast in 4–5 minutes, but larger nuts might require twice this period. They will continue to cook for a few minutes away from the heat. Slicing nuts while they are warm and soft gives you cleaner pieces with fewer crumbs.

1 Melt the butter in a frying pan and add the pear wedges, honey, and sea salt, and fry over a high heat for about 2 minutes until the pears start to caramelize, but are not breaking down. Remove from the pan and set aside, then reduce the heat and fry the goat's cheese in the same pan for 5–6 minutes, until brown and crispy on each side, turning once.

2 To make the dressing, whisk together the mustards, vinegar, and honey, and then gradually add the oil and season to taste.

3 Place the watercress in a large bowl with the caramelized pear wedges, and toss through the dressing. Divide between 4 serving plates and top each with a slice of crispy fried goat's cheese and a scattering of toasted pine nuts.

WARMED GOAT'S CHEESE SALAD WITH WALNUTS AND POMEGRANATE DRESSING

Louise Colley marketing manager and 2007 quarter-finalist

300g (10oz) round goat's cheeses
85g (3oz) walnut pieces, toasted
 (see MasterTip, opposite) and
 slightly crushed
150g (5½oz) rocket leaves
½ tsp salt
1 tsp walnut or olive oil

FOR THE DRESSING
2 tbsp pomegranate molasses
 (see MasterTip, right)
2 tbsp lemon juice
6 tbsp olive oil
1 pomegranate

PREPARATION TIME
5 minutes

COOKING TIME
15 minutes

SERVES 4

1 To make the dressing, whisk together the molasses, lemon juice, and oil. Slice the pomegranate in half and, with a wooden spoon, hit the side of the pomegranate halves. This will release the seeds from the shell more easily. Add the seeds to the dressing, then set to one side until ready to serve.

2 Preheat the grill to low. Cut the goat's cheese rounds into slices, about 2cm (¾in) thick, and transfer to a baking sheet. Top with the toasted walnuts and place under the grill for about 1 minute to warm through, until the cheese starts to soften but still holds its shape.

3 Put the rocket into a large bowl, season with the salt and add the walnut or olive oil to coat the leaves.

4 To assemble, place a handful of rocket in the centre of each plate and place 2 to 3 slices of the goat's cheese on top. Finally, drizzle the pomegranate dressing around the plate.

MASTER TIP
POMEGRANATE MOLASSES

Pomegranate molasses can be difficult to get hold of, so to make your own, mix together 3 tbsp caster sugar with 250ml (8fl oz) pomegranate juice and the juice of 1 lemon.

GLAZED GOAT'S CHEESE AND BEETROOT WITH PEA SHOOTS SALAD

Wendi Peters actress and 2009 Celebrity finalist

3 large beetroots
10 raw baby beets
3 sprigs of thyme, plus 2 tbsp leaves
4 individual goat's cheeses, each
   125g (4½oz)
200ml (7fl oz) olive oil,
   plus 3 tbsp

115g (4oz) caster sugar
2 tsp balsamic vinegar
salt and freshly ground black pepper
150g (5½oz) pea shoots
20g (¾oz) toasted pine nuts (see
   MasterTip, p.40)

PREPARATION TIME
45 minutes

COOKING TIME
30 minutes

SERVES 4

1 Preheat the oven to 200°C (400°F/Gas 6). Bring a saucepan of water to the boil, add the large beetroots, reduce the heat, and simmer for 30 minutes or until tender. Leave to cool, then peel and dice.

2 Wrap the baby beets in a foil envelope with the sprigs of thyme. Place in the oven and bake for 15–20 minutes or until they are tender. Leave to cool, then peel the beets and cut into wedges.

3 Put the goat's cheeses in a bowl with half the thyme leaves and pour over the olive oil. Leave to marinate while you prepare the rest of the ingredients.

4 To make the beetroot purée, melt the sugar in a heavy pan on a moderate heat, then cook for about 5 minutes until the sugar has turned golden brown (see MasterTip, p.314). Add the diced large beetroot and cook for a further 3 minutes, stirring until they are coated with the caramel. Remove from the heat and add the balsamic vinegar. Transfer to a food processor and blend to a smooth consistency.

5 Pour the purée into a muslin-lined colander, set over a bowl and allow the liquid to drain through. Season the liquid to taste and double the volume with olive oil to create a dressing. Also season the purée. Set them both aside.

6 Preheat the grill to hot. Remove the cheeses from the marinade and blot off any excess oil with kitchen paper. Glaze the tops of the cheeses under the grill for 1–2 minutes or until golden brown.

7 Toss the pea shoots in 4 tbsp of the beetroot dressing.

8 To assemble, spread a tablespoon of the beetroot purée on the plate. Add some dressed pea shoots and position a glazed cheese on top. Scatter over the remaining thyme leaves and drizzle around the remainder of the dressing. Add the baby beets and sprinkle with the toasted pine nuts. Serve with soda bread (see MasterTip, right).

MASTER TIP

SODA BREAD

Soda bread is the perfect accompaniment to this salad. To make it, put 400g (14oz) wholemeal flour, 1 tbsp sugar, 1 tbsp bicarbonate of soda, and 1 tsp salt in a large mixing bowl. Add 360ml (12fl oz) buttermilk and mix together with a round bladed knife to form a dough. Knead gently on a floured surface, just enough to smooth the dough, then shape into a round about 23cm (9in) in diameter. Bake for 20 minutes in a preheated oven at 200°C (400°F/Gas 6) until the bread sounds hollow when tapped.

WARM MEDITERRANEAN SALAD WITH BRAISED FENNEL AND PANCETTA CROUTONS

Matt James garden designer and 2007 Celebrity quarter-finalist

PREPARATION TIME
15 minutes

COOKING TIME
15 minutes

SERVES 4

1 radicchio
100g (3½oz) watercress
16 cherry tomatoes, halved
12 black olives, pitted and halved
4 tbsp olive oil
sea salt and freshly ground black pepper

2 bulbs fennel, finely sliced
12 juniper berries, crushed
125g (4½oz) pancetta, cubed
  (see MasterTip)
1 tbsp fennel seeds, toasted
  and crushed

MASTER TIP
PANCETTA

Pancetta comes from the same pork belly cut that gives us streaky bacon, but it is salt-cured and flavoured with nutmeg, fennel seeds, pepper, and garlic, before being air-dried (not smoked) for about 3 months. It can be served in wafer-thin slices or cubed to release its rich flavours in a sauce.

1 Tear the radicchio and watercress leaves into a large salad bowl. Add the cherry tomatoes and olives and then mix the whole lot together with 2 tbsp of the olive oil and a pinch of salt and pepper.
2 Brush or drizzle the remaining olive oil over the fennel slices. Put a non-stick frying pan and a griddle pan on a high heat.
3 When the frying pan is hot, add the juniper berries and, a minute or so later, throw in the pancetta cubes and toss them around until golden. There is no need to add any extra oil; the fat from the pork is more than enough. Transfer to kitchen paper to absorb the excess fat. Discard the juniper berries and leave the pancetta croutons to rest.
4 When the griddle is very hot, add the fennel slices. For a warm but crunchy bite, cook each side for about 3 minutes.
5 To serve, make a bed of salad on each plate, then lay the fennel on top and sprinkle over the pancetta croutons and the fennel seeds.

BAKED GOAT'S CHEESE SALAD
inspired by **David Herbert** restaurateur and 2005 quarter-finalist

PREPARATION TIME
25 minutes, plus marinating time

COOKING TIME
15 minutes

SERVES 4

4 x 1cm (½in) thick slices from
  a goat's cheese log
2 tbsp thyme leaves
1 tbsp chopped rosemary
200ml (7fl oz) extra virgin olive oil
85g (3oz) stale breadcrumbs
sea salt and freshly ground
  black pepper

4 slices sourdough bread
1 tsp sherry vinegar
2½ tbsp walnut oil
250g (9oz) mixed salad leaves, such
  as chicory, curly endive, watercress
1 pear, cored and sliced

1 Marinate the cheese, starting preferably the day before the salad is
to be eaten. Place the slices in a dish just large enough for them to fit
in one layer and scatter over the thyme and rosemary. Pour on the oil,
cover, and chill for anything from 6 hours up to 5 days.
2 Preheat the oven to 200°C (400°F/Gas 6). Remove the cheese from
the oil, reserving it. Season the breadcrumbs and roll the cheese in
them so they are coated all over. Place the crumbed cheese discs on
a non-stick baking sheet and bake in the oven for 12–15 minutes,
turning once, or until golden brown and crispy.
3 Drizzle the slices of sourdough with 2 tbsp of the reserved olive oil
and halfway through cooking, place these on the baking sheet with
the cheese and bake until slightly toasted, turning once.
4 Make the dressing by whisking the sherry vinegar and walnut oil
together with ½ tsp of sea salt and ¼ tsp of pepper. Use it to dress the
salad leaves in a large bowl.
5 To serve, divide the leaves between 4 plates, arrange the pear
slices on top and finish with a baked goat's cheese round and a slice
of the sourdough.

WILD MUSHROOM BRUSCHETTA
Helen Cristofoli PR consultant and 2005 quarter-finalist

8 x 5cm (2in) thick slices from
  a baguette, cut on the diagonal
3 tbsp olive oil
sea salt and freshly ground
  black pepper
1 shallot, thinly sliced

1 garlic clove, crushed
200g (7oz) mixed wild and chestnut
  mushrooms (see MasterTip,
  right), sliced
100ml (3½fl oz) white wine
2 tbsp chopped parsley, to garnish

PREPARATION TIME
10 minutes

COOKING TIME
20 minutes

SERVES 4

1 Preheat the oven to 200°C (400°F/Gas 6). Lightly brush both sides
of the baguette slices with some of the olive oil, sprinkle very lightly
with salt, place on a baking sheet, and bake for 8–10 minutes or until
crisp and lightly browned at the edges.

2 Heat the remaining olive oil in a frying pan and sauté the shallot for
2–3 minutes or until beginning to soften. Add the garlic and
mushrooms, a generous pinch of salt and a good grind of pepper and,
keeping the pan over a high heat, sauté for about 10 minutes until the
mushrooms release their juices and begin to reabsorb them. Continue
to sauté until the mushrooms are golden brown.

3 Add the wine and boil for about 1 minute until the wine is absorbed
into the mushrooms. Check the seasoning.

4 To serve, place 2 bruschetta on each serving plate and top each
with the mushroom mixture. Garnish with the parsley.

MASTER TIP

WILD AND CHESTNUT MUSHROOMS

Chestnut mushrooms,
also known as brown cap
mushrooms, are darker than
button mushrooms and have
a stronger taste and a meatier
flavour. Wild mushrooms have
a stronger taste than the
cultivated variety. Dried wild
mushrooms are a great kitchen
standby that will liven up many a
soup or stew. Dried mushrooms
are also available frozen.

RISOTTO WITH CHANTERELLES AND ROCKET PESTO

Jonny Stevenson single father of two, now head chef and 2008 finalist

PREPARATION TIME
30 minutes

COOKING TIME
50 minutes

SERVES 4

FOR THE MUSHROOM STOCK
200g (7oz) chestnut mushrooms (see MasterTip, p.47), finely chopped
1 carrot, finely chopped
1 celery stick, finely chopped
1 onion, finely chopped
1 leek, finely chopped
1 sprig of thyme
1 dried bay leaf

FOR THE RISOTTO
2 tbsp olive oil
6 banana shallots, finely chopped
300g (10oz) carnaroli rice
120ml (4fl oz) vermouth
60g (2oz) salted butter

60g (2oz) Parmesan cheese, freshly grated
1 tbsp mascarpone cheese
salt and white pepper

FOR THE CHANTERELLES
2–3 tbsp olive oil
2 handfuls small chanterelles
25g (scant 1oz) salted butter

FOR THE ROCKET PESTO
60g (2oz) pine nuts, toasted (see MasterTip, p.40)
1 garlic clove, finely chopped
60g (2oz) Parmesan cheese, freshly grated
100g (3½oz) rocket
150ml (5fl oz) olive oil

1 To make the mushroom stock, place the mushrooms, carrot, celery, onion, leek, thyme, and bay leaf into a large saucepan, cover with 1.5 litres (2¾ pints) cold water and bring to the boil. Boil for about

---

MASTER TIP
MAKING RISOTTO

Risotto, a dish from northern Italy, is simple food at its best. The basic recipe is made by gradually stirring hot stock into rice and softened onions until all the stock has been absorbed and the risotto is creamy with firm, separate rice grains. It is easy to prepare, the secrets being the choice of rice, the quality of the stock, and constant stirring. A basic risotto can be embellished with fish, shellfish, meat, chicken, or vegetables.

1 Choose a heavy saucepan that will be large enough to accommodate the rice and the stock, together with all the other ingredients.

2 Always use risotto rice together with a good, well-flavoured stock – chicken, fish, or vegetable, depending on the type of risotto.

20 minutes, removing the skum every 5 minutes. Strain the stock, reserve the liquid, and keep warm over a low heat. The volume of stock will reduce to about 1.2 litres (2 pints).

2 For the risotto, heat the olive oil in a large saucepan on a low heat, add the shallots and fry gently until translucent. Add the rice and cook, stirring frequently, for about 2 minutes or until the rice grains turn translucent (see also MasterTip, below). Add the vermouth and reduce until evaporated. Then add a ladle of the hot mushroom stock and stir the rice until the stock has been absorbed. Continue ladling in stock until the rice is al dente, which will take about 20 minutes. Beat in the butter and the Parmesan cheese. Finally, fold in the mascarpone cheese and season with salt and white pepper to taste.

3 For the chanterelles, heat a sauté pan over a medium heat and when the pan is hot add the olive oil. Add the chanterelles and fry for 1–2 minutes. Add the butter and fry for another 1–2 minutes or until the mushrooms are softened. Season with salt and white pepper. Stir most of the chanterelles into the creamy risotto, saving some for the garnish.

4 For the rocket pesto, place the pine nuts, garlic, and Parmesan cheese into a food processor and process for 30 seconds. Then add the rocket and process again, while adding the olive oil. Keep pouring in oil until the mixture is smooth but thick. Season with salt and white pepper. Do not process for too long as the friction of the blades will discolour the rocket.

5 To serve, spoon the risotto onto the middle of 4 serving plates, scatter the reserved chanterelles over and around it. Take a tablespoon of pesto and drag it in a straight line alongside the risotto.

3 Keep the stock at a gentle simmer, and the rice at a lively simmer. Stir constantly throughout the cooking process to release the starch in the rice.

4 Constant stirring also gives the risotto its famed creamy texture. Leave the risotto to rest for about 2 minutes before serving.

RICOTTA AND LEMON RAVIOLI
Fiona Marshall teacher and 2006 quarter-finalist

PREPARATION TIME
1 hour

COOKING TIME
5 minutes

SERVES 4

FOR THE PASTA
200g (7oz) "00" pasta flour (see
   MasterTip, p.52)
2 eggs

FOR THE FILLING
150g (5½oz) ricotta cheese
grated zest of 1 lemon
100g (3½oz) Parmesan cheese

50g (1¾oz) Pecorino cheese
½ tbsp chopped thyme
½ tbsp chopped flat-leaf parsley
½ tbsp chopped mint
salt and freshly ground black pepper

FOR THE DRESSING
100g (3½oz) unsalted butter
juice of ½ lemon
1 tbsp chopped sage leaves

1 Make the pasta as described opposite.

2 To make the filling. Place the ricotta, lemon zest, cheeses, and herbs into a bowl and mix – don't be tempted to beat the mixture as this will spoil the texture of the ricotta. Season with pepper and taste before adding any salt as the hard cheeses are quite salty anyway.

3 Remove the pasta dough from the fridge and cut it in half (1 piece each for the top and bottom layers of the ravioli). Roll out a piece of dough into a rectangular shape narrow enough to fit through a pasta machine (see MasterTip, p.190). Pass the dough through the rollers on the widest setting, then fold the long rectangle over in thirds to make it shorter. Pass it through the rollers again, turning it if necessary to keep the best shape. Repeat until the pasta has had 10 passes on the widest setting – this will give you a really silky dough.

4 Reduce the rollers to the next setting and pass the dough through twice. Repeat this process on each roller setting until the last but one. Cut the pasta into more manageable lengths to make it easier. Finally, pass each length of pasta through the thinnest setting just once and lay out flat. Repeat steps 3 and 4 for the other half of the dough.

5 Cut out 24 rounds using a 7cm (2¾in) circular cutter (12 tops and 12 bottoms). Place a rounded teaspoonful of filling in the centre of the bottoms and moisten the edges with a little water. Place the tops over the mixture and seal the edges, trying to expel any air trapped inside as this will cause the ravioli to pop.

6 Bring a large saucepan of salted water to a rapid boil then drop in the ravioli and cook for no more than 2 minutes. Remove and drain.

7 To serve, first make the dressing. Melt the butter in a frying pan, add the lemon juice, salt and pepper, and the sage leaves. Gently bubble on a medium heat for a few seconds so as not to burn the butter, then add the ravioli and coat with the dressing before transferring to serving plates.

1 Pour the flour onto a surface, form a well in the centre, and add the eggs.

2 Beat lightly with a fork, slowly drawing the flour into the eggs.

MAKING PASTA DOUGH

Fresh pasta dough can be made in a food processor or by hand. The former is quicker, but making pasta by hand allows you to get a feel for the dough, adjusting the amount of flour to the particular absorbency of the eggs. To make pasta dough in a food processor, put the flour in the processor and then, with the machine running, add the eggs, lightly beaten, and process until the mixture just begins to form a ball. If it is too dry to do this, add a small amount of water, teaspoon by teaspoon, and continue to process. Knead and chill, as described in steps 5 and 6.

3 Once the eggs are absorbed, push the remaining flour into the centre.

4 Place the dough on a clean surface and knead it until it holds together.

5 Continue to knead for at least 4–5 minutes, until it is silky and smooth.

6 Wrap the dough in cling film and place in the fridge to rest.

SMOKED MOZZARELLA RAVIOLI WITH CHERRY TOMATO SAUCE AND BASIL CREAM

James Nathan barrister turned chef and 2008 champion

PREPARATION TIME
45 minutes, plus resting time

COOKING TIME
60 minutes

SERVES 4

FOR THE PASTA
100g (3½oz) "00" pasta flour
25g (scant 1oz) fine semolina
1 tbsp olive oil
6 egg yolks
1 egg, beaten

FOR THE FILLING
1 large leek, finely shredded
salt and freshly ground black pepper
30g (1oz) unsalted butter
125g (4½oz) smoked mozzarella
　cheese, grated
1 egg white

FOR THE TOMATO SAUCE
1 tbsp olive oil
1 finger-sized red chilli, deseeded
　and sliced
1 garlic clove, crushed
450g (1lb) sweet cherry tomatoes
2 tsp sugar
500ml (16fl oz) chicken stock
　(see MasterTip, p.21)

FOR THE BASIL CREAM
500ml (16fl oz) chicken stock
　(see MasterTip, p.21)
300ml (10fl oz) double cream
2 large bunches of basil, 25g
　(scant 1oz) each, roughly chopped

MASTER TIP

PASTA FLOUR

Because fresh egg pasta is rolled and stretched to a very thin consistency, the flour generally used is milled to a fine gauge which makes the dough especially pliable. Type "00", or *doppio zero*, refers to the fine texture of the flour rather than being an indication of its protein or gluten content, as is sometimes believed.

1 For the ravioli filling, melt the butter in a pan and fry the leek with a good pinch of salt over a low heat for 3–5 minutes or until well softened and translucent but not browned. Remove from the heat and allow to cool slightly.

2 Add the mozzarella and egg white to the cooled leeks. Stir well. Season the mixture and put into a piping bag with a plain nozzle about 1cm (½in) wide.

3 For the pasta, put the flour, semolina, a pinch of salt, olive oil, and egg yolks in a blender with a pulse button. Pulse until the mixture reaches a breadcrumb consistency. Turn the motor on full and trickle in iced cold water until the dough just comes together. Remove the dough and leave to rest for at least 30 minutes.

4 Divide the dough into 3 then roll each piece of dough through a pasta machine on the largest setting. Fold in half and roll again. Repeat twice then roll the pasta out, progressing down through the sizes of the pasta machine to the thinnest setting (see MasterTip, p.190). Lay the pasta "blanket" on a floured work surface. Repeat this process with the remaining dough. Brush half of each piece of pasta with egg wash. Pipe mounds of leek and mozzarella filling the size of a teaspoonful onto the wet half of the pasta, heaping them as tall as possible. Fold the remaining half of the pasta sheet over to cover the mounds of filling.

5 Gently cut around the mounds with a pastry cutter 6cm (2½in) in diameter. Take each individual ravioli and press the air out with your fingers, ensuring that the edges are well sealed and the air is removed. Dust a large plate or tray with fine semolina and lay the ravioli in it. Keep covered. Repeat until you have sufficient ravioli for your guests – this quantity of dough makes about 20 ravioli.

6 For the tomato sauce, heat a large pan or wok over a medium heat. Add the olive oil and quickly fry the chilli and the garlic clove for 1–2 minutes. Add all the tomatoes to the pan with the sugar and ½ tsp salt and cook over a high heat for 5–8 minutes. As the tomatoes start to split, crush them down with a potato masher. When they have cooked down and lost most of their moisture, add the chicken stock. Cook over a high heat for 10–12 minutes or until reduced by half. Season to taste. Blend the mixture in a food processor then sieve to remove the seeds and skins and return to the pan. Cook over a high heat for a further 3–4 minutes to reduce until you have a thick tomato sauce. Season again as necessary.

7 For the basil cream, boil the chicken stock and double cream together for 10–15 minutes or until reduced by half. Add the basil to the boiling cream and stock mixture. Immediately pour it into a blender and blend for about 1 minute or until very finely mixed then pass through a fine sieve, pressing all the juice from the basil through. Heat the sauce again over a high heat for a further 10 minutes or until well reduced and you have a thick green cream. Season to taste and keep warm.

8 To serve, boil a large pan of water, add the ravioli in batches and cook for about 3 minutes until they rise to the surface. Meanwhile, heat the tomato sauce. Drain the cooked pasta thoroughly and gently stir it into the tomato sauce. Spoon delicately into serving bowls, trying not to break the pasta, and drizzle the basil cream around the edge of the bowl.

USHKA WITH BEETROOT AND SOURED CREAM
Michael Pajak communications manager and 2006 quarter-finalist

PREPARATION TIME
60 minutes

COOKING TIME
10 minutes

SERVES 4

2 shallots, finely chopped
30g (1oz) butter
1 garlic clove, crushed
25g (scant 1oz) dried mushrooms,
   preferably porcini, rehydrated (see
   MasterTip, below) and chopped
150g (5½oz) button mushrooms,
   finely diced

sprig of thyme, leaves only
salt and freshly ground black pepper
1 pack fresh wonton skins
150ml (5fl oz) soured cream
about 4 tbsp olive oil
4 golfball-sized cooked beetroot
about 2 tbsp balsamic vinegar,
   to drizzle

MASTER TIP

REHYDRATING DRIED MUSHROOMS

Dried mushrooms such as porcini need to be rehydrated before cooking. Pour some boiling water into a bowl and steep the mushrooms in it for 20–30 minutes – allow plenty of water as they will increase in volume up to three or four times their size when dried. Drain the mushrooms and reserve the water, which is now a very flavoursome addition to dishes such as soups and stews and can be frozen for use later. Strain it carefully to remove any grit remaining from the mushrooms.

1 In a medium frying pan, fry the shallots gently in the butter for 2–3 minutes. Add the garlic and mushrooms. Raise the heat and stir-fry for about 5 minutes until most of the water has been cooked out of the mushrooms. Add the thyme leaves and season with salt and pepper. Allow to cool.

2 Take a wonton skin and place 1 tsp of the mushrooms towards one corner, but not too close to the edge. Wet the edges of the wonton skin and fold over the edge opposite the filling to cover it. Press down to seal. You will now have a triangular shape. Wet the two opposite corners and press them together. Repeat to make approximately 20 or until you have used all the mushroom mixture up.

3 Boil some water in a large pan and poach the ushka for 30 seconds only. Remove and leave to dry on a tea towel. Meanwhile, make the dressing. Thin down the soured cream with a little olive oil, mixing until you are just able to pour it. Season with salt and set aside.

4 Slice the cooked beetroot into rounds about 5mm (¼in) thick. Heat a frying pan until smoking hot, add some olive oil and flash fry the beetroot slices for about 30 seconds each side. When they are almost done, add a generous splash of balsamic vinegar and allow to bubble and reduce around the beetroot. Season, remove from the pan and keep warm. Wipe the pan clean and place back on the heat. Add some more olive oil and fry the ushka for 2–3 minutes or until crispy.

5 Place 3–5 of the caramelized beetroot slices on each plate with 3–5 fried ushka on top of each. Dress each ushka with a little of the soured cream and garnish the plate with a few drops of olive oil and a few drops of balsamic vinegar.

LEEK AND WILD MUSHROOM VOL AU VENT

inspired by **Christopher Souto** IT consultant turned chef and 2005 semi-finalist

350g (12oz) ready-made puff pastry
(or see MasterTip, p.365)
1 egg, lightly beaten
75g (2½oz) Charlotte potatoes (see
MasterTip, p.197), peeled and finely
sliced with a mandolin
salt and freshly ground black pepper
85g (3oz) watercress, stalks removed
2–4 tbsp vegetable stock
250g (9oz) leeks, sliced into thin
julienne strips

1 garlic clove, finely chopped
2 tbsp olive oil
150g (5½oz) assorted wild
mushrooms, sliced
3 sprigs of lemon thyme,
leaves only
10g (¼oz) butter
2 tsp plain flour
100ml (3½oz) double cream

PREPARATION TIME
15 minutes

COOKING TIME
20 minutes

SERVES 4

1 Preheat the oven to 200°C (400°F/Gas 6). Roll out the pastry to
a thickness of 5mm (¼in). Cut out 4 rounds using a 9cm (3½in) plain
cutter and place them on a dampened baking sheet. Using a 7cm
(2¾in) plain cutter, cut part way through the centre of each round.
Prick the inner circle with a fork and brush the outer circle with egg.
Chill for 20 minutes, then bake in the oven for 10 minutes until
well-risen and golden brown. Remove the centre lids and keep warm.
2 Bring a small saucepan of salted water to the boil and add the
potato slices. Cook the potatoes just long enough for them to start
to soften and lose their raw flavour. Drain and reserve.
3 Put the watercress in a colander and pour over enough boiling
water to wilt the watercress but not destroy its vibrant colour.
Liquidize the potato and watercress together with 2 tbsp vegetable
stock. Pass through a fine sieve and, if necessary, loosen with a little
more vegetable stock. Set aside.
4 Heat 1 tbsp olive oil in a frying pan and sweat the leeks and garlic
for about 6 minutes or until soft. Remove from the heat and set aside.
5 Heat the remaining olive oil in a frying pan over a medium heat.
Sweat the mushrooms with the thyme until they are almost tender.
Remove from the heat and set aside.
6 Melt the butter in a small pan over a low heat. Stir in the flour and
mix to a paste. Cook for 1 minute. Add the cream and stir continuously
over a low heat until the sauce thickens. Remove from the heat.
7 Mix the leeks and three-quarters of the mushrooms together.
Fold the white sauce through the vegetables and season to taste.
8 Fill the cavity of the vol au vents with the leek and mushroom
mixture and plate up. Scatter the reserved mushrooms and drizzle
the warm watercress coulis over the plates. Serve immediately.

WARM ROQUEFORT CHEESECAKE WITH OVEN-ROASTED VINE TOMATOES

James Shepherd horse groom turned caterer and 2007 quarter-finalist

FOR THE CHEESECAKE BASE
85g (3oz) fresh white bread
45g (1½oz) unsalted butter
salt and freshly ground black pepper

FOR THE CHEESECAKE FILLING
100g (3½oz) full-fat cream cheese
75g (2½oz) Roquefort cheese
1 large egg yolk
1 tsp cornflour
1 tbsp double cream
squeeze of lemon juice

FOR THE ROASTED TOMATOES
20 cherry tomatoes on the vine
olive oil, for roasting

FOR THE BASIL OIL
30g (1oz) basil
75ml (2½fl oz) olive oil

PREPARATION TIME
20 minutes

COOKING TIME
30 minutes

SERVES 4

1 Preheat the oven to 190°C (375°F/Gas 5). Butter the bases and sides of four 8cm (3in) fluted, loose-bottomed flan tins.
2 For the cheesecake base, put the bread in a food processor and whizz until it has turned into fine crumbs. Melt the butter over a gentle heat in a saucepan, tip in the breadcrumbs and stir to combine. Press the mixture into the bottom and sides of the flan tins, pressing down with the back of a spoon to ensure an even layer. Bake in the oven for about 10 minutes or until the base is golden – keep watch as it can overcook very quickly. Keep the oven on for roasting the tomatoes.
3 For the filling, cream together all the ingredients and divide between the flan tins. Return to the oven and bake for 10–12 minutes or until golden and just set (there should be a slight wobble when you shake the tins). Remove the cheesecakes from the oven and allow them to cool slightly before removing from the tins.
4 Split the tomato vine so there are 5 tomatoes per person. Place them on a baking tray, drizzle over some olive oil and roast in the oven for about 10 minutes or until the skins start to blister.
5 Meanwhile, make the basil oil. Blanch the basil leaves in salted boiling water and then refresh in cold water. Place in a blender with the olive oil and pulse until the liquid is moving freely, adding more oil if necessary. Pour into a muslin-lined sieve over a bowl to drain. Decant the oil into a jug.
6 To serve, place each cheesecake on a plate, top with the cherry tomatoes, and add a drizzle of basil oil.

FIG TART WITH RED ONION JAM

inspired by **William Leigh** designer turned food writer and 2007 semi-finalist

PREPARATION TIME
10 minutes

COOKING TIME
1 hour 45 minutes

SERVES 4

FOR THE RED ONION JAM
50g (1¾oz) butter
1 tbsp olive oil
500g (1lb 2oz) red onions, finely sliced
½ tsp salt
¼ tsp freshly ground black pepper
1 bay leaf
1 tsp thyme leaves
50g (1¾oz) light soft brown sugar
100ml (3½fl oz) dry red wine
75ml (2½fl oz) sherry vinegar

FOR THE FIG TART
375g (13oz) ready-made puff pastry
   (or see MasterTip, p.365)
1 egg, beaten
4 figs, quartered
250g (9oz) Roquefort cheese
   or similar blue, crumbled
2 tbsp olive oil
sea salt and freshly ground
   black pepper

1 For the jam, melt the butter with the oil in a heavy pan. Add the sliced onions and stir well to coat in the butter, then add the salt, pepper, bay leaf, thyme, and sugar and mix everything together.

2 Cook on a medium-low heat for 30–40 minutes, until the onions are very soft and caramelized. Add the wine and vinegar, increase the heat slightly and reduce by about two-thirds to a sticky jam – about another 25–30 minutes. Remove the bay leaf.

3 Preheat the oven to 200°C (400°F/Gas 6). Line two baking sheets with baking parchment.

4 On a floured surface, roll out the pastry and cut out 4 circles about 18cm (7in) in diameter. Score a line about 1cm (½in) in from the edge, and place the discs on the baking sheets. Prick inside the scored area lightly with a fork. Brush with the egg and place in the oven for 7–8 minutes until they are lightly golden and risen. Then remove from the oven, press down inside the scored area, and top with the fig quarters and crumbled cheese. Drizzle with the oil and season, then place back in the oven for 8–10 minutes, or until the pastry is golden brown and the cheese is melted.

5 Serve the tarts with the warm onion jam spooned on top.

MUSSELS À LA PROVENÇALE

inspired by **Luciana Byrne** housewife and mother and 2007 quarter-finalist

3 tbsp olive oil
1 onion, finely chopped
2 garlic cloves, finely chopped
1 celery stick, finely chopped
4 vine-ripened tomatoes, skinned, deseeded, and chopped
1 bay leaf

1 tsp thyme leaves
200ml (7fl oz) dry white wine
2kg (4½lb) live mussels, cleaned (see MasterTip, below)
2 tbsp chopped flat-leaf parsley
2 tbsp chopped basil

PREPARATION TIME
10 minutes

COOKING TIME
15 minutes

SERVES 4

1 Heat the oil in a large saucepan, big enough to take all the mussels, and soften the onion, garlic, and celery.

2 Add the chopped tomatoes, bay leaf, and thyme, then pour in the wine and bring to the boil. Tip in the mussels, place the lid on the pan and turn up the heat, shaking every now and then.

3 Steam the mussels for 4–6 minutes or until most of them are open; discard those that aren't.

4 Stir through the parsley and basil before serving in warmed bowls.

MASTER TIP
CLEANING MUSSELS

You will often find live mussels still have their byssus threads, or "beards", still attached. This is what they use to cling to surfaces in the water and they should be removed before cooking. Steam cooking opens the shells, or they can be shelled by hand and then grilled or stuffed and baked.

1 Scrub the mussels under running water to brush away any grit and scrape off barnacles with a small knife.

2 Pinch the byssus thread with your fingers and firmly jerk it away from the mussel shell.

MUSSELS WITH CHIPOTLES AND CORIANDER
inspired by **Thomasina Miers** food writer turned chef and 2005 champion

PREPARATION TIME
15 minutes

COOKING TIME
20 minutes

SERVES 4

25g (scant 1oz) butter
2 shallots, finely chopped
2 garlic cloves, finely chopped
1 tbsp chipotle chillies in oil
200ml (7fl oz) dry white wine

2kg (4½lb) live mussels, cleaned
  (see MasterTip, p.59)
handful of coriander leaves,
  roughly chopped
75ml (2½fl oz) double cream

MASTER TIP

CHIPOTLE CHILLIES

A feature of Mexican cuisine even before the time of the Aztecs, chipotles are smoked jalapeño chillies. They are relatively mild and can be used in a variety of dishes from soups to salsas.

1 Melt the butter in a large saucepan, big enough to take all the mussels, and sweat the shallots and garlic over a low heat to soften but not colour.
2 Stir in the chipotle chillies, then pour in the wine and bring to the boil. Tip in the mussels, place the lid on the pan and turn up the heat, shaking every now and then. Steam the mussels for 4–6 minutes until most of them are open; discard those that aren't.
3 Finally, stir through the coriander and cream before serving in warmed bowls.

SCALLOPS ON AN APPLE AND WALNUT SAUCE

inspired by **Jayne Middlemiss** presenter and 2009 Celebrity champion

PREPARATION TIME
25 minutes

COOKING TIME
20 minutes

SERVES 4

5 Granny Smith apples
juice of 1 lemon
150ml (5fl oz) apple juice
100g (3½oz) walnut halves
3 tbsp olive oil
2 tbsp chervil

1 tbsp dill
salt and freshly ground black pepper
15g (½oz butter)
12 scallops, removed from shells and
    trimmed of coral (see MasterTip, p.64)

1 Begin by making the sauce: peel, core and slice 4 apples and place in a saucepan along with the lemon juice and apple juice. Bring to a simmer and cook down until the apples are soft – about 10–15 minutes.
2 Cut the remaining apple into matchsticks and sprinkle with lemon juice to prevent it from discolouring.
3 Add half of the walnuts to the pan, along with 2 tbsp of the oil and the herbs, and season well. Transfer everything to a food processor or blender and pulse to a smooth sauce.
4 For the scallops, heat the remaining oil along with the butter in a frying pan until smoking hot, then fry the scallops in 2 batches so as not to overcrowd the pan. Turn after about 2 minutes per side, or until the outside is browned and crispy and the inside is still soft.
5 Serve 3 scallops per portion on a pool of the apple and walnut sauce. Arrange the apple matchsticks in crisscrosses on top of each scallop. Finally, garnish each plate with the remaining walnut halves.

CARAMELIZED SCALLOPS ON CELERIAC PURÉE WITH GARLIC BACON LARDONS

Nadia Sawalha actress and presenter and 2007 Celebrity champion

1 small celeriac, about 400g
    (14oz), cubed
1 garlic clove, whole
2 tbsp double cream
salt and freshly ground black pepper
3 tbsp olive oil

8 scallops, removed from shells and
    trimmed of coral (see MasterTip, p.64)
1 garlic clove, crushed
100g (3½oz) smoked lardons
frisée, rocket or other salad leaves,
    dressed in a little olive oil
    and lemon juice

PREPARATION TIME
10 minutes

COOKING TIME
20 minutes

SERVES 4

1 Boil the celeriac and garlic in salted water for 15–20 minutes until very tender. Drain thoroughly, then add the cream and black pepper to taste and mash to the consistency of smooth mashed potato or use a hand blender to blend until very smooth. Keep warm while you cook the scallops.

2 Heat 2 tbsp of the oil in a heavy frying pan until hot enough to sizzle. Season the scallops then add to the hot pan and do not disturb them for the 1–2 minutes or until golden underneath, otherwise you will not get the delicious caramelized flavour. When they are golden underneath, flip them over and cook on the other side. The whole of the frying should take about 3 minutes, depending on the thickness of the scallops.

3 Meanwhile, in a separate frying pan, heat the remaining oil, add the garlic and bacon lardons and pan-fry for 3–4 minutes or until they are crisp and golden.

4 On each plate, pile a little of the salad in the middle, then put 2 tbsp of celeriac purée either side of it. Place a scallop on each circle of celeriac purée and then sprinkle a few fried lardons around the plate. Serve immediately.

ROASTED SCALLOPS, CAULIFLOWER PURÉE, VEGETABLES À LA GRECQUE

Derek Johnstone junior sous chef and 2008 Professionals champion

PREPARATION TIME
30 minutes

COOKING TIME
35 minutes

SERVES 4

1 large cauliflower, leaves and
  stalk removed
300ml (10fl oz) milk
300ml (10fl oz) double cream
50g (1¾oz) unsalted butter
pinch of celery salt
salt and freshly ground black pepper
10 baby carrots
10 baby leeks
4 banana shallots, thickly sliced
8 radishes, preferably Easter egg
2 tbsp white wine vinegar
100ml (3½fl oz) olive oil
4 tbsp white truffle oil (see MasterTip,
  p.22), plus extra for serving

juice of 1 lemon
1 bunch of thyme
1 garlic clove
2 tsp coriander seeds, cracked
2 pinches of saffron threads
1 clove
1 sprig of rosemary
8 large scallops, removed from
  shells and trimmed of coral
  (see MasterTip, below)
250ml (8fl oz) dry white wine
2 kinds of microgreens, such as
  red amaranth and pea shoots
  (see MasterTip, p.281)

1 Halve the cauliflower and slice half of it thinly. Put the slices in a shallow pan with the milk and cream, cover, and cook for 8–10 minutes or until the cauliflower is soft. Remove the cauliflower from the pan and place in a blender. Add the butter and blend until very smooth, adding a little of the cooking milk and cream if needed to thin down slightly. Pass through a fine sieve and season with the celery salt, salt and pepper.

MASTER TIP
PREPARING SCALLOPS

Scrub the shells of scallops clean before you open them. To open, slide a thin, flexible knife between the top and bottom shells, holding the scallop firmly in the palm of your hand with the flat shell uppermost. Keep the blade as close to the top shell as you can to avoid cutting the meat. Sever the muscle by sliding the knife around the top shell.

1 Remove the top shell and detach the scallop from the bottom shell with the knife, taking care not to damage it.

2 Pull away and discard the viscera and membrane. Remove the coral too if you wish. Rinse the scallop.

2 Blanch the remaining cauliflower, broken into small florets, the leeks and the carrots separately in a large pan of salted water, then refresh immediately in cold water.

3 Place the vegetables in a bowl. Place the vinegar, oils, lemon juice, thyme, garlic, coriander seeds, saffron, clove, rosemary, and wine in a saucepan and bring to the boil. Pour over the drained vegetables and leave to cool completely, then remove the garlic, thyme, and rosemary.

4 Heat a little olive oil in a non-stick frying pan, add the scallops and cook for 1–2 minutes on one side before turning over and cooking for a further 1 minute or until golden and seared.

5 Place a few spoonfuls of the cauliflower purée on serving plates and smooth over to create a smear of purée. Arrange the scallops on top then place the drained vegetables from the marinade on the plate. Sprinkle the microgreens on top and finish with a little truffle oil.

ASPARAGUS AND CRAB TARTLET WITH AVOCADO SORBET

Daniel Gvalda sous chef and 2009 Professionals quarter-finalist

60g (2oz) sugar
2 ripe avocados
salt and freshly ground black pepper
1 sheet ready-rolled puff pastry
250g (9oz) hand-picked crabmeat
  or 2 dressed crabs

1 tbsp crème fraîche
10g (¼oz) dill, snipped
16 asparagus spears (see
  MasterTip, p.221)
chervil, to garnish

PREPARATION TIME
15 minutes

COOKING TIME
15 minutes

SERVES 4

1 Make a syrup by dissolving the sugar in 100ml (3½fl oz) water and bringing it to the boil. Blitz the avocado with the syrup in a blender, add some pepper and transfer to an ice-cream maker to churn and freeze. (If you do not have a machine, see the MasterTip on p.347.)

2 Preheat the oven to 180°C (350°F/Gas 4). Put the puff pastry in between two baking containers to keep it flat – Swiss roll tins are ideal. Place in the oven and bake for about 15 minutes until crisp. Divide into quarters.

3 Mix the crab with the crème fraîche and dill. Season with salt and pepper. Blanch the asparagus in boiling water – about 3–4 minutes depending on the thickness of the spears. Refresh in cold water.

4 To serve, lay the pastry on 4 plates and top with the crab and the asparagus. Spoon the avocado sorbet on the side.

TIAN OF CRAB WITH CORIANDER-INFUSED OIL
Dean Edwards digger driver turned chef and 2006 finalist

PREPARATION TIME
35 minutes, plus cooling time

COOKING TIME
15 minutes

SERVES 4

200–225g (7–8oz) white crabmeat
2 tbsp crème fraîche
1 tbsp chopped coriander
salt and freshly ground black pepper
1 large ripe avocado
juice of 1 small lime

FOR THE CORIANDER OIL
¼ tsp turmeric
1 tsp coriander seeds
1 tsp ground cumin
1 tsp fennel seeds

1 tsp mustard seeds
1 stick cinnamon
4 cardamom pods
1 green chilli, deseeded
1 garlic clove, chopped
200ml (7fl oz) olive oil
35g (1¼oz) coriander

1 To make the coriander oil, place a frying pan over a medium heat and dry fry the spices for about 2 minutes. Add the chilli, garlic, and olive oil and allow to infuse on a low heat for 30 minutes.

2 Meanwhile, blanch and refresh the coriander. Strain the oil and blitz with the coriander in a food processor or blender. Pass through muslin and allow to cool, refrigerating it if you wish to assemble the dish later.

3 Dress the crabmeat with the crème fraîche, coriander, and salt and pepper. Mash the avocado and add lime juice and salt and pepper.

4 Using four 7cm (2¾in) ring moulds, layer the avocado and then the crabmeat on 4 plates. Drizzle the coriander oil around and serve.

LOBSTER RAVIOLI WITH A TARRAGON BUTTER SAUCE

Derek Johnstone junior sous chef and 2008 Professionals champion

PREPARATION TIME
40 minutes, plus chilling time

COOKING TIME
11 minutes

SERVES 4

FOR THE LOBSTER MOUSSE
1 fresh lobster, cooked and deshelled
  (see MasterTip, below), keeping the
  claws for garnish
2 eggs
15g (½oz) Parmesan cheese, grated
10g (¼oz) chervil, chopped
100ml (3½fl oz) double cream
salt and white pepper

FOR THE PASTA
400g (1lb) "00" pasta flour (see
  MasterTip, p.52)
pinch of saffron
4 eggs
3 egg yolks

FOR THE STUFFED TOMATOES
1 tbsp olive oil
50g (1¾oz) baby spinach
2 tbsp double cream
pinch of nutmeg
4 large plum tomatoes

FOR THE SAUCE
250g (9oz) butter
1 shallot, finely diced
1 sprig of thyme
1 bay leaf
100ml (3½fl oz) white wine
60ml (2fl oz) white wine vinegar
100ml (3½fl oz) double cream
10g (¼oz) tarragon

1 Purée half of the lobster meat in a food processor with the eggs and Parmesan. Dice the rest of the body meat and add to the lobster mix with the chopped chervil.

2 In a bowl, whip the double cream until stiff peaks form. Gently fold the lobster mixture into the cream and season to taste with salt and pepper. Allow to chill in the fridge for 1 hour before you begin to make the lobster ravioli.

MASTER TIP

EXTRACTING THE MEAT FROM A COOKED LOBSTER

Rather than buying a live lobster and having to kill and clean it before cooking, you may prefer to buy a whole cooked lobster. Points to look for when buying are a fresh smell and a moist shell; avoid any with loose legs, claws, heads, or tails. Extracting the meat is easy; if you do not have a lobster cracker for the claws, use a small hammer.

1 Take hold of the tail and twist it sharply to detach it.

2 Turn the tail over and cut down the centre with kitchen scissors.

3 To make the pasta, place the sieved flour in a food processor and turn on the motor. Add the saffron and gradually add the whole eggs and egg yolks until well combined. Knead until elastic on a floured board and leave to rest in the fridge for about 1 hour. (Or see MasterTip p.51.)

4 For the stuffed tomatoes, first cook the spinach. Heat the oil in a pan, add the spinach and wilt it over a low heat. Add the cream and reduce until the mixture has thickened. Season with nutmeg and salt.

5 Preheat the oven to 190°C (375°F/Gas 5). Blanch the tomatoes for a few seconds in boiling water, then slice off the top and deseed. Stuff with the spinach mix, place on a baking tray and bake for 5 minutes.

6 Using a pasta machine, roll out the pasta to the thinnest setting (see MasterTip, p.190). Cut 2 rectangular dough sheets and add small scoops of lobster mousse on top of the first sheet at intervals about 5cm (2in) apart. Brush around the filling with a little water and top with the second sheet of dough, covering the filling gently. Using your fingertips, gently press round the filling to remove any air. Cut out the ravioli using a fluted pastry cutter about 5cm (2in) in diameter. Repeat until all the pasta dough and mousse have been used. Cover with cling film until ready to cook.

7 To make the sauce, heat 20g (¾oz) butter in a frying pan and sweat the shallot gently without colouring it. Add the thyme, bay leaf, white wine, and vinegar and reduce by half. Add the cream and reduce again by half. Gently whisk in the remaining butter, a small knob at a time, until totally emulsified. Remove the sprig of thyme and bay leaf. Add the chopped tarragon and season to taste.

8 To cook the ravioli, poach in boiling salted water for about 5 minutes. Serve in bowls on top of the stuffed tomatoes with the sauce drizzled over. Garnish with chopped meat from the crab claws.

3 Pull the shell apart with your thumbs and extract the meat in one piece.

4 To remove the meat from the claws, crack them open with lobster crackers.

CRISPY SQUID WITH GREEN PEPPERCORN AND CHILLI DRESSING

Susie Carter administrator turned food writer and 2006 quarter-finalist

PREPARATION TIME
15 minutes

COOKING TIME
5 minutes

SERVES 4

4 medium squid, cleaned (see
 MasterTip, pp.72–3)
juice of 1 lime
salt and freshly ground black pepper
groundnut oil for deep-frying
3 tbsp cornflour

FOR THE DRESSING
2 tbsp fresh green peppercorns
1 red chilli, deseeded and finely chopped
3cm (1¼in) piece fresh root ginger,
 finely grated

2 garlic cloves, crushed
3 tbsp nam pla (Thai fish sauce)
3 tbsp rice vinegar
75g (2½oz) caster sugar
2 tsp soy sauce
juice of 1 lime

TO SERVE
4 slices of lime
coriander leaves

1 To make the dressing, put all the ingredients in a small pan and simmer, stirring, until the sugar has dissolved and the mixture has thickened. Leave to cool.

2 Open out the body sac of the squid and cut each one into about 8 rectangles. With the inside facing up, score a diamond pattern with a sharp knife, taking care not to cut all the way through. Douse with lime juice, season well with salt and pepper, and leave to cure for 2 minutes.

3 Heat plenty of groundnut oil in a large saucepan or deep fat fryer to 180°C (350°F).

4 Dry the squid thoroughly on kitchen paper then toss with the cornflour. Shake off the excess and deep fry in batches for 2 minutes until golden and crisp. Drain on kitchen paper then quickly toss with a few spoonfuls of the dressing and serve immediately with a slice of lime on the side and coriander to garnish.

STUFFED SQUID WITH SPICY TOMATO SAUCE
Hannah Miles lawyer turned cookbook author and 2007 finalist

PREPARATION TIME
30 minutes, plus proving time

COOKING TIME
55–75 minutes

SERVES 4

6 squid, cleaned (see MasterTip,
  below), pockets 5–7.5cm (2–3in)
  long and tentacles
3 tbsp olive oil
1 small red chilli, deseeded
  and finely chopped
2 garlic cloves, crushed
100ml (3½floz) white wine
400g (14oz) can pomodorini tomatoes
  or chopped tomatoes
vine-ripened cherry tomatoes,
  to garnish

FOR THE FOCACCIA
1½ tsp dried yeast
1½ tsp salt
500g (1lb 2oz) strong white bread flour
90ml (3fl oz) olive oil plus extra
  for drizzling
Halen Môn spiced sea salt

FOR THE FISH STOCK
1 carrot, chopped
1 celery stick, chopped
1 onion, chopped
fish heads and bones
2 bay leaves
salt and 20 black peppercorns

FOR THE SQUID STUFFING
60g (2oz) baby spinach, roughly torn
2 slices of white bread, crusts removed
120ml (4fl oz) milk
10 large raw peeled prawns (see
  MasterTip, p. 75)
1 onion, finely chopped
1 garlic clove, crushed
2 large fresh red chillies,
  deseeded and finely chopped
30g (1oz) salted butter
1 egg yolk
salt and freshly ground black pepper

1 To make the bread, add the yeast to 2 tbsp warm water then leave
to stand for 10 minutes until frothy. Place the flour and salt in a mixer,
add the yeast mixture and olive oil and enough tepid water (about

---

MASTER TIP
CLEANING SQUID

Squid consists of 2 main edible
parts – the body, known as
the mantle, and the tentacles.
The black "ink", contained
within a small silvery black
sac, is also sometimes used
to colour and flavour seafood
sauces, pasta, and rice. Squid
has a single eye and an inner
lining called the quill, which
has a consistency like that
of plastic. Both of these are
removed before cooking.

1 First pull the mantle and tentacles
apart. The head, viscera, and ink sac
will come away with the tentacles.

2 Next, pull the transparent quill out
of the mantle and discard it.

270ml/9fl oz) to form a smooth but not sticky dough, then knead well. Leave to rise for about 30 minutes or until doubled in size. Knead again, prodding it with your fingers, and leave to rise again.

2 Meanwhile, preheat the oven to 230°C (450°F/Gas 8). When the dough is fully risen, make dimples in the top of it using your finger, drizzle with olive oil and spiced sea salt and bake in the oven for 15–20 minutes until golden on top.

3 To make the fish stock, simmer the carrot, celery, onion, fish heads and bones, bay leaves, and peppercorns in 600ml (1 pint) water for 20–30 minutes (see also MasterTip, p. 123). Skim as necessary then strain, discarding the vegetables and fish heads and bones. Season to taste with salt.

4 To make the stuffing, first wilt the spinach in a pan for 1–2 minutes. Soak the bread in milk. Poach the prawns in the fish stock for 2 minutes, then remove the prawns and chop, reserving the fish stock. Pan-fry the onion, garlic, and chilli in the butter until soft. Add the spinach, prawns, bread, and egg yolk and season to taste. Cook for about 3 minutes until the mixture is firm. Put in a piping bag in the fridge to chill.

5 Stuff the squid and secure with cocktail sticks. Pan-fry the squid in olive oil for about 5–8 minutes, turning frequently. When golden, add the chilli and garlic and cook until soft. Add the white wine and cook off the alcohol. Add the reserved fish stock and the tomatoes and simmer for a further 8–10 minutes or until the sauce is thickened.

6 Cut the squid diagonally into slices and lay on the tomato sauce with cherry tomatoes on the vine to garnish and the focaccia to serve.

3 Separate the tentacles from the head, cutting above the eye. Discard the head, viscera, and ink sac.

4 Open the tentacles to pull out the ball-shaped beak. Rinse the tentacles and mantle under cold running water.

THAI FISH CAKES WITH SWEET CHILLI SAUCE

inspired by **Mat Follas** engineer turned chef patron and 2009 champion

PREPARATION TIME
10 minutes

COOKING TIME
50 minutes

SERVES 4

300g (10oz) white fish, such as cod
  or coley, skinned and boned
200g (7oz) raw shelled prawns
  (see MasterTip, opposite)
2 tbsp red Thai curry paste
  (see MasterTip, left)
1 egg
1 tbsp nam pla (Thai fish sauce)
1 tsp palm sugar
2 tbsp chopped coriander
10 French beans, finely sliced
2 kaffir lime leaves, finely sliced
groundnut oil, for deep frying

FOR THE SWEET CHILLI SAUCE
150ml (5fl oz) rice wine vinegar
6–8 red chillies, deseeded and
  finely chopped
2 garlic cloves, crushed
300g (10oz) light soft brown sugar
1 tsp salt
¼ tsp paprika
juice of ½ lime

MASTER TIP

RED THAI CURRY PASTE

To make your own red Thai
curry paste place the following
ingredients in a food processor
and blend:
1 shallot, chopped
1 stalk lemongrass, chopped
1–2 red chillies
4 garlic cloves
2.5cm (1in) piece fresh root
  ginger, sliced
2 tbsp tomato purée
1 tsp caster sugar
1 tbsp ground cumin
½ tbsp ground coriander
3 tbsp nam pla (Thai fish sauce)
2 tbsp chilli powder
enough coconut milk to keep
  the blades turning
2 tbsp lime juice

1 For the sweet chilli sauce, place 150ml (5fl oz) water in a small saucepan, add all the ingredients except the lime juice and bring to a simmer. Stir to dissolve the sugar and salt, and reduce the heat to low. Continue to cook for 40–50 minutes, until the mixture turns syrupy, then remove from the heat and stir in the lime juice to taste.
2 Meanwhile, make the fish cakes. Place the fish, prawns, curry paste, egg, nam pla, sugar, and some salt in a food processor and pulse until smooth and combined. Throw in the coriander and pulse again. Tip the mixture out into a bowl and stir in the beans and lime leaves and mix well.
3 With wet hands, divide the mixture into 16–20 pieces, roll into little balls and flatten slightly. Fry in about 2.5cm (1in) groundnut oil in the base of a wok for 1–2 minutes on each side, until golden brown.
4 Arrange the fish cakes on serving plates and serve with the sweet chilli sauce.

CRISPY BUTTERFLY PRAWNS WITH GINGER AND LIME

Perveen Nekoo wedding cake maker and 2006 quarter-finalist

12 large raw black tiger prawns,
  heads and shells removed,
  tails left on
juice and zest of 1½ limes
1 tsp grated fresh root ginger
½ tsp turmeric
salt
35g (1¼oz) coriander,
  finely chopped

70–75g (2¼–2½oz) fresh
  white breadcrumbs
60g (2oz) plain flour
1 large egg, beaten
60g (2oz) salted butter
2 tbsp olive oil
1 lime

PREPARATION TIME
30 minutes

COOKING TIME
10 minutes

SERVES 4

1 Devein and butterfly the prawns (see MasterTip, below). In a bowl, mix the lime juice, ginger, turmeric, salt, and half the coriander. Add the prawns to this mixture and leave to marinate for 20 minutes.

2 In a separate bowl, mix the remaining coriander with the breadcrumbs and lime zest.

3 Dip the prawns in the flour, then the egg and finally the breadcrumb mixture. Repeat the egg and breadcrumb sequence to give them a good coating.

4 Heat the butter and oil in a pan until they start to sizzle. Add the coated prawns and fry until golden. Remove and drain on kitchen paper. Serve with wedges of fresh lime.

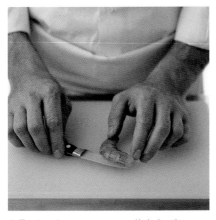

1 To devein a prawn, cut lightly along the back with a paring knife. Remove the vein with your fingers or the knife tip and rinse the prawn in cold water.

2 To butterfly a prawn, cut along the back and splay it open – take care not to cut it right through. Rinse under cold running water and pat dry.

MASTER TIP

PREPARING PRAWNS

When using larger varieties of prawn it is advisable to remove the intestinal vein, or sand line. You can do this either before or after shelling. Butterflying allows prawns to be stuffed and also makes them suitable for coating in breadcrumbs or batter.

OPEN RAVIOLI OF SQUASH AND LANGOUSTINES IN A LANGOUSTINE AND BROAD BEAN SAUCE

Hardeep Singh Kohli comedian and broadcaster and 2006 Celebrity finalist

6 large raw langoustines in their shells
5–6 tbsp olive oil
1 small bulb fennel, finely diced
1 carrot, finely diced
½ leek, finely diced
1 tsp salt
½ small butternut squash, peeled, deseeded and cut into 2.5cm (1in) chunks

200ml (7fl oz) glass Noilly Prat or other dry vermouth
1½ tsp tomato purée
150ml (5fl oz) double cream
400g (14oz) broad beans, shelled
12 x 10cm (4in) squares fresh pasta (see MasterTips, pp.51 and 190–91)

PREPARATION TIME
1 hour

COOKING TIME
30 minutes

SERVES 4

1 Preheat the oven to 200°C (400°F/Gas 6). Remove the flesh from the langoustine shells and set the flesh to one side. Smear the shells, including the heads, with 1 tbsp of olive oil and place them on a roasting tray in the oven for 8 minutes.
2 Meanwhile, heat 2 tbsp of olive oil in a frying pan and add the fennel, carrot, leek, and salt. Sweat them over a low heat while the langoustine shells roast. Remove the shells from the oven and add to the vegetables, smashing them with a potato masher to release as much juice and flavour as possible. Fry together for about 5 minutes, continuing to squeeze every drop of flavour from the shells and head.
3 Toss the squash in a little oil, place in a roasting pan and roast in the oven for 15 minutes until golden brown.
4 Add the Noilly Prat to the vegetable mixture, reduce by half, and add the tomato purée. Cook for 2 minutes, then add the cream. Turn the heat down, simmer for 1–2 minutes, then pass through a sieve.
5 In a small pan, boil some salted water and add the broad beans. Boil until tender – about 8 minutes – then drain and allow to cool before removing the dull green outer skin. Add to the sauce.
6 In a larger pan, boil some salted water, adding a spot of oil. Slide in the squares of pasta and cook for about 3 minutes.
7 Meanwhile, drizzle the langoustines with olive oil and season them. Sear in a hot pan for no more than 60 seconds on each side. Rest for a couple of minutes, then cut 2 of them into 4 diagonal slices each.
8 Drain the pasta and place a square in each of 4 large bowls. Add 4–5 cubes of squash, then place another square of pasta on top followed by 2 langoustine slices. Add the final square of pasta and spoon the sauce and broad beans over. Top with a single langoustine.

GREGG WALLACE

"The deep fish creaminess of the sauce is the first thing you taste, then you get the softness of the langoustines that comes after the beautiful rich sauce."

LANGOUSTINES WITH GREEN CURRY SAUCE AND MANGO PURÉE

Cheryl Avery purchasing manager and 2009 quarter-finalist

PREPARATION TIME
30 minutes

COOKING TIME
6–8 minutes

SERVES 4

2 tbsp olive oil
1 shallot, finely chopped
8 spring onions, cut in half
16 raw langoustines (see MasterTip, opposite), peeled
salt and freshly ground black pepper
1 small very ripe mango
4 tsp finely shredded basil leaves, to garnish

FOR THE SAUCE
3 spring onions, chopped
1 fresh green chilli, deseeded and chopped

1 garlic clove, chopped
2 tsp finely chopped fresh root ginger
2 tsp coriander seeds, dry roasted and crushed
¼ tsp cracked black peppercorns
2 kaffir lime leaves, torn
1 stalk lemongrass, chopped
50g (1¾oz) basil, chopped
25g (scant 1oz) coriander with stalks, chopped
5 tsp olive oil
grated zest and juice of 2 limes
2 tbsp coconut milk

1 First make the sauce. Purée all the ingredients except the coconut milk in a blender. Press the purée through a fine-mesh sieve into a small saucepan. Add the coconut milk and combine. Set aside.
2 To cook the langoustines, heat the oil in a frying pan over a moderate heat. Add the shallots and spring onions and cook for 2 minutes. Add the langoustines, increase the heat to high and cook for 2–3 minutes on each side, or until just cooked through. Remove the langoustines from the pan and season to taste with salt and pepper.
3 Peel the mango and chop into small pieces (see MasterTip, p.160). Place in the blender and purée until smooth.
4 To finish, warm the sauce over a moderately low heat for about 3 minutes until just hot. Cover one side of the plate with a generous amount of the sauce. Place spoonfuls of the mango purée on the other side of the plate. Arrange the langoustines and spring onions on top of the sauce. Garnish with the shredded basil leaves and serve.

WARM SALAD OF LANGOUSTINES AND FENNEL

Becky McCracken teacher and 2006 semi-finalist

500ml (16fl oz) fish stock (see
  MasterTip, p.123)
16 raw langoustines (see MasterTip,
  right) or large prawns in their shells
2 tsp salted butter
2 bulbs fennel, finely sliced and
  the tops reserved
few sprigs of chervil, leaves chopped
few sprigs of dill, leaves chopped

PREPARATION TIME
30 minutes

COOKING TIME
10 minutes

SERVES 4

1 Bring the fish stock up to a slow boil in a large saucepan. Place the langoustines or prawns in the pan with the fish stock and cover with a lid. Leave to cook for 7 minutes, then take out of the stock and put to one side to cool.

2 Melt the butter in a pan on a medium heat and add the sliced fennel. Soften for 3–4 minutes, until it goes slightly translucent. Take 4–6 tbsp of the langoustine broth and pour over the fennel. Set aside.

3 Meanwhile, shell the langoustines or prawns (see MasterTip, p.75), leaving 1 per person with the shell on as they look so pretty.

4 Mix the herbs with the langoustines (or prawns) and fennel, and arrange on the plates. Serve with a slice of ciabatta.

MASTER TIP
COOKING LANGOUSTINES

If you buy langoustines live, check that they are still moving. Cook them as soon as possible, as they soon become unfit to eat. The humane way to cook langoustines is to freeze them for 1–2 hours beforehand.

SMOKED HADDOCK RISOTTO WITH A POACHED HEN'S EGG

Alice Cooper trainee accountant and 2009 quarter-finalist

PREPARATION TIME
10 minutes

COOKING TIME
30 minutes

SERVES 4

1 tbsp olive oil
60g (2oz) salted butter
1 onion, finely chopped
1 celery stick, finely chopped
200g (7oz) arborio rice
150ml (5fl oz) white wine
1 litre (1¾ pints) chicken stock
  (see MasterTip, p.21)

150g (5½oz) fillet of undyed smoked
  haddock (see MasterTip, left), chopped
50g (1¾oz) baby leaf spinach
grated zest and juice of 1 lemon
50g (1¾oz) Parmesan cheese,
  freshly grated
salt and freshly ground black pepper
3 tbsp white wine vinegar
4 eggs

MASTER TIP
SMOKED HADDOCK

When fish is smoked it turns an orangey yellow and haddock is often brined in salted water before smoking, turning it a paler colour. Dyes were used for years to turn smoked fish the deeper, redder colour we associate with smoked food – the flavour was unchanged. Now the trend is towards using the fish in its natural state after smoking, on the grounds that there is no point adding something with no legitimate purpose.

1 Heat the oil and half the butter in a large saucepan. Add the onion and celery and fry on a medium heat until soft. Add the rice, cook for a few minutes and then add the wine. Once the wine has been absorbed, start adding the stock, bit by bit, allowing the rice to absorb all the liquid before adding more.

2 Once the rice is nearly cooked, after about 20 minutes, add the haddock, spinach, and lemon zest. Then, once the rice is done, stir in the lemon juice, Parmesan cheese, and the rest of the butter, and adjust the seasoning. Place a lid on the pan, remove from the heat, and leave to rest for 5 minutes while you cook the eggs.

3 To poach each egg, bring a saucepan of water to the boil and add the vinegar. Create a whirlpool and crack the egg into the centre. Reduce the heat and simmer for 4 minutes or until the white has set. If not using straight away, then place in ice-cold water to arrest the cooking process, so keeping a soft yolk.

4 To serve, spoon out the risotto into a neat round on a plate, using a ring mould if necessary. Top with the poached egg.

PAN-FRIED FILLET OF RED MULLET WITH SCALLOP TARTARE AND CELERIAC PURÉE

Robert Scott head chef and 2008 Professionals quarter-finalist

PREPARATION TIME
20 minutes

COOKING TIME
20 minutes

SERVES 4

4 red mullet fillets, 120–130g
   (4¼–4¾oz) each
1 tbsp olive oil
juice of 1 lemon
30g (1oz) butter
salt and freshly ground
   black pepper

FOR THE PURÉE
50g (1¾oz) butter
1 celeriac, about 500g (1lb 2oz),
   finely grated
200ml (7fl oz) double cream

FOR THE TARTARE
juice of 2 limes
30g (1oz) butter

1 green chilli, deseeded and
   finely diced
2 garlic cloves, crushed
20g (¾oz) fresh root ginger, grated
2 banana shallots, finely chopped
1 small bunch of coriander, chopped
2 plum tomatoes, skinned, deseeded
   and cut into 5mm (¼in) dice
8 large scallops, shelled (see
   MasterTip, p.64) and finely chopped

TO GARNISH
2 punnets of sakura cress
   (see MasterTip, p.281)
2 heads of pak choi

1 To make the purée, melt the butter in a large pan. Add the celeriac, season well with salt and pepper, and sweat slowly for 10–12 minutes until cooked. Add the cream and bring to the boil. Remove from the heat, place in a blender, and whizz until smooth. Check for seasoning, then pass through a fine chinois. Warm to serve.

2 To make the scallop tartare, bring the lime juice to the boil in a small saucepan and remove from the heat. In a frying pan, melt the butter and sweat the chilli, garlic, and ginger. In a bowl, mix together the shallots, coriander, and diced tomato. Add the chilli mix and combine. Add the scallops and lime juice, season to taste, and mix well. Divide the mixture on to 4 serving plates.

3 Remove the scales from the fish fillets, check for bones and remove them. Score the skin across, then dry the fillets. Heat the oil in a large frying pan. Season the fish fillets well, place skin-side down in the pan and cook for 3–4 minutes. Flip over onto the flesh side, add the lemon juice and butter and cook for just 20 seconds.

4 Using a spoon, draw a line of the celeriac purée on each plate, next to the scallop tartare. Place the mullet on top and serve immediately.

PAN-FRIED SEA BREAM WITH ROASTED TOMATOES AND A FENNEL SALAD

Andy Oliver project manager turned chef and 2009 finalist

20 vine-ripened cherry tomatoes
salt and freshly ground black pepper
4 garlic cloves, unpeeled, lightly crushed
2 sprigs of rosemary
pinch of dried chilli flakes
150ml (5fl oz) olive oil
4 sea bream fillets
2 small bulbs fennel, with fronds
  if possible
squeeze of lemon juice
a few fresh basil leaves, finely shredded

PREPARATION TIME
10 minutes

COOKING TIME
20 minutes

SERVES 4

1 Preheat the oven to 180°C (350°F/Gas 4).
2 Season the tomatoes with salt and pepper and place in a roasting tin with the garlic, rosemary, 120ml (4fl oz) olive oil, and a sprinkling of chilli flakes. Put in the oven and roast for 15–20 minutes.
3 Shave the fennel finely on a mandolin and mix with a pinch of salt, 1 tbsp oil, and a squeeze of lemon. Keep the fronds aside for garnish.
4 For the dressing, take some oil from the tomato roasting tin and allow to cool. Add a squeeze of lemon and adjust the seasoning. Add the basil.
5 Trim the bream fillets and score the skin finely. Heat a frying pan until hot and add the remaining olive oil. Season the fish and pan-fry it skin-side down until the skin is crisp and and the flesh is almost totally cooked through, then turn over and cook for a further 20 seconds. Remove from the pan.
6 To serve, place the roasted tomatoes in the middle of the plates. Place the fish on them and put the fennel salad on top of the fish. Drizzle the dressing around the plates and garnish with fennel fronds.

PANCETTA-WRAPPED MONKFISH WITH SAFFRON CHIPS AND TARTARE SAUCE

inspired by **Daniel Mellor** sous chef and 2009 Professionals quarter-finalist

PREPARATION TIME
60 minutes

COOKING TIME
10 minutes

SERVES 4

¼ tsp saffron threads
  (see MasterTip, p.316)
2 large potatoes (see MasterTip,
  p.197), peeled and cut
  into thin chips
90g (3¼oz) pancetta (12 slices)
4 pieces of monkfish tail,
  75g (2½oz) each
vegetable oil for deep frying

FOR THE TARTARE SAUCE
100ml (3½fl oz) crème fraîche
1½ tbsp capers, chopped
½ small shallot, finely chopped
1 tbsp chopped fresh parsley
1 tbsp snipped chives
squeeze of lemon juice
sea salt and freshly ground
  black pepper

TO SERVE
2 tbsp fresh capers
lemon wedges

1 Put the saffron threads in a large bowl, then pour 200ml (7fl oz) boiling water over them and stir. Add the chips and enough cold water to cover them. Soak the chips in the saffron water for 45 minutes until they are tinged with yellow.

2 To make the tartare sauce, simply combine all the ingredients thoroughly in a small bowl, seasoning to taste with the lemon juice, salt and pepper. Keep cool in the fridge.

3 Preheat the oven to 200°C (400°F/Gas 6). Arrange 3 slices of

---

MASTER TIP

FILLETING MONKFISH

Monkfish is often sold with the tough black skin already removed. If it is still present, slide a knife beneath it at the wider end of the tail, take hold of it and pull and cut it away. The flesh is also covered with a translucent connective membrane and you will need to take care to remove this, otherwise the monkfish will become rubbery in texture when you cook it.

1 Slide a long, sharp knife between the backbone and the fillet. Remove the fillet and repeat on the other side.

2 Remove the membrane by sliding your knife between the skin and the flesh, tugging it away with your hand.

pancetta on a baking tray, slightly overlapping them. Top with a piece of monkfish and roll it up in the pancetta. Repeat with the rest of the pancetta and monkfish.

4   Drain and dry the chips on kitchen paper. Heat the vegetable oil in a large saucepan or deep-fat fryer until it reaches the temperature when a small piece of bread will instantly begin to brown and develop little bubbles all around it. Fry the chips for about 10 minutes or until they are light golden brown. Drain them on kitchen paper and toss with sea salt.

5   Meanwhile, cook the fish in the oven for 10 minutes until the pancetta is crispy and the fish is firm.

6   Serve the monkfish with a neat stack of saffron chips and a little tartare sauce on the side. Garnish with capers and a lemon wedge.

STEAMED FILLET OF SEA BASS WITH GARLIC CONFIT AND VANILLA CREAM SAUCE

Daniel Graham sous chef and 2009 Professionals finalist

4 fillets of sea bass, about 150g
  (5½oz) each
grated zest and juice of 1 lemon
3 tbsp light olive oil
1 vanilla pod, deseeded
salt and freshly ground black pepper
125g (4½oz) green beans

FOR THE GARLIC CONFIT
12 garlic cloves
100ml (3½fl oz) vegetable oil

FOR THE VANILLA CREAM SAUCE
25g (scant 1oz) butter
2 large shallots, diced
2 garlic cloves, crushed
100ml (3½fl oz) white wine
  (see MasterTip, p.123)
250ml (8fl oz) fish stock
1 vanilla pod, deseeded and
  seeds reserved
100ml (3½fl oz) double cream

PREPARATION TIME
15 minutes, plus marinating time

COOKING TIME
25 minutes

SERVES 4

1 Rinse the sea bass under cold running water to ensure it is free from pin bones and scales. Trim the fish at the ends and along the belly. Score the skin lightly 4–5 times and place in a shallow tray.

2 In a small bowl, add the lemon zest and juice, the olive oil, vanilla seeds, and salt and pepper. Mix together and then pour the mixture over the sea bass and leave to marinate for 1 hour.

3 To make the garlic confit, place the garlic cloves in a saucepan with the vegetable oil, making sure the garlic is completely covered, and put on a low heat for 20 minutes or until the garlic is soft. Drain the garlic cloves and keep warm.

4 Meanwhile, for the vanilla cream sauce, melt the butter in a heavy pan and add the diced shallots and garlic. Gently cook for 5–6 minutes, until soft. Add the white wine and increase the heat. Let the mixture boil for 8–10 minutes, until reduced by two-thirds. Next, add the fish stock and vanilla seeds and reduce by half. Add the cream and salt and pepper to taste, and reduce by half once again.

5 Once the sauce and the garlic are ready, cook the sea bass. Lay the fillets in a bamboo steamer basket with the skin facing upwards. Place over a pan of boiling water and steam for 7–9 minutes, depending on the size of the fish, until cooked through.

6 For the green beans, top and tail them and then blanch in boiling water for 3 minutes.

7 To assemble, put a pile of the green beans on the centre of each plate and carefully place a sea bass fillet on top. Place 3 cloves of the garlic confit around the plate and finish with a generous drizzle of the vanilla cream sauce.

HOT SMOKED WILTSHIRE TROUT WITH CELERIAC AND APPLE REMOULADE AND GRAIN MUSTARD DRESSING

inspired by **Jamie Barnett** chef and 2009 Professionals quarter-finalist

PREPARATION TIME
10 minutes

SERVES 4

½ celeriac, about 250g (9oz)
2 Cox's apples
1 tbsp grain mustard
6 tbsp olive oil

1 tbsp white wine vinegar
sea salt and freshly ground
  black pepper
4 fillets hot-smoked Wiltshire trout

1 Peel and coarsely grate the celeriac. Then grate the apple and combine with the celeriac in a serving bowl.
2 Whisk together the mustard, oil, and vinegar and season well, then dress the celeriac and apple.
3 Divide the dressed salad between 4 plates and top with the smoked trout fillets.

TAGLIATELLE OF BEETROOT JUICE WITH APPLE AND MINT CREAM

Emily Ludolf 18-year-old student and 2008 finalist

FOR THE TAGLIATELLE
350g (12oz) fresh beetroot, peeled, trimmed, and chopped
2 Cox's apples (or other sharp dessert apples), peeled, cored, and chopped
5 tsp powdered gelling agent such as Texturas Gellan

FOR THE CREAM
250ml (8fl oz) soured cream
2–3 tbsp creamed horseradish (see MasterTip, p.220)

1 tbsp milk
1 small Granny Smith apple, peeled, grated, and sprinkled with fresh lemon juice
1 small bunch (about 12 sprigs) of mint, finely chopped
salt and freshly ground black pepper

TO SERVE
125g (4½oz) sliced smoked salmon, cut into thin strips
lemon juice

PREPARATION TIME
1 hour, plus chilling time

SERVES 4

1 Preheat the oven to its lowest setting. Place a 30 x 20cm (12 x 8in) shallow non-stick baking tray in the oven to warm.
2 Place the beetroot in a juicer and process to extract the juice. Add the chopped apples and process to extract their juice into the same container.
3 Measure out 250ml (8fl oz) of the juice and place in a small saucepan. Measure the gelling agent carefully, levelling off the teaspoon with a knife. Use a balloon whisk to whisk in the gelling agent – it will immediately thicken and appear cloudy. Set the juice over a high heat and keep stirring until you see that it has thinned and cleared. Pour into the warmed baking tray, ensuring it spreads evenly. Place in the fridge until the jelly has set firmly. Once it is cold, loosen a corner with a round-bladed knife and carefully lift it out onto a chopping board. Slice it finely into tagliatelle-like strips. Set aside in a bowl.
4 For the apple, mint, and horseradish cream, mix together all the ingredients in a bowl until completely incorporated. Chill, covered, in the fridge.
5 Season the salmon with pepper and lemon juice. Arrange the tagliatelle and salmon in pretty, loose piles on 4 plates. Place a spoonful of the apple, mint, and horseradish cream on top of each pile, or serve separately if you wish. Serve immediately.

PAVÉ OF SALMON, VEGETABLE TERRINE, CONSOMMÉ OF SAN MARZANO AND QUAIL'S EGG JELLY

Adam Fargin head chef and 2008 Professionals quarter-finalist

2 tbsp olive oil
450–500g (1lb–1lb 2oz) centre-cut
  fillet of salmon, skin on
125g (4½oz) samphire or
  fine asparagus
25g (scant 1oz) unsalted butter
sea salt
white peppercorns

FOR THE CONSOMMÉ
8 quail's eggs
1 kg (2¼lb) San Marzano or
  vine-ripened tomatoes

8–10 basil stalks
8 small or 4 long gelatine
  sheets, soaked

FOR THE TERRINE
2 courgettes, 1 sliced lengthways,
  the other into discs
1 large purple aubergine,
  sliced lengthways
2 red peppers, deseeded and sliced
1 yellow pepper, deseeded and sliced
100g (3½oz) baby carrots, stalks on
35g (1¼oz) basil

PREPARATION TIME
45 minutes, plus chilling time

COOKING TIME
15 minutes

SERVES 4

1 Blanch the quail's eggs in boiling water for 2 minutes, 7 seconds. Refresh in cold water and, once cold, peel under cold water.
2 Reserve 100ml (3½fl oz) consommé (see MasterTip, right) for the vegetable terrine. Line a terrine mould or 600ml (1 pint) loaf tin with cling film, fill with half the consommé and freeze for 30–40 minutes. When semi-hard, put in the quail's eggs and fill to the top with the remaining consommé. Return to the fridge until set (about 1½ hours).
3 In a frying pan, heat the oil to 55°C (131°F). Add the salmon, cover, and keep the temperature constant for 14 minutes, then remove from the pan and allow to cool for 30 minutes. Refrigerate.
4 To prepare the vegetable terrine, chargrill the lengthways-cut courgettes, aubergine, and half the peppers. Place the remaining vegetables in a pan of salted boiling water until cooked (about 10 minutes), drain and refresh in iced water. Line a 1.2 litre (2 pint) loaf tin or terrine with cling film and then add the chargrilled aubergine and courgette. Fill the centre with the boiled vegetables and basil and top with the chargrilled peppers. Pour the reserved tomato consommé jelly over and refrigerate for at least 1½ hours.
5 Allow the salmon to come up to room temperature. Cut into 4 portions. Sauté the samphire in the butter for 2–3 minutes and season. Lay on a cloth to remove any remaining butter. Cut the jellied egg terrine through the eggs and place on the plate with the vegetable terrine and the salmon, topped with the samphire or asparagus.

MASTER TIP
TOMATO CONSOMMÉ

To make the consommé, place the tomatoes in a food processor with the basil stalks and whizz to a pulp. Season with salt and pepper. Place the mixture in muslin or a jelly bag and leave to drip overnight in the fridge – if there is not sufficient time, squeeze very gently occasionally to speed up the process. You should have 600ml (1 pint) consommé.
  Gently heat the consommé in a pan. When slightly hot, add the gelatine leaves and whisk in until broken down. Allow to cool.

SALMON CARPACCIO AND SPRING ONION PANCAKES

Matt Dawson professional rugby player and 2006 Celebrity champion

PREPARATION TIME
30 minutes

COOKING TIME
10 minutes

SERVES 4

1 egg
100g (3½oz) self-raising flour
3 tbsp milk
10g (¼oz) butter
4 spring onions, finely chopped
2 tbsp groundnut oil
salt and freshly ground black pepper
250g (9oz) sushi-grade salmon
50g (1¾oz) daikon, sliced into thin
  julienne strips

25g (scant 1oz) shiso
25g (scant 1oz) mixed leaves such
  as radish and coriander (see
  MasterTip, p.281)

FOR THE DRESSING
juice of 1 lime
50–75ml (1¾–2½fl oz) groundnut oil
2 tsp crushed green peppercorns

1 To make the pancakes, place the egg and flour in a medium bowl and whisk together into a paste. Gradually add the milk and butter, whisking well as you go. Stir in the spring onions and season well.
2 Heat a non-stick frying pan with a little of the oil. When the pan is hot, add tablespoons of batter – about 2 tbsp for an 18cm (7in) pan. Cook for 2–3 minutes until bubbles begin to appear on the surface of the mixture. Turn the pancakes over and cook for a couple of minutes more. Keep warm and continue using up all of the batter. You should have 8 pancakes.
3 Slice the salmon as thinly as you can and then gently tap and flatten it with a rolling pin until it is wafer thin. For the dressing, whisk together the lime and oil then add the peppercorns. Season well.
4 To serve, cut the pancakes into triangles and arrange in the middle of the plate. Lay the salmon over them. Arrange the daikon around the pancakes and sprinkle around the shiso and mixed leaves. Drizzle the dressing over the dish and serve.

SESAME CRUSTED TUNA WITH HORSERADISH MOUSSE

Christopher Souto IT consultant turned chef and 2005 semi-finalist

700g (1½lb) yellow fin tuna
3 tbsp light soy sauce
2 tsp sesame oil
3 tbsp vegetable oil
2 tsp Dijon mustard
3 tbsp olive oil, plus extra for cooking
1 tbsp white wine vinegar
salt and freshly ground black pepper

100ml (3½fl oz) double cream
3 tsp creamed horseradish (see
  MasterTip, p.220)
2 tbsp black sesame seeds
2 tbsp white sesame seeds
50g (1¾oz) rocket
50g (1¾oz) watercress

PREPARATION TIME
20 minutes, plus marinating time

COOKING TIME
4–5 minutes

SERVES 4

1 Cut the tuna into 4 square steaks and put in a single layer in a dish. Mix together the soy sauce, sesame oil, vegetable oil, and one teaspoon of the mustard. Pour over the tuna and leave for 2 hours, or overnight, in the fridge.

2 In a bowl, combine the remaining mustard with the olive oil and the vinegar and blend to make a vinaigrette. Season with salt and pepper to taste.

3 To make the horseradish mousse, combine the cream with the creamed horseradish and then whip using an electric hand whisk until light and fluffy. Season with salt and pepper to taste.

4 Mix together the black and white sesame seeds on a plate. Drain the marinade from the tuna steaks and roll them in the seeds. Add a dash of olive oil to a frying pan and, over a high heat, cook the steaks for 2 minutes on each side.

5 Serve each of the tuna steaks with a quenelle (see MasterTip, right) of mousse and the rocket and watercress salad lightly tossed in the vinaigrette.

MASTER TIP

SHAPING QUENELLES

A quenelle is a term that refers to the shaping of a mousse or creamed fish or meat that is created by using 2 spoons. To make the oval shape, scoop up the mousse with one spoon – which can be either a dessert or tablespoon, depending on the finished size you are aiming for – and pass the ingredients back and forth to achieve the perfect shape. If the mixture is sticking to the spoons, try damping them.

SEARED TUNA WITH CHIPOTLE MAYONNAISE

inspired by **Thomasina Miers** food writer turned chef and 2005 champion

PREPARATION TIME
10 minutes

COOKING TIME
5 minutes

SERVES 4

4 tuna steaks, about 175g (6oz)
  each and about 2.5cm (1in) thick
sea salt and freshly ground
  black pepper
1 tbsp olive oil

FOR THE MAYONNAISE
2 egg yolks
1 tsp Dijon mustard
1 tsp white wine vinegar
250ml (8fl oz) vegetable oil
1 tbsp chipotle chillies in adobo sauce
  (see MasterTip, p.60)

1 For the tuna, season the fish on both sides and rub in the oil.
Heat a griddle pan over a moderately high heat, and sear the tuna for
2 minutes on each side, transferring to a warmed plate as they are
done. Leave to rest for a few minutes.

2 For the mayonnaise, place the egg yolks in a bowl and add the
mustard, vinegar, and a pinch of salt. Whisk together using an electric
hand whisk, and gradually add the oil, starting with little more than
a tablespoon at a time, until the mayonnaise starts to thicken; carry
on until the desired consistency is reached. If the mix is too thick,
let it down with 1–2 tbsp boiling water. Whisk in the chillies in adobo
sauce to taste.

3 Serve the tuna steaks with a spoonful of mayonnaise alongside.

JOHN TORODE "What I like about the flavour is
the meatiness of the tuna and there is also
this sort of lovely meatiness of the sauce.
It's quite a complex dish. It works very, very
well indeed."

SEARED MACKEREL FILLET WITH RED ONION MARMALADE

Peter Bayless ad creative turned author and 2006 champion

4 mackerel fillets,
  about 100g (3½oz) each
olive oil, for brushing the fish
1 lime
small bunch of chives, to garnish

FOR THE ONION MARMALADE
50g (1¾oz) salted butter
splash of olive oil
4 red onions, finely sliced
sea salt and freshly ground
  black pepper
150ml (5fl oz) sherry or red vinegar
25g (scant 1oz) dark soft brown sugar
50g (1¾oz) seedless raisins

PREPARATION TIME
10 minutes

COOKING TIME
50 minutes

SERVES 4

1 To make the onion marmalade, melt the butter with the olive oil in a saucepan and add the onions together with a good pinch of salt and pepper. Cook over a medium heat for about 10 minutes, stirring occasionally until well softened, being careful not to allow the onions to burn or colour too much. Add the vinegar, sugar, and raisins, bring to the boil, reduce the heat and then simmer gently for about 30 minutes, uncovered, or until the marmalade comes together as a mass. Turn out into a dish and keep warm at the side of the hob.
2 Meanwhile, preheat the oven to 200°C (400°F/Gas 6). Heat an ovenproof frying pan to very hot, brush the mackerel fillets on both sides with a little olive oil and lay in the pan, skin-side down. After 3 minutes, sprinkle the flesh side of the fillets with a little salt and pepper and transfer the pan to the oven for 2–3 minutes, depending on the thickness of the fish, until cooked through.
3 Cut the lime in half and then cut four thin slices from the middle. Make a slit in each slice from the centre to the outside edge and give each a half twist. Finely pare the zest from the remaining lime.
4 Place one mackerel fillet onto each serving plate, squeeze the lime juice over and sprinkle with a little of the zest. Place a spoonful of the onion marmalade alongside and garnish with 2 or 3 chives and a twist of lime.

SMOKED MACKEREL PÂTÉ
inspired by **Steven Wallis** creative director and 2007 champion

PREPARATION TIME
20 minutes, plus chilling time

SERVES 4

250g (9oz) cold-smoked
  mackerel fillets
50g (1¾oz) crème fraîche
25g (scant 1oz) mascarpone cheese
3 stems of fennel fronds, plus extra
  to garnish
grated zest and juice of 1 lime
grated zest of ½ orange
fleur de sel (see MasterTip, left)
½ tsp toasted coriander seeds

3 tbsp hazelnut oil
salt and freshly ground black pepper
½ tsp sugar
4 tsp Muscat vinegar
3 chicory heads
25g (scant 1oz) toasted hazelnuts
  (see MasterTip, p.40), finely chopped
baby chervil, to garnish
pea shoot tendrils, to garnish

MASTER TIP

FLEUR DE SEL

Fleur de sel means "flower of salt" as it is felt to be fine and delicate. On the sea-salt beds of west France the crystals that accumulate on the surface of the salt pans are raked off before they can fall lower where the ordinary grey sea salt gathers. This fleur de sel does not carry the particles of sediment of ordinary sea salt, and instead is said to carry traces of algae and other materials to imbue a characteristic aroma.

1 Finely pick through the smoked mackerel to remove any bones, remove the skin, and break the flesh into pieces into a food processor. Add the crème fraîche, mascarpone cheese, fennel fronds, lime and orange zest, and the lime juice. Season with the fleur de sel and blend to a smooth pâté consistency. Chill for 30 minutes.
2 To prepare the vinaigrette, mix together the toasted coriander seeds and hazelnut oil, season with salt and pepper, and add the sugar. Then add the Muscat vinegar, whisk well and set aside.
3 To serve, trim the chicory leaves by cutting a good third of the leaves from the end. Allow 3 leaves per person. Spoon in a neat quenelle of pâté (see MasterTip, p.93) onto the cut end of each leaf. Drizzle over the vinaigrette, and scatter over the chopped hazelnuts. Finish with a pinch of fleur de sel and baby chervil leaves, fennel fronds, and pea shoot tendrils.

JOHN TORODE "Taste delicious. Texture delicious. Combination delicious. Looks fantastic on a plate. This is very, very, very good indeed."

CHICKEN AND ASPARAGUS TORTELLINI WITH POACHED QUAIL'S EGGS

Hannah Payne junior sous chef and 2009 Professionals quarter-finalist

PREPARATION TIME
1 hour 20 minutes

COOKING TIME
10–15 minutes

SERVES 4

3 egg yolks and 2 whole eggs
280g (10oz) "00" pasta flour (see MasterTip, p.52)
salt
4 quail's eggs
1 tsp vinegar

FOR THE CHICKEN MOUSSE
1 skinless chicken breast, trimmed and cut into 1cm (½in) cubes
1 egg
75ml (2½fl oz) double cream

salt and freshly ground black pepper
1 tbsp lemon juice
12 asparagus spears

FOR THE HOLLANDAISE SAUCE
2 egg yolks
115g (4oz) clarified butter
squeeze of lemon juice

FOR THE TRUFFLE FOAM
100ml (3½fl oz) milk
1 tbsp truffle oil (see MasterTip, p.22)

1 Combine the egg yolks and whole eggs in a mixer, using the dough hook. Add salt and the flour one-third at a time. Once the mix is brought together, remove from the mixer and knead until the dough has a glossy texture. Wrap in cling film and rest for 30 minutes in the fridge. (Or see MasterTip p.51.)

2 Blend the chicken in a food processor until smooth. Add the egg till the mix appears shiny, then chill for 20 minutes. Once chilled, stir in the cream slowly. Mix until fluffy and light, season and add lemon juice.

3 Reserve the top 7.5cm (3in) of the asparagus spears and cook the rest in boiling salted water until soft, about 5 minutes. Drain and whizz in a blender. Once cooled, stir into the chicken mousse.

4 Knead the pasta until pliable. Using a pasta machine (see MasterTip, p.190), roll the pasta. Cut into 7.5cm (3in) circles. Place 2 tsp mousse in the centres and fold over. Seal the edges and join opposite corners. Once all the tortellini are made, cover with a tea towel until cooking.

5 To make the sauce, put 2 tbsp of water and 2 egg yolks in a pan. Whisk over a bain marie until thick and frothy. Slowly add the butter until the sauce thickens. Season and add a squeeze of lemon juice.

6 Cut the remaining asparagus spears into 5cm (2in) lengths and cook for 5 minutes in boiling salted water. Cook the tortellini for 5 minutes in boiling salted water, and poach the quail's eggs for 30 seconds in a pan of simmering water with the vinegar added.

7 Put the milk and truffle oil in a small pan and heat to a lukewarm temperature. Season and foam up with a hand blender or whisk.

8 Serve the tortellini topped with a quail's egg and hollandaise. Spoon truffle foam around and garnish with asparagus.

DUCK BREAST ON ASIAN SALAD
inspired by **Paul Young** singer and 2006 Celebrity quarter-finalist

PREPARATION TIME
10 minutes

COOKING TIME
15 minutes

SERVES 4

4 duck breasts, about 200g (7oz) each
sea salt and freshly ground black pepper
60g (2oz) roasted salted cashew nuts
1 lime, cut into wedges, to serve

FOR THE SALAD
2 Little Gem lettuces, leaves separated
½ cucumber, peeled, deseeded,
 and sliced
60g (2oz) radishes, finely sliced
2 spring onions, sliced diagonally
2 handfuls beansprouts

small handful of coriander leaves
small handful of mint leaves

FOR THE DRESSING
juice of 1 lime
2 tbsp golden caster sugar
2 tbsp nam pla (Thai fish sauce)
1 tbsp dark soy sauce
1 tsp chopped fresh root ginger
2 red Thai (bird's eye) chillies,
 deseeded and chopped

1 Preheat the oven to 200°C (400°F/Gas 6). Score the duck skin and fat layer in a criss-cross pattern, being careful not to cut down into the flesh, and season well.

2 Place the duck breasts, skin-side down, in a dry frying pan over a medium-high heat for about 5 minutes, or until the fat starts to run and the skin turns golden brown and crispy. Turn and cook on the other side for 1–2 minutes to seal, then transfer to a roasting tin and cook in the oven for 7–8 minutes until cooked through. Remove from the oven and allow to rest.

3 Make the salad by tossing together the lettuce leaves, cucumber, radishes, spring onions, beansprouts, coriander and mint leaves, and divide among 4 serving plates.

4 Make the dressing with the lime juice, sugar, fish sauce, soy sauce, ginger, and chillies together with 2 tbsp water and drizzle over the top of the salad.

5 Scatter over the cashew nuts, and finish with one duck breast per portion, sliced into 3 pieces, and a lime wedge.

LAMB SAMOSAS
Daksha Mistry housewife turned caterer and 2006 finalist

250g (9oz) minced lamb
½ onion, finely chopped
1 garlic clove, finely chopped
½ tsp curry powder
¼ tsp chilli powder
½ tsp ground turmeric
¼ tsp ground roasted cumin seeds
½ chilli, finely chopped
1 tbsp chopped coriander
¼ tsp grated fresh root ginger
½ tsp salt

freshly ground black pepper
squeeze of lemon juice
1 litre (1¾ pints) sunflower oil,
  for deep frying
4 sprigs of coriander, to garnish

FOR THE PASTRY
110g (4oz) plain flour
1 tsp salt
1 tbsp vegetable oil
about 3 tbsp warm water

PREPARATION TIME
50 minutes

COOKING TIME
15 minutes

SERVES 4

1 To make the pastry, mix the flour and salt in a bowl. Make a well in the centre and add the oil and enough water to make a firm dough. Knead the dough on a floured surface until smooth and roll into a ball. Cover in cling film and set aside at room temperature for 30 minutes.
2 For the filling, put all the ingredients except the oil and coriander sprigs into a bowl and mix thoroughly with your hands.
3 Divide the pastry into 6 equal pieces. Roll each piece into a ball and cover with cling film to stop them from drying out. Roll each ball of pastry into a 12.5cm (5in) circle and then divide into 2 equal semicircles with a knife.
4 Place a level tbsp of the mixture on one half circle of the semicircle of pastry. Then fold the other half circle across the filling to form a triangle. Dampen the edges with water and gently seal the open edges. Repeat for the other samosas.
5 Heat the oil in a large saucepan (see MasterTip, right). To test when the oil is hot enough, put in a small piece of bread and as soon as it starts to sizzle, remove it and start frying the samosas, 4 at a time. Cook each batch for about 5 minutes, turning occasionally, or until the samosas are crisp and brown. Remove them from the pan, drain on kitchen paper and serve 3 samosas per person while still warm, garnished with the coriander.

MASTER TIP
DEEP FRYING

When deep frying foods, always use a fat with a high smoke point and check the temperature of the oil – fat is dangerous when hotter than 190°C (375°F). Cook in small batches to prevent the fat cooling down, and always dry food well before frying to avoid spluttering. Drain cooked food on kitchen paper and do not cover it to keep it warm or it will become soggy. Never move a hot deep-fat fryer and keep the handles away from the front of the hob. Have a fire extinguisher or blanket and a lid in easy reach so that you can smother the flames – never spray them with water.

SEARED BEEF WITH CUCUMBER AND POPPY SEED SALAD

Cassandra Williams food marketer and 2009 quarter-finalist

PREPARATION TIME
15 minutes

COOKING TIME
2 minutes

SERVES 4

1 cucumber
1 tbsp rice vinegar
2 tbsp sunflower oil
1 tbsp poppy seeds
1 tbsp caster sugar
1 mild red chilli, deseeded and
    finely sliced
bunch of coriander, chopped
1 tsp coriander seeds
1 tsp cumin seeds
freshly ground black pepper
1 tsp sea salt

150g (5½oz) fillet of beef
2 tsp sesame seeds
1 tbsp olive oil
handful of purple basil and
    radish sprouts, to serve
    (see MasterTip, left)

FOR THE DRESSING
2 tsp olive oil
1 tsp sesame oil
1 tbsp rice vinegar
1 tbsp light soy sauce

MASTER TIP
SPROUTING SEEDS

Sprouts are very tender seedlings that can be eaten raw or very briefly cooked. Those that are most commonly used come from the bean, grain, cabbage, or onion families. Radish sprouts have the mild peppery flavour of radishes and make a pleasant contrast to other sprouts, which can be rather bland. Buy sprouts as fresh as possible because microbes thrive in the warm, wet conditions in which they are produced. You can also get sprouting jars and packets of seeds to sprout from health food shops. Alternatively, use ready grown beansprouts, although they are not such a strong flavour.

1 Cut the cucumber in half lengthways and remove the seeds. Finely slice the cucumber and place in a bowl with the rice vinegar, 1 tbsp of the sunflower oil and the poppy seeds, caster sugar, chilli, and coriander. Mix with your hands and place in the fridge.

2 Put the coriander seeds and cumin seeds with the black pepper and sea salt in a pestle and mortar, lightly crush, and then scatter the mixture onto a plate. Trim any excess fat or sinew off the fillet then roll in the spices until evenly coated. Put the sesame seeds on another plate.

3 Heat the olive oil in a frying pan until hot, then place the fillet in the pan. Sear on each side for about 1 minute and remove from the pan. Roll in the sesame seeds, then leave to rest for 10 minutes.

4 To make the dressing, whisk together the oils with the rice vinegar and the soy sauce, and add seasoning. Just before serving, toss the basil and radish sprouts into the dressing until they are lightly and evenly coated, then remove.

5 To serve, finely slice the beef and arrange on a plate, positioning slightly to one side. Put a mound of the cucumber salad on the other side and then lightly place the basil and sprouts around the plate.

WINTER SALAD OF PIGEON AND JERUSALEM ARTICHOKES

David Hall IT buyer turned food writer and 2007 semi-finalist

4 tbsp olive oil
1 tbsp thyme leaves
salt and freshly ground black pepper
4 pigeon breasts, about 75g (2½oz)
  each, skin removed
4 Jerusalem artichokes, peeled and
  cut into 2cm (¾in) slices
4 tbsp red wine vinegar
1 tbsp caster sugar
1 garlic clove, thinly sliced
2 small or 1 large beetroot, peeled,
  halved, and very thinly sliced
50g (1¾oz) toasted hazelnuts (see
  MasterTip, p.40), roughly chopped

FOR THE DRESSING
100ml (3½fl oz) dry white wine
1 garlic clove, peeled and left whole
3 tbsp white wine vinegar
2 tbsp olive oil
1 tbsp clear honey

FOR THE SALAD
4 large handfuls of baby spinach leaves
8 Swiss chard leaves, stems cut out
  and sliced into 2.5cm (1in) strips

PREPARATION TIME
15 minutes, plus infusing time

COOKING TIME
20 minutes

SERVES 4

1 Mix 2 tbsp of the olive oil with the thyme and a little seasoning and toss with the pigeon breasts. Set aside.

2 Bring a pan of water to the boil, add the Jerusalem artichoke slices and let simmer for 5 minutes until just soft. Drain and leave to cool.

3 In a bowl, mix the red wine vinegar, sugar, and garlic and toss with the beetroot slices. Leave for 30 minutes.

4 Heat a non-stick frying pan and sear the pigeon breasts for 3–4 minutes on each side. Remove, cover with foil, and set aside to rest.

5 For the dressing, add the wine and garlic clove to the pan, bring to the boil and then leave to simmer to reduce by half. Add the vinegar and reduce by half again. Remove from the heat, add the olive oil and the honey, and season to taste. Remove the garlic clove.

6 Meanwhile, in another non-stick frying pan heat up the remaining olive oil and cook the artichokes for 5–8 minutes, or until they are crisp and golden.

7 To serve, toss the salad leaves in some of the dressing and pile onto plates. Slice the pigeon breasts in half. Arrange the slivers of beetroot, artichoke, and pigeon over the leaves. Top with the hazelnuts and drizzle on any remaining dressing.

SPICED QUAIL SALAD WITH POMEGRANATE SEEDS AND PISTACHIOS

Andy Oliver project manager turned chef and 2009 finalist

PREPARATION TIME
45 minutes, plus marinating time

COOKING TIME
40 minutes

SERVES 4

2 quail
1 garlic clove
salt and freshly ground black pepper
1 tbsp olive oil
2 tsp ras el hanout spice blend
½ tsp cayenne pepper
1 tbsp groundnut or sunflower oil
1 onion, finely sliced
50g (1¾oz) selection of mixed baby salad leaves
25g (scant 1oz) unsalted, skinned pistachio nuts, chopped
1 pomegranate, deseeded and flesh discarded

10g (¼oz) small mint leaves
30g (1oz) micro coriander cress and micro red chard (see MasterTip, p.281)
pomegranate molasses, to serve (see MasterTip, p.41)

FOR THE DRESSING
3 tbsp olive oil
2 tbsp walnut oil
juice of 1 lemon
½ tsp caster sugar
1 garlic clove, finely chopped

GREGG WALLACE

"It's a really terrific-looking dish. You get lemon, and then the meatiness of the quail. Then little bursts of fruit from the pomegranate, and then pepper and spice. That's very clever."

1 Remove the breasts and legs of the quail. Crush the garlic clove in a pestle and mortar with some salt. Add the olive oil and the spice mix and blend. Rub the quail breasts with the marinade, transfer to a tightly sealed container and leave to marinate overnight in the fridge.
2 Preheat the oven to 200°C (400°F/Gas 6). Add the cayenne pepper and extra seasoning to the quail legs. Transfer them to a roasting tin and roast for 25 minutes.
3 Poach the quail breasts in a saucepan of simmering water for 20 minutes.
4 To make the dressing, mix together the ingredients and season with salt and pepper to taste.
5 To finish the quail, heat the groundnut or sunflower oil in a frying pan and cook the onion until crisp. Remove from the pan and drain on kitchen paper. Take the quail breasts out of the poaching liquid, pat dry with kitchen paper, and then fry on each side for 3–4 minutes until browned. Remove the legs from the oven.
6 To serve, place a small handful of salad leaves in the middle of the serving plates. Then divide the legs and breasts between the plates and scatter over the nuts, pomegranate seeds, mint leaves, and micro coriander cress and red chard. Drizzle the dressing over the top and finish with the fried onions and some dots of pomegranate molasses.

GRILLED QUAIL WITH A PISTACHIO AND ORANGE BLOSSOM SAUCE, SERVED ON HOME-MADE FLAT BREAD

Nadia Sawalha actress and presenter and 2007 Celebrity champion

4 quail, each cut into four pieces by
  your butcher, or into two if small
½ small onion, grated
1 tbsp finely chopped parsley
1 tsp ground coriander seeds
1 small green chilli, deseeded and
  finely chopped
2 tbsp olive oil
salt and freshly ground black pepper

FOR THE PISTACHIO SAUCE
60g (2oz) pistachio nuts
60g (2oz) pine nuts

10 large mint leaves, finely chopped
1 tbsp finely chopped coriander
4–5 tbsp extra virgin olive oil
good squeeze of lemon
about 1 tbsp orange blossom water

FOR THE FLAT BREAD
260g (9½oz) white bread flour
pinch of salt
½ tsp dried yeast
200ml (7fl oz) lukewarm water
1 tbsp olive oil

PREPARATION TIME
45 minutes, plus marinating time

COOKING TIME
20 minutes

SERVES 4

1 Put the quail in a bowl and then, in a jug, mix the onion, parsley, coriander, and chilli with the olive oil. Add salt and pepper to season and pour the marinade over the quail. Cover and leave to marinate for a minimum of 1 hour.

2 Preheat the grill to high and cook the quail on a grill pan, for 15–20 minutes, turning them a couple of times, until cooked through.

3 Meanwhile, make the pistachio sauce. Put the nuts in a food processor and blend until they are very finely chopped. Transfer to a bowl and stir in the mint and coriander together with the olive oil and lemon juice. Season with salt and pepper. Add the orange blossom water a teaspoonful at a time, until you like the taste (some people can find it a little overpowering).

4 To make the flat bread, put the flour and salt into a bowl. Dissolve the yeast in the water and pour it gradually into the flour, mixing all the time with your hands or use a dough hook on a food processor. Add the olive oil and knead until the dough is soft.

5 Sprinkle some flour on the work surface. Divide the dough into 4 pieces and roll them out until they are pancake thin. Heat a pancake or omelette pan until hot and then cook the bread rounds, one at a time, for 1–2 minutes on each side, until browned and cooked through.

6 To serve, lay a flat bread on each plate, top with the quail pieces, and drizzle the pistachio sauce over the top.

JOHN TORODE "I think your food looks fantastic. It's just simple, elegant, beautiful, understated-looking food. Every single bit you get is just fantastic."

ROAST QUAIL WITH SCOTCH EGG, MORELS, AND ASPARAGUS

Steve Groves chef de partie and 2009 Professionals champion

PREPARATION TIME
40 minutes, plus chilling time

COOKING TIME
1 hour 30 minutes

SERVES 4

4 whole, oven-ready quail, divided
  into crowns (see MasterTip, below),
  legs saved for Scotch eggs and
  trimmings for vinaigrette
400ml (14fl oz) chicken stock
1 tbsp olive oil
20g (¾oz) salted butter
sea salt and freshly ground
  black pepper

FOR THE QUAIL VINAIGRETTE
about 750ml (1¼ pints) chicken stock
  (see MasterTip, p.21)
3 tbsp olive oil
2 shallots, finely sliced
2 garlic cloves, finely chopped
2 sprigs of thyme
2 bay leaves
150ml (5fl oz) white wine
1 tsp sherry vinegar

FOR THE SCOTCH EGGS
4 quail's eggs
125g (4½oz) skinless, boneless
  chicken breast
2 eggs, 1 white only, 1 beaten
250ml (8fl oz) double cream
2 tbsp plain flour
100g (3¾oz) pancetta (see MasterTip,
  p.44), finely diced
1 tsp chopped tarragon
50g (1¾oz) fresh breadcrumbs
1 litre (1¾ pints) vegetable oil

FOR THE MORELS AND ASPARAGUS
8 asparagus tips
16 morels, cut in half OR 25g (scant
  1oz) dried porcini mushrooms,
  rehydrated (see MasterTip, p.54)
1 shallot, finely diced
20g (¾oz) salted butter
2 tbsp Madeira wine
4 tbsp juices from vinaigrette stock

MASTER TIP
PREPARING QUAIL

The crown of a quail, or any
other bird, is the breastbone,
wishbone, and ribcage
trimmed back to the breasts
alone, so there are no wings,
backbone, or neck left. They
are usually skinned, too. For
a quail, it is possible to prepare
the bird with a sharp pair of
shears, but larger birds, such
as partridge and pheasant, can
be tougher, so it is best to ask
your butcher to prepare the
crown for you.

1 Poach the 4 crowns gently in the chicken stock for 5 minutes.
Remove from the stock and dry on kitchen paper. Set aside.
2 For the vinaigrette, drain the poaching liquid into a measuring jug
and make up to 1 litre (1¾ pints) with the vinaigrette chicken stock.
Heat 1 tbsp of the oil in a saucepan. Add the quail trimmings, reduce
the heat and cook for 10 minutes until the trimmings are a deep brown.
Remove from the pan and allow the fat to drain away from the trimmings.
3 In the same pan, add a further tablespoon of oil, then add the
shallots, garlic, thyme, and bay leaves and cook for about 10 minutes
until well caramelized. Deglaze with the white wine and reduce by half
to a glaze. Return the quail trimmings and cover with the stock. Bring
gently to a simmer and cook for an hour, skimming often.
4 Cook the quail's eggs in boiling water for 2 minutes and refresh in
iced water. Once cooled, leave to sit submerged in vinegar for around
1 hour or until the shells go soft; this makes them easier to peel.
5 Meanwhile, for the Scotch eggs, make a chicken mousse. Blend
the chicken meat with a generous pinch of salt in a food processor,

then add the egg white and, while the machine is running, gradually add the cream.

6 Mix the quail leg meat and pancetta with the tarragon and then add the chicken mousse and a good seasoning of salt and pepper. Lightly oil 4 squares of cling film, then spread some of the mixture onto each to form a circle about 3mm (⅛in) thick and large enough to wrap around each egg. Put in the fridge to chill for about 1 hour.

7 Return to the quail crowns and pan-fry them in the oil and butter for 5–6 minutes, until golden all over. Allow to rest for 5 minutes and then remove the breasts from the crowns and set aside. Season with a little salt.

8 Once the sauce has cooked for long enough, pass it through muslin and reduce once again until it has a very deep flavour and begins to lightly coat a spoon. Remove the sauce from the heat, check the seasoning, and add a few drops of the vinegar for some acidity. Finally, add 1 tbsp or so of olive oil so that it splits the sauce and forms a vinaigrette.

9 To finish the Scotch eggs, remove the quail meat wraps from the fridge and wrap around the eggs, removing the cling film and nipping off any excess at the join. Put the beaten egg into a shallow bowl and the breadcrumbs into a separate shallow bowl. Roll the covered eggs lightly in flour to form a nice ball, then dip in the egg and finally roll in the breadcrumbs.

10 Pour the oil into a large saucepan and heat to 180°C (356°F) (see MasterTip, p.101). You can test the temperature using a deep-fry thermometer, or a more traditional route would be to dip a wooden chopstick into the hot oil. If it sizzles vigorously, the oil is hot enough. Deep fry the Scotch eggs for 8–10 minutes until golden.

11 Meanwhile, prepare the morels and asparagus. Blanch the asparagus tips in boiling salted water for 3–4 minutes until just tender. Remove from the water and drain.

12 Over a medium-high heat, sauté the morels (or rehydrated porcini mushrooms) and shallot in the butter for 1–2 minutes. Add the Madeira wine and reduce by half to a glaze, add 4 tbsp of juices from the vinaigrette stock and again reduce by half to a glaze. Toss the asparagus through this mixture then check the seasoning.

13 To serve, spoon the asparagus and morels onto serving plates, top with the roasted quail breasts and quail Scotch eggs, cut in half. Drizzle over the quail vinaigrette.

MICHEL ROUX JR
"I think it's inspired to have used a quail's egg as a Scotch egg. Beautifully cooked supreme of quail. Perfectly seasoned. Tremendous sauce with bags of flavour. Very, very good."

CARPACCIO OF VENISON WITH WATERCRESS SALAD AND A RASPBERRY VINAIGRETTE

Angela Kenny administrator turned chef and 2009 semi-finalist

1 tbsp dried thyme, finely chopped
salt and freshly ground black pepper
200g (7oz) loin of venison
1 tbsp olive oil
85g (3oz) watercress

FOR THE VINAIGRETTE
30g (1oz) raspberries
4 tbsp balsamic vinegar
90ml (3fl oz) olive oil

PREPARATION TIME
35 minutes

COOKING TIME
2 minutes

SERVES 4

1 Preheat a frying pan until hot. Season the thyme with salt and pepper and spread on a plate. Rub the venison with some of the olive oil and roll it in the herb mixture.

2 Place the venison in the hot drying pan and sear all the edges. Remove from the pan and leave to rest for around 30 minutes.

3 Meanwhile, make the vinaigrette by puréeing the raspberries with a hand blender and pass through a sieve to remove any pips. Mix the raspberry purée with the balsamic vinegar and olive oil, and add salt and pepper to taste.

4 Thinly slice the venison (see MasterTip, right), arrange on a serving plate and sprinkle with salt and pepper. Arrange the watercress in the centre and drizzle the dressing over the top.

MASTERTIP
CARPACCIO

The word "carpaccio" refers to any thinly sliced meat or fish, such as beef, veal, venison, salmon, or tuna, that is eaten raw. To make it easier to slice thinly and evenly, freeze the meat or fish after searing.

GREGG WALLACE "The vinaigrette gives sharpness and sweetness to the wonderful deep richness of venison. The peppery addition of watercress is inspirational."

TRIO OF WILD RABBIT WITH PANCETTA CRISPS AND FOIE GRAS SAUCE

Mat Follas engineer turned chef patron and 2009 champion

PREPARATION TIME
10 minutes

COOKING TIME
35 minutes

SERVES 4

1 wild rabbit, with prepared racks, tenderloin, and kidneys
8 stems wild young nettles
10 strips fine cut pancetta (see MasterTip, p.44)
150ml (5fl oz) double cream
25g (scant 1oz) foie gras, cut into slices

25g (scant 1oz) salted butter, plus extra for the nettles
freshly ground black pepper
1 tsp puréed wild garlic flowers or 1 tsp garlic purée (see MasterTip, p.206)
4 fennel fronds, to garnish

1 Preheat the oven to 200°C (400°F/Gas 6). Pick off the nettle leaves, blanch them for 2 minutes in boiling water, then put in a bowl of iced water. Drain, dry, and set aside.

2 For the pancetta crisps, place half the pancetta onto a baking tray and place another tray on top to flatten the pancetta. Bake in the oven for 10–15 minutes, or until crisp. Remove from the tray, place on kitchen paper, and leave to cool. Cut them into small rectangles.

3 To make the foie gras sauce, bring the cream to the boil in a pan and add the foie gras. Heat gently until the foie gras is warmed through and the sauce has thickened and coats the back of a spoon. Push the creamed foie gras through a sieve and set aside.

4 To prepare the rabbit loin, wrap the remaining pancetta around it. Melt the butter in a non-stick frying pan and fry the loin for 10 minutes or until the pancetta is cooked and crisp. Remove the loin from the pan, unwrap the pancetta and leave the loin to rest. Discard the pancetta or, if that seems too wasteful, serve on the side.

5 Season the racks with salt and pepper and cook in the same pan with the pancetta fat for 5–8 minutes until browned on all sides. Remove from the pan and leave to rest with the loin. Halve the kidneys and then cook in the same pan for 1 minute or until slightly browned. Remove from the pan and leave to rest with the other pieces of rabbit.

6 Mash the nettles with a fork, adding a tiny amount of puréed wild garlic flowers (or garlic purée) to taste. Fry the nettles in a frying pan in the remaining butter, just long enough to heat them through.

7 To serve, make a circle of hot smashed nettles in the centre of each plate. Place 1 tbsp of foie gras sauce to the right of the nettles and drag downwards with the spoon. Place the crisps to the left of the nettles. Slice the loin into 4 and place on top of the pancetta crisps and put the kidneys on the foie gras sauce. Slice the rack and pile the pieces into a tower on top of the nettles. Garnish with a frond of fennel.

JOHN TORODE

"Salty pancetta and soft loin. The nettle just kicks in. The flavours are unbelievably extraordinary. I never thought I'd see a dish as beautiful as that. I love it."

BRAISED WILD HARE
WITH PEARL BARLEY RISOTTO

Gillian Wylie property developer turned chef and 2007 quarter-finalist

30g (1oz) unsalted butter
1 tbsp olive oil
1 onion, roughly chopped
1 small leek, roughly chopped
2 carrots, roughly chopped
1 leg of wild hare, skinned
few sprigs of thyme
1 bay leaf
3 garlic cloves, roughly bashed
sea salt and white pepper
300ml (19fl oz) dry white wine

30g (1oz) finely snipped chives
85g (3oz) watercress, to garnish

FOR THE RISOTTO
500ml (16fl oz) chicken or game stock
115g (4oz) unsalted butter
1 tbsp olive oil
2 shallots, finely chopped
200g (7oz) pearl barley
375ml (13fl oz) white wine
juice of ½ lemon

PREPARATION TIME
15 minutes

COOKING TIME
1 hour 5 minutes

SERVES 4

1 Preheat the oven to 180°C (350°F/Gas 4). Heat the butter and oil in a flameproof casserole and sauté the onion, leek, and carrots for 5 minutes or until the onion is translucent. Transfer to a separate dish using a slotted spoon.

2 Remove as much of the sinewy film covering the hare leg as possible without damaging the flesh too much. Fry the leg in the casserole for 1 minute on each side or until browned. Return the onion, leek, and carrots to the pan. Add the thyme, bay leaf, and garlic and season with sea salt and white pepper.

3 Pour in enough wine to cover the leg. Bring to the boil, put on the lid and transfer to the oven for at least 1 hour or until the hare is tender and falling from the bone.

4 To make the pearl barley risotto, heat the stock. Melt 85g (3oz) of the butter and the oil in a large saucepan and fry the shallots gently for 5 minutes, or until translucent. Add the pearl barley and stir for 1 minute. Add a splash of white wine and wait until it is absorbed, then add alternate ladlefuls of stock and wine until the barley has swelled and resembles traditional rice risotto (this should take 15–20 minutes). The barley will still be quite firm and nutty, but it shouldn't be too chewy. Stir in the lemon juice.

5 Take the risotto pan off the heat and beat in the remaining butter with a wooden spoon, season, and leave to rest for a few minutes.

6 Remove the hare leg from the casserole and shred the meat into a bowl. Add 4 tbsp of stock and half of the chives. Check the seasoning. To serve, spoon some of the risotto into a 9cm (3½in) ring mould on each plate, then top with shredded hare. Sprinkle with more chopped chives and garnish with watercress.

MASTER TIP
THE PERFECT RISOTTO

For some hints and tips on cooking the perfect risotto, see pages 48–49. Recipes for chicken and game stock are given on pages 21 and 275.

STARTERS

VEGETABLES & FISH

POULTRY

MEAT

GAME

DESSERTS

SPINACH AND RICOTTA RAVIOLI WITH WALNUT PESTO, AND A CREAM AND BASIL SAUCE

Chris Gates civil servant turned junior sous chef and 2009 finalist

PREPARATION TIME
1 hour 20 minutes

COOKING TIME
10 minutes

SERVES 4

FOR THE PASTA
150g (5½oz) "00" pasta flour (see MasterTip, p.52), plus extra to dust
350g (12oz) semolina flour
2 large eggs
10 egg yolks

FOR THE FILLING
20g (¾oz) butter
200g (7oz) spinach
salt and freshly ground black pepper
350g (12oz) ricotta or soft goat's cheese
grated zest of 1 lemon

FOR THE PESTO
30g (1oz) walnuts
1 bunch of basil
1 garlic clove, chopped
25g (scant 1oz) Parmesan cheese, freshly grated
olive oil

FOR THE SAUCE
1 shallot, finely chopped
1 tbsp olive oil
500ml (16fl oz) double cream
juice of 1 lemon

MASTER TIP

MAKING THE RAVIOLI

Be as gentle as you can when laying the second dough sheet over the first, otherwise you may displace the filling and it is a fiddly job to reposition the scoops. Ensure the edges are well pressed together so the filling does not fall out when the ravioli are cooked.

1 To make the pasta, blitz all of the ingredients in a food processor until you have a mixture the consistency of breadcrumbs. Empty onto a floured surface and knead into a silky dough. Wrap in cling film and leave to rest in the fridge for about 1 hour. (Or see MasterTip, p.51.)

2 Meanwhile, make the filling. Melt the butter in a large pan and wilt the spinach. Season with salt and pepper. Squeeze out any water and place in a bowl. Add the ricotta and lemon zest and season to taste.

3 For the pesto, toast the walnuts in a dry pan until golden (see MasterTip, p.40). Using a pestle and mortar, break them up with the garlic and basil leaves, reserving the stalks. Add the Parmesan, loosen with oil, and season.

4 For the cream sauce, sauté the chopped shallot in a pan with the oil until softened. Add the reserved basil stalks and soften for 3–4 minutes. Add the cream and allow to reduce slightly. Season with salt and pepper and add the lemon juice.

5 Using a pasta machine, roll out the pasta to the thinnest setting (see MasterTip, pp.190–91). Make 2 rectangular dough sheets. Place scoops of the filling on top of the first dough sheet at intervals about 5cm (2in) apart. Brush round the filling with a little water and top with the second sheet of dough. Using your fingers, press round the filling to remove any air. Cut out the ravioli, using a fluted pastry cutter about 5cm (2in) in diameter.

6 Cook the ravioli in boiling salted water for about 5 minutes. Drain and serve on warm plates with the cream sauce and pesto spooned over and a scattering of basil leaves as a garnish.

WILD MUSHROOM RISOTTO WITH TRUFFLED BRIE

Dan Cameron head chef and 2008 Professionals semi-finalist

PREPARATION TIME
30 minutes

COOKING TIME
1 hour

SERVES 4

FOR THE MUSHROOM STOCK
35g (1½oz) dried mushrooms
6 sprigs of thyme
1 Spanish onion, roughly chopped
1 garlic bulb, cut in half horizontally
  through the middle

TO SERVE
175g (6oz) truffled brie (see
  MasterTip, left)
bunch of chives, to garnish
bunch of chervil, to garnish

FOR THE RISOTTO
2 tbsp olive oil
4 large banana shallots, finely sliced
300g (10oz) arborio rice
4 tbsp groundnut oil
500g (1lb 2oz) wild mushrooms (see
  MasterTip, p.47), larger ones sliced,
  including slicing a cep into 4,
  to garnish
knob of butter (optional)
150g (5½oz) Parmesan cheese,
  freshly grated
juice of 1 lemon
sea salt and white pepper

MASTER TIP

TRUFFLED BRIE

For the truffled brie, take a segment of a ripe but not runny cheese, cut in half and spread sliced truffle on the inside. Put back together, wrap and keep refrigerated until it is needed.

MICHEL ROUX JR "I like it. In fact, I like it so much I would pay top money for it – and it's a great idea."

1 To make the mushroom stock, put the dried mushrooms into a saucepan and cover with 2 litres (3½ pints) of water. Add the thyme, onion, and garlic and bring to the boil, then reduce the heat and simmer for 30 minutes or until the mushrooms have softened. Strain and keep the stock hot.

2 Heat the olive oil in a large saucepan on a low heat, add the shallots and fry gently until translucent. Add the rice and stir, cooking for 3–4 minutes.

3 Start adding the stock, a ladle at a time, stirring the rice all the time. Once the stock has dried up, add another ladle and continue doing so until the rice is *al dente*, which takes about 20 minutes (see MasterTip, p.48–9).

4 Just before the rice is ready, heat up a frying pan and add the groundnut oil and all the risotto mushrooms and brown them off quickly. You may need to add a knob of butter to help this. Add a small ladle of stock to the hot pan and boil. This will emulsify the fats to make a thick, intense, mushroom-flavoured liquid, which will really bring the risotto to life. Add the contents of this pan – except for the cep slices, which should be reserved for the garnish – to the risotto and stir in gently. Add the Parmesan and lemon juice, and combine. Generously season to taste.

5 Place a large spoonful of risotto in 4 soup plates, then garnish each with slices of truffled brie, some chopped chives and chervil leaves, and a slice of the reserved cep.

BAKED RICOTTA CAKE WITH ROASTED CARDAMOM VEGETABLES

inspired by **Rani Price** presenter and 2007 Celebrity quarter-finalist

½ red pepper
½ yellow pepper
½ red onion
½ aubergine
½ courgette
250g (8oz) ricotta cheese
200g (7oz) Pecorino cheese,
  freshly grated
freshly grated nutmeg
3 garlic cloves, crushed and
  finely chopped

3 eggs, beaten
100ml (3½fl oz) single cream
handful of pine nuts
50g (1¾oz) rocket

FOR THE DRESSING
seeds from 10 green cardamom pods
3 tbsp clear honey
3 tbsp olive oil
salt and freshly ground black pepper

PREPARATION TIME
30 minutes

COOKING TIME
1 hour 20 minutes

SERVES 4

1 Preheat the oven to 220°C (425°F/Gas 7).
2 To mix up the dressing, place all of the ingredients into a lidded jar and shake. Leave to infuse while you cut all of the vegetables into equal-sized chunks of about 2.5cm (1in) in size.
3 Place the vegetables on a large baking sheet and drizzle the dressing over them. Use your hands to mix and coat the vegetables thoroughly with the dressing. Roast the vegetables in the oven for about 30 minutes, turning every 10 minutes until soft, brown, and shiny.
4 Reduce the oven temperature to 190°C (375°F/Gas 5). Put the ricotta in a large bowl and mix in the Pecorino, nutmeg, garlic, eggs, and cream. Season then place into a lightly greased 20cm (8in) springform tin. Cook in the oven for about 40 minutes until golden brown and firm when gently pressed.
5 Scatter the pine nuts on a baking sheet and dry roast in the oven for 2–3 minutes until lightly golden (see MasterTip, p.40). Leave to cool, then scatter over the roasted vegetables.
6 Once the ricotta cake is cooked, remove from the oven and leave to stand for about 5 minutes. Gently turn out of the tin, divide into 4 and serve each portion on a bed of rocket with the roasted vegetables on top, finished with a drizzle of olive oil.

GNOCCHI WITH BLUE CHEESE, GREEK YOGURT, AND PINE NUT SAUCE

inspired by **Midge Ure** musician and 2007 Celebrity finalist

PREPARATION TIME
30 minutes

COOKING TIME
40 minutes

SERVES 4

500g (1lb 2oz) floury potatoes, left whole
   and peeled
salt and freshly ground black pepper
1 egg
150g (5½oz) "00" pasta flour (see
   MasterTip, p.52)
rocket, to serve

FOR THE SAUCE
250ml (8fl oz) white wine
125g (4½oz) Dolcelatte cheese, chopped
3 tbsp Greek yogurt
1 tsp clear honey
60g (2oz) pine nuts, toasted (see
   MasterTip, p.40)

1 To make the gnocchi, place the potatoes in a large pan of cold water, add a sprinkling of salt and bring to the boil for 25–30 minutes, or until the potatoes are cooked all the way through. Don't be tempted to peel and chop them to speed this up – the skins help to prevent the potatoes taking on any water and making the mixture too soggy. Once they are cooked, drain and allow to cool slightly, then peel with a knife.
2 Pass the potatoes through a potato ricer and then press through a sieve. Season with salt and beat in the egg. Add half of the flour and mix in well until smooth, then tip out onto a lightly floured surface and incorporate the remaining flour while kneading the mixture into a dough. Form into a roll and cut crossways into quarters. Cover with cling film. To make the gnocchi, see the MasterTip, below.
3 Place the finished gnocchi on a floured tray ensuring that, until

---

MASTER TIP

GNOCCHI

Gnocchi is made by forming a rough dough out of cooked potato, eggs, flour, and also sometimes flavourings such as Parmesan cheese. The key to successful gnocchi, delicate rather than stodgy, is not to handle the potato too much but work the dough with a lightness of touch.

1 Take each piece of dough and roll back and forth on a lightly floured work surface to form a cylinder that is about as thick as your forefinger.

2 Cut the rolled dough into 3cm (1¼in) pieces, shape into crescents, and press onto the back of a fork to form the distinctive indentations.

you are ready to cook them, they do not touch each other or they will stick together. To cook, bring a large pan of salted water to the boil and slide the gnocchi into the water from the tray. Cook for about 2 minutes, or until they start to float to the surface, then drain well.

4 To make the sauce, bring the wine to the boil in a saucepan, lower the heat and leave the wine to reduce by about a third. Stir in the Dolcelatte until melted, and then the yogurt, honey, and some seasoning. Finally, add two-thirds of the toasted pine nuts.

5 Serve the sauce poured over the gnocchi, with the remaining pine nuts sprinkled over the top together with some rocket leaves.

MUSHROOM, LEEK, AND ALE PIE
Richard Arnold presenter and 2007 Celebrity semi-finalist

PREPARATION TIME
30 minutes

COOKING TIME
1 hour

SERVES 4

2 tbsp olive oil
25g (scant 1oz) butter
1 onion, finely chopped
4 leeks, cut into 2.5cm (1in) pieces
2 garlic cloves, crushed
½ tsp cayenne pepper
500g (1lb 2oz) mixed mushrooms, cleaned and cut into chunky pieces
250ml (8fl oz) ale of the sweeter variety, such as Newcastle Brown

250ml (8fl oz) double cream
small bunch of chives, finely chopped
small bunch of flat-leaf parsley, finely chopped
2–3 potatoes, about 150g (5½ oz) in weight, peeled and very finely sliced on a mandolin
30g (1oz) butter
salt and freshly ground black pepper

1 Preheat the oven to 180°C (350°F/Gas 4). In a very large deep pan, melt the oil and butter together and gently fry the onions and leeks for 8–10 minutes or until soft and translucent but not coloured. Add the garlic and cayenne and cook for a further 2–3 minutes. Tip in the mushrooms, turn up the heat and cook for a further 3–5 minutes or until softened slightly but still retaining some bite.

2 Pour in the ale and allow to bubble down for 2–3 minutes to reduce by half, then add the cream and simmer gently for a further 2–3 minutes until thickened. Stir in the herbs and season to taste with salt and pepper.

3 Divide the mushroom mixture between 4 ovenproof dishes and arrange the potato slices on top, overlapping them slightly. Dot each dish with a little of the butter and season well with salt and pepper.

4 Bake in the oven for 30–35 minutes, or until the potato goes golden brown. Serve immediately with a vegetable of your choice.

CAULIFLOWER AND BROCCOLI FLAN

Julia Paterson client service advisor and 2007 quarter-finalist

FOR THE PASTRY
250g (9oz) plain flour
pinch of salt
1½ tsp paprika, plus extra
  for sprinkling
¼ tsp dried thyme
100g (3½oz) margarine

FOR THE FILLING
175g (6oz) broccoli,
  cut into small florets
175g (6oz) cauliflower,
  cut into small florets
1 tbsp vegetable oil
1 onion, finely chopped
15g (½oz) butter
20g (¾oz) plain flour
200ml (7fl oz) milk
75g (2½oz) Scottish Cheddar
  or Gruyère cheese, grated

PREPARATION TIME
20 minutes

COOKING TIME
20 minutes

SERVES 4

1 Preheat the oven to 190°C (375°F/Gas 5). To make the pastry, sift the flour and salt into a bowl with the paprika and thyme. Rub in the margarine with your fingertips to make a breadcrumb consistency, then add sufficient cold water to make a dough (about 3–4 tbsp).
2 Roll out onto a floured surface and line 4 small pastry tins, 10cm (4in) in diameter. Prick in several places with a fork and line with baking beans to bake blind (see MasterTip, pp.368–9). Place in the oven and bake for 10–12 minutes.
3 Cook the broccoli and cauliflower florets in a large pan of salted boiling water for 3–4 minutes, then drain.
4 Melt the oil in a pan and cook the onion over a medium heat until softened but not coloured – about 7 minutes.
5 To make a white sauce, melt the butter in a pan over a medium heat – do not allow it to brown. Remove from the heat and stir in the flour to make a smooth paste. Return to the heat and add the milk a little at a time, stirring as you go. Turn the heat to low and allow the sauce to cook for 7–10 minutes.
6 Stir in the cheese, reserving a little for topping, and allow it to melt. Add the broccoli, cauliflower, and onion, stir the sauce and then pour it into the pastry cases. Sprinkle with a little extra cheese and paprika, place in the oven and bake for 10 minutes until the cheese bubbles. Serve with a salad of your choice.

SEAFOOD TAGINE WITH FLAT BREAD
Andy Oliver project manager turned chef and 2009 finalist

PREPARATION TIME
35 minutes

COOKING TIME
2 hours

SERVES 4

2 black bream or 2 bream-sized red snappers, filleted with the skin left on and pin-boned, reserving the bones for stock
12 large raw king prawns (not tiger prawns), peeled, leaving heads and tails on
12 fresh clams

FOR THE FLAT BREAD
250g (9oz) very strong plain or wholemeal flour or a mix of both, plus extra for dusting
½ tsp dried yeast
2 tbsp olive oil, plus extra for drizzling
sea salt

FOR THE STOCK
fish bones
1 celery stick
small bunch of parsley stalks
1 slice bulb fennel
½ onion
2 bay leaves
6 fennel seeds
6 coriander seeds
6 peppercorns
2 slices lemon
2 star anise

FOR THE PASTE
2 banana shallots, halved
2cm (¾in) piece fresh root ginger
2 garlic cloves
2 long mild red chillies, seeds removed
small bunch of coriander, with stalks
½ tsp ground coriander
½ tsp ground cumin

FOR THE TAGINE
2 bay leaves
1 cinnamon stick
2 tbsp olive oil
500g (1lb 2oz) waxy potatoes, preferably Cyprus (see MasterTip, p.197), peeled and sliced
a pinch of saffron threads
100g (3½oz) medium purple pitted olives
2 large plum tomatoes, peeled and diced
4 small preserved lemons, cut into wedges, pips removed, reserving some for garnish

TO SERVE
2 tbsp finely chopped mint
2 tbsp finely chopped flat-leaf parsley
2 fresh lemons, cut into wedges
a strong fruity extra virgin olive oil for drizzling

1 First make the flat bread. Mix the flour and yeast in a large mixing bowl. Gradually pour in the olive oil and 125ml (4 fl oz) water and stir slowly with one hand, bringing the flour into the middle until it all comes together to form a dough. Using the ball of your hand, knead until the dough is elastic and smooth. Alternatively, place all the ingredients in the bowl of a large electric mixer and knead using the dough hook until the dough is elastic and smooth. Shape into a ball, place in a bowl, cover with cling film and leave to rest for 1–2 hours in a warm, dry place.
2 To make the stock, place the fish bones, celery, parsley, fennel, onion, bay leaves, fennel seeds, coriander seeds, peppercorns, lemon, star anise, and salt in a large pan. Cover with 1 litre (1¾ pints) water; bring to the boil and leave to simmer gently for 30 minutes. Strain

through a very fine sieve and taste. If it is too bland, return to the heat and reduce until it is more concentrated in flavour.

3 Make the paste by blending the shallots, ginger, garlic, chillies, coriander stalks, ground coriander, and ground cumin.

4 For the tagine, fry the bay leaves and cinnamon in the olive oil in a large sauté pan or tagine with a lid, add the paste and fry gently for 5 minutes. Add about half the stock, the potatoes, and saffron and simmer for 20–25 minutes until the potatoes are nearly cooked.

5 Meanwhile, to cook the flat bread, heat a griddle pan. Divide the dough into 4 equal pieces and roll each one out to 5mm (¼in) or less thick. Rub the dough on each side with extra virgin olive oil and sprinkle with sea salt. Lay the pieces carefully on the hot griddle to grill for 3–4 minutes on each side until golden.

6 When the potatoes are nearly cooked, add the olives, tomatoes, and preserved lemon wedges to the tagine. Add the remaining stock and season with salt. Lay the fish fillets, prawns, and clams on top. Bring to the boil, cover with a lid and gently simmer for 5 minutes until the fish has turned opaque, the prawns are pink all over, and the clams have opened. Discard any clams that have not opened. Peel the skin off the fish.

7 Spoon the potatoes, seafood, and sauce onto a plate, add the tomatoes and olives, sprinkle with herbs and garnish with fresh and preserved lemon wedges. Drizzle with extra virgin olive oil. Serve with the warm flat bread.

MASTER TIP
MAKING FISH STOCK

Fish bones for stock are easily available from a fishmonger, who will have plenty left over from the filleting of much of the fresh fish on sale. The bones of white fish such as turbot, sole, whiting, and hake are best; otherwise, slightly oily fish such as salmon and bass. Avoid those from oily fish such as herring and mackerel. Sweating the bones in butter before adding liquid intensifies the flavour of the stock.

1 Melt the butter in a large saucepan or stockpot. Add the bones and stir until they smell of cooked fish, taking care that they do not burn.

2 Add water, vegetables, and seasoning and bring to the boil. Skim away any foam and simmer for 30–40 minutes before straining through a fine sieve.

ROASTED COD WITH MASH AND CURLY KALE

Caroline Brewester banker turned food writer and 2005 finalist

PREPARATION TIME
1 hour 30 minutes

COOKING TIME
1 hour

SERVES 4

4 portions cod fillet, each about 160g (5¾oz) and 2.5cm (1in) thick
1 tbsp plain flour
2 tbsp sunflower oil
15g (½oz) butter
4 small bunches cherry tomatoes on the vine (2–3 tomatoes per bunch), to serve

FOR THE MASHED POTATO
600g (1lb 5oz) floury white potatoes (see MasterTip, p.197), peeled and cut into large chunks
45g (1½oz) butter
4 tbsp milk, plus extra if needed
2 tbsp double cream
grated nutmeg
salt and freshly ground black pepper

FOR THE KALE
800g (1¾lb) curly kale, thick stalks removed
30g (1oz) butter
1 small garlic clove, crushed
squeeze of lemon juice

FOR THE SAUCE
2 shallots, finely chopped
225g (8oz) cold salted butter, cut into 1cm (½in) cubes
80ml (2¾fl oz) white wine vinegar
120ml (4fl oz) white wine
150ml (5fl oz) fish stock (see MasterTip, p.123)
2 tbsp double cream
1–2 tbsp wholegrain mustard
salt and white pepper

1 First put the potatoes in a large saucepan of cold salted water and bring to the boil. Reduce the heat and simmer until just tender. Drain and leave to stand in a colander to steam dry for 2–3 minutes. Push the potatoes through a ricer back into the saucepan and put over a low heat. Add the butter, milk, and cream and beat well until smooth, adding more milk as necessary to give creamy mashed potatoes. Season to taste with nutmeg, salt, and pepper and keep warm.

2 Bring a large saucepan of salted water to the boil. Add the kale, bring back to the boil and cook for 2–3 minutes until just tender. Drain and immediately plunge into iced water until cold. Remove from the iced water and drain. Pat dry and set aside.

3 To make the sauce, gently cook the shallots in a saucepan with 15g (½oz) of the butter until soft but not coloured. Add several grinds of white pepper and the vinegar and boil until reduced to 1 tbsp. Add the white wine and stock and boil again until reduced by three-quarters. Strain and transfer the reduced liquid to a clean pan.

4 Put the pan over a medium heat and bring the liquid to the boil, then stir in the double cream. Reduce the heat slightly then vigorously whisk in the remaining cubes of cold butter, 1 at a time, making sure each is fully incorporated before adding a new cube.

5 Add the mustard 1 tsp at a time, tasting between additions, until the sauce is as piquant as you like. Season to taste. Transfer to a heatproof bowl and set the bowl over a saucepan of warm (not boiling) water. Whisk the sauce occasionally to prevent it from splitting.

6 To cook the cod, preheat the oven to 200°C (400°F/Gas 6). Line a baking sheet with baking parchment. Pat the cod fillets dry with kitchen paper, dust with flour, patting off any excess, and season with salt and pepper. Heat the oil and butter in a frying pan until just sizzling and fry the cod, skin-side down, for 2–3 minutes until the skin is brown and crisp. Transfer to the baking sheet, skin side up, and roast for 5–6 minutes, until the fish is just cooked through.

7 Meanwhile, melt the butter for the kale in a wok or large frying pan, add the garlic and cook for 1 minute. Add the kale and cook for 2–3 minutes to warm through. Season to taste with salt, pepper, and a squeeze of lemon juice.

8 To serve, put a quenelle (see MasterTip, p.93) of mashed potato onto each plate and sit a piece of cod, skin-side up, on the mash. Spoon the mustard butter sauce around and top each piece of cod with a bunch of cherry tomatoes. Serve with the kale alongside.

ROAST COD AND CLAMS WITH BACON MASH, CREAMY SHALLOT SAUCE, AND SPINACH

Sarah Whittle detective sergeant and 2008 semi-finalist

PREPARATION TIME
1 hour 30 minutes

COOKING TIME
1 hour

SERVES 4

4 thick cod fillets, 160g (5¾oz) each
sea salt and white pepper
75g (2½oz) unsalted butter
2 tbsp rapeseed oil
750g (1lb 10oz) baby spinach

FOR THE BACON MASH
6 rashers smoked dry-cure streaky
   bacon, rind removed
1.5kg (3lb 3oz) Maris Piper potatoes
   (see MasterTip, p.197), cut into
   7.5cm (3in) pieces
50g (1¾oz) unsalted butter
white pepper

FOR THE SHALLOT SAUCE
1kg (2¼lb) venus or palourde clams,
   scrubbed and soaked for 2 hours
   in salted water (use cockles if clams
   are unavailable)
½ large glass of dry white wine
   (nothing "oaky")
2 shallots or 1 small onion, very
   finely chopped
300ml (10fl oz) double cream
1 heaped tbsp thyme leaves
juice of ½ lemon

1 Preheat the oven to 180°C (350°F/Gas 4). Put the bacon on a non-stick baking tray in the oven for about 10 minutes until crisp. Cool and crumble, reserving a few rashers for garnish. Boil the potatoes for about 20 minutes until tender. Drain, return to the pan, add the butter and mash well. Season with pepper and stir in the bacon.

2 To make the sauce, put the clams in a large pan with the wine and half the shallots. Cook, covered, over a high heat, shaking from time to time, for about 4–5 minutes until the clams have opened – discard any that haven't. Drain into a colander over a bowl to catch the juice. Reserve 12 of the clams in their shells for garnish and shell the rest.

3 Pour the clam juice into a pan and add the remaining shallot. Simmer for 10 minutes until reduced slightly, then add the cream. Simmer for a further 5 minutes then, if you wish to, blend until smooth using a hand blender. Add the thyme and clam meat and check the seasoning, adding a little lemon juice. Keep the sauce warm.

4 To cook the cod, coat the skin side with seasoned flour. Put 50g (1¾oz) butter and the oil in a non-stick ovenproof frying pan over medium heat until frothing. Put the fish in, skin-side down, and cook until the fish turns white halfway up its sides. Baste with the oil and butter once, then put it in the oven for 7–8 minutes or until opaque. In the meantime, heat the remaining butter and add the washed spinach. Cook until wilted, then season and drain it.

5 To serve, spoon mash on each plate. Top with 3 clams in their shells, spinach, a piece of cod, and bacon. Pour the sauce around and on top.

COD FILLET IN HERB CRUST WITH SABAYON OF WHOLEGRAIN MUSTARD

Cassandra Williams food marketer and 2009 quarter-finalist

PREPARATION TIME
1 hour 45 minutes

COOKING TIME
1 hour

SERVES 4

120g (4¼oz) white mushrooms, finely sliced
2 tsp whipping cream
2½ tbsp olive oil
1 garlic clove, finely diced
4 shallots, finely diced
2 large ripe tomatoes, skinned, deseeded and diced
sprig of thyme
100g (3½oz) fresh white bread
40g (1¼oz) Gruyère cheese, grated
30g (1oz) flat-leaf parsley, chopped
65g (2¼oz) salted butter, softened
salt and freshly ground black pepper
1.5kg (3lb 3oz) Maris Piper potatoes (see MasterTip, p.197), peeled and cut into chunks

freshly grated nutmeg
4 cod fillets, 175g (6oz) each
4 tsp Dijon mustard
100ml (3½fl oz) white wine
100ml (3½fl oz) fish stock
a squeeze of lemon juice

FOR THE SABAYON
15g (½oz) butter
250ml (8fl oz) white wine
250ml (8fl oz) dry vermouth
500ml (16fl oz) fish stock
3 tbsp whipping cream
2 egg yolks
50g (1¾oz) butter, warmed
3 tbsp double cream
1–2 tsp wholegrain mustard

MASTER TIP
MAKING THE SABAYON

To make the sabayon, place the egg yolks in a round-bottomed glass bowl with a few drops of water and gently beat over a bain marie. As the egg yolks thicken and cook, add the warm butter and remove from the heat. Add the velouté with the double cream, whipped with the wholegrain mustard.

1 Preheat the oven to 220°C (425°F/Gas 7). To make the sabayon, first make a velouté by melting the butter in a large pan and cooking 3 of the shallots until softened but not coloured. Deglaze the pan with the white wine and Noilly Prat and boil to reduce to a syrup. Add the fish stock and boil to reduce by half. Add the cream, bring to the boil, and simmer for 5 minutes until the sauce coats a spoon. Pass through a sieve and then reduce by half again.

2 Place the mushrooms in a frying pan and heat up to draw out the moisture. Add the whipping cream and mix. Transfer to a bowl to cool.

3 Heat 2 tbsp oil in a pan and sweat the garlic and remaining shallot without colouring. Add the tomatoes and thyme. Cook over a low heat until the moisture has been removed. Blend with a hand blender.

4 To make the herb crust, whizz the bread, Gruyère, parsley, 60g (2oz) butter, and seasoning in a blender. Place in another small bowl.

5 Boil the potatoes until soft. Pass through a sieve and add pepper, nutmeg, and the remaining butter. Keep warm over a bain marie.

6 Season the cod. Spread with 1 tsp mustard followed by 1 tsp tomato purée and 1 tsp mushroom reduction, then top with the herb crust. In a small pan, heat the wine, stock, remaining olive oil, and lemon juice until the mixture boils. Line an ovenproof dish with greaseproof paper. Place the fish in the centre and pour the stock around it. Place in the oven for 7 minutes. Meanwhile, finish the sabayon (see MasterTip, left).

7 To serve, pipe a base of mash into the centre of 4 large white plates. Gently place the cod on top and pour the sabayon around. Place under a preheated grill until the crust and sauce are a golden brown.

HARISSA PAN-FRIED COD WITH ROASTED ROOTS AND A FRESH CORIANDER SAUCE

Matt James garden designer and 2007 Celebrity quarter-finalist

3 large King Edward potatoes, peeled
  and sliced into finger-sized chips
2 large carrots, sliced into
  finger-sized chips
2 medium parsnips, sliced into
  finger-sized chips
1 tbsp extra virgin olive oil
sea salt and freshly ground
  black pepper
4 pieces of cod loin, 175g (6oz) each,
  boned but not skinned
4 tsp harissa paste
lemon slices, to garnish

FOR THE SAUCE
1 medium onion, finely diced
1 garlic clove, finely diced
knob of butter
large glass of medium-dry white wine
284ml (10fl oz) double cream
1 bunch of coriander, finely chopped

PREPARATION TIME
1 hour

COOKING TIME
30 minutes

SERVES 4

1 Preheat the oven to 180°C (350°F/Gas 4). Parboil the potatoes, carrots, and parsnips in salted water for 10 minutes, drain, then spread thinly on a baking tray. Drizzle olive oil and a little sea salt over the top then place in a hot oven. Roast until golden brown, turning occasionally.

2 Heat a little oil in an ovenproof frying pan. Season the cod on both sides then smear harissa paste on the fleshy side. Now place each piece skin-side down in the pan. Fry for 4–5 minutes before flipping over. Sear the flesh for only 2 minutes before transferring the pan to the oven. Cook the cod on the shelf below your roasted roots for about 6 minutes.

3 To make the sauce, sweat the onion and garlic in a pan with the butter until translucent. Pour in the wine and simmer gently for 4–5 minutes. Stir in the cream and warm through before adding the coriander. Serve the steaks skin-side up on top of a neat pile of roots and pour the sauce over the top. Garnish with lemon slices.

MASTER TIP
HARISSA

A favoured ingredient in North African cuisine, harissa is also used as a condiment. It is sold as a sauce or a paste and although the exact ingredients may vary, chilli is always the main one. Rose harissa, which contains rose petals, may be made from 40 or so spices, but it is easy to make a simpler harissa at home by simply blending red chilli peppers with garlic, salt, olive oil, cumin, coriander, and caraway seeds.

SAUTÉED COD WITH COD CAKES AND CLAM CHOWDER

Jonny Stevenson single father of two, now head chef and 2008 finalist

PREPARATION TIME
1 hour 30 minutes

COOKING TIME
1 hour

SERVES 4

4 cod steaks, 200g (7oz) each
1 tbsp olive oil

FOR THE COD CAKES
300g (10oz) cod trimmings
450g (1lb) potatoes (see MasterTip, p.197)
small bunch of spring onions, finely chopped
45g (1½oz) unsalted butter, plus extra for frying
1 egg, beaten
1 tsp Dijon mustard

chopped flat-leaf parsley
pinch of cayenne pepper
salt and freshly ground black pepper

FOR THE CLAM CHOWDER
25g (scant 1oz) salted butter
1 shallot, finely chopped
2 garlic cloves, diced
sprig of thyme
splash of white wine
24 clams (if unavailable use 500g/1lb 2oz mussels)
500ml (16fl oz) double cream

1 First make the cod cakes. Place the trimmings in a pan with a small volume of water and bring to a boil with the lid on. Turn off the heat, leave for 5 minutes, then drain and break into flakes.

2 Boil the potatoes in salted water for about 20 minutes until soft. Drain and return to the pan over moderate heat for 2–3 minutes to evaporate excess moisture. Mash and keep warm. In a small frying pan, sauté the spring onions in 15g (½oz) butter until soft.

3 Mix the flaked fish, potatoes, remaining butter, and spring onions together using a fork, then mix in the egg, mustard, parsley, and cayenne pepper. Season to taste. When the mixture has cooled enough to handle, use floured hands to make 8 cod cakes. Heat enough butter to coat a frying pan, preferably non-stick, and cook over medium heat until each side is golden and the cakes are heated through. You can refrigerate them for up to 6 hours if you are not cooking them immediately.

4 To cook the pan-fried cod, season with salt and pepper on both sides. Using a non-stick pan, heat the olive oil and place the cod into the hot oil skin-side up for 2 minutes. Flip over and continue to cook for a further 3–4 minutes, being careful not to overcook.

5 To make the clam chowder, heat the butter in a pan and sweat the shallot and garlic with the thyme . Add the white wine and reduce to a glaze. Add the clams and cream, then reduce to sauce consistency and season to taste.

6 To serve, place 2 cod cakes on warmed plates, top with the pan-fried cod, skin-side up, and pour the clam chowder around the fish.

STEAMED SEA BASS WITH SPICED BROTH
Matt Dawson professional rugby player and 2006 Celebrity champion

10g (¼oz) unsalted butter
4 shallots, chopped
4 garlic cloves, crushed
1kg (2¼lb) lobster, chopped into large
  pieces, or shell-on prawns
600ml (1 pint) chicken or fish stock
  (see MasterTips, p.21 or p.123)
4 sea bass fillets, about 150g
  (5½ oz) each
16–20 asparagus spears
300g (10oz) purple sprouting broccoli
10g (¼oz) mint, leaves only,
  finely shredded

FOR THE SPICE PASTE
2 tbsp tamarind paste (see MasterTip,
  p.152)
30g (1oz) cumin seeds
3 red chillies, deseeded
5–6cm (2–2½in) piece fresh root ginger
75g (2½oz) peanuts, chopped
100ml (3½fl oz) coconut milk (see
  MasterTip, p.25)
15g (½oz) coriander seeds

PREPARATION TIME
30 minutes

COOKING TIME
35 minutes

SERVES 4

1 First whizz all of the spice paste ingredients in a food processor until you achieve a coarse paste. Set aside.

2 Heat the butter in a wide, deep frying pan. Sweat the shallots for about 5 minutes until soft but not coloured then add the garlic and lobster or prawns and cook for 10 minutes.

3 Add 4 tbsp of the spice paste and fry for 5 minutes. Add the chicken or fish stock and cook for 15 minutes.

4 Using a bamboo steamer, double pan or a sieve over a pan, steam the sea bass for 6 minutes or until just cooked.

5 Meanwhile, blanch the asparagus and broccoli in boiling salted water for 4–5 minutes and drain.

6 To serve, lay the vegetables on the base of 4 soup plates like a raft. Place the fish on top. Using a hand blender, blend the broth then pass through a sieve. Pour around the fish so that it appears to be suspended in broth and sprinkle the mint over it. Serve with a bowl of jasmine rice on the side.

SEA BASS WITH A TAHINI SAUCE, CARROT AND ONION SEED SALAD, AND SAFFRON RICE

Nadia Sawalha actress and presenter and 2007 Celebrity champion

PREPARATION TIME
45 minutes

COOKING TIME
35 minutes

SERVES 4

4 sea bass fillets, skin on
1 tsp ground cumin
¼ tsp cinnamon
1 tbsp olive oil
sea salt and freshly ground
   black pepper

FOR THE SALAD
4 tbsp vegetable oil
250g (9oz) onions, finely sliced
250g (9oz) carrots, finely grated
salt
juice of ½ lemon
½ tbsp mustard seeds (optional)
½ tbsp nigella seeds (black
   onion seeds)

FOR THE TAHINI SAUCE
1 tsp salt
1 garlic clove
100ml (3½fl oz) tahini
juice of 1 lemon
2 tbsp finely chopped
   flat-leaf parsley

FOR THE SAFFRON RICE
pinch of saffron threads
400ml (14fl oz) hot chicken stock
   (see MasterTip, p.21)
25g (scant 1oz) butter
50g (1¾oz) whole blanched almonds
200g (7oz) basmati rice
1 tsp baharat spice
50g (1¾oz) raisins

1 To make the salad, fry the onions in half the oil until golden and caramelized. Meanwhile, put the carrots in a bowl and add salt and lemon juice. Fry the mustard and nigella seeds in the remaining oil for a few seconds until they begin to pop. Tip over the salad and mix well, then stir in the onions.

2 To make the sauce, put the salt into a mortar and pound with the garlic until really smooth. Pour in the tahini and mix with a whisk. Add the lemon juice and whisk until sticky, then whisk in 75ml (2½fl oz) of warm water. When it looks like thick double cream, stir in the parsley.

3 Put the saffron in the stock. Melt half the butter in a heavy pan and fry the almonds gently. When they are golden, remove and set aside. Put the remaining butter in, add the rice and spice, stir, and add the raisins. Pour in the hot stock, season, bring to the boil, give it one more stir and then put the lid on and reduce the heat to as low as possible. Cook for about 15–20 minutes. Mix the fried almonds through.

4 Dry the sea bass fillets with kitchen paper. Rub the spices over them and season well. Gently heat the olive oil in a heavy frying pan and slide the fish in, skin-side up. After about 3 minutes turn the fillets over and cook on the other side for another 3 minutes or so, depending on their thickness. To serve, form the rice into a mound on the plates and place the fish on it. Top with the salad and drizzle the sauce around.

SEA BASS IN A FENNEL VANILLA SAUCE WITH FONDANT POTATO

Jonny Stevenson single father of two, now head chef and 2008 finalist

PREPARATION TIME
45 minutes

COOKING TIME
30 minutes

SERVES 4

2 tbsp olive oil
4 wild sea bass fillets,
 skin on, pinboned
salt and white pepper
25g (scant 1oz) butter

FOR THE FONDANT POTATO
2 large Maris Piper potatoes (see
 MasterTip, p.197), peeled
3 tbsp olive oil
about 45g (1½oz) butter

FOR THE PARSNIP CREAM
3 large parsnips, core
 removed, chopped

200ml (7fl oz) double cream
pinch of freshly grated nutmeg

FOR THE SAUCE
1 tbsp olive oil
2 large bulbs fennel, finely chopped
100ml (3½fl oz) hot fish stock (see
 MasterTip, p.123)
100ml (3½fl oz) double cream
½ vanilla pod, seeds only
25g (scant 1oz) butter

TO SERVE
175–200g (6–7oz) fresh baby spinach
15g (½oz) butter

1 Preheat the oven to 190°C (375°F/Gas 5). For the fondant potato, halve the potatoes and trim to about 4cm (2½in) high. Cut with a 5cm (2.5in) pastry cutter and trim around the sharp edges.

2 Heat the oil in an ovenproof pan over a medium-high heat. Add the potatoes and when golden-brown on one side, turn over, add a knob or 2 of butter and 100ml (3½fl oz) water, and season. Bring to a simmer then put in the oven and cook for about 25 minutes or until tender in the centre. Remove from the oven and keep warm.

3 For the parsnip cream, place the parsnips in a medium-sized pan and add the cream and 200ml (7fl oz) water, or enough to cover the parsnips. Bring to the boil and slowly simmer until tender, about 15 minutes. Drain, reserving the liquid. Put the parsnips in a blender with a few tablespoons of cooking liquid. Blend until smooth, adding more cooking liquid as necessary to reach a smooth consistency. Season with salt, white pepper, and a small grating of nutmeg.

4 For the fennel vanilla sauce, heat the olive oil in a saucepan, add the fennel and fry gently for 8–10 minutes, or until softened but not browned. Add the fish stock, bring to the boil and then simmer until reduced by half. Add the cream and again bring to the boil, then turn down to a simmer and cook until reduced by half. Remove from the heat and place in a food processor with the vanilla seeds. Process until fine and then whisk in the butter. To foam, simply whisk with a hand blender and skim the foam with a spoon.

5 For the sea bass, heat a non-stick frying pan over high heat and add the oil. Season the fish with salt and white pepper and place in the oil skin-side down. Cook for 2–3 minutes, turn over, add the butter and cook for another 1–2 minutes.

6 Wilt the spinach in a pan with the butter, then drain. To serve, spoon a circle of parsnip cream in the centre of a serving plate and top with the wilted spinach and fondant potato. Place the sea bass on top and spoon the foam around the plate.

STEAMED SEA BASS AND RICE WRAPPED IN LOTUS LEAF
Mark Moraghan actor and 2008 Celebrity finalist

225g (8oz) glutinous rice
1 tsp salt
1 tsp sesame oil
1 large lotus leaf
3 tbsp vegetable oil
1 whole sea bass, about 500g (1lb 2oz)

2 spring onions, halved lengthways
1 tbsp thinly shredded fresh root ginger
2 tbsp light soy sauce
1 tbsp rice wine
2 spring onions, thinly shredded
fresh coriander leaves, to garnish

PREPARATION TIME
25 minutes

COOKING TIME
25 minutes

SERVES 4

1 Wash the rice once, then place in 500ml (16fl oz) boiling water with the salt and sesame oil. Bring back to the boil and stir. Reduce the heat to low and cook, covered, for 10 minutes until the water is absorbed and the rice is soft but still has some bite.

2 Soak the lotus leaf in boiling water for 15 minutes until soft. Dry with kitchen paper, cut into 4 and rub with 1 tbsp vegetable oil. Place a portion of rice on each piece, fold the leaf over to make a package and place in a hot steamer for 15 minutes.

3 Meanwhile, clean and dry the fish. With a sharp knife, make diagonal scores down to the bone on both sides, 2.5cm (1in) apart. Rub the inside and outside of the fish with salt and sesame oil.

4 Lay the spring onion halves on a platter and place the fish on top. Scatter the ginger inside and outside the fish and put the platter in a hot steamer over high heat for 15 minutes.

5 Remove the shredded ginger and transfer the fish to a serving dish. Sprinkle the soy sauce, rice wine, and shredded spring onions over the cooked fish. Heat the remaining vegetable oil and pour over the fish. Garnish with coriander and serve with the rice packages.

HALIBUT WITH A WALNUT CRUST ON LEEKS AND COCKLE SAUCE

David Hall IT buyer turned food writer and 2007 semi-finalist

PREPARATION TIME
15 minutes

COOKING TIME
20 minutes

SERVES 4

4 pieces of halibut fillet, 200g (7oz)
  each, skinned
4 small or 2 large leeks, finely sliced
25g (scant 1oz) butter
3 tbsp olive oil
salt and freshly ground black pepper

FOR THE WALNUT CRUST
50g (1¾oz) softened butter
100g (3½oz) walnut halves
2 tbsp flat-leaf parsley, finely chopped

FOR THE SAUCE
175ml (6fl oz) white wine
2 shallots, halved and sliced thinly
200g (7oz) fresh cockles in shells
100ml (3½fl oz) double cream
knob of butter
squeeze of lemon

1 To make the walnut crust, mash together the butter, walnuts, parsley and a little seasoning in a bowl. Spoon into the centre of a large rectangle of baking parchment. Fold it in half and roll out using a rolling pin until the butter is thin. Place in the freezer until frozen. Once frozen, peel back and place the fish fillets onto the butter. Cut out 4 pieces of butter, tracing round the fillets. Set both aside.

2 Heat the butter and 1 tbsp olive oil in a frying pan, add the leeks and cook gently for 10 minutes, stirring regularly, until soft but not coloured. Season with salt and pepper.

3 To make the sauce, bring the wine and shallots to the boil in a large pan. Gently simmer for about 5 minutes until the shallots have softened. Whisk in the cream, butter, and lemon juice. Add the cockles to the sauce, bring to the boil, season with salt and pepper and remove from the heat. Keep warm.

4 Preheat the grill to a medium setting. Season the halibut fillets. Heat the remaining olive oil in a frying pan and cook the halibut fillets for 2 minutes on each side until starting to colour. Arrange the walnut butter on the fillets and place under the grill for about 1 minute until the crust is golden brown.

5 Heap a large spoonful of leeks in the centre of each serving bowl. Arrange the halibut with the walnut crust on top and the cockle sauce spooned over and around.

1 Cut along the stomach with a sharp knife and pull out the guts and any roe.

2 Cut off the fins with kitchen scissors, taking care not to cut into the body.

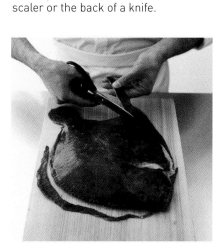

3 Scrape off the scales with a fish scaler or the back of a knife.

4 Cut off the gills with scissors, then rinse the fish under running water.

5 To skin flat fish, first cut off the fins about 5mm(¼in) from the body.

6 Slide a knife under the skin at the tail end and pull the dark skin away.

MASTER TIP
PREPARING FLAT FISH

The first step in gutting and trimming a fish is to remove the viscera (guts) so that there is no possibility of cutting into them during the trimming process. If you wish to serve the fish without the head, lay it dark side up and cut a V shape all the way round the head. Grasp the head and pull it away with a quick twist; the guts and gills should come away with it. Rinse the cavity under cold running water to remove any blood and guts.

ROAST HALIBUT WITH CRAB AND A TOMATO AND SAFFRON VINAIGRETTE

Steve Groves *chef de partie and 2009 Professionals champion*

PREPARATION TIME
15 minutes

COOKING TIME
1 hour 10 minutes

SERVES 4

400g (14oz) Jersey Royal potatoes or
   new potatoes (see MasterTip, p.197)
3 tbsp olive oil
150g (5½oz) white crabmeat
salt and freshly ground black pepper
2 tbsp olive oil
25g (scant 1oz) butter
8 baby bulbs fennel
4 pieces of halibut, 150g (5½oz) each,
   with skin
few sprigs of chervil, chopped
few sprigs flat-leaf parsley, chopped

FOR THE VINAIGRETTE
500g (1lb 2oz) crab shells
75ml (2½fl oz) olive oil
30g (1oz) onion, chopped
30g (1oz) carrot, chopped
30g (1oz) celery stick, chopped
1 tsp tomato purée
2 tomatoes
100ml (3½fl oz) white wine
1 bay leaf
few sprigs of thyme
small pinch of saffron threads
juice of ½ lemon
2 plum tomatoes, skinned, deseeded
   and diced

1 Boil the potatoes in a large pan of salted water for about 10 minutes until tender. Drain then, while still hot, scrape off the skins and put the potatoes in a bowl with 1 tbsp oil, the crabmeat, herbs and seasoning. Lightly crush and mix together.

2 Blanch the fennel in boiling salted water for 4–5 minutes until just tender. Drain and toss in a pan with a little olive oil and seasoning.

3 For the vinaigrette, fry the crab shells in 1 tbsp oil in a heavy saucepan over a medium heat for 5 minutes. Remove from the pan then add the vegetables and fry for about 7 minutes until nicely coloured. Add the tomato purée, tomatoes, wine, and herbs and reduce until most of the wine has evaporated.

4 Return the crab shells to the pan and add water to cover. Bring to a simmer and cook for 30–40 minutes. Pass through a sieve, add the saffron then reduce the sauce to about 200ml (7fl oz), tasting often to ensure it does not become over-reduced and bitter. Stir in the lemon juice, plum tomatoes, and remaining oil and check the seasoning.

5 Season the fish with salt and pepper. Heat 1 tbsp oil in a non-stick frying pan and fry the fish on the flesh side for 1½–2 minutes. Turn over, add the butter and cook for a further 1½–2 minutes, spooning the butter over while doing so.

6 Pile a mound of potatoes and crabmeat in the centre of each plate. Top with a halibut fillet, arrange the fennel around the outside, and drizzle with the vinaigrette. Garnish with chervil and parsley.

TURBOT WITH FENNEL HOLLANDAISE

Patrick Zahara property manager and 2006 quarter-finalist

4 portions of turbot fillet off the bone,
  about 150g (5½oz) each
2 heaped tsp sea salt
freshly ground black pepper
1 tbsp light olive oil
75g (2½oz) unsalted butter
juice of ¼ lemon
4 crispy potato rostis
  (see pp.274–5), optional
4 heaped tbsp cooked, drained, and
  seasoned spinach, kept warm

FOR THE HOLLANDAISE
25g (scant 1oz) unsalted butter
½ tbsp olive oil
½ medium bulb fennel, trimmed
  and finely chopped
1½ tbsp tarragon vinegar
1 shallot, finely chopped
7 black peppercorns
3 parsley stalks
2 garlic cloves, bruised
115g (4oz) lightly salted butter, melted
1 large egg yolk
juice of ¼ lemon

PREPARATION TIME
25 minutes

COOKING TIME
12 minutes

SERVES 4

1 To make the sauce, melt the butter and oil together in a lidded saucepan and add the fennel and a pinch of salt. Cover the pan and cook over a low heat for about 20 minutes until the fennel is very soft but not coloured, stirring occasionally. While the fennel is still hot, blend into a purée using a hand blender and push through a fine sieve. Set aside.

2 Put the vinegar, shallot, peppercorns, parsley stalks, and garlic in a pan and boil until the liquid is reduced to about 2 tsp. Sieve the liquid into the fennel purée. Add the egg yolk, put the purée into a blender and turn it on. While the blender is running, slowly pour in the melted butter until all is combined. Add the lemon juice and blend again. Taste the sauce and adjust the seasoning with lemon, salt and pepper as necessary. Keep warm.

3 Preheat the oven to 200°C (400°F/Gas 6). Season the fish with the salt and a generous amount of pepper. Heat a large ovenproof frying pan until hot, add the oil and then the fish. After about 1 minute add the butter and when it is melted and foaming flip the fish over. Put in the oven for about 5 minutes or until the skin of the fish comes off easily and a cocktail stick goes through the flesh without resistance. Squeeze the lemon over the fish and allow to rest for 2 minutes.

4 To serve, put a mound of the warmed spinach onto each plate and place the fish on top. Pour a generous amount of the fennel hollandaise on the fish and place the potato rostis beside it, if using.

ROAST TURBOT WITH LOBSTER AND LOBSTER CREAM SAUCE

Wendi Peters actress and 2009 Celebrity finalist

PREPARATION TIME
10 minutes

COOKING TIME
45 minutes

SERVES 4

1 lobster, cooked, deshelled and sliced
 (keep the shells for the sauce)
4 turbot fillets, 125g (4½oz)
 each, skinned
2 tbsp light olive oil
25g (scant 1oz) unsalted butter
salt and freshly ground white pepper

FOR THE CREAM SAUCE
1 tbsp light olive oil
2 tbsp chopped carrot
2 tbsp chopped onion
2 garlic cloves, crushed
1 tbsp tomato purée
2 tbsp brandy
150ml (5fl oz) white wine
300ml (10fl oz) double cream

FOR THE VINAIGRETTE
½ tsp Dijon mustard
1½ tbsp white wine vinegar
salt and cracked black pepper
90ml (3fl oz) extra virgin olive oil
½ tsp crushed garlic
1 tsp chopped tarragon
½ tbsp chopped flat-leaf parsley
½ tbsp snipped chives
1 plum tomato, skinned, halved,
 deseeded and cut into 5mm (¼in) dice

TO SERVE
3 large King Edward potatoes,
 peeled and cut into chunks
20g (¾oz) butter
3 tbsp double cream, warmed

1 To make the sauce, heat the oil in a very large pan until smoking. Roughly chop the lobster shells, toss into the pot and sauté over a high heat for 3 minutes. Add the vegetables and garlic and cook for a further 2 minutes. Stir in the tomato purée, brandy, and wine and simmer until the wine is reduced by half. Add 600ml (1 pint) of boiling water, reduce the heat and simmer for 20 minutes. Strain through a fine sieve into a clean pan then simmer to reduce to about 250ml (8fl oz). Add the cream and boil until thick and creamy, then set aside.

2 Bring a large pan of salted water to the boil, add the potatoes and simmer for 20 minutes until cooked. Drain, mash, and season with salt and pepper. Add the butter and warmed cream. Keep warm.

3 To make the vinaigrette, whisk together the mustard, vinegar, and some seasoning. Whisk in the oil, then the garlic and herbs. Stir in the tomato dice. Transfer to a pan.

4 Season the turbot. Heat the oil in a large heavy frying pan until almost smoking. Add the butter and as it begins to foam put the turbot into the pan. Sauté for about 3 minutes on each side. Meanwhile, gently heat the sliced lobster in the vinaigrette.

5 To serve, put the mash on warmed plates and place the turbot on top. Spoon the lobster and vinaigrette alongside and drizzle the plates with lobster cream sauce.

TURBOT WITH PETIT POIS BONNE FEMME AND SAUTÉED POTATOES

Daniel Graham sous chef and 2009 Professionals finalist

PREPARATION TIME
5 minutes

COOKING TIME
40 minutes

SERVES 4

1 tbsp olive oil
4 portions of turbot, 150g (5½oz) each,
   with skin
25g (scant 1oz) salted butter

FOR THE POTATOES
100g (3½oz) salted butter
1 large sweet potato, sliced into
   1cm (½in) thick discs and cut out
   with 5cm (2in) cutter
1 large floury potato (see MasterTip,
   p.197), the same size as sweet
   potato, prepared the same way
1 garlic clove, finely sliced

FOR THE PETIS POIS
25g (scant 1oz) salted butter
50g (1¾oz) pancetta, diced

50g (1¾oz) baby silverskin onions,
   blanched and peeled
250g (9oz) frozen petit pois
2 tbsp finely chopped mint

FOR THE SAUCE
15g (½oz) salted butter
1 onion, finely chopped
1 garlic clove, finely chopped
175ml (6fl oz) white wine
175ml (6fl oz) fish stock
   (see MasterTip, p.123)
175ml (6fl oz) double cream
salt and freshly ground black pepper

TO GARNISH
1 leek, sliced into thin julienne strips
2 tbsp cornflour
vegetable oil for deep-frying

MICHEL ROUX JR

"The sauce is delicious – it makes a perfect accompaniment for the turbot. And I really like the crispy fried leeks."

1 To make the sauce, heat the butter in a large pan and sweat the onion and garlic for 3–4 minutes. Add the white wine and reduce by two-thirds, then add the fish stock and reduce again by two-thirds. To finish, add the cream, season to taste and simmer for 8–10 minutes.
2 For the potatoes, melt the butter in a heavy frying pan and sauté both potatoes with the garlic for 20 minutes or until golden brown all over and tender. There should be enough butter to foam up over them.
3 For the petit pois bonne femme, place a saucepan over a medium heat, add the pancetta and colour slightly. Add the silverskin onions and allow them to colour lightly, then add the petits pois and the cream sauce. Bring to the boil. Season and add the mint.
4 To cook the fish, oil and season it and place it skin-side down in a pan over a medium-high heat. Cook for 6 minutes then add the butter and turn it over for a further 2 minutes.
5 For the garnish, shake the leeks in a frozen food bag with the cornflour to coat them. Deep-fry for 1-2 minutes until they are golden and crispy.
6 To serve, spoon the petit pois bonne femme onto 4 plates, arrange the sautéed potatoes next to the bonne femme, then place the fish on top and finish with a handful of the crispy leeks.

TILAPIA WITH MANGO SALSA AND CORN SHAK

Daksha Mistry housewife turned caterer and 2006 finalist

½ tsp ground turmeric
salt to taste
1 tsp ground coriander
1 tsp ground cumin
½ tsp garam masala
½ tsp red chilli powder
1 garlic clove, crushed
1 tsp grated fresh root ginger
1 tsp lemon juice
1 tbsp sunflower oil
4 tilapia fish fillets, scaled
  and pin-boned

FOR THE MANGO SALSA
1 tsp white wine vinegar
1 tsp light soft brown sugar
1 star anise

1 medium semi-ripe mango,
  finely diced (see MasterTip, p.160)
1 small red onion, finely chopped
juice and zest of 1 lime
small bunch of coriander,
  finely chopped
1 tsp ground cumin
salt and freshly ground black pepper

FOR THE CORN SHAK
240g can sweetcorn
1 tbsp sunflower oil
1 tsp black mustard seed
1 garlic clove, finely chopped
½ tsp ground cumin
½ tsp ground turmeric
1 tbsp coriander, finely chopped

PREPARATION TIME
20 minutes

COOKING TIME
8 minutes

SERVES 4

1 To make the marinade for the tilapia, mix the turmeric, salt, coriander, cumin, garam masala powder, chilli powder, garlic, grated ginger, and lemon juice together. Rub into the fillets and leave to stand for a minimum of 15 minutes.
2 To make the salsa, put the vinegar, sugar, and 2 tbsp water in a saucepan and simmer until reduced by half. Add star anise and leave to infuse for 10 minutes.
3 In a bowl, combine the mango, onion, the lime juice and zest, coriander, cumin, and salt and pepper. Leave to infuse for 10 minutes, then combine with the vinegar mixture and set aside.
4 To make the corn shak, sauté the sweetcorn in sunflower oil with the mustard seed. Cook for 2 minutes before adding the garlic. Add the cumin and turmeric and stir for a further 4 minutes. Finally, add the chopped coriander and seasoning.
5 Heat 1 tbsp sunflower oil in a hot frying pan and cook the fish, skin-side down, for 4–5 minutes. Turn the fish over, take the pan off the heat, and leave the fish to finish cooking in the pan for a further 1 minute.
6 To serve, place the fish fillets on the plates with the corn shak and mango salsa served alongside.

DOVER SOLE SERVED WITH TOMATO CHUTNEY, BASIL CRISPS, AND LEMONGRASS VELOUTÉ

Chris Georgiou father of two and 2009 semi-finalist

PREPARATION TIME
60 minutes

COOKING TIME
5 minutes

SERVES 4

4 large Dover sole fillets
  (lemon sole if unavailable)
1 tbsp olive oil
1 tbsp clarified butter

FOR THE FISH STOCK
2 tbsp olive oil
1 small onion, chopped
½ celery stick, chopped
1 bulb fennel, chopped
1 small leek, sliced
sea salt and freshly ground
  black pepper
1kg (2¼lb) white fish bones and
  trimmings (ideally turbot, sole,
  or haddock, but no fish heads)
75ml (2½fl oz) dry white wine

FOR THE VELOUTÉ
1 banana shallot, sliced
½ tsp white peppercorns

½ tsp coriander seeds
1 garlic clove
1 bay leaf
handful of thyme, leaves only
3 lemongrass stalks, halved lengthways
125ml (4¼ fl oz) Noilly Prat
  or dry Martini
250ml (8fl oz) double cream
1 bunch of chervil, leaves only,
  finely chopped

FOR THE TOMATO CHUTNEY
2 tbsp olive oil
300g (10oz) ripe tomatoes, skinned,
  deseeded and finely chopped
a few thyme sprigs

FOR THE BASIL CRISPS
8 basil leaves
olive oil

1 First prepare the fish stock. Heat the olive oil in large pan and add the onion, celery, fennel, leek, and a little salt and pepper. Stir over a medium heat for 3–4 minutes to soften but not brown the vegetables. Add the fish bones and wine and bubble to reduce right down. Pour in enough cold water to cover and bring to the boil, skimming regularly. Lower the heat and simmer for 20 minutes, then remove from the heat and allow to settle for 20 minutes. Pass the stock through a sieve into a bowl.

2 Now make the velouté by putting the shallot, peppercorns, coriander seeds, garlic, bay leaf, thyme, lemongrass, and Noilly Prat in a wide sauté pan and bringing to the boil. Reduce to a syrupy glaze and then add 250ml (8fl oz) fish stock and boil to reduce by half. Add the cream and simmer until the sauce has reduced to coating consistency. Adjust the seasoning and strain the sauce through a fine sieve into bowl. Just before serving, reheat and add the chervil.

3 To make the tomato chutney, heat the olive oil in a saucepan and add the tomatoes, thyme, and seasoning. Cook for 15 minutes until the tomatoes are soft and pulpy. Remove the thyme.

4 For the crisps, stretch a sheet of cling film tightly over a deep plate. Rub olive oil over each basil leaf and press flat onto the cling film. Microwave for 3 minutes until crisp and then store in an airtight container until serving.

5 Season the sole fillets with salt and pepper and lightly dust in flour. Heat a large non-stick frying pan over a medium heat and add the olive oil and clarified butter. Place the sole in the pan skin-side down and sauté for 2 minutes, then turn and cook for a further 1–2 minutes.

6 Serve the sole with a little sauce over the top and a spoonful of tomato chutney. Garnish with the basil crisps and place the remaining sauce in a sauceboat.

MASTER TIP

SKINNING DOVER SOLE

Dover sole is prepared for cooking in a different way to other flat fish. When the fish is to be cooked whole the dark skin is left on, but it is usually removed before filleting is done. The more delicate white skin remains intact during filleting and is only scaled. You need to pull off the dark skin sharply, parallel to the flesh, and it helps to use a towel or to dip your fingers in salt to give you a firmer hold.

1 With a sharp knife, make a small incision through the dark skin at the tail end, cutting at an angle.

2 Using a towel to give you some grip on the slimy skin, pull the skin away, while holding the tail.

RED MULLET WITH PURPLE SPROUTING BROCCOLI AND COURGETTE GRATIN

Christopher Souto IT consultant turned chef and 2005 semi-finalist

PREPARATION TIME
35 minutes

COOKING TIME
10–15 minutes

SERVES 4

16–20 medium Charlotte
  potatoes (see MasterTip,
  p.197), peeled
salt and freshly ground black pepper
125g (4½oz) clarified butter
4 medium red mullet, filleted,
  skin on, or 4 pink trout fillets

FOR THE GRATINS
400g (14oz) medium-sized courgettes
400g (14oz) purple sprouting
  broccoli florets
25g (scant 1oz) clarified butter

good pinch of paprika
2 tbsp double cream
good pinch of grated nutmeg

FOR THE SAUCE
75 ml (2½fl oz) white wine
1 tbsp white wine vinegar
2 tbsp Noilly Prat or other dry vermouth
75g (2½oz) butter

TO GARNISH
½ tsp salmon caviar
4 chervil or flat-leaf parsley leaves

1 Cut the potatoes to an even barrel shape. Parboil in salted water for about 7–8 minutes, then drain and dry off. Melt 100g (3½oz) clarified butter in a medium-sized frying pan. Cook the potatoes for about 8–10 minutes until evenly browned and crisp on the outside and soft inside. Keep warm.

2 For the gratins, finely slice half the courgettes lengthways, using a mandolin or potato peeler. Blanch them for 30 seconds in salted boiling water and refresh in iced water. Drain well and set aside.

3 Chop the purple sprouting broccoli florets and leaves into smallish pieces. Discard any slightly thick stems. Melt the clarified butter in a frying pan or wok and stir-fry the broccoli for 2 minutes, stirring constantly. Sprinkle with 2–3 tbsp hot water and continue to stir for another 1–2 minutes until the broccoli is tender and wilted down. Remove from the heat and season well with the paprika, salt, and pepper. Set aside.

4 Peel and dice the remaining courgettes. Blend with the double cream and season generously with pepper and grated nutmeg. Set aside.

5 Preheat the grill to very hot. To assemble the gratins, butter four 7cm (2¾in) metal cooking rings or ring moulds. Cut out and butter 4 squares of greaseproof paper, a little larger than the cooking rings. Lay them on a baking sheet and put the cooking rings on top. Line the base and sides of the rings with the blanched courgette slices, ensuring there are no gaps. Layer them with the purple sprouting broccoli, pressing the mixture down well into the rings. Cover with

the puréed courgette, filling the cooking ring to the top. Smooth over. Cook the gratins under a hot grill for about 7–8 minutes until hot, and the puréed courgette has just started to colour.

6 To make the sauce, put the wine, vinegar and Noilly Prat in a saucepan and reduce by two-thirds. Gradually whisk in the butter until smooth and glossy. Keep warm.

7 Melt the remaining 25g (scant 1oz) clarified butter and use to brush the fish fillets. Season and pan-fry over a medium-high heat, skin-side down, for about 3 minutes or until the fish just begins to turn opaque.

8 To serve, put the butter-sautéed potatoes on 4 warmed serving plates and place the fish fillets on top. Carefully invert the vegetable gratins onto the plates and garnish with the salmon caviar. Drizzle the vermouth butter sauce over the fish and garnish with chervil.

SALMON EN PAPILLOTTE WITH BRAISED FENNEL AND A CREAMY CAPER SAUCE

Chris Gates civil servant turned junior sous chef and 2009 finalist

PREPARATION TIME
15 minutes

COOKING TIME
35 minutes

SERVES 4

4 salmon fillets, 200g (7oz) each,
  skin removed
1 bulb fennel, sliced
1 lemon, sliced
25g (scant 1oz) butter
about 120ml (4fl oz) white wine
salt and freshly ground black pepper

FOR THE SAUCE
1 shallot, finely chopped
25g (scant 1oz) butter
1 tbsp capers, drained
200ml (7fl oz) double cream
1 tbsp fresh chopped dill

1 Preheat the oven to 190°C (375°F/Gas 5). Fold 4 sheets of baking parchment in half and fold over 2 of the edges twice, leaving the remaining edge open to make a bag.

2 Place a salmon fillet in the bag with 2 slices of fennel, 2 slices of lemon, a knob of butter and 2 tbsp white wine. Season with salt and pepper. Close the bag by folding the baking parchment over twice on the remaining side. Repeat to fill 3 more bags. Place the bags on a baking tray and cook in the oven for about 20 minutes until the fish is ready – it should be slightly paler in colour and just set.

3 To make the sauce, soften the shallot in the butter for 10 minutes until translucent. Add the capers and cream and simmer gently for 5 minutes until the sauce has thickened. Season and stir in the dill just before serving.

4 Once the fish is just cooked, cut open the bags and transfer the salmon fillets to warmed plates. Spoon over the fennel and juices left in the bag, discarding the lemon. Drizzle some of the caper sauce around the salmon and serve while hot.

1 Slide a knife into the flesh at the tail, cutting next to the skin at an angle.

2 Turn the knife almost flat, keep it in place and pull the skin away.

3 Lay the fish on one half of the wrapping and fold the other half over.

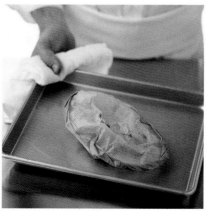

4 The parcels will puff up in the oven. Cut them open and remove the fish.

MASTER TIP

COOKING EN PAPILLOTTE

Enclosing fish in a parcel with vegetables and seasonings keeps the fish moist and succulent, infused with the accompanying flavours. The traditional wrapping is baking parchment, but you can also use foil or leaves such as lotus. Since there is no risk of the fish burning on the bottom, it is often skinned.

HERB-MARINATED SALMON IN COCONUT CURRY SAUCE

Andy Oliver project manager turned chef and 2009 finalist

PREPARATION TIME
10 minutes, plus marinating

COOKING TIME
15 minutes

SERVES 4

3 tbsp Greek-style yogurt
handful of coriander
handful of mint
4 pieces of salmon fillet, about
    150g (5½oz each, skinned (see
    MasterTip, p.151)

FOR THE MARINADE
1 onion, roughly chopped
2 tsp grated fresh root ginger
4 garlic cloves, roughly chopped
3 medium-hot green chillies,
    roughly chopped

2 tsp ground turmeric
2 tsp ground coriander
4 tsp garam masala

FOR THE SAUCE
1 tsp sunflower oil
400ml (14fl oz) coconut milk
    (see MasterTip, p.25)
1 tbsp thick tamarind paste
    (see MasterTip, left)
200g (7oz) baby spinach, washed
salt and freshly ground black pepper

MASTER TIP

TAMARIND PASTE

Tamarind paste is popular in Asian and Oriental dishes and is readily available in Asian food stores and supermarkets. It is easy and cheaper, however, to make your own from blocks of tamarind. Simply soak the block in the quantity of water specified for about 30 mins and then push through a sieve to strain. The paste will keep for up to a week in the fridge.

1 Preheat the oven to 200°C (400°F/Gas 6).
2 To make the marinade, whizz the onion, ginger, garlic, and chillies in a food processor with a good pinch of salt and 1 tbsp of water to help bind the paste. Mix in the spices.
3 Take out half of this paste and set aside. Add the coriander and mint leaves to the remaining paste in the food processor, reserving some to garnish. Whizz again until smooth. Mix in the yogurt and rub this mixture over the salmon. Leave to marinate for 30 minutes.
4 Place the salmon on a greased baking tray and cook in the oven for 5–10 minutes, depending on the thickness.
5 Meanwhile, make the sauce. Fry the remaining paste in the sunflower oil for 3 minutes, then add the coconut milk and 4 tbsp of water. Simmer for 5 minutes then add the tamarind paste and spinach. Season to taste and cook until the spinach has wilted.
6 To serve, spoon the curry sauce into wide bowls and place the salmon fillets on top. Garnish with coriander and mint leaves.

POACHED SALMON IN AN ASIAN BROTH

inspired by **Mat Follas** engineer turned chef patron and 2009 champion

1 litre (1¾ pints) fish stock (see MasterTip, p.123)
2 lemongrass stalks, chopped
2.5cm (1in) piece of galangal or fresh root ginger, sliced into matchsticks
1 banana shallot, sliced
3–4 bird's eye chillies, deseeded and finely chopped
1 tsp golden caster sugar

4 kaffir lime leaves, roughly shredded
¼ tsp salt
1 tbsp nam pla (Thai fish sauce)
4 salmon fillets, 175g (6oz) each, skinned
2 heads of pak choi, quartered lengthways
juice of 1 lime
1 handful of coriander leaves, roughly chopped

PREPARATION TIME
25 minutes

COOKING TIME
35 minutes

SERVES 4

1 Bring the stock to the boil in a large saucepan with the lemongrass, galangal or ginger, shallot, chillies, sugar, salt, and 2 of the lime leaves. Simmer for 10–15 minutes.

2 Stir in the nam pla, then gently lower the salmon into the liquid, followed by the pak choi, and turn the heat down to low. Cover with a lid and poach for 8–10 minutes, then remove the fish to warmed bowls.

3 Add the remaining lime leaves, lime juice, and coriander leaves to the broth and taste for seasoning. Ladle the broth over the salmon to serve, with some cooked noodles if desired.

SEARED TUNA WITH AN ASIAN GLAZE

Angela Kenny administrator turned chef and 2009 semi-finalist

4 carrots
4 courgettes
8 tbsp dark soy sauce
4 limes
6 tbsp demerara sugar
12–16 Charlotte potatoes
  (see MasterTip, p.197), peeled
  and sliced into discs

60ml (2fl oz) white miso paste (see
  MasterTip, right)
60ml (2fl oz) mirin
90ml (3½fl oz) dry sake
2 tbsp rice wine vinegar
1 tbsp oil
4 tuna steaks, 175–200g (6–7oz) each
salt and freshly ground black pepper

PREPARATION TIME
20 minutes

COOKING TIME
8 minutes

SERVES 4

1 With a potato peeler, shave the carrots and courgettes into long strips. Place in a mixing bowl with 3 tbsp soy sauce, the juice and zest of 1½ limes, and 4 tbsp sugar.

2 Put the potatoes in a large pan with boiling water to cover and the white miso paste. Cook for about 10 minutes until the potatoes are tender and then drain.

3 Place the mirin, sake, remaining sugar and soy sauce, rice wine vinegar, and the juice and zest of the remaining limes in a frying pan over a medium heat and reduce to a syrup consistency – about 10 minutes.

4 Season the tuna with salt and pepper. Heat another frying pan until hot, add the tuna and sear on both sides for about 3 minutes.

5 Once the tuna is cooked, transfer it to the frying pan containing the glaze and turn to coat it. Heat the ribbon vegetables in the glaze for 2 minutes, then serve with the tuna and potatoes.

MASTER TIP
MISO PASTE

Miso paste is a Japanese seasoning made by fermenting barley, rice, or soya beans, the last being the most common. It is used in a variety of dishes and makes excellent soup. The flavour depends on the region in which it is produced and the main ingredient, but white miso is a common type found throughout Japan and worldwide.

POACHED SEA TROUT WITH ASPARAGUS, MASHED POTATO, AND SORREL SAUCE

Andy Oliver project manager turned chef and 2009 finalist

PREPARATION TIME
25 minutes

COOKING TIME
30 minutes

SERVES 4

4 sea trout fillets 200g (7oz) each,
  skin on
1 banana shallot, sliced
a small bunch parsley stalks
2 bay leaves
6 white peppercorns
salt
1 tsp fennel seeds
½ lemon, thinly sliced
1 litre (1¾ pints) fish stock
  (see MasterTip, p.123)
400g (14oz) asparagus spears
  (see MasterTip, p.221)

FOR THE MASHED POTATO
4 large floury potatoes such as
  King Edwards or Maris Piper
  (see MasterTip, p.197), peeled
100ml (3½ fl oz) whole milk, hot
knob of butter
splash of double cream

FOR THE SAUCE
15g (½oz) butter
1 banana shallot, finely diced
splash of dry vermouth or good-quality
  white wine
100ml (3½fl oz) fish stock
3 tbsp double cream
1 small bunch of fresh sorrel, shredded

1 First cut the potatoes into even-sized pieces. Bring to the boil in a saucepan and then simmer for 20–30 minutes until tender. Pass the potatoes through a ricer or use a masher until completely smooth. Beat in the hot milk, butter, and a little cream.

2 To poach the fish, place the fillets skin-side down in a wide frying pan with the shallot, parsley stalks, bay leaves, peppercorns, salt, fennel seeds, and a couple of thin lemon slices. Pour over enough fish stock to cover the fish and bring to a gentle simmer. Poach the fish for about 5 minutes, until opaque and just set. Drain and remove the skin.

3 To make the sauce, melt the butter in a pan and cook the shallot until softened but not coloured. Add the dry vermouth or wine and reduce. Pour in the fish stock and reduce by half, then add the cream and reduce again until the sauce reaches the desired consistency. Add the shredded sorrel and keep warm.

4 Steam or cook the asparagus in boiling salted water for 5–6 minutes until tender. Drain. Make quenelles of mashed potato by placing it between two identical tablespoons and moulding into a rugby ball shape (see MasterTip, p.93).

5 To serve, place a quenelle of mash on the centre of each plate, arrange the fish on top and the asparagus around the outside. Pour the sauce around.

MACKEREL FILLETS ON SALT COD AND BUTTERBEAN SALAD WITH SALSA VERDE

Susie Carter administrator turned food writer and 2006 quarter-finalist

8 mackerel fillets
olive oil for frying

FOR THE SALAD
200g (7oz) pre-soaked salt cod
3 tomatoes, deseeded and chopped
1 banana shallot, very thinly sliced
420g can butterbeans, drained
  and rinsed
small bunch of flat-leaf parsley
1 tbsp capers
1 tbsp sherry vinegar
4 tbsp olive oil

FOR THE SALSA VERDE
1 large bunch of basil
1 large bunch of flat-leaf parsley
a few mint leaves
1 tbsp capers, drained and rinsed
6 anchovy fillets in oil
8 pitted green olives
1 large garlic clove, crushed
½ lemon, juiced
sea salt and freshly ground
  black pepper
olive oil

PREPARATION TIME
25 minutes

COOKING TIME
5 minutes

SERVES 4

1 First make the salad. Drain the salt cod and cut or tear into thin slivers. Combine with the rest of the salad ingredients and taste for seasoning.

2 To make the salsa verde, put all the salsa ingredients except for the lemon juice and oil on a large chopping board and chop until finely minced and well mixed. Resist the urge to use a blender – you will end up with a nasty green sludge rather than a delicate green relish.

3 Transfer the salsa to a bowl and add half the lemon juice, a big pinch of sea salt, and about 15 turns of the pepper mill. Stir in enough olive oil to give it a pesto-like consistency and taste for seasoning. If it is too sharp, add more oil; if there is not enough zing, add more lemon or try a little more salt, which helps to bring out sharp flavours.

4 Season the mackerel fillets and fry skin-side down in a frying pan with a little olive oil over a high heat for 2–3 minutes. Carefully turn the fillets over and cook for a further 2 minutes until cooked through.

5 Use a 7cm (2¾in) ring mould to serve the salad. Top with 2 mackerel fillets per person, and spoon a little salsa on the side.

STARTERS
VEGETABLES & FISH
POULTRY
MEAT
GAME
DESSERTS

PAN-FRIED CHICKEN BREAST WITH SESAME SEEDS AND A MANGO HOLLANDAISE

Jaye Wakelin interior designer and 2007 quarter-finalist

PREPARATION TIME
15 minutes

COOKING TIME
20 minutes

SERVES 4

4 chicken breasts, skinned
2 large egg yolks
salt and freshly ground black pepper
1 tbsp lemon juice
1 tbsp white wine vinegar
125g (4½oz) salted butter

1 ripe mango, peeled, stoned
  and chopped (see MasterTip, left)
2 tbsp sesame seeds
1 tbsp groundnut oil
25g (scant 1oz) butter
400g (14oz) purple sprouting broccoli

MASTER TIP
PREPARING MANGOES

Mangoes have such large amounts of sticky juice it is sometimes said they are best peeled in the bath. It helps to be methodical, though. One way to do it is to slice off the flat sides as close to the stone as possible, score the flesh down to the peel in cube shapes, then press with your thumbs to push the flesh forward from the skin. The other common method is to pare away the peel then make a series of cube-shaped cuts through the flesh so that it is more easily cut from the stone.

1 Remove the chicken from the fridge at least 30 minutes before preparation.
2 To make the hollandaise, place the egg yolks in a blender with salt and pepper to taste and blend thoroughly. Heat the lemon juice and vinegar to simmering point in a small saucepan, then remove the pan from the heat. Switch on the blender again and pour the hot lemon liquid through the vent in the top of it in a steady stream. Switch off the blender.
3 In the same saucepan, melt the butter over a low heat. With the blender running as before, add the butter to the egg mixture in a steady stream. The mixture should now look like runny mayonnaise. Pour it out into a clean bowl.
4 Add the chopped mango to the blender and blitz until smooth and puréed. Stir into the hollandaise, cover with cling film and set aside.
5 Spread the sesame seeds over a plate and press the chicken breasts onto them, coating each one evenly. Melt the oil and butter in a frying pan over a medium heat, taking care that the butter doesn't brown. Add the chicken breasts and fry gently on both sides until cooked through – about 5–8 minutes on each side. At this point the butter in the pan will look brown but will not have burnt. Meanwhile, steam the broccoli until tender – about 8 minutes.
6 Return the mango hollandaise to a clean saucepan and reheat gently, taking care not to let it bubble and separate. Put the sliced chicken breasts on plates and serve with the hollandaise spooned over. This dish goes well with any stir-fried Chinese greens or purple sprouting broccoli with a little soya sauce.

CHICKEN BREAST FILLED WITH LIVER SERVED WITH MADEIRA CREAM SAUCE
James Nathan barrister turned chef and 2008 champion

PREPARATION TIME
2 hours

COOKING TIME
1 hour 30 minutes

SERVES 4

4 chicken breasts, fillets removed
 and reserved
20 large spinach leaves
4 chicken livers, weighing about
 50g (1¾oz) in total
fine sea salt in a pot, tub or bowl
 but not a grinder
freshly ground white pepper
freshly ground black pepper
100g (3½oz) unsalted butter,
 at room temperature

FOR THE COURGETTE ROSTI
3 medium courgettes
25g (scant 1oz) melted butter
1 garlic clove, chopped
2 medium egg whites
1 tbsp olive oil

FOR THE COURGETTE FLOWERS
4 dry-cured smoked back
 bacon rashers
100ml (3½fl oz) whipping cream
4 courgette flowers
2 garlic cloves
1 lemon
2 tbsp cornflour
2 tbsp plain flour

150ml can Slimline tonic water
vegetable oil for deep-frying

FOR THE PASTA
150g (5½oz) "00" pasta flour (see
 MasterTip, p.52)
50g (1¾oz) semolina flour
3 egg yolks
1 tbsp olive oil
small pinch of saffron powder
3–4 tbsp still mineral water
1 egg, beaten

FOR THE FILLING
25g (scant 1oz) unsalted butter,
 at room temperature
4 shallots, finely chopped
50g (1¾oz) chestnut mushrooms,
 finely chopped
50–75ml (1¾–2½fl oz) double cream

FOR THE SAUCE
25g (scant 1oz) dried porcini mushrooms
400ml (14fl oz) chicken stock (see
 MasterTip, p.21)
100ml (3½fl oz) sweet, dark Madeira
75ml (2½fl oz) double cream
dash of lemon juice

1 To make the pasta, put 100g (3½oz) "00" flour, 25g (scant 1oz) semolina flour, the egg yolks, olive oil, saffron and a pinch of salt in a food processor bowl. Process to fine breadcrumb consistency then add the still mineral water until the mixture starts to come together. Tip out onto a lightly floured work surface. Knead for 3–4 minutes until smooth, firm, and easy to manage. (Or see MasterTip, p.51.)
2 For the filling, melt the butter in a small pan and add the shallots. Cover and sweat until soft but not coloured. Add the chestnut mushrooms and sweat until all the moisture is absorbed. Season with salt and pepper. Turn up the heat and loosen the mixture with double cream. Cook until the mixture thickens and the cream starts to bubble. Set aside and cool until needed.

3 Using a pasta machine, roll out the pasta dough to the finest setting (see MasterTip, pp.190–91) and lay the pasta sheet on a floured surface. Brush half of it with egg glaze. Using a teaspoon, place about 20 small but tall mounds of the mushroom filling onto the egg-glazed pasta, making sure they are well spaced. Fold the unglazed half of the pasta sheet over the mounds of filling and cut out with a 4–5cm (1¾–2in) pastry cutter. Work your fingers around the edge of each ravioli, ensuring the air is squeezed out and the filling is sealed in. Place on a plate lightly dusted with semolina flour and cover with a tea towel.

4 To make the courgette flowers, cut the leanest parts of the smoked bacon and dice finely. Also finely dice the fillets from the chicken breast; you want 3 times more chicken meat than bacon. Put the meats in a blender, season with salt and white pepper, then blend to a smooth paste. Chill to relax the mixture. When it is rested, gently fold in the whipping cream with a fork over a bowl of ice.

5 Remove the stamens from the courgette flowers, taking care not to damage the petals. Using teaspoons dipped in hot water, shape 4 rough quenelles (see MasterTip, p.93) of the mousse. Insert the mousse into the flowers and twist the petals to seal it inside.

6 To make tempura batter, mix the cornflour and plain flour and season with salt and white pepper. Mix to a light frothing batter with the tonic water and use immediately. Gently roll the flowers in the mixture then cook in a deep-fat fryer for 2–3 minutes at 180°C (350°F) until lightly golden brown. Drain on kitchen paper and keep warm.

7 For the stuffed chicken breast, put the chicken in between cling film and flatten gently using the base of a pan or a rolling pin.

8 Blanch the spinach leaves and refresh in iced water. Season the

---

MASTER TIP

STUFFING A CHICKEN BREAST

There are several ways to stuff a chicken breast but the crucial point is to ensure the stuffing doesn't spill out during the cooking process. Resist the temptation to be too generous with the stuffing or you will not be able to pull the edges of the meat together. Here we show how to stuff by making a pocket in the chicken breast (see also p.167).

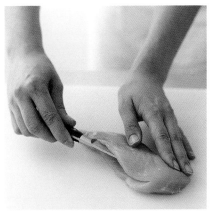

1 With a sharp knife, cut a pocket about 4cm (1½in) deep in the side of the breast fillet.

2 Holding back one side of the chicken breast, press the stuffing in firmly and then roll the flesh back.

liver all over with salt and pepper then sear in butter on all sides in a smoking hot non-stick frying pan. Pour off the fat and deglaze the frying pan with Madeira. Drain the livers on kitchen paper then wrap in the blanched spinach leaves. Lay the wrapped livers on the chicken breasts and roll up like a Swiss roll. Brush with butter and season. Wrap in non-PVC cling film and form into neat cylinders. Cook in simmering water for 10–12 minutes. Leave to rest in the cling film for 5 minutes while you cook the ravioli for 3–4 minutes in the same water, then unwrap and fry the chicken breasts briefly in hot butter to colour the outside. Slice into rounds to serve.

9 To make the sauce, soak the porcini for 15 minutes in 150ml (5fl oz) warm water. In a small pan, heat the chicken stock and reduce by half. Add the soaked mushrooms and reduce by half again. Add the deglazed juice from the pan used to cook the liver. Reduce to a rich brown residue. Add the double cream and reduce to a thick, rich, glossy sauce. Add a few drops of lemon juice to thin the sauce if required. Season the sauce as it cooks – remember that the flavours intensify as the volume decreases.

10 Preheat the oven to 180°C (350°F/Gas 4). To make the courgette rosti, peel strips from the courgettes to remove half of the green skin in bands. Grate the courgettes coarsely in a food processor, sprinkle liberally with fine salt and set in a colander to drain for 30 minutes. Squeeze any excess water out of the courgettes by wringing them out in a tea towel. Put them into a bowl and add the melted butter, chopped garlic, and egg white and season with salt and pepper. Put two 7cm (2¾in) plate rings into a hot, non-stick, ovenproof, heavy saucepan and add the olive oil. Press the courgette mixture into the rings and fry on both sides until golden brown. Put the pan into a hot oven for about 15 minutes to cook through.

11 To serve, place a rosti on each of 4 large plates. Top with the sliced chicken breast and coat with sauce. Lay a courgette flower and 5 ravioli by the side.

CHICKEN WITH AUBERGINE STUFFING

Angela Kenny administrator turned chef and 2009 semi-finalist

4 chicken breasts, skin on
1 tbsp olive oil
salt and freshly ground black pepper

FOR THE STUFFING
1 tbsp olive oil
½ red onion, finely chopped
7 chestnut mushrooms, finely chopped
¼ aubergine, finely chopped
30g (1oz) black olives, finely chopped
small bunch of basil, finely chopped
1 pickled walnut, finely chopped
3 garlic cloves, finely chopped
grated zest of ½ lemon
3 tbsp polenta
100g (3½oz) pork mince
30g (1oz) pine nuts, finely chopped
chicken stock to moisten

FOR THE POTATO CAKE
100g (3½oz) potato such as
  Maris Piper (see MasterTip. p197),
  cut into chunks
25g (scant 1oz) walnuts, chopped
25g (scant 1oz) rocket, chopped
25g (scant 1oz) plain flour
1 egg, beaten
polenta for dusting
3 tbsp olive oil

FOR THE SAUCE
2 ripe peaches, cut into wedges
100ml (3½fl oz) white wine
100ml (3½fl oz) chicken stock
  (see MasterTip, p.21)
small knob of butter
large bunch of basil, chopped

PREPARATION TIME
1 hour, plus chilling time

COOKING TIME
1 hour

SERVES 4

1 Remove and reserve the chicken skin. Flatten the flesh between
2 sheets of cling film with a rolling pin. Run the back of a knife across
the skin, stretching it as much as you can without tearing.
2 For the stuffing, heat the oil in a pan and gently fry the onion,
mushrooms, and aubergine until golden. Allow to cool. Mix with the
other stuffing ingredients and divide between the chicken breasts.
Roll up tightly. Wrap the chicken skin around the breast, then wrap
firmly with foil or cling film to make a sausage. Chill for 30 minutes.
3 Preheat the oven to 200°C (400°F/Gas 6). Heat 1 tbsp olive oil in a
frying pan, remove the foil or cling film and brown the chicken. Transfer
to a roasting tin, drizzle with oil and put in the oven for 25–30 minutes.
4 Put the potatoes in a pan of simmering water for 10–15 minutes
until tender. Meanwhile, make the sauce. Brown the peaches in the
same pan used for the chicken. Once lightly cooked, add the wine
and stock then reduce. Add a knob of butter and stir in the basil.
5 Drain the potatoes and put through a potato ricer. Add the walnuts
and rocket, season to taste, and add the flour and an egg to bind the
mixture. Shape into 4 rounds and dust with polenta. Heat a frying pan
with the olive oil and fry the potato cakes until brown on each side.
6 Remove the chicken from the oven and allow to rest for 5 minutes,
then slice into rounds. Place a potato cake on each plate and top with
chicken. Lay the peach slices on the plate and drizzle with the sauce.

CHICKEN BREAST STUFFED WITH PESTO AND MOZZARELLA ON A BED OF MUSHROOMS

inspired by **Midge Ure** musician and 2007 Celebrity finalist

PREPARATION TIME
30 minutes

COOKING TIME
40 minutes

SERVES 4

4 chicken breasts, skinned
8 slices Parma ham
2 tbsp olive oil

FOR THE STUFFING
40 basil leaves, about 15g (½oz)
25g (scant 1oz) pine nuts, toasted (see MasterTip, p.40)
1 small garlic clove, finely chopped
25g (scant 1oz) Parmesan cheese finely grated
100ml (3½fl oz) olive oil
salt and freshly ground black pepper
2 balls mozzarella cheese, chopped

FOR THE MUSHROOM CAPS
1 tbsp olive oil
15g (½oz) butter
2 shallots, finely chopped
450g (1lb) mixed mushrooms such as chestnut, Portobello, and button, destalked and sliced
1 garlic clove, crushed
75ml (2½fl oz) dry sherry
salt and freshly ground black pepper
3 tbsp flat-leaf parsley, chopped
2 tbsp double cream

1 Preheat the oven to 200°C (400°F/Gas 6). Lay the chicken breasts smooth side down on a board. With a sharp knife, remove the small fillet of meat from the breasts. Make 2–3 slashes in the breasts, cutting halfway through, and open out the meat. Lay cling film over the top and, using a rolling pin, bash out the meat until it is about 1.5cm (¾in) thick. Flatten the fillets in the same way.

2 To make the pesto, place the basil, pine nuts, garlic, Parmesan, and oil in a food processor and pulse until smooth. Season. Spread 2 tbsp pesto over each chicken breast and scatter a quarter of the mozzarella in a line along one side of the breast, keeping the filling 2.5cm (1in) away from the edge. Place the fillet over the top and roll up the chicken into a torpedo shape, tucking in the ends. Season the outside generously and rub in the oil.

3 Lay the slices of Parma ham on the board and roll 2 around each chicken breast, then sear in a hot frying pan on all sides with a touch more oil for 1–2 minutes, seal side down first, so that the ham turns crispy. Transfer to a baking sheet and bake for 20–25 minutes.

4 For the mushrooms, heat the oil and butter in a frying pan, add the shallots and sauté gently for 5 minutes before adding the mushrooms and garlic. Cook until the mushrooms start to release their liquid, then turn up the heat, pour in the sherry and reduce by half. Season, stir in the parsley, add the cream, and bring to a gentle bubble.

5 To serve, slice each chicken breast into 3 pieces and lay on a bed of the mushroom caps.

CHICKEN WITH A MEDITERRANEAN STUFFING AND A ROSEMARY VERMOUTH QUINCE SAUCE

Katherine Haworth housekeeper and 2005 quarter-finalist

4 chicken breasts, skinless
50g (1¾oz) butter
1 garlic clove, finely chopped

FOR THE STUFFING
2 slices prosciutto, finely chopped
10 green or black olives, finely chopped
6 sun-dried tomatoes in oil, drained
  and finely chopped

2 tbsp finely chopped fresh oregano
  leaves or ½ tsp dried
salt and freshly ground black pepper
1 tbsp olive oil

FOR THE SAUCE
250ml (8fl oz) Noilly Prat or other
  dry vermouth
2 tbsp quince jelly
1 tbsp finely chopped rosemary

PREPARATION TIME
40 minutes

COOKING TIME
40 minutes

SERVES 4

1 Cut the small fillets off the chicken breasts and chop very finely. In a small pan, melt 25g (scant 1oz) of the butter and add the garlic. Cook for 1 minute then add the chopped chicken fillets, cook for another 2 minutes and remove from the heat. Stand in a bowl of cold water to cool quickly.

2 Mix the prosciutto, olives, tomatoes, and oregano with the chopped chicken fillets and garlic and season to taste with salt and pepper. With a sharp, narrow-bladed knife, cut a pocket in the thickest part of the chicken breasts, push the stuffing mix into it and bring the meat together around it (see MasterTip, p.163).

3 Preheat the oven to 190°C (375°F/Gas 5). Lay 4 large squares of foil on a baking sheet. Heat the remaining butter and the olive oil in a small frying pan and brown the chicken breasts on all sides, then lift them out and place on the foil squares. Lift up the foil round the sides but do not seal up yet.

4 Put the dry vermouth, quince jelly, and rosemary into the frying pan, return to the heat and simmer until the jelly has melted. Pour over the chicken and seal up the parcels. Place in the oven for about 20–25 minutes. At the end of the cooking time, remove from the oven and open a small hole at one end of the parcels. Carefully pour the juices into a small pan, reseal the hole, put the chicken in a warm place to rest and boil the juices until reduced by half.

5 To serve, place the chicken breasts on to 4 plates and pour the juices over them.

CHICKEN STUFFED WITH WILD MUSHROOMS AND HAZELNUTS WITH PAN HAGGERTY

David Hall IT buyer turned food writer and teacher and 2007 semi-finalist

PREPARATION TIME
45 minutes

COOKING TIME
40 minutes

SERVES 4

FOR THE STUFFING
2 tbsp butter
150g (5½oz) wild mushrooms,
  finely chopped
2 tbsp thyme leaves, finely chopped
50g (1¾oz) hazelnuts, coarsely chopped
2 chicken livers, finely chopped
2 tbsp finely chopped flat-leaf parsley
2 good-quality pork sausages,
  skin removed
salt and freshly ground black pepper

FOR THE CHICKEN
4 tbsp olive oil
4 chicken legs, boned, with skin on

FOR THE PAN HAGGERTY
50g (1¾oz) butter
3 large Desirée potatoes, peeled
  and thinly sliced
200g (7oz) onion, thinly sliced
50g (1¾oz) Cheddar cheese, grated

FOR THE GRAVY
400ml (14fl oz) fruity red wine
200ml (7fl oz) port
1 shallot, finely diced
1 tbsp balsamic vinegar
1 tbsp dried mushrooms, rehydrated
  (see MasterTip, p.54)
2 sprigs of thyme
1 bay leaf
400ml (14fl oz) chicken stock
  (see MasterTip, p.21)
50g (1¾oz) butter

FOR THE CARAMELIZED TURNIP
1 turnip, diced
50g (1¾oz) butter
50g (1¾oz) light soft brown sugar

FOR THE KALE
300g (10oz) curly kale, shredded
50g (1¾oz) butter

1   First make the stuffing. Heat the butter in a non-stick pan and gently cook the wild mushrooms for 5 minutes. In a bowl, mix the cooked mushrooms, thyme, hazelnuts, chicken livers, parsley, and sausage meat. Season to taste with salt and pepper.

2   For the stuffed chicken, prepare 4 large squares of foil, drizzle with 2 tbsp olive oil and lay the boned chicken legs, skin-side down, on the foil. Season with salt and pepper. Divide the stuffing into 4 portions then, using your hands, roll each portion into a sausage shape and place along the length of the chicken legs. Carefully roll the chicken firmly in the foil and twist the ends of the foil up tightly so that it resembles a Christmas cracker – it is important to make a water-tight parcel.

3   Bring a large pan of water to the boil and add the chicken parcels to the pan. Simmer for 20 minutes, or until the chicken is cooked all the way through, then set aside.

4   Meanwhile, to make the pan haggerty, melt the butter in a large non-stick ovenproof frying pan, layer the potatoes and onions and

season with salt and pepper. Sprinkle with the grated cheese and cover with a tight fitting lid. Simmer gently over a low heat for 20–25 minutes or until the potato is cooked.

5 To make the gravy, bring the wine and port to the boil in a small pan, along with the shallot, balsamic vinegar, dried mushrooms, thyme, and bay leaf. Cook over a moderate heat for 15 minutes or until the liquid has reduced by half.

6 Pour in the chicken stock and simmer for 10 minutes to reduce by half again. Remove from the heat, strain through a sieve into a clean pan and season with salt and pepper. Reheat the gravy and then whisk in the butter. Set aside and keep warm.

7 To make the caramelized turnip, bring a pan of water to the boil and simmer the turnip for 5 minutes. Drain thoroughly. Melt the butter in a non-stick frying pan, add the sugar and turnip and shake the pan continuously until the outside of the turnip pieces are caramelized. Set aside and keep warm.

8 To finish off the chicken, remove from the foil and place in a hot frying pan with 2 tbsp olive oil. Cook for 2 minutes or until the skin is crispy and golden brown. Set aside and keep warm.

9 When the pan haggerty has cooked, remove the lid and place the pan under a hot grill until the cheese is bubbling and golden.

10 To cook the kale, bring a pan of water to the boil and simmer the kale for 3–4 minutes. Drain well and return to the pan. Add the butter to the pan and mix well. Season to taste with salt and pepper.

11 To serve, slice the chicken and arrange on 4 warm serving plates with the pan haggerty, turnip, and kale. Finish by drizzling some gravy around the plate.

POACHED POUSSINS WITH SWISS CHARD AND BALSAMIC-GLAZED BABY ONIONS

Mark Moraghan actor and 2008 Celebrity finalist

2 poussins, 500g (1lb 2oz) each
  (preferably corn-fed)
8 bay leaves
4 sprigs of thyme
2 sprigs of sage
1 litre (1¾ pints) chicken stock
  (see MasterTip, p.21)
1 tsp sea salt
1 tbsp olive oil
2 onions, thickly sliced

FOR THE GLAZED ONIONS
16 baby onions, peeled
2 bay leaves
3 tbsp white wine vinegar
2 sprigs of thyme

6 juniper berries
10g (¼oz) salted butter
3 tbsp balsamic vinegar

FOR THE BEURRE BLANC
500ml (16fl oz) chicken stock
3 tbsp white wine
50g (1¾oz) butter
salt and freshly ground black pepper

FOR THE SWISS CHARD
200g (7oz) Swiss chard, stalks and
  leaves separated
25g (scant 1oz) butter
2 tbsp olive oil

PREPARATION TIME
30 minutes

COOKING TIME
1 hour 15 mins

SERVES 4

1 Fill the cavity of each poussin with bay leaves, thyme, and sage. Bring the chicken stock to just below boiling point then immerse the poussins in it. Cook, covered, for 30 minutes at the same temperature.
2 Preheat the oven to 180°C (350°F/Gas 4). Remove the poussins from the stock and drain for 3 minutes then dry with kitchen paper. Season with salt, drizzle with olive oil and lay on top of the onions in a baking tray so the birds do not touch the bottom of the tray. Roast for 20 minutes then leave to rest for 3 minutes before serving.
3 Blanch the baby onions for 3–5 minutes in boiling water seasoned with salt, bay leaves, and vinegar. Transfer to a hot dry frying pan to caramelize the exterior. Add the thyme, juniper berries, and butter, return to the heat and allow the butter to foam and flavour the onions. After basting the onions, add the balsamic vinegar. When reduced almost to caramel consistency (about 15 minutes), check the onions – they should be al dente. If they need more cooking add some chicken stock. Meanwhile, cook the beurre blanc (see MasterTip, right).
4 Peel the Swiss chard stalks and cut into dice about 5mm (¼in) square. Slice the leaves finely. Blanch the stalks in boiling salted water, adding the leaves after 1 minute. Cook until al dente then drain. Season with the butter, oil, and a pinch of sea salt. Serve a leg and a breast from each poussin for each person. Arrange on plates with the baby onions and a spoonful of chard. Drizzle with the beurre blanc.

MASTER TIP

MAKING BEURRE BLANC

For the chicken beurre blanc, reduce the stock in a wide, shallow pan until it is very concentrated and only one-tenth of its previous volume, which will take about 20 minutes. Add the white wine and reduce again. To finish, whisk in the butter and season to taste.

CHICKEN SUKKA WITH SWEET RICE
Michelle Peters university researcher and 2009 semi-finalist

PREPARATION TIME
20 minutes

COOKING TIME
45 minutes

SERVES 4

FOR THE BAFAT SPICE MIX
5 long mild dried red chillies
10cm (4in) cinnamon stick
1 tbsp peppercorns
1 tbsp cloves
1 tbsp cumin seeds
4 tbsp coriander seeds
½ star anise

FOR THE CHICKEN SUKKA
90ml (3fl oz) vegetable oil or ghee
200g (7oz) onion, chopped
2.5cm (1in) piece of fresh root ginger,
   finely chopped
2 garlic cloves, crushed
1 green chilli, deseeded
   and finely chopped
4 large tomatoes, roughly chopped
½ tsp turmeric
4 tbsp tomato ketchup
salt and freshly ground black pepper

500g (1lb 2oz) boned chicken thighs,
   cut into bite-sized pieces
200g (7oz) fresh coconut, finely grated
1 long red chilli
sprig of curry leaves
1 garlic clove, whole, unpeeled
   and smashed
30g (1oz) coriander, chopped

FOR THE RICE
450g (1lb) basmati rice
5 tbsp ghee or clarified butter
2 tbsp caster sugar
salt
200g (7oz) onion, thinly sliced
50g (1¾oz) raisins
50g (1¾oz) mixed nuts (skinned
   almonds, unsalted cashew nuts)
1 whole green cardamom
5 whole cloves
2 x 2.5cm (1in) pieces cinnamon stick

1 To make the bafat spice mix, toss all the ingredients in a hot heavy frying pan for 2 minutes, stirring constantly. Remove the mixture from the pan, place in a coffee or spice grinder, and blend until finely powdered. This makes enough spice mix to make the recipe twice – store in an airtight tin.

2 Heat 3 tbsp oil in a heavy frying pan and fry the onion for about 10 minutes over a low heat until it is a light golden colour. Add the ginger, garlic, and green chilli and fry gently for another 2 minutes.

3 Add the tomatoes and cook for about 10 minutes until they soften. Sprinkle in 3 tbsp bafat spice mix and add the turmeric, tomato ketchup, and salt and pepper to taste. Fry the mixture over a gentle heat for 5 minutes, stirring so that it does not stick to the pan. Add a dash of water if it gets too dry.

4 Add the chicken pieces to the pan and stir in so that they are well coated with the other ingredients. Pour in 200ml (7fl oz) hot water, cover, and cook over a moderate heat for 20–25 minutes or until the chicken is cooked. If the sauce is too watery, cook uncovered until it thickens. Add the grated coconut and let it absorb the sauce – the dish should be quite dry.

5 Put the remaining oil in a small heavy pan. Bring it to a high heat and fry the red chilli, curry leaves, and garlic for about 30 seconds until the garlic is light brown. Pour over the chicken and cover the pan. Just before serving, stir the dish and garnish with chopped coriander.

6 While the chicken is cooking, soak the rice for 5 minutes in cold water then drain and dry out on a large plate for about 10 minutes.

7 Heat 2 tbsp ghee in a large pan; add the rice and fry, stirring, until the rice is opaque and very lightly coloured. Pour 600ml (1 pint) boiling water into the rice, along with the sugar and a couple of generous pinches of salt. Cover tightly, turn the heat low and allow to cook for around 15 minutes or until the rice is cooked.

8 In a separate pan, melt 2 tbsp ghee over a moderate heat, add the onion and cook gently for 10 minutes until it is caramelized and golden. Remove from the pan.

9 In the same pan, melt the remaining ghee and stir in the raisins and nuts. Fry gently for 5 minutes until lightly coloured, remove from the pan and set aside. Put the cardamom, cloves, and cinnamon in the same pan and sauté for about 2 minutes over a moderate heat.

10 When the rice is cooked, open the lid and stir in the raisins, nuts, and whole spices. Turn off the heat and place the caramelized onions over the rice to serve with the chicken.

SPICED BLACKENED POUSSIN WITH AUBERGINE RAITA AND WHOLEWHEAT PUFFS

Perveen Nekoo wedding cake maker and 2006 quarter-finalist

PREPARATION TIME
25 minutes

COOKING TIME
50 minutes

SERVES 4

2 poussins
2 tbsp toasted sesame seeds

FOR THE MARINADE
4 tbsp tomato purée
1 bunch of spring onions,
  finely chopped
2 garlic cloves
5cm (2in) piece of fresh root
  ginger, grated
4 tsp ground cumin
2 tbsp toasted sesame seeds
2 tsp ground cinnamon
2 tsp sweet paprika
2 green bird's eye chillies
salt and freshly ground black pepper
4 tbsp olive oil

FOR THE RAITA
1 medium purple aubergine,
  cut into small cubes
2 tbsp sunflower oil
1 tsp ground cumin
1 tsp cumin seeds
2 tsp clear honey
300ml (10fl oz) Greek-style yogurt
15cm (6in) piece of cucumber,
  finely diced
200g (7oz) red onion, finely diced
10 vine-ripened cherry
  tomatoes, quartered
20g (¾oz) mint, chopped

FOR THE WHOLEWHEAT PUFFS
60g (2oz) wholemeal flour
250ml (8fl oz) sunflower oil

1 Preheat the oven to 200ºC (400ºF/Gas 6). Place all the marinade ingredients in a bowl and blitz using a hand blender until the mixture resembles a thick paste. Spread all over the poussins, place them in a roasting tin and roast in the oven for 50 minutes (no marinating time is necessary). Remove from the oven and sprinkle with sesame seeds.
2 To make the raita, season the aubergine and toss in a little oil. Roast for 15–20 minutes in the oven at the same temperature until the aubergine is golden on the outside and soft to the touch. Remove from the oven and toss in the ground cumin and cumin seeds. Drizzle with honey, return to the oven for 5 minutes and then set aside.
3 Place the yogurt in a bowl and stir in the cucumber, red onion, tomatoes, and mint. Season with salt and pepper then layer with the aubergine into a small serving dish. Refrigerate until needed.
4 To make the wholewheat puffs, place the flour, 1 tsp oil, 3 tbsp water and salt in a bowl and mix with a palette knife to form a dough. Place the dough on a lightly floured board and knead for 2 minutes. Roll out and cut out 12 circles using a 7.5cm (3in) round cutter.
5 Heat the remaining oil in a pan and deep-fry the wholewheat puffs for 30–45 seconds on each side or until each one puffs up (see MasterTip, p.101). Drain on kitchen paper and serve immediately with the poussins and raita.

ROAST POUSSIN WITH WILD MUSHROOMS AND CARAMELIZED SHALLOT SAUCE

Gillian Wylie property developer turned chef and 2007 quarter-finalist

PREPARATION TIME
40 minutes

COOKING TIME
30 minutes

SERVES 4

4 poussins, 500–600g
  (1lb 2oz–1lb 5oz) each
100g (3½oz) unsalted butter
4 tbsp olive oil
2 carrots, chopped
1 onion, chopped
1 celery stick, chopped
500ml (16fl oz) chicken stock (see
  MasterTip, p.21)
2 tbsp Madeira

6 black peppercorns
1 bay leaf
20 small shallots, skinned (see
  MasterTip, below)
salt and freshly ground white pepper
150g (5½oz) fresh wild mushrooms
½ cauliflower (500g/1lb 2oz),
  cut into small florets
600ml (1 pint) milk
1 tbsp double cream

MASTER TIP
SKINNING SHALLOTS

A speedy way to skin shallots is to place them in a bowl and cover with boiling water. Leave for 2 minutes, drain and peel the skin off.

1 Preheat the oven to 200°C (400°F/Gas 6). Cut the wings from the birds, trim the wing tips off and discard them. Remove both drumsticks then cut the breasts away from the carcass, keeping the skin on, and taking the thighs with them. Cut the thigh meat off the bone, keeping the flesh in one piece. Trim any ragged edges from the breasts. Chop up the carcass. Repeat with the other birds.

2 Melt 25g (scant 1oz) butter and 1 tbsp olive oil in a large pan. Sauté the bones for 10–15 minutes or until they are golden. Add the carrots, onion, and celery and fry until softened and tinged brown. To make the jus, pour in the Madeira and enough stock to just cover, scraping the bottom of the pot as you do so. Add the peppercorns and bay leaf. Let it bubble until the liquid is reduced by half. Strain and keep warm.

3 In a wide frying pan, brown the poussins all over in 25g (scant 1oz) butter and 1 tbsp olive oil. With a slotted spoon, transfer to a roasting tin and roast for 20–30 minutes or until there are no pink juices.

4 Fry the shallots in the butter and oil used for the poussin with a pinch of salt until golden brown. Heat the remaining oil in a frying pan and sauté the mushrooms with a pinch of salt over a high flame until any water has evaporated and the edges are starting to crisp.

5 Cook the cauliflower gently in the remaining butter for 10 minutes, then cover with milk and simmer for 15–20 minutes until very tender. Drain and blitz to a smooth paste in a food processor, then let down to a purée consistency with the cream. Season with salt and pepper.

6 Put 2 tbsp of the purée in the centre of shallow soup bowls. Pile a breast, thigh, drumstick, and wing on the purée, sprinkle with the mushrooms and shallots and pour some of the reserved Madeira jus around the edges. Serve the remaining jus in a sauceboat.

POACHED QUAIL'S EGGS WITH DUCK SAUSAGE

Belinda Fife investment banker and 2009 quarter-finalist

16 cherry tomatoes
2 tsp tomato purée
1 tsp red wine vinegar
200g can cannellini beans
2 garlic cloves, minced
1 tsp lemon zest
2 tsp lemon juice
salt and freshly ground black pepper
pinch of sugar
4 tbsp olive oil
½ tsp white truffle oil (see MasterTip, p.22)
4 tbsp finely chopped flat-leaf parsley, plus extra parsley sprigs to garnish

4 large Portobello mushrooms
2 tbsp ground sumac berries
1 tbsp white wine vinegar
8 quail's eggs

FOR THE SAUSAGES
1 duck breast (skin and fat on)
6 rashers streaky bacon
1 small onion, finely diced
2 garlic cloves, crushed
2 quail's eggs, lightly beaten
4 slices lean prosciutto cotto

PREPARATION TIME
20 minutes

COOKING TIME
20 minutes

SERVES 4

1 First, make the sausages. In a food processor, combine the duck breast (flesh and fat), bacon, onion, garlic, and quail's eggs. Mould portions of the mixture into 4 sausages, wrap with cling film and gently poach in boiling water for 5 minutes. Remove from the water and set aside to cool. When cooled, wrap in the prosciutto cotto.

2 Meanwhile, bring the tomatoes to the boil in enough water to cover. Strain then mash through a sieve, removing the skins and seeds. Combine the tomato flesh with the tomato purée, red wine vinegar, cannellini beans, garlic, lemon zest, lemon juice, a pinch of salt and a pinch of sugar and heat in a saucepan until just simmering. Remove the saucepan from the heat and stir.

3 Combine the olive oil, white truffle oil, and parsley and brush over the mushrooms. Roll the edge of the mushrooms in the sumac.

4 Preheat the grill to medium. Grill the sausages for 5–6 minutes, turning frequently until the prosciutto cotto around them is crisp. At the same time, grill the mushrooms for 2–3 minutes each side.

5 Meanwhile half fill a frying pan with water, bring to the boil and reduce to a very gentle simmer. Add the white wine vinegar. Gently break each quail's egg into the water, then turn off the heat. Allow the eggs to poach in hot water for 1½ minutes.

6 To assemble, place a mushroom in the bottom of each of 4 large shallow dishes, stalk side up. Top with one of the sausages, sliced lengthways, 3 tbsp cannellini bean purée, 1–2 sprigs of parsley and 2 of the quail's eggs. Season with salt and pepper and serve.

ORANGE AND MAPLE-GLAZED DUCK BREAST WITH VANILLA CELERIAC PURÉE

James Hollister chef de partie and 2008 Professionals quarter-finalist

PREPARATION TIME
1 hour 30 minutes

COOKING TIME
25 minutes

SERVES 4

4 duck breasts, preferably
  large Gressinghams
vegetable oil for frying

FOR THE SAUCE
30g (1oz) coriander seeds
30g (1oz) cashew nuts, roughly chopped
40g (1¼oz) white sesame seeds
50g (1¾oz) desiccated coconut
1 tbsp tamarind paste
2 litres (3½ pints) duck or chicken
  stock (see MasterTip, p.21)
juice of 1 navel orange
10g (¼oz) unsalted butter

FOR THE GLAZE
3 tbsp clear honey
5 tbsp maple syrup
juice of 2 navel oranges
2 star anise
1cm (½in) piece fresh root
  ginger, grated

1 long red chilli, deseeded
  and roughly chopped
3 tbsp water

FOR THE PURÉE
1 celeriac root, about 550g (1¼lb),
  roughly chopped
500ml (16fl oz) skimmed milk
1 vanilla pod, deseeded
100ml (3½fl oz) double cream
4 tbsp maple syrup

FOR THE GARNISH
1 medium potato, preferably
  Desirée or other starchy variety
  (see MasterTip, p.197), peeled
1 black truffle potato, peeled
50g (1¾oz) morel mushrooms, sliced
  lengthways into rings
20g (¾oz) unsalted butter
2 tsp mild olive oil
250g (9oz) garlic leaf

1 Remove any excess skin from the duck breasts and cut into strips. Deep-fry at 180°C (350°F) until crispy and golden, then set aside. Score the skin of the breasts in a criss-cross and leave in the fridge.
2 To make the sauce, lightly heat the coriander seeds and cashew nuts in a frying pan for 4 minutes, tossing occasionally. Add the sesame seeds and desiccated coconut and heat for a further 4–5 minutes until golden brown, stirring often. Put this mixture in a blender with the tamarind paste and blitz with a little water until a paste is formed. Put the paste into a pan and add the stock. Reduce until of a gravy-like consistency, then pass through a sieve.
3 For the glaze, place all the ingredients in a pan and reduce until golden and of a light syrup consistency. Sieve and set aside.
4 To make the purée, put the celeriac in a non-stick pan with the milk and vanilla pod. Bring to the boil then simmer for 12 minutes, or until the celeriac is cooked. Take off the heat, remove the vanilla pod and blitz the celeriac in a blender, adding the cream and maple syrup. Pass through a sieve, return to a clean pan and reheat before serving.

5 For the garnish, slice the Desirée potato into 1mm thick slices, then cut into matchstick-sized strips. Pat dry with kitchen paper, then deep-fry at 180°C (350°F) until golden and crispy. Slice the black truffle potato as thinly as possible and pat dry with kitchen paper, then deep-fry at 180°C (350°F) until crispy. Sprinkle both with salt then set aside on kitchen paper. Keep warm.

6 Preheat the oven to 200°C (400°F/Gas 6). Heat an ovenproof frying pan until it is smoking hot. Place the duck breasts in, skin-side down, for about 4–5 minutes, until the skin is brown and crispy. Remove the duck breasts and pour away the excess fat. Put them back in the pan flesh-side down. Pour the glaze over the duck skin and cook in the oven for 6 minutes (longer if you prefer them more well-done). Take them out of the oven and baste with the glaze. Leave to rest for 10 minutes.

7 To finish the garnish, heat half the butter in a frying pan and fry the morels for 2 minutes until softened. Heat a separate frying pan with the remaining butter and the olive oil and fry the garlic leaf until soft.

8 Reheat the sauce and add a little of the orange juice and the butter and stir until shiny. To serve, spoon the celeriac purée onto 4 plates. Slice each duck breast and place beside the purée. Surround with sauce and garnish with garlic leaf, crispy potatoes, and morels.

PAN-FRIED DUCK WITH SALSA VERDE

Chris Gates civil servant turned junior sous chef and 2009 finalist

4 duck breasts
salt and freshly ground black pepper

FOR THE SALSA VERDE
2 tbsp chopped capers
2 tbsp chopped gerkins
3 anchovy fillets, chopped

1 tsp Dijon mustard
1 tsp red wine vinegar
1 small bunch of basil, chopped
1 small bunch of flat-leaf
  parsley, chopped
1 small bunch of mint, chopped
about 90ml (3fl oz) olive oil to taste

PREPARATION TIME
15 minutes

COOKING TIME
17 minutes

SERVES 4

1 To cook the duck breasts, score the skin and season with salt and pepper. Place the duck skin-side down in a cold pan and cook over a medium to hot heat for 10 minutes to allow the fat to render out. Turn the duck over and continue cooking for a further 6–8 minutes.

2 Mix all of the salsa verde ingredients together, loosen with the olive oil and season to taste.

3 Serve with seasonal vegetables such as steamed green beans and carrots, tossed in the salsa verde.

MASTER TIP
SUCCESSFUL SALSA

Mint and basil quickly turn black and watery if they are finely chopped. Aim for just a medium chop and do not make the salsa in advance – it must be fresh.

SLOW-ROASTED DUCK WITH CABBAGE AND GOOSEBERRY JAM

Hardeep Singh Kohli comedian and broadcaster and 2007 Celebrity finalist

PREPARATION TIME
10 minutes

COOKING TIME
2 hours 5 minutes

SERVES 4

4 duck legs
a few sprigs of rosemary
6 peppercorns

FOR THE GOOSEBERRY JAM
200g (7oz) gooseberries,
  topped and tailed
100g (3½oz) demerara sugar

TO SERVE
1 Savoy cabbage, roughly chopped
knob of butter
freshly ground black pepper

1 Preheat the oven to 200°C (400°F/Gas 6). Place the duck legs in a roasting pan and tuck in a few rosemary sprigs and peppercorns. Roast for 30 minutes and then turn the oven to 150°C (300°F/Gas 2) and cover with foil. Cook the duck for another 1½ hours, basting occasionally. Leave to rest, saving the juices from the tin.
2 Place the gooseberries and demerara sugar in a saucepan with 2–3 tbsp water. Slowly bring to the boil, cover with a lid, and simmer for 20 minutes, removing the lid for the last 10 minutes, stirring occasionally. The gooseberries will form a sticky, sweet jam.
3 Steam or cook the cabbage in boiling salted water for 4–5 minutes until tender. Drain and toss in butter and pepper.
4 To serve, pile a spoonful of buttered cabbage in the centre of the plates and place the slow-roasted duck on top, with a spoonful of the rosemary-flavoured pan juices and a generous spoonful of the gooseberry jam on the side.

PAN-ROASTED BREAST OF GRESSINGHAM DUCK WITH PORT SAUCE, ARTICHOKE FOUR WAYS, AND WILTED GREENS

Robert Scott head chef and 2008 Professionals quarter-finalist

PREPARATION TIME
3 hours

COOKING TIME
1 hour 15 minutes

SERVES 4

4 Gressingham duck breasts, about
   200g (7oz) each
salt and freshly ground black pepper
125g (4½oz) unsalted butter
2 garlic cloves
sprig of thyme
pinch of sea salt

FOR THE ARTICHOKE
1kg (2¼lb) Jerusalem artichoke
juice of 1 lemon
500ml (16fl oz) double cream
125g (4½oz) unsalted butter
250ml (8fl oz) semi-skimmed milk
grapeseed oil for deep-frying

FOR THE PORT SAUCE
2 small shallots, sliced
1 garlic clove, sliced
½ red chilli, sliced
1 tbsp vegetable oil
300ml (10fl oz) port wine

1 star anise
1 litre (1¾ pints) veal stock
   or chicken stock (see MasterTip, p.21)
2 sprigs of thyme

FOR THE VEGETABLE GARNISH
200g (7oz) fine green beans,
   chopped into 3
200g (7oz) girolle mushrooms, sliced
handful of chervil, finely chopped
handful of tarragon, finely chopped
handful of chives, finely chopped
handful of flat-leaf parsley,
   finely chopped
125g (4½oz) unsalted butter

FOR THE WILTED GREENS
125g (4½oz) unsalted butter
200g (7oz) curly kale, stalks removed,
   cut into small pieces
salt and freshly ground black pepper

1 Preheat the oven to 180°C (350°F/Gas 4). Remove any feathers and sinew from the duck breasts and trim off fat. Score the top of the skin across the breast, season both sides well and set aside until ready to cook.
2 Peel the artichokes and place in cold water with the lemon juice. Put the skins in a pan, cover with water, bring to the boil. Skim and then pass through a fine chinois or sieve and retain the stock.
3 Reserve 2 artichokes and use the rest to make 20 batons measuring 2.5 x 1 x 1cm (1 x ½ x ½in), reserving all the trimmings. Blanch the batons for 4 minutes and set aside.
4 Take the trimmings and any remaining artichokes other than the reserved ones and chop up into rough pieces. Place in a pan and cover with the stock made earlier. Bring to the boil and reduce before adding the cream and butter. Bring back to the boil then blend with a hand blender and pass through a chinois or sieve. Divide into 2 and

use one half for purée; to the other half add the milk, bring to the boil and foam using a hand blender.

5 For the sauce, place the shallots, garlic, and chilli in a heavy saucepan with the oil and sweat for 4–5 minutes without colouring. Add the port and star anise, bring to the boil and simmer for 20–30 minutes until the port is reduced by two-thirds. Then add the veal stock or chicken stock and thyme and simmer for 30–45 minutes until the sauce is of a thicker consistency. Remove the thyme sprigs before serving.

6 For the vegetable garnish, blanch the green beans for 2 minutes. Put the artichoke batons in a hot dry frying pan until they begin to colour and then add the butter, girolles, and green beans. Season well, toss lightly and add the herbs. When the vegetables are cooked, place on kitchen paper to drain.

7 Slice the 2 reserved artichokes thinly, using a mandolin. Deep-fry in oil until light brown. Remove from the oil, drain on kitchen paper and sprinkle with salt.

8 For the wilted greens, melt the butter in a heavy pan on a medium heat. Add the greens and season well. Saute for 4–5 minutes, adding water if required. Drain through a colander before serving.

9 Place the duck breasts in a medium-hot ovenproof frying pan, skin-side down. When the skin has browned, turn the breast over and cook for 3–5 minutes on the flesh side, then turn back over onto the skin side. Add the butter, garlic, and thyme to the pan, cover with foil and cook in the oven for 12–14 minutes, then remove from the oven and lift off the foil. Turn the breasts back onto the flesh side to avoid the skin softening. Cover with foil and leave to rest for 5–8 minutes then, for serving, slice and sprinkle a small amount of sea salt over.

10 To serve, arrange the greens, artichoke purée, and foam on 4 serving plates. Place the duck on top and drizzle the sauce over. Sprinkle with vegetable garnish and top with artichoke crisps.

DUCK BREAST WITH BUTTERED BABY TURNIPS AND DUCK JUS

Steven Wallis creative director and 2007 champion

PREPARATION TIME
1 hour

COOKING TIME
1 hour 30 minutes

SERVES 4

70cl bottle Pinot Noir
300ml (10 fl oz) Madeira wine
1 duck carcass, as much fat removed
   as possible
2 litres (3½ pints) chicken stock
   (see MasterTip, p.21)
1 carrot, finely diced
1 leek, finely diced
1 celery stick, finely diced
2 banana shallots, diced
bouquet garni of bay leaf, sprig thyme,
   few parsley stalks and star anise
25g (scant 1oz) unsalted butter
pinch of finely chopped rosemary

FOR THE VEGETABLES
1 leek, white parts only, sliced into
   julienne strips
100ml (3½fl oz) whole milk

about 45g (1½oz) rice flour
8–10 baby turnips depending on size
handful of Swiss chard leaves, torn
vegetable oil for deep-frying
500ml (16fl oz) chicken stock
knob of unsalted butter, melted

FOR THE POTATOES
225g (8oz) small waxy potatoes
50g (2oz) oak chips for smoking
drizzle of extra virgin olive oil
2 tsp snipped fresh chives
salt and freshly ground black pepper

FOR THE DUCK BREASTS
2 large duck breasts, skin scored
pinch of fleur de sel (see MasterTip,
   p.96) or other sea salt

1 Preheat the oven to 220°C (425°F/Gas 7). Pour both wines into a heavy pan, and simmer to reduce by a third. Meanwhile, roast the duck carcass in the oven for 20 minutes. Place the carcass in a large pan and add the stock, vegetables, and bouquet garni. Bring to the boil and skim off any froth. Add the wine and simmer until the liquor is reduced by half. Strain the stock through a fine sieve. Pour half into a clean pan (freeze the rest for another time) and reduce again by half.
2 Soak the leek in the milk for 10 minutes. Drain and coat in the flour.
3 Boil the potatoes in salted water for 15–20 minutes until tender. Drain, return to the pan, cover with cling film and leave until the skins will slide off easily. Smoke (see MasterTip, p.196) and set aside.
4 Place the duck breasts in a cold frying pan, skin-side down. Cook over a medium heat for about 10 minutes, or until the skin is crispy. Turn over and cook for 5 minutes. Leave to rest for 10 minutes.
5 Poach the baby turnips in the chicken stock for 20 minutes or until tender. Lift out and keep warm. Blanch the chard leaves in the stock for 5 minutes or until tender. Heat the oil in a deep-fat fryer and fry the leek julienne until crisp. Drain on kitchen paper. Crush the potatoes in a small pan with a drizzle of olive oil. Season and stir in the chives.

6 Reheat the duck jus and when bubbling whisk in the unsalted butter. Add the rosemary, taste and adjust seasoning.
7 Spoon the potatoes on to warm plates and top with Swiss chard. Slice the duck breasts, sprinkle with a little fleur de sel and arrange on top of the chard. Arrange the baby turnips around the plate and glaze with a little melted butter and chicken stock. Spoon the duck jus over and around and finish with a neat pile of leek crisps on top.

DUCK BREASTS WITH SWEET POTATO MASH
Christopher Bisson actor and 2007 Celebrity quarter-finalist

PREPARATION TIME
30 minutes

COOKING TIME
1 hour

SERVES 4

4 duck breasts, 225g (8oz) each
1 bunch of watercress, to serve

FOR THE CABBAGE
1 small red cabbage, cored and
 finely chopped
1 large or 2 small red onions,
 finely chopped
100g (3½oz) unsalted butter,
 cut into cubes
150ml (5fl oz) red wine vinegar
50g (1¾oz) clear honey
100g (3½oz) demerara sugar

1 bay leaf
few sprigs of thyme
salt and freshly ground black pepper

FOR THE SWEET POTATO MASH
500g (1lb 2oz) sweet potatoes, peeled
 and cut into large chunks
2 garlic cloves, whole
olive oil
500g (1lb 2oz) Maris Piper potatoes,
 peeled and cut into pieces
25g (scant 1oz) butter
splash of double cream

1 Preheat the oven to 200°C (400°F/Gas 6). Place all the braised red cabbage ingredients in a roasting tin and mix well. Cover with foil and put in the oven for about 1 hour, stirring from time to time.
2 Put the sweet potato on a baking tray with the garlic. Toss with oil and salt and pepper and put in the oven for about 40 minutes, until soft. Boil the Maris Piper potatoes in salted water until soft.
3 Meanwhile place the duck breasts skin-side down in a cold ovenproof frying pan. Fry over a medium heat for 5–6 minutes, until golden brown. Turn over and cook for another 2 minutes. Transfer to the oven for 8 minutes, then allow to stand for about 3 minutes.
4 Mash the sweet potatoes with the Maris Piper potatoes, leaving the garlic in. Beat in the butter and cream and check the seasoning. Leave in the pan with the lid on and reheat over a low heat before serving.
5 To serve, cut each duck breast into 3 equal slices diagonally. Serve on a bed of watercress. Remove the bay leaf and thyme from the cabbage and serve in individual ramekins.

DUCK WITH CHERRY SAUCE AND PARSNIP PURÉE

Emily Ludolf 18-year-old student and 2008 finalist

2 large parsnips, cored and chopped
4 duck breasts
salt and freshly ground black pepper
300ml (10fl oz) chicken stock (see MasterTip, p.21)
300ml (10fl oz) port

sprigs of thyme
200g (7oz) cherries, pitted and halved
100ml (3½fl oz) whipping cream, lightly whipped
85g (3oz) butter

PREPARATION TIME
25 minutes

COOKING TIME
35 minutes

SERVES 4

1 To make the parsnip purée, boil the parsnips in lightly salted water for 8–10 minutes or until tender, then drain. Place in a food processor and purée to a smooth consistency, then transfer to a bowl.
2 Using a sharp knife, lightly score the skin of the duck breasts, then rub over with salt and pepper. Heat a heavy pan over low heat. Add the duck breasts, skin-side down, and cook for about 10 minutes until the fat is nearly all extracted and the skin is golden brown and crisp.
3 Meanwhile, put the chicken stock, port, and thyme into a heavy saucepan and bring to the boil. Let it bubble away until the mixture is reduced to a third, which will take 10–15 minutes. Remove the thyme sprigs then add the halved cherries and simmer for another 5–10 minutes until the sauce has thickened.
4 Meanwhile, turn over the duck breasts, increase the heat and cook the flesh side for 3–4 minutes; if you want the meat cooked to medium, it should feel slightly springy when pressed. Remove to a plate and set aside to rest for 5 minutes.
5 Gently reheat the cherry sauce if need be and add 60g (2oz) butter, one piece at a time, whisking until it has melted before adding the next piece. The sauce will turn rich and glossy. Season to taste with salt and pepper.
6 To serve the parsnip purée, fold in the whipped cream and the remaining butter and adjust the seasoning – the consistency should be very light and creamy. Transfer the duck breasts to warm serving plates, spoon the sauce over and arrange spoonfuls of the parsnip purée beside them.

MASTER TIP
CHERRIES

Use fresh cherries for this dish when they are in season. At other times, substitute the semi-dried cherries available in supermarkets.

SPICED MAGRET OF DUCK WITH ROASTED ROOT VEGETABLES

Michael Pajak communications manager and 2006 quarter-finalist

PREPARATION TIME
30 minutes

COOKING TIME
40–45 minutes

SERVES 4

4 duck breasts, at room temperature
1 tbsp ground ginger
1 tbsp coriander seeds
1 star anise
1 tbsp Sichuan peppercorns
1 tsp ground cinnamon
2 tbsp sherry, apple, or cider vinegar
250ml (8fl oz) apple juice
30g (1oz) unsalted butter, chilled

FOR THE VEGETABLES
2 carrots
2 parsnips
½ swede
4 baby beetroots
4 baby turnips
2 onions, red or white
olive oil, to drizzle
salt and freshly ground black pepper
5–6 bay leaves
few sprigs of rosemary

1 Preheat the oven to 180°C (350°F/Gas 4). Chop the vegetables to a size where they will all cook evenly: leave thin carrots or parsnips whole, cut thick ones lengthways, halve and cut into 2.5cm (1in) dice; cut the swede into 2.5cm (1in) dice; trim the beetroots and turnips but leave whole. Quarter the onions, leaving the root end attached.

2 Put the vegetables in a large roasting tin. Drizzle with a little olive oil and toss to coat them evenly. Season well with salt and add the bay leaves and rosemary sprigs. Cook in the oven, turning the vegetables once or twice, until they are tender and golden brown – about 40–45 minutes. Check the seasoning and add a few grinds of black pepper.

3 Meanwhile, cook the duck breasts. Grind all the spices as finely as you can. Score the skin of the duck with a sharp knife and rub the spice mix all over the breast. Put the duck breasts skin-side down in a cold frying pan (preferably ovenproof), bring up to a medium-high heat and cook for about 10 minutes.

4 Season the flesh side with salt and pepper and put the frying pan in the preheated oven for about 8 minutes until cooked to medium rare. If you do not have a suitable pan, add the duck to the vegetables.

5 Take the frying pan from the oven, remove the duck and allow it to rest while you make the sauce. Pour off some fat from the pan and place on a medium heat. Add the vinegar to deglaze the pan. Scrape the bottom and let the vinegar reduce by two-thirds. Add the apple juice and let it reduce by about one-third. Remove the pan from the heat, whisk in the cold butter and check the seasoning.

6 Divide the roasted vegetables between 4 plates. Either slice up the duck breasts into about 5 thick slices and fan out over the vegetables, or serve whole. Pour over a little of the sauce and serve.

GLAZED DUCK BREAST WITH DUCK LEG RAVIOLI AND EXOTIC MUSHROOMS

Andy Oliver project manager turned chef and 2009 finalist

PREPARATION TIME
40 minutes, plus chilling time

COOKING TIME
1 hour 15 minutes

SERVES 4

1 duck leg, skin removed
1 tbsp olive oil
4 duck breasts
2 tbsp Chinese five-spice powder

FOR THE BRAISING LIQUOR
500ml (16fl oz) chicken stock (see
   MasterTip, p.21)
finely grated zest and juice of 1 orange
4 star anise
a few white peppercorns
1 cinnamon stick, broken
a few whole cloves
a few coriander seeds
1 dried long red chilli
10g (¼oz) dried shiitake mushrooms
1 bunch of spring onions, roughly
   chopped, reserving 4 for filling
2 kaffir lime leaves, roughly torn
1cm (½in) fresh root ginger, chopped
1 garlic clove, sliced
1 lemongrass stalk, trimmed and
   roughly chopped
1 tbsp rice wine
1 tbsp dark soy sauce
1 tbsp ketjap manis (see MasterTip, p.192)

FOR THE PASTA
150g (5½oz) "00" pasta flour (see
   MasterTip, p.52)
pinch of salt
1 whole egg
1 egg yolk
1 tbsp olive oil

TO FINISH
1 tsp tamarind paste (see MasterTip,
   p.152)
2½ tbsp plum sauce, preferably
   a Thai brand
1 tsp clear honey
1 tsp cornflour
150g (5½oz) exotic mushrooms such
   as oyster, king oyster, shimeji, honey
   mushrooms, fresh shiitake, and enoki
1 tbsp olive oil
1 tbsp roughly chopped coriander
1 tbsp shredded Thai basil
60g (2oz) beansprouts
1 bunch choi sum, shredded (if
   unavailable, use pak choi, mustard
   greens, Swiss chard, sorrel, or spinach)

USING A PASTA MACHINE

While rolling pasta dough by hand is satisfyingly traditional, a machine makes the process less time-consuming. By rolling the dough partially through the machine then lifting the other end to press the edges of the dough together you can create a loop. This avoids the need to keep removing the dough from the machine and feeding it back in.

1 Flatten the pasta dough into a circle and pass through the machine 3 times.

2 Fold into thirds, flatten, and pass through the machine. Repeat 6 times.

1 Preheat a shallow frying pan to hot. Add the oil and then the duck leg and sauté for 3–5 minutes or until well browned. Add the braising liquor ingredients then bring to the boil, cover, and reduce the heat to a simmer. Cook for 35–40 minutes or until the duck is very tender.

2 Make the pasta dough by placing the flour and salt into a food processor. At a low speed, add the whole egg, egg yolk, olive oil, and a little cold water if needed to make into a smooth but not sticky dough. Turn out onto a lightly floured surface and knead for about 10 minutes. Cover and rest in the fridge for 30 minutes. (Or see MasterTip, p.51.)

3 Wipe the duck breasts with kitchen paper, rub the five-spice powder into the flesh and skin and set aside to marinate.

4 When the duck leg is cooked, remove from the cooking liquor along with the shiitake mushrooms. Take the meat off the bone and shred it finely, chopping with the shiitake mushrooms and reserved spring onions to make the ravioli filling. Stir in a spoonful or so of the cooking liquor to keep the mixture moist and leave to cool slightly.

5 Remove the pasta from the fridge and divide in half. Take a piece and roll to the thinnest setting on your machine (see MasterTip, below). Place on a lightly floured surface. Repeat with the remaining dough.

6 Brush half of each piece of pasta with egg wash then place spoonfuls of the duck leg filling along the egg-washed side. Fold the other half over the top then, using a 6cm (2½in) round cutter, cut out the ravioli. Press the edges of each together until well sealed then place on a large tray lightly dusted with semolina flour. Repeat until all the ravioli have been made – you should end up with about 12.

7 Drain 300ml (10fl oz) of the cooking liquor into a clean pan and boil for about 3–5 minutes or until reduced by half. Then add the tamarind paste, 1 tsp plum sauce and the honey. Stir the cornflour into a small

3 Continue to roll, decreasing the thickness setting each time.

4 Press the edges of the pasta sheet together to create a loop.

amount of cold water until blended then stir into the sauce and heat for 1–2 minutes until thickened. Adjust the seasoning and keep warm.
8 Preheat the oven to 190°C (375°F/Gas 5). Preheat a frying pan then add the duck breasts skin-side down and cook for about 10 minutes or until most of the fat has been rendered out. Then transfer the duck to an ovenproof dish, brush with extra plum sauce and a sprinkling of five-spice powder and cook in the oven for 5–10 minutes. Remove from the oven and leave to rest for 5 minutes under a piece of foil.
9 Bring a large saucepan of water to the boil then reduce the heat and cook the ravioli a few at a time for about 3 minutes or until they rise to the surface.
10 Stir-fry the mushrooms in olive oil for 2–3 minutes. Add the basil, coriander, beansprouts, and choi sum and stir-fry for 1–2 minutes.
11 To serve, slice the duck thinly. Place the choi sum with the mushrooms on top in the middle of each plate, with the ravioli around the edge and the sliced duck in the centre, drizzled with a little sauce.

TEA-SMOKED DUCK BREAST ON EGG NOODLES
Mark Rigby salesman and 2005 quarter-finalist

PREPARATION TIME
10–15 minutes

COOKING TIME
20 minutes

SERVES 4

115g (4oz) loose jasmine tea
115g (4oz) long grain rice
115g (4oz) soft dark brown sugar
4 duck breasts, skinned and
  fat removed

2 heads of pak choi, halved
500g (1¼lb) fresh medium egg noodles
splash of ketjap manis (see
  MasterTip, left)
splash of sesame oil

MASTER TIP
KETJAP MANIS

This sauce, often found as an ingredient in Indonesian food or used as a condiment, resembles dark soy sauce but is much sweeter. It is available from Asian food stores.

1 Place the tea, rice, and sugar in a small bowl and mix together. Cut a 30cm (12in) disc of foil and place it in the bottom of a wok. Empty the mixture onto the foil and heat with the lid on over a medium heat until it starts to smoke – about 5 minutes. Remove the lid and place a wire trivet over the smoking mixture. Place the duck breasts on the trivet, replace the lid and smoke for 12–16 minutes until cooked.
2 Place the pak choi in a steamer and set over boiling water in a second wok. Cover and steam until tender (about 4–5 minutes).
3 Remove the duck from the wok and leave to rest for a few minutes. Stir-fry the noodles in a pan for 2–3 minutes, then drizzle with the ketjap manis and sesame oil and toss to combine. To serve, slice the duck breasts and place on a bed of noodles accompanied by pak choi.

ROASTED DUCK BREAST ON POTATO AND APPLE ROSTI

Nadia Sawalha actress and presenter and 2007 Celebrity champion

4 large duck breasts
salt and freshly ground black pepper
4 Desirée or Romano potatoes (see MasterTip, p.197), scrubbed
1 tbsp lemon juice
25g (scant 1oz) unsalted butter
3 Granny Smith apples

pinch of grated nutmeg
25cl bottle Shiraz red wine
100g (3½oz) blueberries
1 tbsp quince jam
30g (1oz) unsalted butter

PREPARATION TIME
20 minutes

COOKING TIME
50 minutes

SERVES 4

1 Preheat the oven to 150°C (300°F/Gas 2).

2 Dry the skin of the duck breasts and season with salt. Heat a frying pan until hot. Place the duck breasts, skin-side down, into the hot pan. Fry until the skin is crisp and golden brown.

3 Remove the duck breasts from the pan and place in a roasting tin. Cover with foil and cook in the oven for 30–40 minutes, depending how rare or well done you like your duck to be. Remove from the oven and leave to rest.

4 Increase the oven heat to 220°C (425°F/Gas 7). Place the potatoes whole in a saucepan and add some salt and boiling water to just cover. Boil for 8 minutes, then leave to cool while you prepare the apples.

5 Place the lemon juice in a shallow dish, then peel, core, quarter, and grate the apples, using the coarse side of a grater placed directly over the bowl. When all the apple is grated, quickly toss it well in the lemon juice to prevent it turning brown.

6 Peel the potatoes and coarsely grate into a large bowl. Squeeze the juice out of the apple with your hand and add to the potatoes. Give everything a good seasoning of salt, pepper, and some nutmeg and toss to combine as evenly as possible.

7 Using your hands, shape the mixture, squeezing firmly to form little cake shapes with nice raggedy edges. Dust each one lightly with flour and return to the plate. Cover with cling film and refrigerate until needed.

8 Brush a baking tray with melted butter, place the rosti on it and brush the tops with melted butter. Put them on a high shelf in the oven and cook for 10 minutes, then, using a fish slice, turn them over and cook for another 10–15 minutes.

9 Place the wine, blueberries, and quince jam in a saucepan and bring to the boil. Simmer until the fruit is soft and the sauce has reduced. Add the butter to the sauce and whisk. Slice the duck and serve with the sauce and potato and apple rosti.

STARTERS
VEGETABLES & FISH
POULTRY
MEAT
GAME
DESSERTS

LAMB CUTLETS WITH SMOKED MASHED POTATOES AND PAN-FRIED VEGETABLES

Mat Follas engineer turned chef patron and 2009 champion

PREPARATION TIME
1 hour

COOKING TIME
1 hour 10 minutes

SERVES 4

8 lamb cutlets
3 Desirée potatoes (see MasterTip, opposite)
25g (scant 1oz) salted butter
100ml (3½fl oz) double cream
salt and freshly ground black pepper
1 tbsp olive oil

FOR THE MADEIRA SAUCE
3 shallots, sliced
30g (1oz) salted butter
100ml (3½fl oz) Madeira wine
300ml (10fl oz) beef stock

FOR THE PAN-FRIED VEGETABLES
4 carrots, sliced
2 beetroot, sliced
2 tsp toasted sesame seeds
2 tbsp maple syrup
1 Romaine lettuce, divided into separate leaves
25g (scant 1oz) toasted flaked almonds (see MasterTip, p.40)
1 tbsp sesame oil
1 tsp balsamic vinegar

MASTER TIP
SMOKING FOOD

To make your own smoker, cut a 35cm (14in) square of foil, add some oak chips, and fold the foil into an open parcel. Set in the base of a saucepan, cover, and put over a medium-high heat. When the oak chips begin to smoke, remove the pan from the heat and stand the food to be smoked over the pan in a covered steamer.

1 Preheat the oven to 220°C (425°F/Gas 7). Peel and cut the potatoes into 2cm (¾in) chunks. Bring a saucepan of water to the boil and add the potatoes. Reduce the heat and cook the potatoes for about 20 minutes until tender. Drain and leave to steam off excess moisture.

2 Meanwhile, prepare the smoker (see MasterTip, left). Put the potatoes into a steamer, set over the smoke, and seal tightly with foil or a lid. Smoke the potatoes for 5–10 minutes, depending on how strong you like the smoky flavour. Return the potatoes to the saucepan and mash with the butter and cream. Season with salt and pepper to taste and then pass through a sieve.

3 Heat the oil in a frying pan and seal the cutlets on each side. Transfer to an ovenproof dish and put them in the oven for 15 minutes.

4 Make the Madeira sauce in the lamb pan. Fry the shallots in 15g (½oz) of the butter until soft and then add the Madeira. Let it simmer until the alcohol has evaporated and then add the stock. Let the sauce reduce by two-thirds, adding the rest of the butter and seasoning with salt and pepper to taste.

5 Cook the carrots and beetroot together in boiling water for about 15 minutes until tender. Drain and add the maple syrup. Heat for 1–2 minutes until the vegetables are coated, then add the sesame seeds.

6 In a separate frying pan, cook the lettuce leaves with the flaked almonds in sesame oil for about 5 minutes until wilted, adding the balsamic vinegar to finish.

7 To serve, put the lamb cutlets on roundels of smoked mash with vegetables surrounding and drizzle over the Madeira sauce to finish.

LAMB CUTLETS WITH BUTTER-MASHED POTATOES, SAVOY CABBAGE, LEEKS, AND WORCESTERSHIRE SAUCE

Mark Moraghan actor and 2008 Celebrity finalist

12 lamb cutlets, about 60g (2oz) each
4 large King Edward potatoes (see MasterTip, right), peeled and diced
4 tbsp single cream
50g (1¾oz) salted butter, plus extra for serving
4 leeks, about 125g (4½oz) each

salt and freshly ground black pepper
2 tbsp olive oil
400g (14oz) Savoy cabbage, roughly chopped
Worcestershire sauce, to serve

PREPARATION TIME
15 minutes

COOKING TIME
20 minutes

SERVES 4

1 Preheat the oven to 200°C (400°F/Gas 6). Bring a saucepan of water to the boil and add the potatoes. Reduce the heat and cook the potatoes for about 20 minutes until tender. Drain them and then mash, adding the cream, half the butter, and seasoning. Keep warm.
2 Meanwhile, cut the leeks from top to root and thinly slice them on the diagonal. Put a large pan over a medium heat, add the remaining butter and let it melt. Add the leeks and plenty of seasoning and stir to coat in the butter. Reduce the heat to low, cover the pan and cook the leeks gently for about 15 minutes, stirring half way through until they are tender. Serve with extra butter.
3 Season the lamb cutlets with salt and pepper. Heat some of the oil in an ovenproof frying pan and fry the lamb cutlets on each side to seal. Transfer to the oven and cook for 12 minutes or until brown on the outside but slightly pink in the middle.
4 Steam the cabbage, or cook in a saucepan of boiling salted water for 4–5 minutes, until tender. Drain and toss in butter and pepper.
5 To assemble, pile a spoonful of mash in the centre of 4 plates and balance 3 cutlets upright over the potato. Serve the leeks and Savoy cabbage on the side with Worcestershire sauce to taste.

MASTER TIP
CHOOSING POTATOES

There are thousands of varieties of potato, of which about 80 are commercially grown. They vary enormously in flavour and texture. A major difference is between the moist, waxy styles that keep their shape well, such as Charlotte and Maris Peer, and floury varieties with a fluffier texture that mash well, such as Estima, King Edward, Maris Piper, and Desirée. If in doubt, go for one that is in season.

NEW SEASON LAMB WITH ROSEMARY AND LEMON ZEST CRUST, SHERRY SAUCE, SAUTÉED NEW POTATOES, AND CAPONATA

inspired by **Luciana Byrne** housewife and mother and 2007 quarter-finalist

PREPARATION TIME
45 minutes

COOKING TIME
2 hours

SERVES 4

4 boneless lamb loins, about 150g
  (5½oz) each, trimmed
3 tbsp olive oil
60g (2oz) fresh breadcrumbs
1 tbsp finely chopped rosemary
grated zest of ½ lemon
sea salt and freshly ground
  black pepper
1 tbsp Dijon mustard

FOR THE SHERRY SAUCE
1 tbsp olive oil
15g (½oz) salted butter
60g (2oz) onion, finely diced
60g (2oz) celery, finely diced
60g (2oz) carrots, finely diced
2 sprigs of thyme
1 bay leaf
4 tbsp sweet sherry
250ml (8fl oz) beef stock
1 tsp balsamic vinegar
1 tbsp double cream

FOR THE POTATOES
500g (1lb 2oz) new potatoes (see
  MasterTip, p.197)
2 tbsp olive oil
15g (½oz) salted butter
2 tbsp chopped flat-leaf parsley

FOR THE CAPONATA
1 aubergine, roughly chopped
3 tbsp olive oil
½ onion, chopped
1½ celery sticks, thickly sliced
225g can plum tomatoes, chopped
45g (1½oz) green olives, pitted
  and chopped
1½ tbsp drained capers, chopped
1½ tbsp red wine vinegar
½ tbsp caster sugar
1½ tbsp chopped flat-leaf parsley

1 Preheat the oven to 200°C (400°F/Gas 6). To prepare the lamb, heat 2 tbsp of the oil in a frying pan until smoking hot and then sear the lamb for about 5 minutes, browning on all sides. Remove from the pan and allow to cool.

2 Prepare the crust by scattering the breadcrumbs over a baking sheet and drizzling with the remaining oil. Place in the oven to crisp up for a few minutes, shaking once or twice during cooking. Allow to cool, then mix in the rosemary, lemon zest, and some seasoning.

3 To make the sherry sauce, heat the oil and butter in a pan and then gently fry the onion, celery, and carrots with the thyme and bay leaf for about 10 minutes, or until they start to brown and caramelize.

4 Pour in the sherry, reduce well and add the stock. Bring to the boil and simmer for 10–15 minutes, or until reduced by half. Pass through a sieve, pushing down the vegetables and thyme to extract any last drops of sauce, then pour back into a clean saucepan and add the balsamic vinegar and seasoning to taste. Stir through the cream.

5 Bring the potatoes to the boil in a pan of salted water and cook for 12–15 minutes until tender. Drain, and cool slightly so you can handle them to slice into rounds about 5mm (¼in) thick. Heat the oil and butter in a frying pan and fry the potato slices with a generous amount of seasoning for 10–15 minutes over a medium heat, flipping often to ensure they turn golden brown on both sides. Finally scatter over the chopped parsley.

6 For the caponata, fry the aubergine in batches in 2 tbsp of the oil until browned all over, and set aside to cool. In the remaining oil, fry the onion and celery for about 5 minutes to soften, then add the tomatoes and simmer for a further 10 minutes. Season well and stir through the olives and capers.

7 In a small bowl, mix together the vinegar and sugar and stir to dissolve. Add this to the pan along with the fried aubergine and about 1½ tbsp water. Cover with a lid and cook everything for about 10 minutes, until most of the liquid has been absorbed. Stir through the parsley to finish.

8 Now come back to the lamb. Brush each piece of loin with some of the mustard and then press onto the rosemary and lemon zest crust. Place on a baking sheet, crumb-side up, and place in the oven to cook on the high shelf for 6–8 minutes.

9 Remove the lamb from the oven and leave to rest for a few minutes before slicing each piece into 3 and arranging on a bed of sautéed potatoes. Spoon some caponata onto each plate, and finally drizzle around the sherry sauce to serve.

GREGG WALLACE "This is rather special. It is like your palate is on a carousel ride. The flavours that keep coming in and out of your mouth. Incredible. Cor!"

RACK OF LAMB WITH A CABBAGE PARCEL, SHALLOT PURÉE, AND RED WINE JUS

Simon Walker sous chef and 2009 Professionals quarter-finalist

PREPARATION TIME
55 minutes

COOKING TIME
1 hour 50 minutes

SERVES 4

2 racks of lamb (3 ribs each), trimmed
   of fat (see MasterTip, p.203)
1 tbsp vegetable oil

FOR THE RED WINE JUS
1.2 litres (2 pints) red wine
1.2 litres (2 pints) chicken stock
   (see MasterTip, p.21)
1 large bay leaf
few sprigs of thyme

FOR THE SHALLOT PURÉE
150g (5½oz) salted butter
450g (1lb) banana shallots, chopped
300ml (10fl oz) chicken stock

150ml (5fl oz) double cream
sea salt, white pepper and freshly
   ground black pepper

FOR THE CABBAGE PARCELS
7 large leaves of Savoy cabbage,
   blanched (see MasterTip, left)
20g (¾oz) duck fat
100g (3½oz) pancetta, very finely diced
100g (3½oz) carrots, very finely diced
100g (3½oz) parsnips, very finely diced
50g (1¾oz) celery, very finely diced
50g (1¾oz) banana shallots,
   finely chopped
2 garlic cloves, finely chopped

MASTER TIP
BLANCHING VEGETABLES

Blanching vegetables preserves their colour, flavour, and texture. Plunge them into boiling salted water for about 1 minute. Cook in batches to keep the water temperature high, and then put the vegetables into iced water straight away to halt the cooking process.

1 Place a large saucepan on a high heat. Add the red wine, chicken stock, bay leaf, and thyme, bring to the boil and then reduce by three-quarters, which should take 1 hour.

2 For the shallot purée, heat a third of the butter in a saucepan, add the shallots and let sweat for 5 minutes. Add the chicken stock and reduce until all the liquid has evaporated. Finally, add the cream and cook for 5 minutes. Place in a food processor and blend to a purée. Season with salt and white pepper and then strain and set aside.

3 To make the cabbage parcels, cut three of the cabbage leaves into julienne strips. Heat the duck fat in a large frying pan and add the pancetta. Cook for 5 minutes until crispy, then add the vegetables, the garlic, and some thyme. Lightly cook and season, then empty into a dish and chill for about 20 minutes. Take each blanched cabbage leaf, and place onto cling film. Spoon a quarter of the vegetable mixture onto each and wrap into a round parcel shape with the cling film.

4 Preheat the oven to 200°C (400°F/Gas 6). Season the lamb with salt and black pepper. Heat the vegetable oil in a non-stick frying pan, add the lamb and sear on all sides. Transfer to a roasting tin and roast the lamb in the oven for 15 minutes for a medium-pink finish. When cooked, remove from the oven and let the meat rest for 5 minutes.

5 Steam the cabbage parcels in a steamer for 10 minutes.

6 To serve, arrange the shallot purée, cabbage parcels, red wine jus, and carved lamb cutlets on individual plates.

RACK OF LAMB WITH WILD MUSHROOMS AND BUTTERBEAN MASH

Hannah Miles lawyer turned cookbook author and 2007 finalist

PREPARATION TIME
25 minutes

COOKING TIME
55 minutes

SERVES 2

2 racks of lamb (4–6 ribs each), trimmed (see MasterTip, opposite)
2 tbsp olive oil
4 sprigs of thyme
3 sprigs of rosemary
3 garlic cloves, crushed
1 large banana shallot, peeled with the root still intact and cut into quarters
400g (14oz) exotic mushroom mix, roughly chopped
20g (¾oz) dried porcini mushrooms, soaked for 20 minutes in port
250ml (8fl oz) full-bodied red wine
150ml (5fl oz) chicken stock (see MasterTip, p.21)

FOR THE RED WINE SAUCE
2 shallots, finely chopped
300ml (10fl oz) full-bodied red wine
400ml (14fl oz) beef stock
20g (¾oz) butter
salt and freshly ground black pepper

FOR THE BUTTERBEAN MASH
410g can of cooked butterbeans
1 sprig of thyme
4 tbsp chicken stock
1 tbsp olive oil

Savoy cabbage (optional, see MasterTip, left)

MASTER TIP

SAVOY CABBAGE

Savoy cabbage braised in chicken stock is the perfect accompaniment to this recipe. To make, heat 2 sprigs of rosemary and 2 chopped garlic cloves in 1 tbsp olive oil in a large saucepan. Add half a finely shredded Savoy cabbage and pan-fry for 5 minutes. Add 200ml (7fl oz) chicken stock and a small knob of butter and seasoning, then cover the pan and simmer for 5–8 minutes, until the cabbage is tender.

1 Preheat the oven to 180°C (350°F/Gas 4). In a large frying pan, heat half the olive oil with the herbs, garlic, and shallot for 2–3 minutes until the shallots have softened. Add the fresh mushrooms and cook over a low heat. Strain the dried mushrooms, finely chop, and add to the pan. Cook for about 5 minutes until they smell woody and earthy.
2 Add a third of the red wine and cook over a low heat for a few minutes. Season the mushrooms. Remove the rosemary and thyme sprigs, place the mushrooms in an ovenproof dish and set aside.
3 Season the lamb. Then heat the remaining oil in a frying pan and brown the lamb on all sides. Add the remaining red wine and cook off the alcohol. Place the lamb on top of the mushrooms and pour over the red wine juices. Add the stock and cook for 20–25 minutes for a medium finish. Remove from the oven and let it rest for 10 minutes.
4 To make the red wine sauce, simmer the shallots in the red wine for about 10 minutes until the wine has almost evaporated. Add the meat stock and simmer until the liquid has reduced to one-third. Strain, whisk in the butter and season with salt and pepper.
5 Simmer the butterbeans and thyme in the chicken stock for 5 minutes. Strain and remove the thyme and then mash the butterbeans with the olive oil and season with salt and pepper.
6 To assemble, carve the lamb ribs and present on a bed of the exotic mushrooms drizzled with the red wine sauce. Serve the Savoy cabbage, if using, and butterbean mash alongside.

RACK OF LAMB WITH PARSNIP MASH AND A RED WINE SAUCE

Gary Heath ICT technician and 2007 quarter-finalist

2 racks of lamb (6 ribs each), trimmed
  (see MasterTip, right)
2 tbsp olive oil
130g (4¾oz) unsalted butter
2 carrots, peeled and sliced
1 bulb fennel, peeled and chopped
3 parsnips, peeled and chopped

3 tbsp double cream, warmed
salt and freshly ground black pepper
1 shallot, chopped
1 sprig of thyme
250ml (8fl oz) red wine
150ml (5fl oz) beef or lamb stock

PREPARATION TIME
10 minutes

COOKING TIME
30 minutes, plus resting time

SERVES 4

1 Preheat the oven to 190°C (375°F/Gas 5). Heat some olive oil in a frying pan and seal the lamb on all sides. Transfer to a roasting tin and cook in the oven for 20–25 minutes, depending on how your lamb is preferred.

2 Add 50g (1¾oz) of the butter to the frying pan and sauté the carrots and fennel, covered, on a low heat, for about 30 minutes or until they are tender.

3 Meanwhile, bring a saucepan of water to the boil, add the parsnips, reduce the heat and cook for about 15 minutes until tender. Drain, add 20g (¾oz) of the butter and 2 tbsp of the warmed cream and mash. Season with salt and pepper to taste. Keep warm.

4 Purée the carrot and fennel mixture in a food processor, also adding 20g (¾oz) of the butter and the remaining cream.

5 Heat 20g (¾oz) of the butter in the same frying pan, add the shallot and thyme leaves and sauté for 3–4 minutes. Then add the red wine and deglaze the pan. Increase the heat and reduce the wine by half, then add the stock, reduce further and finally add another 20g (¾oz) of butter to thicken. Remove the sprig of thyme.

6 Remove the lamb from the oven and leave to rest for 5 minutes.

7 To assemble, use a ring mould to arrange some mashed parsnip in the centre of each plate and add some carrot and fennel purée on top. Carve the lamb and arrange 3 ribs per person on the plates, spooning the red wine sauce over the lamb.

MASTER TIP
LAMB CUTS

Rack of lamb is also known as best end of neck and is roasted on the bone or boned and rolled. Before roasting, the outer skin and chine bone (the spine) are removed and fat and meat trimmed to expose the ends of the bones. With an English trim, the bones are cleaned 2.5cm (1in) from the ends. The French trim exposes the bones to their ends by about 5–6cm (2–2½in) to just below the line of the meat.

ROAST LAMB WITH SPINACH MOUSSE, WILD GARLIC PURÉE, MUSHROOM DUXELLES, FONDANT POTATO, AND BALSAMIC JUS

Christos Georgakis head chef and 2008 Professionals quarter-finalist

PREPARATION TIME
30 minutes

COOKING TIME
55 minutes

SERVES 4

FOR THE SPINACH MOUSSE
400g (14oz) baby spinach
250g (9oz) cooked and chilled
  skinless chicken breasts, chopped
200ml (7fl oz) double cream
50g (1¾oz) crème fraîche
salt and freshly ground black pepper

FOR THE CANNON OF LAMB
2 fillets of lamb, about 280g
  (10oz) each
4 tbsp olive oil
small bunch of tarragon, chopped
small bunch of chervil, chopped
small bunch of chives, chopped
50g (1¾oz) Dijon mustard
60g (2oz) salted butter
500g (1lb 2oz) caul (see
  MasterTip, below)
200g (7oz) spinach leaves

FOR THE GARLIC CONFIT
12 garlic cloves
3 sprigs of thyme
3 tbsp olive oil
25g (scant 1oz) sea salt

FOR THE FONDANT POTATO
2 large Maris Piper potatoes, peeled
3 tbsp corn oil
150g (5½oz) salted butter
2 garlic cloves

FOR THE BALSAMIC-SCENTED JUS
1 garlic clove, chopped
1 tbsp redcurrant jelly
juice of 1 lemon
4 tsp balsamic vinegar
4 sprigs of thyme
12 vine-ripened tomatoes
300ml (10fl oz) lamb stock

FOR THE WILD GARLIC PURÉE
200g (7oz) wild garlic leaves
  (see MasterTip, overleaf)
3 tbsp double cream
50g (1¾oz) unsalted butter
3 tbsp water

FOR THE DUXELLES
50g (1¾oz) salted butter
3 large shallots, chopped
300g (10oz) wild mushrooms,
  trimmed and finely chopped

MASTER TIP
CAUL

Caul is the lacy, fatty membrane that encases the stomach of a pig. It can be ordered from the butcher – 2 pieces are generally enough to wrap any joint of meat. Caul seals the meat and stuffing and, because it renders its fat during roasting, it makes the meat very moist.

1 Preheat the oven to 180°C (350°F/Gas 4). To make the spinach mousse, blanch the spinach in salted hot water for 1 minute, then refresh in cold water. Drain the leaves and leave it to dry. Put the chicken in a food processor, season with salt and pepper and blend to a purée. Add the spinach and start the food processor again. Mix together the cream and crème fraîche and pour slowly into the spinach and chicken until it combines to make a mousse. Place it in a metal bowl and leave in the fridge until you need it.

2 For the cannon of lamb, trim and remove excess fat from the fillets. Season with salt and pepper and, in a large frying pan, sauté in the olive oil over a high heat for 1 minute on each side. Meanwhile, mix

MASTER TIP
WILD GARLIC

Wild garlic thrives in woodland and other semi-shady areas from late winter to the end of spring. It has a garlic-like smell and long leaves, similar to Lily of the Valley. Unlike cultivated garlic, it is the leaves, and sometimes the flowers (see p.110), of wild garlic that are mainly eaten, either raw or cooked. Although the bulbs are edible, they grow in small quantities.

the chopped herb leaves in a bowl with salt and pepper. Remove the fillets from the pan and wipe off the fat with kitchen paper. Brush the fillets with the Dijon mustard and cover with the herb mixture.

3 Lay out a 30cm (12in) square of caul and cover with half the spinach leaves. Spoon a generous amount of spinach mousse over one side of the fillet and place this side down on top of the spinach leaves. Cover the other side of the fillet with spinach mousse and then carefully wrap the pork caul around the fillet, tucking the ends round and under. Transfer to a roasting tin, and repeat for the second lamb fillet. Cook for 12–14 minutes, depending on how pink you prefer your lamb. Remove from the oven and allow the lamb fillets to rest for 10 minutes before serving.

4 Meanwhile, make the garlic confit. Put all the ingredients in a square of foil and fold to make a parcel, ensuring all edges are sealed. Bake in the oven for 15–20 minutes until softened. Drain the oil and remove the thyme sprigs and keep warm until serving.

5 For the fondant potato, cut each potato into two slabs 4cm (1½in) thick. In a saucepan, heat the oil and fry the potatoes for 4–5 minutes on each side until golden brown. Add the butter, garlic cloves, seasoning, and 250ml (8fl oz) of water. Bring to a simmer, cover the pan and let the potatoes cook for 15–20 minutes or until soft in the centre. Drain and keep warm.

6 To make the balsamic-scented jus, combine all the ingredients in a small saucepan and simmer for 30 minutes. Leave it to infuse in a warm place and strain before serving.

7 For the wild garlic purée, blanch the garlic leaves in boiling water for 30 seconds, remove from the water and refresh in cold water. Bring the cream, water, and butter to the boil in a saucepan. Put the garlic leaves into a blender, add the liquid and blend to a smooth purée.

8 Then make the Duxelles mushrooms. Melt the butter in a frying pan, add the shallots and mushrooms and season with salt and pepper. Cook over a medium to low heat for 8–10 minutes until the vegetables are brown and the water from the mushrooms evaporated.

9 To assemble, slice the lamb and arrange 3–4 thick slices on a bed of Duxelles mushrooms. Serve the potato fondant alongside together with a pool of wild garlic purée and some of the garlic confit. Pour over the jus and serve immediately.

LOIN OF LAMB WITH POMMES ANNA AND SHALLOT PURÉE

Adrian Martin chef de partie and 2008 Professionals quarter-finalist

4 loins of lamb, about 175g (6oz) each
25g (scant 1oz) salted butter
15 slices Parma ham

FOR THE POMMES ANNA
225g (8oz) salted butter, melted
10 Maris Piper potatoes (see
   MasterTip, p.197), about 900g (2lb),
   peeled and thinly sliced

FOR THE DUXELLES
25g (scant 1oz) salted butter
3 banana shallots, diced
300g (10oz) button mushrooms,
   finely chopped
bunch of thyme
1 whole nutmeg
salt and freshly ground black pepper

FOR THE SHALLOT PURÉE
25g (scant 1oz) unsalted butter
8 large banana shallots, finely diced
4 tbsp double cream

FOR THE SPICED RED WINE SYRUP
1 onion, sliced
1 garlic clove, chopped
knob of butter
25g (scant 1oz) plain flour
300ml (10fl oz) stock
300ml (10fl oz) Cabernet Sauvignon
2 tbsp clear honey
grated zest of 1 orange
½ star anise
¼ cinnamon stick
3 juniper berries
¼ vanilla pod

PREPARATION TIME
1 hour 10 minutes

COOKING TIME
2 hours 20 minutes

SERVES 4

1 Preheat the oven to 200°C (400°F/Gas 6). Layer the potatoes in a deep, non-stick, ovenproof pan, pouring over the melted butter and adding plenty of salt and pepper to each layer. Bake in the oven for 1 hour until the potatoes are tender.

2 To make the Duxelles, heat the butter in a pan and sweat the shallots and mushrooms for a few minutes. Add the thyme leaves and a grating of nutmeg. Cook for 10 minutes or until the mix is nearly dry. Blend until smooth and season.

3 Trim and season the lamb, and seal in a hot pan in foaming butter. Cover each with the Duxelles and wrap in the Parma ham. Bake in the oven for 8–10 minutes until the ham is crispy. Remove from the oven and leave to rest for a few minutes.

4 For the shallot purée, sweat the shallots in the butter for 10 minutes and then add the cream. Cook slowly for 6–7 minutes, then blend until smooth and season to taste. Keep warm.

5 To make the syrup, fry the onion and garlic in the butter in a frying pan. Add the flour and slowly add the stock followed by the rest of the ingredients. Bring to the boil and reduce to a syrup. Season to taste.

6 To serve, place 1 tbsp of the shallot purée onto each plate and put a loin of lamb on top, sliced in 3 and fanned out, with a portion of the pommes Anna. Serve with the sauce in a sauceboat.

CANNON OF LAMB WITH ROASTED AUBERGINE, WILD GARLIC, AND THYME JUS

Steve Groves chef de partie and 2009 Professionals champion

PREPARATION TIME
30 minutes, plus chilling time

COOKING TIME
2 hours

SERVES 4

2 cannons of lamb, about 250g (9oz) each
2 tbsp olive oil
4 baby aubergines
few sprigs of thyme
2 garlic cloves, halved
200g (7oz) baby spinach
200g (7oz) wild garlic leaves
   or baby spinach leaves
30g (1oz) butter

FOR THE THYME JUS
1 tbsp olive oil
200g (7oz) lamb trimmings

1 shallot, chopped
2 garlic cloves, halved
75ml (2½fl oz) white wine
500ml (16fl oz) lamb stock
sprig of thyme, leaves removed
salt and freshly ground black pepper

FOR THE AUBERGINE PURÉE
2 large aubergines
15g (½oz) salted butter
1 shallot, chopped
2 tbsp double cream
salt and freshly ground black pepper

1 For the thyme jus, heat the oil in a large pan and fry the lamb trimmings for 8–10 minutes until a deep brown. Remove from the pan and set aside. Add the shallot and garlic and cook for 1–2 minutes until golden, scraping the pan bottom to release the stuck-on lamb flavour.
2 Deglaze the pan with the wine, then reduce the sauce until almost entirely evaporated. Add the stock and return the lamb trimmings to the pan. Simmer gently for around 1 hour, skimming regularly. Strain and, for the best results, chill overnight so it sets and any fat can be removed. Otherwise, return to a clean saucepan and reduce by about half until it starts to become glossy. Add some thyme leaves, cover with cling film and leave to infuse for 5 minutes.
3 To cook the lamb, preheat the oven to 200°C (400°F/Gas 6). Heat 1 tbsp of the oil in a roasting tin on the hob. Add the lamb cannons and seal on all sides then transfer to the oven and cook for 10–15 minutes until well browned but still slightly pink in the very centre. Remove from the oven and let the lamb rest in a warm place for 5–10 minutes.
4 Halve the baby aubergines, place in a roasting tin, drizzle with the remaining olive oil and season with salt and pepper. Roast for 15 minutes with the thyme and garlic. Wilt the spinach and wild garlic (or baby spinach) leaves quickly in a frying pan in the butter for 2–3 minutes. Drain off any excess moisture and season. Keep warm.
5 To make the purée, place the whole aubergines in a dry hot pan and cook on medium to high heat for about 15 minutes, turning frequently, until burnt all over and completely soft inside. Leave the

aubergines to stand for a few minutes before handling. Then carefully slit them open and, using a spoon, scoop out the softened flesh, wiping off any excess moisture.

6 Melt the butter and sweat the shallot for 1–2 minutes. Then add the aubergine flesh and continue cooking for a further 3–4 minutes or until the mixture is fairly dry. Add the cream to loosen, season to taste, then purée in a blender. Pass through a sieve and keep warm.

7 To serve, divide the wilted spinach and garlic and the baby aubergines between 4 plates and top each with some of the aubergine purée. Cut the cannons into slices and divide between the plates topping the baby aubergine and finish with a drizzle of the thyme jus.

LAMB WITH FENNEL AND A MADEIRA JUS
Dean Edwards digger driver turned chef and 2006 finalist

600g (1lb 5oz) rump of lamb
5 tbsp olive oil
4 garlic cloves, chopped
2 sprigs of thyme
2 bulbs fennel, sliced
250ml (8fl oz) chicken stock (see MasterTip, p.21)
30g (1oz) salted butter
1 tbsp olive oil
1 onion, diced

1 carrot, diced
2 celery sticks, diced
1 garlic clove, chopped
2 sprigs of thyme
1 bay leaf
1 tsp sherry vinegar
500ml (16fl oz) Madeira wine
500ml (16fl oz) chicken stock (see MasterTip, p.21)
salt and freshly ground black pepper

PREPARATION TIME
15 minutes, plus marinating time

COOKING TIME
1 hour 30 minutes

SERVES 4

1 Mix 3 tbsp of the olive oil with the garlic and thyme and pour over the lamb in a bowl. Leave to marinate for at least 30 minutes.

2 Preheat the oven to 200°C (400°F/Gas 6). For the Madeira jus, heat the olive oil in a wide saucepan and add the onion, carrot, and celery and sauté for a few minutes to colour and soften. Add the garlic, thyme, and bay leaf. Then add the vinegar and Madeira wine and let the sauce reduce by two-thirds. Add the stock and reduce by two-thirds once more. Strain and keep warm.

3 To cook the lamb, heat 1 tbsp of olive oil in a roasting tin and, when hot, seal the lamb on all sides. Transfer to the oven and cook for about 20 minutes for a medium finish. Allow to rest for 5–10 minutes.

4 Colour the fennel in the remaining olive oil in a hot pan. Add the stock and butter and cover. Braise for 15 minutes or until softened.

5 To serve, slice the lamb and serve with the fennel and jus.

ROAST MOROCCAN LAMB WITH COUSCOUS AND HARISSA SAUCE

Helen Gilmour 2007 quarter-finalist

PREPARATION TIME
1 hour, plus marinating time

COOKING TIME
30 minutes

SERVES 4

2 cannons of lamb, about 350g (12oz) each

FOR THE MARINADE
200ml (7fl oz) olive oil
juice of ½ lemon
1 onion, finely chopped
3 tbsp chopped flat-leaf parsley
3 tbsp chopped mint
5 tbsp chopped coriander
1½ tsp ground cumin
1 tsp paprika
1 tsp sea salt and freshly ground black pepper

FOR THE COUSCOUS
100g (3½oz) medium grain couscous
6 dried apricots, chopped
50g (1¾oz) golden sultanas
25g (scant 1oz) salted butter
200ml (7fl oz) chicken stock
25g (scant 1oz) flaked almonds
20g (¾oz) mint, finely chopped
20g (¾oz) coriander, finely chopped
200g can chickpeas
25g (scant 1oz) nibbed pistachios
½ tsp ground cinnamon
3 tbsp olive oil (optional)

FOR THE HARISSA SAUCE
3 tbsp rose harissa paste
2 tbsp plain yogurt

MASTER TIP

CACIK

Cacik is the Turkish version of the better-known Greek tzatziki and is the perfect accompaniment for the lamb and harissa sauce in this recipe. To make, peel and halve 1–2 small cucumbers, scrape out the seeds, finely slice into half moons and put in a colander. Sprinkle with salt and leave for about 20 minutes for the juices to run out. Then rinse, drain, and dry on kitchen paper. Mix together 125g (4½oz) plain yogurt, ½ finely chopped garlic clove, and a small bunch of chopped mint leaves together with ½ tsp dried mint and some sea salt. Add the cucumber, stir together and chill.

1 Combine all the marinade ingredients, pour over the lamb and set aside to marinate for a minimum of 2 hours, or overnight if you can.

2 Prepare the couscous. Place the couscous, apricots, and sultanas in a bowl. Add the butter and pour over the chicken stock so there is just enough to cover the grains. Cover with cling film and set aside for 10 minutes to allow the stock to be absorbed.

3 Toast the almonds in a dry pan until golden and set aside in a bowl. Add the mint and coriander.

4 Fluff the couscous with a fork and add half the chickpeas and stir through. Add the almonds and herbs, and then the pistachios and mix thoroughly. Finally, add the cinnamon and season with salt and pepper, and add some olive oil, if required.

5 For the harissa sauce, mix the harissa paste with the yogurt and warm it in a small saucepan over a low heat, but do not overheat as it may split.

6 Heat a frying pan until hot and cook the lamb for 8–10 minutes. Remove from the pan, cover with foil and leave to rest for 5 minutes.

7 To assemble, divide the couscous between 4 plates and place slices of lamb and a spoonful of the harissa sauce alongside. A spoonful of cacik is the perfect accompaniment (see MasterTip, left).

ROASTED CROWN OF LAMB WITH MINTED PEA PURÉE

Christopher Souto IT consultant turned chef and 2005 semi-finalist

PREPARATION TIME
30 minutes

COOKING TIME
30 minutes

SERVES 4

2 racks of lamb (6 ribs each), French-trimmed (see MasterTip, p.203)
8 Charlotte potatoes
4 tbsp olive oil
2 garlic cloves
salt and freshly ground black pepper
200g (7oz) frozen peas

4 sprigs of mint
1 tsp red wine vinegar
200ml (7fl oz) chicken stock (see MasterTip, p.21)
2 tbsp melted butter
3 sprigs of rosemary
300ml (10fl oz) red wine

MASTER TIP
RESTING MEAT

Roasted meat must be rested before serving. This lets heat reach the centre of the joint to cook it more evenly, and gives the hot juices time to flow through the joint. The muscle fibres will also relax, making the meat easier to carve and more tender to eat.

1 Preheat the oven to 200°C (400°F/Gas 6). Boil the potatoes with their skins on in lightly salted water for 15–20 minutes until almost cooked through. Drain and peel. Using a 2cm (¾in) pastry cutter, cut the potatoes into cylinders and then slice into 1cm (½in) thick discs.
2 Heat half the olive oil in a frying pan over a high heat. Cut the garlic cloves in half and rub into the surface of the lamb (keep the garlic for the potatoes). Season the lamb with salt and pepper then place in the frying pan and sear for about 2 minutes until browned on all sides. Place the lamb in the oven in a roasting tin for 18–20 minutes. Remove from the oven and leave to rest.
3 Meanwhile, cook the peas in salted boiling water for about 3 minutes. Drain and tip into a blender with the mint leaves and vinegar. Purée the peas, adding a little of the chicken stock to achieve the required consistency. Season the purée with salt and pepper to taste. Keep warm until ready to serve.
4 In a large frying pan, heat the butter and remaining olive oil over a medium heat together with 2 sprigs of the rosemary and the reserved garlic. Cook the potato disc until golden on both sides. Remove the rosemary and garlic and season to taste.
5 To make the sauce, heat the wine in a saucepan with the remaining rosemary and reduce by two-thirds. Add the rest of the chicken stock and reduce by half. Season the sauce to taste and remove the rosemary.
6 To serve, carve the rack into individual cutlets and place 3 on each plate. Add a swipe of pea purée and a line of sautéed potatoes. Drizzle the sauce over the lamb and serve.

SPICED BEST END OF LAMB ON A BED OF WILD RICE WITH THYME JUS

Elisa Zaccour fashion buyer and 2009 quarter-finalist

2 best end of lamb racks (4–6 ribs)
  (see MasterTip, p.203)
1 tsp cumin seeds
1 tsp coriander seeds
1 tsp dried chilli flakes
4 large garlic cloves
4 tbsp olive oil
salt and freshly ground black pepper
150g (5½oz) wild rice mixed with
  basmati rice
360ml (12fl oz) lamb stock or water
75g (2½oz) pine nuts
50g (1¾oz) blanched and
  peeled almonds

FOR THE AUBERGINE
2 large aubergines, halved lengthways
1 tbsp light olive oil

FOR THE THYME JUS
500ml (16fl oz) lamb stock
3 sprigs of thyme, leaves removed
  and chopped

FOR THE TURNIPS
8 baby turnips
knob of butter
salt and freshly ground black pepper

PREPARATION TIME
15 minutes

COOKING TIME
35 minutes

SERVES 4

1 Preheat the oven to 240°C (475°F/Gas 9). In a hot frying pan, dry roast the cumin seeds and coriander seeds for 1–2 minutes, adding the chilli flakes at the end for 30 seconds. Put in a pestle and mortar with the garlic cloves and crush. Add 1 tbsp of olive oil and combine. Score the fat on the lamb and rub with the spices, salt, and pepper.
2 Heat 1 tbsp of olive oil in a frying pan and sear the lamb all over. Move it to a roasting tin and roast in the oven for 20–25 minutes for medium to well done. Leave to rest for 10 minutes before serving.
3 To prepare the aubergines, cut two 1cm (½in) slices from each of their middles. Put into a colander and salt well. Leave for 20 minutes.
4 For the jus, put the stock in a saucepan on a medium heat and let it reduce by two-thirds. Remove from the heat and add the thyme.
5 Cook the rice (see MasterTip, right). Heat another tbsp of the oil in a frying pan. Add the pine nuts and fry until golden. Then fry the almonds until golden, remove from the pan to avoid burning, and combine with the rice.
6 Rinse the aubergine slices of salt and pat dry. Heat the olive oil in a frying pan and fry for 2–3 minutes on each side, until browned.
7 Cook the turnips in boiling water for 3 minutes, then drain and toss in a little butter. Season and keep warm until ready to serve.
8 To assemble the dish, lay an aubergine slice on each of 4 plates and top with the carved lamb ribs. To the side of this spoon the rice and nuts into an 8cm (3¼in) ring mould, with the buttered baby turnips alongside. Drizzle the jus over the ribs of lamb and serve.

MASTER TIP
COOKING THE RICE

Cooking rice to perfection isn't always easy. This method gives the desired end result. Heat 1 tbsp of olive oil in a saucepan, add the wild and basmati rice and sauté for a few minutes. Then add the stock or water and bring to the boil. Reduce the heat and cook for about 20 minutes or until the rice is cooked through. Drain well, and leave to stand for 3 minutes. Before serving, lightly fork through the grains.

FILLET STEAK WITH WASABI SAUCE AND PAK CHOI

Andi Peters presenter and producer and 2008 Celebrity finalist

PREPARATION TIME
5 minutes

COOKING TIME
30 minutes

SERVES 4

4 fillets of beef steak, about 175g (6oz) each
salt and freshly ground black pepper
2 tbsp olive oil
15g (½oz) salted butter
2 heads pak choi, halved lengthways

FOR THE WASABI SAUCE
25g (scant 1oz) salted butter
2 shallots, chopped
1 garlic clove, chopped
3 tbsp white wine
200ml (7fl oz) double cream
1 tbsp wasabi paste

MASTER TIP
WASABI SAUCE

Wasabi is the light green paste that accompanies sushi and is made from the Japanese equivalent of the horseradish plant. Fresh wasabi is in short supply but there are Japanese brands of tubed wasabi that combine the real thing with western horseradish. The best flavour is achieved by adding it to a sauce just before use.

1 Bring the steaks to room temperature. Season the meat well and rub with 1 tsp olive oil per steak. Place 2 at a time into a hot frying pan along with the butter, cooking for 2–2½ minutes on each side, depending on how you like it cooked. This timing is for rare. Allow to rest in a warm place for 5 minutes.

2 Meanwhile, to make the sauce, heat half of the butter in a saucepan. Add the shallots and garlic and sweat for about 5 minutes to soften but not colour.

3 Add the remaining butter and continue to infuse for 2–3 minutes. Stir in the white wine, a little at a time, and then add the cream. Season with salt and pepper to taste and then add the wasabi paste and bring the sauce to a gentle simmer.

4 To cook the pak choi place in a steamer basket over a pan of boiling water. Cover and steam for 6–8 minutes or until tender.

5 To serve, strain the wasabi sauce and pour over the steaks and add the pak choi alongside.

MUSTARD AND CUMIN SEED CRUSTED FILLET STEAK WITH BEETROOT RELISH AND POTATO GRATIN

Jo Seward surgeon's PA and 2005 quarter-finalist

4 fillets of beef steak, about 115g (4oz) each
1 garlic clove
1 tbsp mustard seeds
1 tbsp cumin seeds
1 tbsp olive oil
150g (5½oz) crème fraîche
½ tsp fresh horseradish, finely grated

FOR THE POTATO GRATIN
400g (14oz) Maris Piper potatoes, peeled and very thinly sliced
150ml (5fl oz) double cream

150ml (5fl oz) whole milk
salt and freshly ground black pepper

FOR THE BEETROOT RELISH
1 tbsp olive oil
1 tbsp mustard seeds
1 tbsp cumin seeds
4 shallots, finely chopped
200g (7oz) beetroot, peeled and diced
1 dried chilli, crumbled
1 garlic clove, chopped
4 tbsp red wine vinegar
400g (14oz) cherry tomatoes

PREPARATION TIME
10 minutes

COOKING TIME
45 minutes

SERVES 4

1 Heat the oven to 200°C (400°F/Gas 6). Cut the garlic clove in half and rub the cut side around a 15cm (6in) square ovenproof dish. Then butter the dish liberally and finely chop the garlic.

2 For the potato gratin, mix the cream, milk, chopped garlic, and salt and pepper in a jug. Layer the potatoes in the buttered dish. Tip in the milk and cream until it just reaches the top of the potatoes. Bake in the oven for 40 minutes, or until the potatoes are soft.

3 To make the relish, heat the oil in a saucepan and add the seeds. Fry for 1–2 minutes until you start to smell them, then add the shallots, beetroot, chilli, and garlic. Add the vinegar, tomatoes, and 6 tbsp water. Stir, cover, and cook for 40–45 minutes on a low heat, until the beetroot is tender. Stir occasionally and add water if required.

4 Dry fry the rest of the mustard and cumin seeds, then crush in a pestle and mortar. Tip onto a plate and roll the edges of the fillets in it. Rub the olive oil onto the top and bottom of the steaks. Heat a griddle pan until really hot and fry the steaks for 2 minutes on each side for medium-rare. Let them rest for 5–10 minutes.

5 Meanwhile, mix the crème fraîche with the horseradish. Taste to check strength and add a little more of either to adjust. Season with salt and pepper to taste.

6 To assemble, cut the potato gratin into 4 square portions and transfer to plates. Serve the steak alongside the gratin with a spoon each of beetroot relish and the creamy horseradish to the side.

MASTER TIP
CHERRY TOMATOES

The cherry tomatoes in the beetroot relish pulp down and the skins come off, so you may wish to remove these at the end of cooking. Alternatively, use a tin of chopped tomatoes in place of the fresh tomatoes.

FILLET STEAK WITH BEETROOT ROSTI AND RED WINE JUS

Cheryl Avery purchasing manager and 2009 quarter-finalist

PREPARATION TIME
25 minutes

COOKING TIME
45 minutes

SERVES 4

4 fillets of beef steak, about 150g
  (5½oz) each
1 tbsp olive oil
50g (1¾oz) curly kale

FOR THE RED WINE JUS
4 garlic cloves
1 tbsp olive oil
100ml (3½fl oz) red wine
100ml (3½fl oz) beef stock

FOR THE BEETROOT ROSTIS
2 beetroot, peeled and grated
2 large potatoes (see MasterTip, p.197),
  about 200g (7oz) each, peeled and
  coarsely grated
1 small onion, coarsley grated
salt and freshly ground black pepper
1 large egg, beaten
1–2 tbsp vegetable oil

1 Preheat the oven to 190°C (375°F/Gas 5). For the jus, toss the garlic cloves in the olive oil, then roast on a small baking tray for 15–20 minutes until very soft. Set aside.

2 Meanwhile, to make the rostis, mix together the beetroot and potato, then squeeze out any excess liquid. Stir in the onion and season with salt and pepper. Add enough of the egg to bind everything, then shape into 4 thin rounds.

3 Heat a large, ovenproof frying pan until hot then pour in the oil. Add the rostis and fry for 4–5 minutes on each side or until crisp and golden. Transfer to the oven for 6–8 minutes or until cooked through.

4 To cook the steaks, heat a frying pan until hot. Rub the steaks with a little olive oil and season. Put the steaks in the hot pan and fry for 2½–3 minutes on each side for a medium-rare finish. Remove from the pan and leave to rest.

5 Put the kale in a steamer over a pan of boiling water. Steam gently for 4–5 minutes or until tender. Add seasoning, put to one side and keep warm.

6 To finish the jus, pour the red wine into the frying pan that the steak was cooked in. Stir in well to deglaze. Squeeze the flesh from the roasted garlic, mash until smooth and stir into the red wine. Then stir in the beef stock. Simmer for 1–2 minutes to reduce slightly.

7 To serve, place a rosti on each plate, layer with curly kale and a steak, and then drizzle the jus over the steak and around the plate.

FILLET OF BEEF WITH HONEYED PARSNIPS AND HORSERADISH, MUSHROOM, AND MARSALA SAUCE

William Leigh retail designer turned food writer and 2007 semi-finalist

PREPARATION TIME
20 minutes

COOKING TIME
30 minutes

SERVES 4

4 fillets of beef steak, about 175g (6oz) each
2 large parsnips, peeled and trimmed
60g (2oz) salted butter
2 tbsp clear honey
2 shallots, finely chopped
100g (3½oz) small chanterelles
1 tbsp olive oil
115g (4oz) peas
¼ Savoy cabbage, cored and finely shredded
200ml (7fl oz) Marsala wine
300ml (10fl oz) crème fraîche
5 tbsp horseradish sauce

1 Preheat the oven to 190°C (375°F/Gas 5). Cut each parsnip in half widthways, then cut the top halves into 4 and remove the core, and cut the bottom halves into 2, so that you end up with 12 even-sized pieces of parsnip.

2 Put half of the butter and all the honey in a roasting tin and place in the oven for about 2 minutes to melt. Add the parsnips and toss until well coated. Cook for 20–25 minutes or until crisp and golden, turning halfway through cooking.

3 Heat the remaining butter in a frying pan and fry the shallots and mushrooms for 2–3 minutes, or until softened. Remove from the pan and set aside.

4 Put the steaks in the hot pan and fry for about 3 minutes on each side for a medium rare finish.

5 Meanwhile, steam the peas and Savoy cabbage for 3–4 minutes, or until tender.

6 Remove the steaks from the pan and leave to rest on warmed plates. Return the shallots and mushrooms to the pan and add the Marsala wine.

7 Mix together the crème fraîche and horseradish sauce in a bowl, then stir into the mushroom and Marsala sauce and heat for 3–5 minutes or until thickened slightly and piping hot.

8 Remove the vegetables from the steamer, stir into the mushroom, marsala, and horseradish sauce and serve with the steak and honeyed parsnips.

FILLET OF BEEF WITH HORSERADISH MASH, COURGETTES, AND GRAVY

Helen Cristofoli PR consultant and 2005 quarter-finalist

4 fillets of beef steak, about 200g (7oz) each and 4cm (1½in) thick
4 courgettes, cut diagonally into 6 slices about 1cm (½in) thick
3 tbsp olive oil
300ml (10fl oz) beef stock
100ml (3½fl oz) full-bodied red wine

FOR THE HORSERADISH MASH
550g (1¼lb) Desirée or King Edward potatoes (see MasterTip, p.197), peeled and diced
salt, white and black pepper
100ml (3½fl oz) whole milk, warmed
15g (½oz) salted butter
1 tbsp horseradish sauce, plus 4 tsp to serve

PREPARATION TIME
40 minutes

COOKING TIME
1 hour

SERVES 4

1 Heat the oven to 130°C (250°F/Gas ½). For the horseradish mash, rinse the potato pieces under water to get rid of some of the surface starch. Put into cold water and then bring to the boil in a saucepan with a pinch of salt. Boil for about 15 minutes, or until the potatoes are tender. Then drain them in a colander and put the colander on top of a pan on the hob so the potatoes dry out a little.

2 Transfer to a bowl and cream the potatoes with the warm milk, some salt and white pepper, and the butter, using either a potato masher or an electric whisk. Add the horseradish sauce and stir through. Place in the oven to keep warm.

3 To cook the courgettes, brush with 2 tbsp of the olive oil and sprinkle with salt and black pepper. Sear in batches on a griddle pan for 5 minutes on each side, or until cooked. Keep warm in the oven.

4 Put the stock and wine into a saucepan and bring to the boil. Lower the heat and let the gravy reduce by half.

5 Meanwhile, rub the beef steaks with the remaining olive oil and season with salt and pepper. Heat a frying pan for 5 minutes to very hot and sear the steaks on all sides, then cook them for a further 3 minutes on each side for a medium rare finish. Remove from the pan and leave to rest.

6 To assemble the dish, place a mound of horseradish mash in the middle of each plate, top with a spoon of horseradish sauce, and then put a steak on top of this. Pile the courgettes around the potato to one side and pour the gravy on the other.

FILLET OF BEEF WITH TOMATO AND GARLIC CRUST, ASPARAGUS, FONDANT POTATO, AND HORSERADISH SAUCE WITH A RED WINE JUS

James Nathan barrister turned chef and 2008 champion

PREPARATION TIME
1 hour, plus marinating time

COOKING TIME
40 minutes

SERVES 4

700g (1lb 4oz) fillet of beef
2 tbsp creamed horseradish (see MasterTip, left)
3–4 tbsp crème fraîche

FOR THE TOMATO AND GARLIC CRUST
3 anchovy fillets in oil
75ml (2½fl oz) whole milk
8 sun-dried tomatoes in oil
2 garlic cloves, chopped
3 tbsp olive oil
2 tbsp warm water
salt and freshly ground black pepper

FOR THE JUS
1 tbsp olive oil
½ onion, roughly chopped
1 celery stick, roughly chopped
1 carrot, roughly chopped
3 shallots, roughly chopped
300ml (10fl oz) veal or beef stock
400ml (14fl oz) Beaujolais

FOR THE VEGETABLES
4 King Edward potatoes (see MasterTip, p.197)
60g (2oz) salted butter
200ml (7fl oz) chicken stock (see MasterTip, p.21)
2 bunches of asparagus

MASTER TIP

CREAMED HORSERADISH

Freshly made creamed horseradish would add a real kick to this recipe. Put 250ml (8fl oz) soured cream, 45g (1½oz) grated horseradish, 1 tbsp Dijon mustard, 1 tsp white wine vinegar, and seasoning into a mixing bowl. Whisk until smooth and creamy. Place in the fridge for at least 4 hours or overnight to allow the flavours to meld.

1 Mix together the creamed horseradish and crème fraîche in a bowl and keep in the fridge until required.

2 To make the tomato and garlic crust, soak the anchovy fillets in the milk for about 30 minutes and then drain. Put the anchovies together with the sun-dried tomatoes, garlic, olive oil, and the warm water into a deep jug and use a hand blender to combine them. Set the purée aside.

3 To make the jus, heat the olive oil in a wide, heavy saucepan on a low heat. Add the vegetables and sweat for about 4 minutes. Add the stock and Beaujolais, bring to the boil and then simmer for 15–20 minutes. Strain the mixture, return it to the pan, and reduce to about 8 tbsp of liquid. Keep warm.

4 Dry the meat with kitchen paper. Season on all sides and rub with olive oil. Heat a frying pan over a high heat, add a drizzle of oil and sear the beef all over, which takes about 6 minutes. Transfer the meat to a shallow ovenproof dish and rub with the sun-dried tomato purée, ensuring it sticks. Cover the fillet and let it marinate for 20 minutes.

5 Preheat the oven to 190°C (375°F/Gas 5) and start preparing the potatoes. Cut a cylinder out of each potato with either a metal pastry cutter or turning knife. Trim the cylinders at each end so they are neat and symmetrical.

6 Before you start to cook the potatoes, put the meat into the oven to roast for 30–40 minutes, depending how rare you want it. Remove from the oven and leave the beef to rest for at least 15 minutes.

7 To cook the potatoes, melt the butter in a heavy ovenproof pan over a medium heat. Cook for about 15 minutes, basting them constantly with butter until they start to brown. Add enough hot chicken stock so the level comes one-third of the way up the sides of the potatoes. Put into the oven and cook for about 30 minutes until the stock has mostly evaporated and the potatoes are tender all the way through.

8 To prepare the asparagus see MasterTip, below. Boil a saucepan full of salted water. Add the asparagus spears and cook for 3–4 minutes, until tender. Drain and keep warm until required.

9 Slice the beef thickly and arrange on 4 plates. Place a fondant potato and some asparagus alongside and spoon the hot jus onto the beef. Serve the creamed horseradish separately.

MASTER TIP

PREPARING ASPARAGUS

Asparagus needs little preparation, apart from trimming off the ends of the stalks. However, if the spears are larger, you may want to peel them. Cook asparagus by boiling or steaming, or try roasting or chargrilling them.

1 With a chef's knife, cut the hard ends from the asparagus spears. If the ends are woody, you can snap them off.

2 Holding the tip of a spear, use a vegetable peeler to peel off a thin layer of skin from all sides of the stalk.

FILLET OF BEEF IN A RED WINE JUS WITH COLCANNON, CARROTS, AND BROCCOLI

Jonny Stevenson single father of two, now head chef and 2008 finalist

PREPARATION TIME
20 minutes

COOKING TIME
40 minutes

SERVES 4

4 fillets of beef steak, about
  175g (6oz) each
1 tbsp olive oil

FOR THE COLCANNON
550g (1¼lb) white potatoes of good
  mashing variety (see MasterTip,
  p.197), peeled and chopped
100g (3½oz) salted butter
3 tbsp whole milk, warmed
200g (7oz) curly kale, cut into
  small strips
salt and freshly ground black pepper

FOR THE RED WINE JUS
25g (scant 1oz) salted butter
1 shallot, halved
1 tbsp caster sugar
150ml (5fl oz) red wine
100ml (3½fl oz) beef stock

FOR THE VEGETABLES
12 Chantenay carrots, cut in
  half lengthways
50g (1¾oz) salted butter
1 tbsp light soft brown sugar
1 large head broccoli, chopped
50g (1¾oz) unsalted butter

MASTER TIP
COLCANNON

Made from mashed potatoes, kale or cabbage, and butter, salt, and pepper, colcannon is a traditional Irish dish. Sometimes cream, leeks, ham, or Irish bacon are added for variety and extra flavour.

1 To make the colcannon, bring a large saucepan of salted water to the boil. Add the potatoes and simmer for about 20 minutes, or until very soft. Drain and pass through a ricer. Then add the butter and milk. Bring another large pan of salted water to the boil and add the kale. Cook for 10 minutes until it is tender but not soft, then drain thoroughly. Add to the mash, mix and season with salt and pepper and keep warm.
2 For the red wine jus, heat most of the butter in an ovenproof frying pan. Add the shallot halves and a pinch of the sugar and stir. Leave to sweat for 20 minutes on a low heat. Add the wine to the pan and simmer for 1–2 minutes. Then add the stock, the remaining sugar and butter, and season well with salt and pepper. Reduce to a sauce-like consistency that coats the back of a spoon and pass through a sieve.
3 For the vegetables, put the carrots in a saucepan with the butter and the brown sugar. Cover the pan and let the carrots steam in their own juices for about 10 minutes until tender. Bring another saucepan of salted water to the boil and blanch the broccoli for 5 minutes until just cooked. Refresh in iced water and drain. When ready to serve, reheat quickly in boiling water.
4 Season the beef on both sides and rub with the oil. Heat a frying pan to very hot and then sear the beef and cook for 3 minutes on each side for a medium-rare finish. Leave to rest for a few minutes.
5 Arrange a serving of colcannon on each plate, top with a fillet steak, and arrange the vegetables attractively around the edge. Either pour a little jus over the steaks or serve in a separate sauceboat.

ROASTED FILLET OF BEEF WITH TROMPETTES NOIRES, CELERIAC, AND FONDANT POTATO

Murray Wilson sous chef and 2008 Professionals finalist

4 fillets of beef steak, about 175g (6oz) each
50g (1¾oz) unsalted butter
1 tbsp olive oil
250g (9oz) *trompette noire* mushrooms, trimmed
10 sprigs of tarragon, leaves only
truffle oil, to drizzle (see MasterTip, p.22)

FOR THE CELERIAC
1 large celeriac, peeled and thinly sliced
200ml (7fl oz) whole milk
200ml (7fl oz) double cream

25g (scant 1oz) unsalted butter
salt and freshly ground black pepper

FOR THE FONDANT POTATOES
4 large Desirée potatoes (see MasterTip, p.197), peeled
3 tbsp duck fat
100ml (3½fl oz) chicken stock (see MasterTip, p.21)

FOR THE JUS
500ml (16fl oz) red wine
200ml (7fl oz) chicken stock
1 tbsp tomato purée

PREPARATION TIME
20 minutes

COOKING TIME
1 hour

SERVES 4

1 To cook the celeriac, put the celeriac slices, milk, and cream in a saucepan, bring to the boil and then simmer for 15 minutes until the celeriac is soft. Add the butter, let it melt, then purée in a blender and pass through a sieve. Season with salt and pepper and keep warm.
2 Cut the potatoes into cylindrical pieces with an apple corer. Heat the duck fat in a saucepan, add the potato pieces and fry until brown on all sides. Add the stock, cover and cook for about 10 minutes until soft.
3 To make the jus, pour the wine into a saucepan, bring to the boil and then simmer until reduced by three-quarters. Add the stock and reduce again by half. Season well with salt and pepper and the tomato purée, and keep warm.
4 To cook the steaks, season them with salt and pepper. Heat half the butter and all the olive oil in a frying pan until hot, add the steaks and cook for 3 minutes on each side for a medium-rare finish.
5 In a separate pan, sauté the mushrooms with the chopped tarragon in the remaining butter and season.
6 To serve, arrange the steaks, celeriac, and fondant potatoes on 4 plates. Add a serving of the *trompettes noires* and pour over the jus.

MASTER TIP
TROMPETTES NOIRES

Trompettes noires are also known as "horns of plenty" rather than the direct French translation of "trumpets of death", and as "false truffles" because their dark colour mimics that of their famous fungi cousin. The mushrooms are grey or black with a thin, lightly ruffled cap, and have a rich, nutty flavour.

BEEF WELLINGTON WITH MASH, CREAMED SAVOY CABBAGE, AND AN OXTAIL JUS

Liz McClarnon singer and 2008 Celebrity champion

4 fillets of beef, about 175g (6oz) each
3 Maris Piper potatoes (see MasterTip, p.197), peeled and chopped
4 large stoneless prunes
4 tsp mango chutney
2 streaky bacon rashers, cut in half
250g (9oz) ready-made puff pastry (or see MasterTip, p.365)
200g (7oz) chestnut mushrooms, chopped
75g (2½oz) salted butter
salt and freshly ground black pepper
2 tsp truffle oil (see MasterTip, p.22)

½ Savoy cabbage, shredded
400ml (14fl oz) double cream
1 tbsp olive oil
3 sprigs of thyme
2 sprigs of rosemary

FOR THE OXTAIL JUS
2 garlic cloves, chopped
1 shallot, chopped
1 tbsp olive oil
3 sprigs of flat-leaf parsley, chopped
300ml (10fl oz) port
200ml (7fl oz) oxtail stock, plus 4 tbsp

PREPARATION TIME
40 minutes

COOKING TIME
1 hour

SERVES 4

1 Preheat the oven to 200°C (400°F/Gas 6). Bring a large saucepan of salted water to the boil, add the potatoes and simmer for 20 minutes, or until cooked. Drain and keep warm.

2 For the oxtail jus, put the garlic cloves and shallot in a frying pan with the oil and parsley. Add the port, bring to the boil and reduce by three-quarters. Then add the stock and reduce by half. Keep warm.

3 Fill the hole in each prune with the chutney and roll in a piece of streaky bacon. Pierce with a cocktail stick and cook on a baking tray in the oven for 7 minutes. Remove from the oven and keep warm.

4 Roll out the pastry and cut out four 8cm (3¼in) diameter circles. Put them on a floured baking sheet, glaze with a little milk, then cook in the oven for 12 minutes, until golden. Remove and keep warm.

5 Meanwhile, cook the mushrooms in 25g (scant 1oz) of the butter in a saucepan, add seasoning and the truffle oil. Keep warm.

6 Put the cabbage in 300ml (10fl oz) of the double cream in a saucepan, and add seasoning. Cook for 10–12 minutes until tender.

7 Mash the potatoes with the rest of the double cream and butter.

8 Cover the beef in the olive oil and salt and pepper. Heat a frying pan and when hot seal the beef for a few seconds on each side. Transfer to a roasting tin, add the thyme and rosemary and spoon the extra stock over the top. Put in the oven for 6 minutes.

9 To assemble, place a puff pastry circle on each plate. Score a circle in the top, push it down, and fill with mushrooms. Add some creamed cabbage, a prune in bacon, and quenelles of mash (see MasterTip, p.93). Place a fillet of beef on top, add the jus and serve.

GREGG WALLACE
"Deep, soft, meaty, creamy, rich. This may be one of the best dishes I've ever tasted on MasterChef. I am truly, truly knocked out by it."

STEAK AND KIDNEY PIE WITH MASH AND BROCCOLI

Peter Bayless ad creative turned author and 2006 champion

PREPARATION TIME
45 minutes

COOKING TIME
1 hour 50 minutes

SERVES 4

500g (1lb 2oz) lean braising steak
200g (7oz) ox or lamb kidney
  (see MasterTip, opposite)
2 tbsp plain flour
salt and freshly ground black pepper
1 tsp mustard powder
25g (scant 1oz) salted butter, plus extra
  for mash
2 tbsp sunflower oil
1 onion, finely chopped

600ml (1 pint) hot brown stock
3 Maris Piper potatoes (see MasterTip,
  p.197), peeled and chopped
1 large head broccoli, chopped

FOR THE SUET CRUST PASTRY
225g (8oz) self-raising flour
125g (4½oz) shredded beef suet
pinch of salt
1 egg, beaten

1 Trim off and discard the fat and any sinews from the steak and cut it into cubes of about 4cm (1½in). Cut out and discard the white core from the kidneys and cut them into pieces no smaller than 2.5cm (1in); if using lamb's kidneys, cut each into 8 pieces.

2 Make up a bowl of seasoned flour, by adding a good pinch of salt, at least 20 twists of freshly ground black pepper, and the mustard powder to the flour. Give this a good mix and toss the meats in it to coat.

3 Melt the butter and half the oil in a large saucepan and, when sizzling, add the onion with a little salt and pepper and fry until transparent. Use a slotted spoon to remove the onion to a bowl.

4 In the same pan, begin to sauté the pieces of steak and kidney, a few at a time. The meat needs to be well browned on all sides so don't try to cook too many pieces at once or they will begin to boil rather than fry and you will get a horrible sticky mess in the pan. As each batch of meat is done, transfer to a bowl and continue until all the meat is browned. If the pan starts to dry up, add the remaining oil.

5 Return the meat and onions into the pan and pour over the stock. Bring the pan up to the boil giving it all a good stir to scrape up the brown bits from the bottom.

6 Cover and simmer for about 1 hour. Check and stir every so often to make sure it is not becoming too thick and, if necessary, add a little boiling water to loosen the mixture. When cooked, transfer to a 1.2 litre (2 pints) pie dish and set aside to cool completely. Preheat the oven to 200°C (400°F/Gas 6).

7 For the pastry, sift the flour into a mixing bowl, add the suet and salt and give it a good mix. Gradually add 6–7 tbsp cold water until you have a firm dough. Turn out onto a floured work surface and knead briefly until smooth.

8 Roll out to a thickness of about 5mm (¼in) and quite a bit larger than the top of your pie dish.

9 Place a pie funnel or an upside-down eggcup into the centre of the meat, pushing it well down to the bottom. Moisten the rim of the dish with a little water and cut some strips of pastry, about 1.5cm (⅝in) wide, from around the outer edge. Carefully line the rim of the pie dish with these strips, pushing down to make sure they stick. Moisten them with water and cover the dish with the pastry.

10 Use kitchen scissors to trim off the excess pastry but leave 5–10mm (¼–½in) extra over the edge of the dish. Use the palm of your hand to gently roll this lip of pastry down over the rim of the pie dish. Crimp the edges of the pastry all round using the back of a fork. Cut a small cross over the centre of the pie funnel (or inverted eggcup), brush the whole top with beaten egg and place in the oven for about 30 minutes until the crust is crisp and golden brown.

11 For the mashed potatoes, bring a large saucepan of salted water to the boil, add the potatoes and simmer for 20 minutes, or until cooked. Drain the potatoes and then mash with some butter and add seasoning to taste.

12 Meanwhile, bring another saucepan of salted water to the boil and blanch the broccoli for 5 minutes until just cooked. Refresh in iced water and drain. When ready to serve, reheat quickly in boiling water.

13 When the pie is cooked, serve it immediately with the mashed potatoes and broccoli.

MASTER TIP
PREPARING KIDNEYS

While you can always ask your butcher to prepare kidneys, it is something that can successfully be done at home. Start by pulling away and discarding the white fat that surrounds the whole kidney. It should come away quite easily. Then follow the steps to the right before slicing the kidney into bite-sized pieces and cutting out the fatty cores.

1 Lay the kidney upside down. With the point of a sharp knife, cut around the fatty core, pull it away, and discard.

2 Peel the membrane off the whole kidney – it will slip off easily when you pull it back with your fingers.

THAI BEEF MASSAMAN CURRY WITH JASMINE RICE

Alix Carwood IT consultant and 2008 quarter-finalist

PREPARATION TIME
25 minutes

COOKING TIME
55 minutes

SERVES 4

500g (1lb 2oz) lean rump steak,
  cut into bite-sized chunks
5 cloves
10 cardamom pods
3 tbsp vegetable oil
400ml can coconut milk
2 tbsp nam pla (Thai fish sauce –
  see MasterTip, left)
175ml (6fl oz) beef stock
60g (2oz) unsalted skinned peanuts
1 large Maris Piper potato (see
  MasterTip, p.197), peeled and cut
  into chunks
1.5cm (½in) piece fresh root ginger
1–2 tbsp palm sugar
1–2 tbsp tamarind paste

FOR THE CURRY PASTE
1 red chilli
1 stalk of lemongrass
1cm (½in) galangal or 1 tsp galangal
  in sunflower oil
5 cloves
1 cinnamon stick
10 cardamom pods
3 garlic cloves
3 shallots
large handful of coriander
3 tbsp olive oil

TO SERVE
300g (10oz) jasmine rice
unsalted, skinned peanuts
coriander leaves, to garnish

MASTER TIP

NAM PLA

Nam pla is the Thai version of fish sauce. This is an intensely flavoured salty seasoning from Southeast Asia made by fermenting whole small fish in salt. Fish sauce has a long history: much of the cuisine of the ancient Romans included their similar fish sauce called garum. Fish sauce is said to provide the savoury umami flavour that is known as the fifth taste.

1 To make the curry paste, put all the ingredients in a food processor with a little olive oil and blend until they form a paste.
2 For the beef curry, put the cloves and cardamom in a frying pan and dry fry to release the fragrance. Remove and place on the side.
3 Put a little of the vegetable oil in the pan and fry 5 tbsp of the curry paste over a medium heat for 5 minutes until the fragrance is released. Add the beef and also fry until browned. Then add the remaining ingredients to the pan and bring to the boil. Reduce to a simmer and cook for about 45 minutes until the beef is tender and the sauce is reduced.
4 Bring a pan of water to the boil. Add a pinch of salt and then the jasmine rice. Reduce the heat and leave to simmer for about 10 minutes until the rice is cooked through.
5 Serve the curry in a bowl, sprinkled with peanuts, with the jasmine rice to one side, garnished with coriander.

VEAL ROULLES STUFFED WITH SPINACH AND GRUYÈRE

Matt Barker sales director and 2008 quarter-finalist

PREPARATION TIME
40 minutes

COOKING TIME
55 minutes

SERVES 4

4 escalopes of veal, about 125g (4½oz) each
8 small shallots, peeled
500ml (16fl oz) veal or beef stock
100ml (3½fl oz) port
salt and freshly ground black pepper
4 carrots, chopped
200g (7oz) swede, chopped

50g can of anchovies in oil, drained and finely chopped
125g (4½oz) unsalted butter, softened
75g (2½oz) Gruyère cheese, grated
25g (scant 1oz) baby spinach leaves
8 asparagus spears, trimmed (see MasterTip, p.221)
1 tbsp olive oil

1 To make the jus, put the shallots into a large saucepan. Pour in the stock and port and simmer for 8–10 minutes or until the shallots are cooked. Remove the shallots and reserve. Increase the heat and reduce the stock to 8 tbsp. Season and set aside.

2 Bring a saucepan of salted water to the boil and cook the carrots and swede for 15–20 minutes or until soft. Drain the water and mash using 50g (1¾oz) of the butter and season liberally.

3 Meanwhile, to make the roulles, lay the veal on a chopping board, cover with cling film and, using a rolling pin or meat tenderizer, bash the meat until it is about 5mm (¼in) thick. Mix the anchovies into 25g (scant 1oz) of the butter. Remove the cling film and spread the butter thinly over the escalopes. Sprinkle the Gruyère evenly over the top and then lay the spinach leaves on the cheese. Gently roll the escalopes from one edge, forming a tight tube. Secure with cocktail sticks.

4 Preheat the oven to 200°C (400°F/Gas 6). Steam the asparagus spears in a steamer for 5–8 minutes or until tender.

5 Heat 25g (scant 1oz) of the butter with a dash of olive oil in a frying pan and, when hot, sear each roulle for 20–30 seconds on each side until brown. Transfer to a baking tray and cook in the oven for 8–10 minutes. Remove from the oven and leave to stand for 1 minute.

6 Return the shallots to the reduced stock, heat for 1–2 minutes and thicken it by whisking in the remaining 25g (scant 1oz) of butter.

7 To assemble, place a quenelle (see MasterTip, p.93) of the carrot and swede in the centre of each plate. Lay 2 asparagus spears on top of the mash. Remove the cocktail sticks from the veal and cut the roulles diagonally in the centre and lean the ends of the roulles against the side of the mash. Place a few shallots around the outside and drizzle over the jus.

FILLET OF VEAL WITH A CREAMY TRUFFLE SAUCE, MUSHROOMS, AND ASPARAGUS

Andy Oliver project manager turned chef and 2009 finalist

2 fillets of veal, about 200g (7oz) each, trimmed of fat and sinew
salt and freshly ground black pepper
6 slices lardo (see MasterTip, below), about 3mm (⅛in) thick
40g (1½oz) salted butter
1 tbsp extra virgin olive oil
12 small girolles or chanterelles
12 asparagus spears, trimmed

FOR THE TRUFFLE SAUCE
30g (1oz) salted butter
200g (7oz) veal trims
1 white onion, sliced
½ head of garlic, cut in half horizontally
small bunch of thyme
600ml (1 pint) chicken stock (see MasterTip, p.21)
150ml (5fl oz) double cream
1 small black truffle (see MasterTip)
1cm (½in) piece of fresh root ginger

PREPARATION TIME
20 minutes

COOKING TIME
50 minutes

SERVES 4

1 To start the sauce, melt the butter in a large saucepan, add the veal trims and sauté for 3–5 minutes until browned. Then add the onion and garlic and sauté for a further 3 minutes or until softened. Add the thyme and stock, simmer for 15 minutes and then boil rapidly until reduced by at least half. Strain the sauce, pressing the pulp through the sieve to extract as much flavour as possible. Return to the pan and continue to boil until reduced to about 200ml (7fl oz).

2 Meanwhile, preheat the oven to 180°C (350°F/Gas 4). Season the veal and wrap each in lardo, using string to tie up at intervals. Heat a non-stick, ovenproof frying pan to high, then add the lardo-wrapped veal fillets and sear all over for 4–5 minutes, turning frequently. Transfer the frying pan to the oven and cook for 10–15 minutes. Remove from the oven and rest.

3 For the vegetables, heat half of the butter and the olive oil in a sauté pan and add the mushrooms with a little seasoning. Sauté for 3–5 minutes, then remove and set aside. Add the asparagus to the pan with the remaining butter and cook with the lid on for 4–5 minutes, or until tender and slightly coloured.

4 Meanwhile, to finish the sauce, add the cream and boil for 4–5 minutes or until well reduced and it has reached a thickish sauce consistency. Finely grate in some black truffle. Grate the ginger, squeeze the juice from the grated ginger, and add this to sauce. Taste for seasoning and adjust.

5 Remove the string from the meat, cut off the lardo, and quickly sauté this in a pan until well coloured, tipping away the excess fat. Serve the fillets cut into slices with the mushrooms and asparagus to the side, the sauce on top, and the crispy lardo to accompany.

MASTER TIPS
TRUFFLES AND LARDO

Truffles grow underground and survive by emitting a scent to attract animals which will eat them and spread their spores. This is why they have such a musky aroma that is as important as their delicate flavour. Black truffles pass their earthy essence into other ingredients when they are cooked together gently and slowly. When buying truffles, look for genuine black (*tuber melanosporum*) or white (*tuber magnatum*) varieties and avoid *tuber aestivum*. This particular summer truffle looks great, but it lacks the fabled flavour of its rarer cousins.

Lardo is cured pork fat that has been seasoned with garlic and herbs and aged for 4–6 months. It is also sometimes called Italian bacon and is sold in strips.

VEAL AND THYME BOUDIN BLANC, WITH VEAL SWEETBREADS, SERVED WITH CORN-FED CHICKEN TORTELLINI

Semone Bonner head chef and 2008 Professionals quarter-finalist

PREPARATION TIME
1 hour 20 minutes, plus chilling time

COOKING TIME
1 hour 10 minutes

SERVES 4

FOR THE PASTA
150g (5½oz) "00" pasta flour (see MasterTip, p.52)
1 egg, beaten
1 egg yolk
1 tbsp olive oil

FOR THE BOUDIN BLANC
1 tbsp olive oil
1 small banana shallot, finely chopped
2 garlic cloves, crushed
450g (1lb) veal meat
75ml (2½fl oz) double cream
few sprigs of thyme, leaves removed
salt and freshly ground black pepper

FOR THE PASTA FILLING
1 tbsp olive oil
1 banana shallot, finely chopped
1 garlic clove, crushed
1 corn-fed chicken breast, about 175g (6oz), skin removed and very finely chopped
1 tbsp double cream
1 small courgette, very thinly sliced
vegetable oil for deep frying

FOR THE SWEETBREADS
300g (10oz) veal sweetbreads
2 tbsp clear honey
1 tbsp olive oil

FOR THE SAUCE
100ml (3½fl oz) sweet sherry
250ml (8fl oz) veal or chicken stock
75ml (2½fl oz) double cream
4 sage leaves, finely chopped
knob of butter

1 Make the pasta dough as described in the MasterTip on p.51, adding the olive oil to the eggs.

2 To make the boudin blanc, heat the oil in a small frying pan, add the shallot and garlic and sauté for 2–3 minutes or until softened. Remove from the heat and leave to cool slightly.

3 Transfer two-thirds of the veal to the clean food processor and process with the cream until smooth and of a mousse consistency. Transfer to a bowl.

4 Finely slice the remaining veal and stir into the mousse with the thyme leaves and season to taste. Then stir in the shallot and garlic mixture. Roll into a sausage shape and wrap very tightly in cling film. Add to a wide pan of simmering water and poach for 25 minutes or until firm to the touch and cooked through. Remove from the pan and allow to stand for at least 5 minutes.

5 Meanwhile, make the pasta filling by heating the oil in a frying pan. Add the shallot and garlic and sauté for 1–2 minutes. Then stir in the chopped chicken and sauté for a further 5–6 minutes or until well cooked. Season to taste, stir in the cream, and leave to cool slightly.

6 Heat enough vegetable oil in a small saucepan to come no more than two-thirds up the sides of the pan. When hot enough – and you can test this by adding a piece of bread to it and it should crisp up quickly – add the courgette slices in batches and deep-fry for 1 minute or until golden and crispy. Remove with a slotted spoon and drain on kitchen paper.

7 For the sweetbreads, soak them in cold water for 10 minutes and then remove the film membrane and any fatty parts from the outside and discard. Wipe on kitchen paper, then toss together with the honey and some seasoning. Heat the oil in a non-stick frying pan and sauté the sweetbreads over a medium heat, stirring frequently, for 10–12 minutes or until golden and cooked through.

8 Divide the rested pasta dough into 2 then, using a pasta machine, roll half of the dough through the widest setting. Fold in half and repeat. Work the pasta through the settings, starting at the widest down to the thinnest, making sure the dough is well floured at all times (see also the MasterTip on p.190–91). Lay the dough out on a surface lightly dusted with flour and repeat with remaining dough.

9 Using a 6cm (2½in) round cutter, cut out approximately 24 discs and brush each one with a little beaten egg. Place a slice of courgette slightly off centre then add 1 tsp of the chicken mixture and enclose it by folding one half of the pasta to the other to form a half moon shape. Bring the two corners of the moon together to form the tortellini. Repeat with each disc of pasta.

10 Bring a large pan of lightly salted water to the boil, reduce the heat to a simmer and poach the pasta in batches for 5–6 minutes. Drain thoroughly and keep warm.

11 To make the sauce, place the sherry in a small saucepan and boil for 1–2 minutes or until reduced by half. At the same time, boil the stock in another pan for 5–6 minutes, or until reduced by half, and add to the sherry. Stir in the cream and sage and whisk in the butter to thicken slightly. Boil for a further 1–2 minutes or until thickened and then season to taste and keep warm.

12 To assemble, unwrap the boudin blanc and cut into thick slices and arrange on serving plates. Add some honeyed sweetbreads around the edge, alternating with the tortellini and then drizzle the sauce over and serve.

LOIN OF PORK STUFFED WITH SWEET PEPPERS WITH AUBERGINE PURÉE, CHOI SUM, AND STAR ANISE AND GINGER SAUCE

Simon Small construction company owner and 2009 quarter-finalist

PREPARATION TIME
1 hour

COOKING TIME
1 hour 45 minutes

SERVES 4

1kg (2¼lb) lean loin of pork on the
  bone, with a good layer of fatty skin
1 tsp five spice

FOR THE STUFFING
1 tbsp groundnut oil, plus extra
  for frying
1 tbsp sesame oil
1 red pepper, halved and deseeded
I orange pepper, halved and deseeded
1 yellow pepper, halved and deseeded
salt and freshly ground black pepper
1 tbsp chopped coriander
½ tsp sesame seeds

FOR THE AUBERGINE PURÉE
2 large aubergines, halved lengthways
½ tsp five-spice powder

FOR THE SAUCE
150ml (5fl oz) red wine
75ml (2½fl oz) rice wine
2 tbsp rice wine vinegar
3 tbsp shiitake extract
2 tbsp dark soy sauce
2 tbsp dark soft brown sugar
3 star anise
1 stalk lemongrass
2 garlic cloves
4 kaffir lime leaves
½ tsp dried chilli flakes
4 spring onions, sliced into 2cm
  (¾in) lengths
10cm (4in) piece fresh root ginger,
  roughly peeled and cut into strips

TO SERVE
1 tsp sesame seeds
2 large stalks choi sum, quartered
1 mild red chilli, thinly sliced

MASTER TIP
BONING A PORK LOIN

Removing the meat from the bone makes it easier to stuff, roll, tie, and then carve. To do this, guide a sharp knife along the bone, making short sharp slits between the bone and the flesh. You will then be able to separate them. Alternatively, ask your butcher to do it for you when you buy the meat.

1 Preheat the oven to 230°C (450°F/Gas 8). To prepare the stuffing, mix the groundnut and sesame oils in a bowl and use to brush the peppers. Season with salt and place them skin-side up on a baking tray. Cook for about 25 minutes or until the skins have blackened. When cool enough to handle, peel off the skin and slice the peppers.
2 Repeat the process with the aubergines, but place skin-side down and score some of the flesh to allow the salt and oil to penetrate. Put in the oven for 25 minutes until soft. Remove from the oven.
3 Prepare the pork by removing the bone (see MasterTip, left) to enable it to be stuffed. Carefully remove the skin from the remaining meat, retaining the fat. Score the skin, rub in salt and sprinkle with five-spice. Place the fat in a roasting tin and roast for about 1 hour until crispy. Leave to cool. Cut into matchsticks.
4 Reduce the heat of the oven to 190°C (375°F/Gas 5). Mix together the sliced peppers, coriander, and sesame seeds and season. Lay the pepper mixture in the centre of the open pork loin, roll, and tie up

with string. Heat a frying pan to hot and then sear the pork on all sides in the pan. Transfer to a roasting tin and roast for 35–45 minutes until there are no pink juices. Remove from the oven and leave to rest.

5 To make the sauce, pour the red wine into a medium-sized saucepan and then add the remaining ingredients, including most of the ginger. Bring to the boil, reduce the heat and simmer until reduced by three-quarters.

6 When the aubergines are cool enough to handle, scoop out the flesh and mash up with some five-spice, pass through a sieve, season with salt and pepper to taste, and keep warm.

7 Clean out the pan from the pork searing and then dry fry the sesame seeds to toast them and lightly fry the remaining ginger slices, cut into strips.

8 Stir-fry the choi sum in some groundnut oil and plate up the aubergine into the centre of each serving plate. Place the choi sum around the aubergine and slice 2 rounds of pork and place on top. Strain the ginger sauce and spoon plenty over the dish. Dress the pork with the ginger, chilli slices, crispy crackling, and sesame seeds.

PORK TENDERLOIN ON PARSNIP MASH WITH CARAMELIZED APPLES AND WATERCRESS SALAD

Rachel Thompson mother of three and 2009 quarter-finalist

450g (1lb) tenderloin of pork
¼ tsp allspice
cracked black pepper
2 tbsp olive oil

FOR THE PARSNIP MASH
250g (9oz) parsnips, peeled and cut
 into chunks
250g (9oz) Desirée or King Edward
 potatoes (see MasterTip, p.197),
 peeled and cut into chunks
100ml (3½fl oz) whole milk
salt and freshly ground black pepper
20g (¾oz) salted butter
1 tbsp crème fraîche

FOR THE CARAMELIZED APPLE
20g (¾oz) unsalted butter
50g (1¾oz) caster sugar
2 Granny Smith apples, cored
 and quartered
juice of 1 lemon

FOR THE WATERCRESS SALAD
2 tbsp balsamic vinegar
4 tbsp olive oil
juice of 1 lemon
75g (2½oz) watercress

PREPARATION TIME
25 minutes

COOKING TIME
30 minutes

SERVES 4

1 Preheat the oven to 200°C (400°F/Gas 6). Place the parsnips and potatoes in a pan with the milk and add enough water to cover the vegetables. Season well and bring to the boil. Reduce the heat and simmer for 20 minutes or until soft. Drain off the liquid and add the butter and crème fraîche. Using a hand blender, process until smooth. Season with salt and pepper to taste.

2 Rub the pork with the allspice and plenty of cracked pepper and drizzle with the oil. Heat a heavy griddle pan, add some of the olive oil and, when hot, seal the pork on all sides. Then place in the oven and roast for 10–20 minutes, or until the pork is cooked through. Let it rest for 10 minutes.

3 Meanwhile, caramelize the apples (see MasterTip, right).

4 For the salad, mix together the balsamic vinegar and olive oil. Add lemon juice and dress the watercress.

5 To serve, put the parsnip and potato mash onto the plates, add the pork and apple and serve with the watercress salad alongside in a small bowl or beside the pork.

MASTER TIP

CARAMELIZING FRUIT

Caramelizing fruit in butter and sugar intensifies its flavour. Put the specified amount of butter and caster sugar in a frying pan and cook over a gentle heat for about 10 minutes, until the sugar dissolves and the caramel is golden in colour. Add the fruit and cook for 3–4 minutes over a low heat – don't be tempted to stir it, just let it cook in the sugar or it won't caramelize. When the fruit starts to caramelize, turn the pieces over and cook for a further 3–4 minutes. Add some lemon juice and simmer for about 1 minute until the fruit has browned. Turn the fruit once again and cook until softened.

PORK TENDERLOIN ON A BED OF FENNEL

inspired by **Thomasina Miers** food writer turned chef and 2005 champion

PREPARATION TIME
15 minutes, plus marinating time

COOKING TIME
1 hour 10 minutes

SERVES 4

2 tenderloins of pork, about 250g
  (9oz) each
½ tsp coarse sea salt
½ tsp black peppercorns
1 garlic clove, finely chopped
2 tsp fennel seeds
2 tbsp olive oil
15g (½oz) butter

FOR THE FENNEL
2 large bulbs fennel
2 tbsp olive oil
3 sprigs of rosemary
200ml (7fl oz) white wine
250ml (8fl oz) chicken stock
  (see MasterTip, p.21)
sea salt and freshly ground
  black pepper

1 Preheat the oven to 180°C (350°F/Gas 4). For the pork, grind the salt and pepper to a coarse powder in a pestle and mortar, then add the garlic and fennel seeds and grind a little more. Brush the pork with the oil and rub in the fennel seed mixture. Cover and leave for at least 2 hours to allow the pork to absorb the flavours.

2 To braise the fennel, quarter the bulbs lengthways and trim away some of the root end, leaving just enough to hold the layers together. Cut each quarter in half again, and fry in batches in the oil in a frying pan for 6–8 minutes over a medium heat, turning to brown evenly on all sides.

3 Arrange the fennel in a single layer in a large gratin dish and bury the rosemary among it. Pour the wine and stock into the pan used to brown the fennel, and bring to the boil. Tip this over the browned fennel, season well and cover with foil, shiny side down. Bake on the lower shelf of the oven for about 1 hour, until the fennel is tender.

4 When you are ready to cook the pork, about 40 minutes into the fennel's cooking time, seal one tenderloin at a time in a hot frying pan. Seal on all sides, using a drop more oil, and transfer to a roasting tin. Place in the oven to cook for 10–12 minutes, until cooked through, then remove and leave to rest for about 10 minutes.

5 Tip the pork juices from the tin and the fennel's braising juices into the frying pan that the pork was sealed in and reduce rapidly by about a half. Finally, whisk in the butter to finish.

6 Serve the pork sliced diagonally, fanned out on a bed of the braised fennel with the gravy over the top.

PORK FILLET WITH PANCETTA, MACERATED SWEDE, AND MARSALA SAUCE

Matt Dobson head chef and 2009 Professionals semi-finalist

2 fillets of pork, about 325g (11oz) each, both cut into two
1 tbsp olive oil
15g (½oz) butter

FOR THE MARSALA SAUCE
250ml (8fl oz) Marsala wine
250ml (8fl oz) chicken stock (see MasterTip, p.21)
150ml (5fl oz) double cream
salt and freshly ground black pepper

FOR THE VEGETABLES
1 small swede, each half peeled and cut into 16 equal pieces

1 tbsp olive oil
60ml (2fl oz) sherry vinegar
2 large carrots, finely diced
4 tbsp double cream
pinch of grated nutmeg

FOR THE PANCETTA
15g (½oz) salted butter
3 shallots, finely sliced
85g (3oz) pancetta (see MasterTip, p.44), cubed
12 button mushrooms, each cut into quarters
1 garlic clove, crushed
sprig of thyme

PREPARATION TIME
30 minutes, plus chilling time

COOKING TIME
1 hour 5 minutes

SERVES 4

1 Trim the fillets of pork, removing any fat and roll tightly in cling film. Leave in the fridge for 1 hour.

2 Pour the Marsala wine into a saucepan, bring to the boil and then reduce for 10 minutes until it is syrupy. Add the chicken stock and reduce again for a further 10 minutes. Add the cream and simmer for a further 10 minutes to a rich and creamy consistency. Adjust the seasoning and keep warm. Preheat the oven to 220°C (425°F/Gas 7).

3 Boil the swede and carrots in separate pans in salted water for 15 minutes until tender and drain. Fry the swede in the oil for 5 minutes until brown. Add the vinegar and reduce for 5 minutes, allowing the swede to absorb the liquid. Remove from the pan. For the carrots, add the cream and blend with nutmeg and seasoning. Keep both warm.

4 For the pancetta, heat the butter in a frying pan and cook all the ingredients for about 15 minutes until golden, turning occasionally. Season with pepper. Discard the thyme and keep the vegetables warm.

5 Unwrap the pork and seal all sides in the oil in an ovenproof frying pan. Transfer to the oven for 10 minutes. Return to the hob set at high, add the butter and spoon it over for 2 minutes or until the pork is cooked. Remove from the heat, cover and leave to rest for 10 minutes.

6 To serve, divide the pancetta mixture between 4 serving plates. Slice each fillet into 1cm (½in) diagonal wedges and place on top of the pancetta. Put a spoonful each of the carrot and swede alongside and finally spoon the Marsala sauce onto the pork fillet slices.

PORK BAFAT WITH OKRA PACHADI AND RICE BREAD

Michelle Peters university researcher and 2009 semi-finalist

PREPARATION TIME
20 minutes, plus soaking and marinating time

COOKING TIME
1 hour 45 minutes

SERVES 4

500g (1lb 2oz) shoulder pork, diced
4 large onions, chopped
2 tbsp tomato ketchup

FOR THE MARINADE
25g (1oz) tamarind
60ml (2fl oz) boiling water
2 tbsp bafat powder (see MasterTip, p.172)
1 tsp garam masala
½ tsp ground nutmeg
7.5cm (3in) piece root ginger, chopped
2 garlic cloves, chopped
2 bay leaves, torn
5 green chillies, chopped
pinch of salt
100ml (3½fl oz) red wine vinegar
5 cloves, 5 cardamom pods, and 2.5cm (1in) piece of cinnamon tied in muslin

FOR THE OKRA PACHADI
1 tbsp vegetable oil
1 tsp black gram
1 tsp mustard seeds
1 tsp cumin seeds
3 mild dried red chillies, finely chopped
1 tsp Bengal gram (split yellow peas)
sprig of curry leaves
8 okra, chopped
200g (7oz) plain yogurt

FOR THE RICE BREAD (SANNA)
250g (9oz) idli rice or pudding rice
65g (2¼oz) basmati rice
45g (1½oz) cleaned white urad dal
25g (scant 1oz) beaten rice (optional)
3 tbsp sugar
1 tsp yeast dissolved in 2 tbsp warm water

MASTER TIP

RICE BREAD BATTER

To prepare the rice bread ingredients, soak the idli rice, basmati rice, urad dal, and beaten rice (if using) in a bowl for about 4 hours. Drain all the water out. Then use a powerful grinder, such as a coffee grinder (in batches if necessary), to grind the soaked mixture with the sugar and salt, using enough water to achieve the consistency of double cream. Pour the batter into a large bowl and stir in the dissolved yeast. Leave in a warm place for at least 4 hours, but preferably overnight to ferment and rise.

1 Prepare the rice bread ingredients a day ahead (see MasterTip, left).
2 Soak the tamarind in the boiling water for 20–30 minutes, breaking up the block as it softens. Strain the paste into a bowl. Add the pork, 200ml (7fl oz) water, and the remaining marinade ingredients. Leave to marinate for about 1 hour. Transfer the pork and the marinade to a saucepan, cover and gently cook for 1 hour 15 minutes, without adding any more water. Mix in the onions halfway through the cooking process. After that time, stir in the ketchup and simmer for about 30 minutes until the pork is tender, adding water if necessary.
3 To cook the okra, heat the oil in a heavy frying pan and add the rest of the ingredients except the yogurt. Cook on a low heat for 20 minutes or until the okra is soft. Add salt to taste and then the yogurt.
4 To steam the sannas, grease six 150ml (5fl oz) ramekins with a little vegetable oil. Fill each ramekin one-third full with the batter so there is room for it to rise. Steam in a steamer for 8 minutes. To check they are ready, poke a cocktail stick into one – it shouldn't have wet batter sticking to it. Carefully remove the ramekins and leave them to cool. Turn the ramekin upside down and the rice bread should slide out easily. Remove the bay leaves and spices in muslin from the pork and serve the bafat with the okra and warmed rice bread.

STUFFED LOIN OF PORK WITH BUBBLE AND SQUEAK AND A CIDER SAUCE

Gary Heath ICT technician and 2007 quarter-finalist

PREPARATION TIME
45 minutes

COOKING TIME
1 hour 50 minutes

SERVES 4

1kg (2¼lb) loin of pork with a good
   layer of fat, scored by your butcher
½ tbsp olive oil
½ small onion, finely chopped
25g (scant 1oz) gooseberries or finely
   chopped Bramley apple
1 tbsp finely chopped sage
1 tbsp finely chopped flat-leaf parsley
½ egg yolk, lightly beaten
25g (scant 1oz) fresh white
   breadcrumbs
salt and freshly ground black pepper
1 tbsp sunflower oil

325g (11oz) baby carrots, trimmed
knob of butter

FOR THE BUBBLE AND SQUEAK
250g (9oz) Maris Piper potatoes
   (see MasterTip, p.197), peeled
   and chopped
3 tbsp milk
25g (scant 1oz) salted butter
¼ Savoy cabbage, finely sliced

FOR THE CIDER SAUCE
200ml (7fl oz) cider
1 tbsp caster sugar

1 Preheat the oven to 220°C (425°F/Gas 7). Heat the oil in a saucepan and cook the onion for 5 minutes or until soft. Then add the gooseberries (or apple) and cook for a further 2 minutes. Take off the heat and let it cool before mixing in the herbs, egg yolk, breadcrumbs, and seasoning.

2 To prepare the pork, make a hole in the centre of the loin by using the point of a large knife to drive right through the meat and turn the knife 360 degrees. Spoon in the stuffing.

3 Rub the pork fat with the sunflower oil and season with salt. Place in a roasting in the oven for 30 minutes to crackle the skin. Reduce the temperature to 190°C (375°F/Gas 5) and cook for a further 1½–2 hours. To test for doneness, pierce a knife into the meat and the juices will run clear. Remove from the oven and leave to rest for 20 minutes.

4 To make the bubble and squeak, simmer the potatoes for about 20 minutes in boiling water until cooked. Drain and add the milk and half the butter. Mash and set aside. Blanch the cabbage in boiling water for 5 minutes and drain. Heat the remaining butter in a frying pan and add the cabbage. Cook for 3–5 minutes until slightly softened but still keeping its shape. Mix into the mash, add seasoning and keep warm.

5 Add the carrots to boiling water and cook for 15–20 minutes until tender. Drain, add 1 teaspoon of butter and cover.

6 Heat the pan you cooked the pork in on a high heat, add the cider and sugar and reduce by a third, scraping any meat from the pan.

7 To serve, slice the pork and place on plates, add scoops of bubble and squeak and baby carrots and spoon the sauce around the meat.

ROAST PORK WITH CARAMELIZED APPLES AND ROSEMARY

Alison Reynolds student and 2006 quarter-finalist

700g (1lb 8oz) thick tenderloin of pork
4 large garlic cloves, very thinly sliced
2 sprigs of rosemary
100g (3½oz) salted butter, plus extra for the mash and cabbage
4 tbsp cider vinegar
6 large shallots, thinly sliced
2 Granny Smith apples, peeled, cored, and each cut into 6 slices

2 tbsp demerara sugar
3 Maris Piper potatoes (see MasterTip, p.197), peeled and chopped
1 Savoy cabbage, roughly chopped
salt and freshly ground black pepper
400ml (14fl oz) cider
4 tbsp double cream or crème fraîche

PREPARATION TIME
15 minutes

COOKING TIME
40 minutes

SERVES 4

1 Preheat the oven to 220°C (425°F/Gas 7). Cut small slits all over the pork and place slices of garlic in each one. Bruise the rosemary sprigs by crushing lightly with a rolling pin on a chopping board to release the flavours.

2 Heat the butter in a saucepan until melted and add the cider vinegar and 1 rosemary sprig cut into 2 pieces. Stir and leave to infuse for a couple of minutes. Brush the meat generously with the butter mixture.

3 Place the shallots on a roasting tin and lay the buttered pork on top. Put the apples around the pork and pour the remaining butter over them. Sprinkle the sugar and remaining rosemary over the pork and apples and place in the oven for 20–30 minutes until the pork is tender. To check for doneness, pierce a skewer or knife into the meat and the juices will run clear. Remove the roasting tin from the oven, transfer the pork to a plate and leave to rest.

4 For the mashed potatoes, bring a large saucepan of salted water to the boil, add the potatoes and simmer for 20 minutes, or until cooked. Drain the potatoes and then mash with some butter and add seasoning to taste.

5 Meanwhile, steam or cook the cabbage in boiling salted water for 4–5 minutes until tender. Drain and toss in butter and pepper.

6 Place the roasting tin on the hob and deglaze by adding a splash of the cider to the tin. Then pour the apples, shallots, and sauce into a saucepan and add the remaining cider. Allow the cider sauce to reduce by a third and then take it off the heat. Whisk in the cream or crème fraîche and season with salt and pepper to taste.

7 Cut the pork into slices and divide among 4 plates together with some mashed potato and cabbage. Pour over the cider sauce and serve immediately.

PORK AND TARRAGON TART WITH CABBAGE AND SMOKED BACON
Simon Spindley service manager and 2006 quarter-finalist

PREPARATION TIME
25 minutes, plus chilling time

COOKING TIME
25 minutes

SERVES 4

FOR THE PASTRY
100g (3½oz) cold butter
200g (7oz) plain flour
pinch of salt

FOR THE FILLING
1 red onion, finely chopped
1 garlic clove, chopped
3 tbsp olive oil
225g (8oz) fillet of pork, trimmed
  and finely diced
100g (3½oz) fine green
  beans, chopped
½ red chilli, finely chopped

1 tbsp balsamic vinegar
75ml (2½fl oz) full-bodied red wine
2 tbsp clear honey
1 tbsp chopped tarragon
1 Granny Smith apple, peeled and diced
1 courgette, thinly sliced
sea salt and freshly ground black pepper
1 tsp Dijon mustard, plus extra to serve

FOR THE CABBAGE AND SMOKED BACON
4 smoked bacon rashers, cut into thin strips
½ Savoy cabbage, very finely shredded
1 tbsp double cream

1 Preheat the oven to 180°C (350°F/Gas 4). Grease four 10cm (4in) round, loose-bottomed tart cases. Rub the butter into the flour and salt in a bowl. Add some cold water until a soft dough is formed. Cover in cling film and chill for 30 minutes. Divide into 4 balls, then roll out each one to 5mm (¼in) thick and line the tart cases, trimming off any excess. Bake blind for 12 minutes (see MasterTip, p.368–69), remove the paper and beans, and cook for 2–3 minutes until crisp.
2 In a large saucepan, fry the red onion and garlic in 1 tbsp of the oil for 2–3 minutes or until softened. Add the pork, green beans, and chilli and cook for 5–8 minutes or until the pork is well cooked. Add the vinegar and most of the wine. Reduce the liquid to virtually nothing, then add the remaining wine and reduce again to nearly dry. Remove the pan from the heat and add the honey, tarragon, and apple.
3 In a frying pan, fry the courgette slices in the remaining oil and some sea salt for a few minutes on each side until lightly coloured. Remove from the heat and drain the courgettes on kitchen paper. Thinly spread a film of mustard on one side of the courgettes.
4 Spoon the meat mixture into the pastry cases and arrange the courgette slices over the top, mustard-side down. Cook in the oven for 8–10 minutes, or until piping hot.
5 Dry fry the bacon for 3–4 minutes, or until crisp, and steam the cabbage for 3–5 minutes, or until tender. Stir the bacon and cream into the cabbage, heat through, and season to taste. Serve alongside each tart with a spoonful of mustard.

ROAST BELLY OF PORK WITH BUBBLE AND SQUEAK CAKE, AND CLAMS IN A CREAM CALVADOS SAUCE

Chris Gates civil servant turned junior sous chef and 2009 finalist

PREPARATION TIME
30 minutes

COOKING TIME
1 hour 30 minutes

SERVES 4

1kg (2¼lb) belly of pork, bone removed (see MasterTip, p.234), skin scored
salt and freshly ground black pepper
175ml (6fl oz) white wine
small bunch of thyme

FOR THE BUBBLE AND SQUEAK CAKES
2 large Desirée potatoes (see MasterTip, p.197), peeled and chopped
2 tbsp olive oil
2 shallots, chopped

1 garlic clove, chopped
½ green cabbage, about 400g (14oz), cored and chopped
50g (1¾oz) salted butter
2 tsp wholegrain mustard

FOR THE CLAMS
16 clams, cleaned and any that are open discarded
3 tbsp Calvados
200ml (7fl oz) double cream

1 Preheat the oven to 180°C (350°F/Gas 4). Place the pork on a rack in a roasting tin and season all over with salt and pepper. Pour the wine and 175ml (6fl oz) of water into the tin and add the thyme. Cover the whole tin with a piece of baking parchment and then a piece of foil and cook in the oven for at least 2 hours.

2 Remove the pork from the oven and increase the temperature to 220°C (425°F/Gas 7). Discard the water, wine, and herbs. Place the pork in a clean roasting tin and press by placing a piece of baking parchment and a dish on top of the pork and adding some weights, such as full cans. Leave it for about 10 minutes, remove the weights and return to the oven for 30 minutes, or until the crackling is crispy.

3 Meanwhile, make the bubble and squeak. Cook the potatoes in a saucepan of boiling water for 20 minutes or until soft. Drain the liquid and mash the potatoes. Heat the oil in another saucepan and add the shallots and garlic and soften for a few minutes. Add the cabbage and season with salt and pepper. Cook for another 3 minutes. Add the mash, half the butter, and the mustard, mix and check the seasoning. Shape into 4 cakes using a palette knife. Fry in the remaining butter for about 5 minutes on each side until golden. Keep warm.

4 For the sauce, heat a pan until smoking hot. Add the clams and cook for 1 minute. Then add the Calvados, cover and continue to cook for 2–3 minutes until the clams have opened. Discard any that haven't opened, add the cream, and check the seasoning. Bring to a simmer.

5 To serve, place the cakes onto 4 plates. Cut up the meat, place on top of the cakes, and spoon around the clams and sauce.

PAN-FRIED CALF'S LIVER WITH MUSTARD POTATO AND MARSALA SAUCE

Steven Waslin entrepreneur and 2009 quarter-finalist

500g (1lb 2oz) calf's liver
110g (4oz) thin slices pancetta
75g (2½oz) salted butter
300g (10oz) spinach, stalks removed

FOR THE MARSALA SAUCE
900ml (1½ pints) beef stock
300ml (10fl oz) Marsala wine
300ml (10fl oz) Cabernet Sauvignon
2 tbsp balsamic vinegar
25g (scant 1oz) salted butter

FOR THE MUSTARD POTATO
600g (1lb 5oz) King Edward potatoes
   (see MasterTip, p.197)
50g (1¾oz) salted butter
3 tbsp double cream
2 tbsp whole milk
1 tsp English mustard

FOR THE ONION PURÉE
50g (1¾oz) salted butter
3 red onions, halved and thinly sliced
2 tbsp balsamic vinegar
1 tbsp granulated sugar

PREPARATION TIME
40 minutes

COOKING TIME
1 hour 15 minutes

SERVES 4

1 For the sauce, combine the stock, wines, and vinegar in a saucepan, bring to the boil and simmer until reduced and thickened slightly to give you about 150ml (5fl oz) of sauce. Whisk in the butter and keep warm.

2 Preheat the oven to 190°C (375°F/Gas 5). Bake the potatoes on a baking tray for 1 hour or until tender when pressed.

3 Meanwhile, for the onion purée melt the butter in a large, shallow pan. Add the onions and sauté for 8–10 minutes or until very soft. Add the balsamic vinegar and sugar and cook gently, stirring frequently, for a further 10 minutes, or until the onions have caramelized. Transfer to a blender and process into a smooth purée. Keep warm.

4 Remove the cooked potatoes from their skins and pass through a potato ricer or mash until smooth. Then mix with the butter and the cream, milk, and mustard until smooth. Also keep warm.

5 Place the slices of pancetta on a large baking tray and heat in the oven for 3–4 minutes or until they are very crispy.

6 Meanwhile, melt 50g (1¾oz) of the butter in a pan and pan-fry the calf's liver for 3–4 minutes, turning over halfway through.

7 In a separate pan, melt the remaining butter and pan-fry the spinach for 2–3 minutes or until just wilted and piping hot.

8 To assemble, place spoonfuls of the mustard mash on 4 plates, top with the spinach, caramelized onion purée, calf's liver, and a few pieces of crispy pancetta and serve with the sauce.

HONEYED CALF'S LIVER WITH GLAZED SNAPS AND DAUPHINOISE POTATO

Natasha Shergold IT manager and 2007 quarter-finalist

PREPARATION TIME
30 minutes

COOKING TIME
40 minutes

SERVES 4

4 slices calf's liver, about 175g
  (6oz) each
plain flour, for dusting
25g (scant 1oz) butter
1 tbsp vegetable oil
115g (4oz) sugar snap peas
knob of butter
1 tsp wholegrain mustard
4 tbsp red wine vinegar
4 tbsp chicken stock (see MasterTip, p.21)
2 tbsp clear honey

FOR THE DAUPHINOISE POTATO
150ml (5fl oz) double cream
150ml (5fl oz) whole milk
1 garlic clove, crushed
4 Desirée or Maris Piper potatoes
  (see MasterTip, p.197), about 200g
  (7oz) each
salt and freshly ground black pepper

1 Preheat the oven to 200°C (400°F/Gas 6). Butter a small ovenproof dish measuring about 23 x 16cm (9 x 6¼in) and season lightly.
2 To make the Dauphinoise potato, place the cream, milk, and garlic in a saucepan and slowly bring to the boil. Remove from the heat and let the liquid cool a little while you peel the potatoes and cut them into 2mm (⅛in) thin slices, using a mandolin or sharp knife.
3 Arrange the slices of potato over the bottom of the ovenproof dish, slightly overlapping them and seasoning each layer until all the potato is used. Pour the milk mixture over, covering the potatoes. Cover with foil and bake in the oven for 35–40 minutes, removing the foil for the last 10 minutes.
4 Meanwhile, wipe the liver with damp kitchen paper, then season both sides and dust lightly with the flour, shaking off any excess.
5 Melt 15g (½oz) of the butter with the oil over a high heat in a large, heavy frying pan, swirling to blend. Add the liver to the pan and cook for 1–2 minutes until browned on one side, then turn and cook for a further minute. Transfer to warmed serving plates and keep warm.
6 While the liver is browning, bring a small pan of slightly salted water to the boil and add the sugar snap peas. After 2 minutes, drain and set aside. Melt a knob of butter in the small pan, stir in the mustard and return the snaps to the pan, tossing until coated in the glaze. Put on the serving plates next to the liver.
7 Put the vinegar, stock, and honey into the frying pan and boil rapidly, stirring constantly for 1–2 minutes, until reduced slightly. Add the remaining butter, whisking until melted and smooth.
8 To serve, cut rounds of potato with a ring mould and put on 4 plates with the calf's liver, glazed sugar snaps, and the sauce poured over.

PAN-FRIED LAMB'S LIVER WITH PANCETTA AND HORSERADISH MASH

Chris Gates civil servant turned junior sous chef and 2009 finalist

300g (10oz) lamb's liver, trimmed
  and sliced
2 tbsp olive oil
5 pancetta slices
small bunch of sage, leaves removed
1 onion, thinly sliced
plain flour, to dust
knob of salted butter
2 tbsp red wine vinegar

FOR THE HORSERADISH MASH
3 large King Edward potatoes
  (see MasterTip, p.197), peeled
  and chopped
20g (¾oz) salted butter
salt and freshly ground black pepper
about 2 tbsp creamed horseradish
about 100ml (3½fl oz) double
  cream, warmed

PREPARATION TIME
15 minutes

COOKING TIME
25 minutes

SERVES 4

1 Bring a large saucepan of salted water to the boil. Add the potatoes and simmer for about 20 minutes until soft.

2 Meanwhile, in a large frying pan heat half the oil and fry the pancetta for 4–5 minutes or until crisp. Remove from the pan and put to one side. Then fry the sage leaves until crisp and also put to one side. Finally, fry the onion for 12–15 minutes over a medium-low heat until caramelized. Set aside.

3 Dust the sliced liver with a little flour. In a large frying pan, heat the remaining olive oil and fry the liver over a high heat for 1–2 minutes on each side until sealed. Return the pancetta, sage leaves, and onion to the pan. Add a knob of butter and the vinegar and heat through.

4 Drain and mash the potatoes and season with salt and pepper. Add the creamed horseradish and double cream to taste.

5 Serve the horseradish mash in large bowls with the liver on top. Spoon over the onion, sage, and pancetta mix.

STARTERS
VEGETABLES & FISH
POULTRY
MEAT
GAME
DESSERTS

ROAST SQUAB PIGEON WITH RAVIOLI OF WILD MUSHROOM, CELERIAC PURÉE, AND SPINACH

Matthew Street sous chef and Professionals quarter-finalist

PREPARATION TIME
1 hour 30 minutes

COOKING TIME
1 hour 30 minutes

SERVES 4

4 squab pigeons, 800g (1¾lb) in total
100ml (3½fl oz) red wine
2 sprigs of thyme
1 carrot, chopped
1 banana shallot, chopped
2 celery sticks, chopped
1 garlic clove, chopped
25g (scant 1oz) butter
500g (1lb 2oz) baby spinach
250ml (8fl oz) chicken stock (see
  MasterTip, p.21)
250ml (8fl oz) port

FOR THE FILLING
1 tbsp olive oil
2 sprigs of thyme, leaves only
200g (7oz) wild mushrooms, chopped
1 banana shallot, finely diced
1 garlic clove, finely diced

FOR THE PURÉE
1 celeriac, about 600g (1lb 5oz),
  roughly chopped
500ml (16fl oz) milk
150ml (5fl oz) double cream

FOR THE PASTA
250g (9oz) "00" pasta flour (see
  MasterTip, p.52)
2 eggs
2 tbsp olive oil
1 tsp salt

1 Preheat the oven to 220°C (420°F/Gas 7). Prepare the pigeon for cooking, removing the giblets, wing bones, and legs. Put the pigeon bones in a roasting tin and roast in the oven until browned – no oil is needed. Transfer to the hob and deglaze the roasting tin with the wine. Add the carrot, thyme, shallot, and garlic, cover with 500ml (16fl oz) water and simmer for at least 40 minutes to make a stock.

2 To make the pasta, whizz all of the ingredients in a food processor until the mixture clings together into a ball, adding a little cold water if needed. Remove and leave to rest for 30 minutes in the fridge. (Or see MasterTip, p.51.)

3 For the filling, heat the oil in a frying pan and sauté the shallot and garlic until softened but not browned. Add the thyme and mushrooms and cook for a further 10 minutes until the mushrooms have reduced down and there is no liquid left. Add the chopped offal from the squab if you wish – it will take only a minute to cook. Allow to cool.

4 To make the ravioli, cut the dough in half and roll out as thinly as possible (see MasterTip, pp.190–91). Brush 1 sheet with a little water, then place dessertspoonfuls of filling about 4cm (1¾in) apart. Lay the second sheet over, pressing gently around the filling. Cut into ravioli. Lay on a tray sprinkled with a little semolina flour until needed.

5 Simmer the celeriac in milk for about 20 minutes until soft. Drain, then purée with a hand blender, enriching with double cream.

6 In a hot pan, melt the butter and wilt the spinach. Season and set aside until serving.

7 In a pan, reduce the chicken stock by half and add your pigeon stock to it. In another pan, reduce the port to 200ml (7fl oz), then add the combined stocks and reduce by three-quarters until your sauce reaches the desired consistency.

8 Preheat the oven to 180°C (350°F/Gas 4). Seal the squab pigeons in a well-seasoned heavy frying pan. Transfer to a roasting tin and cook in the oven for 15–20 minutes. Remove from the oven, rest for about 15 minutes and then remove the breasts. Keep warm.

9 Cook the ravioli in a large sauce pan of boiling salted water for about 5 minutes until the pasta is cooked through but is still *al dente*.

10 To serve, heat the purée and the spinach. Spoon into soup plates and top with the pigeon breasts then the ravioli. Finish with the sauce.

PAN-FRIED BREAST OF WOOD PIGEON WITH A FRICASSÉE OF WILD MUSHROOMS, PANCETTA, AND GARDEN PEAS

Leon Dodd head chef and 2008 Professionals finalist

4 wood pigeon breasts, skin on
1 tbsp olive oil
50g (1¾oz) salted butter
1 sprig of thyme, leaves removed and chopped

FOR THE FRICASSÉE
½ banana shallot, finely chopped
1 garlic clove, finely chopped
200g (7oz) wild mushrooms, broken into bite-sized pieces
1 sprig of thyme, leaves removed and chopped
75g (2½oz) smoked pancetta, cut into small lardons

1 tbsp olive oil
50g (1¾oz) salted butter
3 tbsp dry white wine
175ml (6fl oz) double cream
50g (1¾oz) frozen garden peas, defrosted
salt and freshly ground black pepper

FOR THE POMMES PURÉE
2 floury potatoes (see MasterTip, p.197), peeled and cut into chunks
50g (1¾oz) salted butter
3 tbsp double cream

PREPARATION TIME
20 minutes

COOKING TIME
50 minutes

SERVES 4

1 To make the fricassée, sauté the shallot, garlic, mushrooms, thyme, and pancetta in the oil and butter for 5 minutes or until golden brown. Deglaze the pan with the wine and reduce until it is almost gone but the pan is not dry. Add the cream and reduce by half so that

it is just coating the mushrooms and pancetta. Add the peas and heat through. Season to taste with salt and pepper.

2 For the pommes purée, boil the potatoes in salted water in a saucepan for 20 minutes or until tender. Drain, replace in the pan and dry them over a very low heat, then pass them through a potato ricer or mouli. Melt the butter in a small saucepan, add the cream and bring to the boil. Pour into the potato and whisk until smooth. Season to taste.

3 Brush the pigeon breasts with olive oil and season with salt and pepper. Heat the oil in a frying pan and sauté the pigeon breasts skin-side down for about 3 minutes. Turn over, add the butter and the thyme, and continue to cook for a further 4–5 minutes, basting continually. Remove from the pan and allow to rest for 5 minutes in a warm place.

4 To serve, spoon 2 tbsp of pommes purée into the centre of 4 wide shallow bowls. Top with a wood pigeon breast and pour a little mushroom fricassée around the outside.

ROAST TEAL WITH SWEET POTATO MASH AND CHILLI AND CHOCOLATE GRAVY

inspired by **Thomasina Miers** food writer turned chef and 2005 champion

PREPARATION TIME
1 hour 30 minutes

COOKING TIME
1 hour 30 minutes

SERVES 4

4 teal
1 tbsp olive oil
salt

FOR THE SWEET POTATO MASH
2 large sweet potatoes, about
  450g (1lb) each
25g (scant 1oz butter)
freshly ground black pepper

FOR THE GRAVY
200g (7oz) mole poblano paste
  (see below)
400ml (14 floz) chicken stock
  (see MasterTip, p.21)
15g (½oz) butter

FOR THE MOLE POBLANO PASTE
75–100g (2½–3½oz) lard
1 tomato, halved
1 small onion, halved
5 garlic cloves, skin left on

½ brioche bun
50g (1¾oz) cashew nuts
50g (1¾oz) natural roasted peanuts
50g (1¾oz) whole almonds
50g (1¾oz) sesame seeds
1 corn tortilla, crumbled
5cm (2in) cinnamon stick
3 cloves
8 allspice berries
1 bay leaf
1 tsp freshly grated nutmeg
½ ripe plantain, peeled and sliced
50g (1¾oz) dried apricots, chopped
50g (1¾oz) stoned prunes, chopped
50g (1¾oz) raisins
1½ tbsp each dried ancho, mulato,
  and pasilla chillies, diced
2 tbsp chipotle chillies in adobo sauce
½ tsp salt
100g (3½oz) dark chocolate (70%
  cocoa – see MasterTip, p.351)
50ml (2fl oz) chicken stock if required

1   Preheat the oven to 200°C (400°F/Gas 6).

2   First, make the mole poblano paste. Melt 25g (1oz) lard in a large frying pan which you will then use to fry the remaining ingredients, and pour over the tomato and onion in a roasting tin. Scatter in the garlic cloves, toss together to ensure everything is well coated, then roast in the oven for about 30 minutes, basting once or twice during cooking. Tip into a large mixing bowl. While the oven is on, bake the brioche bun on a low shelf until golden brown and crispy and add to the bowl.

3   Melt another 25g (1oz) lard in the pan and fry the nuts separately until golden brown and then the sesame seeds. Transfer to the bowl as you go, draining the fat each time, reserving it for the next ingredient. Repeat with the crumbled tortilla until golden brown. Melt some more lard in the pan, add the spices and stir, cooking until they start to toast and release their aromas, then grind roughly in a pestle and mortar before adding to the bowl.

4   Now fry the sliced plantain in the fat left coating the pan, adding more if necessary. When both sides are a dark golden colour, transfer to your bowl. Next, put the dried fruits in the pan and stir well to coat in the lard. Cook gently for 5–10 minutes, then tip into the bowl with the rest of the ingredients.

5   Fry the dried chillies in a little more lard until they start to pop slightly; add to the bowl along with the chipotle in adobo and salt. Finally, grate the chocolate – or break into pieces and pulse in a food processor – and add to the bowl with all the other fried ingredients. Mix everything together well.

6   In batches, blend the ingredients to a paste in a food processor and tip back into the bowl, adding a drop of chicken stock if the mixture is not damp enough.

7   Brush the teal with the olive oil and place on a roasting tray. Sprinkle with salt and roast in the oven at 200°C (400°F/Gas 6) for 12–15 minutes, then remove from the oven to rest for 5–7 minutes.

8   For the sweet potato mash, peel the potatoes and chop into 4cm (1½in) cubes. Place into boiling water to cook for 10–12 minutes, or until tender throughout. Drain and mash with the butter and seasoning.

9   For the gravy, place the mole poblano paste in a small saucepan and gradually add the stock, whisking to avoid lumps. Pass this through a sieve and tip back into the saucepan. Bring to a gentle simmer and finally whisk in the butter to finish.

10   Serve the teal on a bed of sweet potato mash, with the gravy spooned around the outside.

MASTER TIP
MOLE POBLANO PASTE
The recipe here produces 600g (1lb 5oz) mole paste, which can be stored in sealed jars in the fridge for up to 1 month and used for a variety of Mexican dishes.

QUAIL PARCELS OF CHICKEN LIVER WITH ONION SOUBISE AND SPINACH AND PEAR PURÉE

Steven Wallis creative director and 2007 champion

4 boned quails (ask your butcher to
  bone them), at room temperature
salt and freshly ground black pepper
a few sprigs of thyme, leaves only
4 large chicken livers
2 tbsp olive oil
60ml (2fl oz) Cognac
100ml (3½fl oz) port or red wine
200ml (7fl oz) chicken stock (see
  MasterTip, p.21)
60g (2oz) butter

FOR THE SOUBISE
500g (1lb 2oz) onions, finely sliced
40g (1¼oz) salted butter
3 tbsp olive oil
freshly ground white pepper

FOR THE PURÉE
500g (1lb 2oz) mature spinach leaves
20g (¾oz) salted butter
2 large Comice pears, peeled and cored
½ tsp grated nutmeg

PREPARATION TIME
30 minutes

COOKING TIME
35 minutes

SERVES 4

1   First prepare the soubise: add the onions to a pan with the butter, oil, salt, and a few grinds of white pepper. Cook down on a low heat, ensuring the onions don't colour. Cut a cover made from greaseproof paper to fit over the onions and cook for 20–30 minutes until they are soft. Purée in a food processor, return to the pan and keep warm.
2   Preheat the oven to 200°C (400°F/Gas 6). Open out the quails, season, and scatter with thyme. In a small pan, flash fry the chicken livers in 1 tbsp oil for a few seconds, add the Cognac, and burn off the alcohol. Remove from the heat and season well.
3   Place the livers inside the quails and close the cavities with wooden cocktail sticks. In the same pan, flash fry the quails for a few minutes to seal them. Place on a baking tray and cook in the oven for 15 minutes until the quail juices run just clear when the breast meat is stabbed with a skewer. Cover with foil and allow to rest for 5 minutes.
4   Reheat the pan in which you cooked the quail and deglaze with port. Add the stock and reduce until syrupy, then whisk in the butter.
5   For the purée, wilt the spinach in a pan with the butter, squeeze out as much water as possible and set aside. Poach the pears in water until soft – about 15 minutes. Drain and then add to a food processor, along with the spinach, nutmeg, and seasoning. Blitz to a fine purée.
6   To serve, add 1 tbsp of soubise to each plate, tapering it into an elegant sweep across the plate. Add a whole bird per plate, removing the cocktail sticks and placing crown side up, tucking in the wings and legs. Add a quenelle (see MasterTip, p.93) of the pear and spinach purée on one side and then spoon the port wine jus over.

GUINEA FOWL WITH A BALLOTINE OF THE LEG, MADEIRA JUS, BABY LEEKS, MASHED POTATO, AND SUMMER TRUFFLE

Marianne Lumb private chef and 2009 Professionals finalist

PREPARATION TIME
1 hour

COOKING TIME
1 hour 10 minutes

SERVES 4

2 guinea fowl
40g (1½oz) dried morels
3 litres (5 pints) chicken stock
  (see MasterTip, p.21)

FOR THE BALLOTINES
2 garlic cloves, crushed
10g (¼oz) chopped chervil, plus some
  sprigs to garnish
salt and freshly ground black pepper
12 thin slices pancetta
salt and freshly ground black pepper

FOR THE JUS
300ml (10fl oz) Madeira wine
3 sprigs of thyme

FOR THE VEGETABLES
16 skinny baby leeks, trimmed
60g (2oz) unsalted butter
4 Desirée potatoes (see
  MasterTip, p.197)
1 tbsp olive oil
150ml (5fl oz) whipping cream
ground white pepper

TO SERVE
2 summer black truffles
  (see MasterTip, p.231)
2 tbsp white truffle oil (see
  MasterTip, p.22)
sprigs of chervil, to garnish

1 Place the morels in a small bowl and cover with boiling water to hydrate for 20–30 minutes.

2 Heat the chicken stock in a large saucepan until boiling. Then reduce the heat and leave to simmer.

3 Remove the legs from the guinea fowl and cut away the backbone leaving just the breasts and the wings attached to the breastbone creating a crown. Set the legs aside and place the crowns in the stockpot with the chicken stock. Poach for about 20 minutes to render the fat in the skin. Remove and place on a roasting tin big enough to fit the crowns comfortably. Set aside.

4 To make the stuffing for the ballotines, take the legs and cut into the drumsticks and thighs. Remove the bones from the thighs and place the bones in the stock. Also remove any sinew and skin and discard. Take the drumsticks and remove the bones and skin. Drain the morels, reserving the soaking liquid. Place the drumstick meat in a food processor with the morels, garlic, and chervil. Blend until nearly smooth and season well.

5 For the ballotines, place the thigh meat between cling film and bash gently with a rolling pin to flatten. Lay out 3 slices of the pancetta so they are just overlapping and place the thigh meat on top.

Season the meat and place a quarter of the stuffing mix in a log across the thigh. Roll the pancetta tightly around the thigh. Repeat with the others, then roll them up in cling film and poach for 10 minutes in the stock. Remove and keep warm.

6 To make the jus, pour the Madeira wine into a saucepan, bring to the boil and then reduce by three-quarters. Add 300ml (10fl oz) of the stock with the thyme and reserved mushroom water. Reduce this by three-quarters until you have a rich dark sauce. Preheat the oven to 200°C (400°F/Gas 6).

7 Cook the baby leeks in 200ml (7fl oz) of boiling water and 25g (scant 1oz) of the butter and a pinch of salt for 7–8 minutes until just cooked. Set aside and keep warm.

8 Cook the potatoes in their skins in lightly salted water for about 20 minutes, or until they are soft in the centre. Remove from the water and, when cool enough to handle, peel and push through a drum sieve, mouli, or ricer. Keep warm.

9 Season the crowns and ballotines and pan-fry briefly in the oil to gain some colour. Then return to the roasting tin and roast the crowns for 10 minutes and the ballotines for 15–20 minutes. Remove from the oven and allow to rest for at least 10 minutes.

10 For the potatoes, heat the cream and remaining butter in a medium pan, add the mashed potato, and cook until smooth. Season with salt and ground white pepper. Remove the leeks from the butter water and drain.

11 To serve, place a quenelle of mash on each plate (see MasterTip, p.93), followed by 4 leeks each. Slice the ballotines into 1cm (½in) thick pieces and place in a curved line underneath the mash. Slice the breast and place on top of the mash. Spoon over the jus, grate over lots of truffle, and drizzle over a little truffle oil. Garnish with chervil sprigs and serve immediately.

GUINEA FOWL WITH BRAISED PEARL BARLEY AND LEMON AND THYME SAUCE

Fiona Marshall teacher and 2006 quarter-finalist

PREPARATION TIME
15 minutes

COOKING TIME
35 minutes

SERVES 4

150g (5½oz) cold unsalted butter
2 tbsp olive oil
1 onion, finely diced
2 garlic cloves, peeled and crushed
100g (3½oz) pearl barley
500ml (16fl oz) dry white wine
1.2 litres (2 pints) chicken stock
  (see MasterTip, p.21)

4 guinea fowl breasts, skin on
8 slices pancetta (see MasterTip, p.44)
1 leek, finely sliced
2 tbsp thyme leaves
juice of ½ lemon
salt and freshly ground black pepper

1 Preheat the oven to 200°C/400°F/Gas 6. Heat 25g (scant 1oz) butter and 1 tbsp olive oil in a non-stick frying pan. Add the onion and garlic and cook gently over a low heat for 5 minutes until the onions are softened but not coloured.

2 Add the barley, wine, and 900ml (1½ pints) stock. Bring to the boil then reduce the heat to a simmer for about 20 minutes until the barley is tender. Stir from time to time, adding an extra 50ml (2fl oz) of stock if needed to maintain a soupy consistency.

3 Meanwhile, season the guinea fowl breasts, then heat the remaining oil in a frying pan and quickly seal and brown the breasts, skin-side down first to get it crispy. Place the breasts on a baking tray then lay slices of pancetta flat beside them. Roast in the oven for 15 minutes or until the breasts are cooked, then remove from the oven and rest.

4 In a small saucepan, blanch the leek in 250ml (8fl oz) stock for 2 minutes. Remove the leek from the pan, drain, and set aside, leaving the stock in the pan. Return the pan to the heat, bring the stock to the boil and then simmer for 10 minutes or until it is reduced by three-quarters.

5 To make the sauce, add the thyme and lemon juice to the reduced stock and then gradually, over a low heat, whisk in 100g (3½oz) cold butter until it turns silky and smooth.

6 To serve, stir the leek through the pearl barley along with the remaining butter. Taste and season with salt and pepper. Present in large bowls, placing the guinea fowl breast on top of the barley with the sauce pooled around the sides. Top with the crispy pancetta.

POT-ROASTED PARTRIDGE WITH SPICED PEAR, CABBAGE PARCELS, AND CHESTNUTS

Daksha Mistry housewife turned caterer and 2006 finalist

4 oven-ready plump partridges, about 250g (9oz) each
25g (scant 1oz) thyme
thinly peeled zest of 1 lemon
4 thin streaky bacon rashers
50g (1¾oz) salted butter
1 tbsp olive oil
1 celery stick, chopped
1 shallot, finely chopped
1 leek, finely chopped
1 carrot, chopped
1 garlic clove, crushed
1 tsp finely chopped flat-leaf parsley
1 tsp finely chopped thyme
100g (3½oz) roasted and ready-to-use chestnuts, roughly chopped

FOR THE CABBAGE PARCELS
225g (8oz) Savoy cabbage
4 tsp olive oil
30g (1oz) butter
1 garlic clove, crushed

1 shallot, chopped
2 tbsp finely chopped belly pork
2 tbsp sausagemeat
½ carrot, very finely diced
1 tbsp finely chopped chestnuts
1 tsp chopped sage
2 tsp chopped flat-leaf parsley
salt and freshly ground black pepper

FOR THE SAUCE
15g (½oz) salted butter, plus 1 tsp
½ tsp white wine vinegar
500 ml (16fl oz) full-bodied red wine
120 ml (4fl oz) Madeira wine
4 tbsp redcurrant jelly

FOR THE SPICED PEAR
2 pears
15g (½oz) butter
2 tbsp caster sugar
1 star anise
½ cinnamon stick

PREPARATION TIME
1 hour 20 minutes

COOKING TIME
45 minutes

SERVES 4

1 Preheat the oven to 220°C (425°F/Gas 7). Remove the core from the Savoy cabbage and blanch 8 leaves in salted boiling water for 5 minutes. Drain and refresh in cold water for 5 minutes, then drain well. Cut circles in the leaves using cutters in 3 different sizes: 2.5cm (1in), 5cm (2in), and 6cm (2½in). Then layer the rounds on top of each other in descending size, with the largest at the bottom.
2 For the stuffing, heat the oil and butter in a heavy pan. Add the garlic and shallot and cook for 2 minutes. Add the belly pork and cook for about 5 minutes until golden. Then add the rest of the ingredients and cook for 5 minutes. Place 1 tsp of the filling into the blanched cabbage rounds, wrap the leaf tightly around the filling, then wrap each parcel with cling film. Steam for 10 minutes. Keep warm.
3 Prepare the partridges by seasoning with salt and pepper inside and outside. Stuff with the thyme and strips of lemon zest, wrap the streaky bacon on the breast side and tie them up.
4 In an ovenproof roasting pot, heat the butter and olive oil. Add the chopped vegetables and herbs and cook gently for 10 minutes to

soften the vegetables, but do not allow them to brown. Place the birds on top of the vegetables and roast in the oven for 30 minutes until cooked through, but still moist. Remove the partridges from the dish and also remove the string and keep them warm.

5 For the sauce, add all the ingredients to the vegetables left in the roasting tin. Bring to the boil and reduce by half to thicken. Strain the liquid and then add the 1 tsp of butter for shine.

6 To make the spiced pears, peel, halve, and core the pears. Melt the butter and sugar in a shallow pan and sauté the pear halves, cut-side down, for about 10 minutes until golden brown.

7 Heat the chestnuts quickly in some melted butter in a pan.

8 To serve, place a partridge on each plate, unwrap the cabbage parcels and arrange 3 parcels on each plate with half a spiced pear. Scatter over the chestnuts and serve the sauce separately.

ROAST PARTRIDGE WITH GAME JUS

Gillian Wylie property developer turned chef and 2007 quarter-finalist

PREPARATION TIME
1 hour

COOKING TIME
1 hour

SERVES 4

4 whole young partridges, crowns prepared by your butcher (keep the trimmings), and feet, heads, and necks removed (see also MasterTip, p.106)
2 large Maris Piper potatoes (see MasterTip, p.197)
4 tbsp olive oil
12 strips of lard or streaky bacon rashers
sea salt and finely ground black pepper
60g (2oz) salted butter

FOR THE SALSIFY AND CEPS
200ml (7fl oz) game stock (see MasterTip, p.275)

3 sprigs of thyme
juice of ½ lemon, plus the ½ lemon itself
1 garlic clove, crushed
2 roots black salsify (see MasterTip, opposite)
4 large ceps
15g (½oz) salted butter, plus a knob
1 tbsp olive oil
2 shallots, finely chopped

FOR THE GAME JUS
300ml (10fl oz) game stock
about 4 tbsp Armagnac
8 pitted prunes

1 To make the salsify and ceps, put the game stock in a saucepan along with 2 sprigs of thyme, lemon juice, half lemon, and garlic. Bring to a simmer.

2 Peel the salsify and cut into lengths to fit the pan. Add the salsify to the stock along with enough hot water to cover the salsify. Simmer for 20–25 minutes until tender, drain and cut the salsify into halves lengthwise and then into 2.5cm (1in) pieces on the diagonal.

3 Trim the bases off the ceps, then shave the stalks (top to bottom) with a knife to clean them up. Cut the nicest looking 2 in half lengthways through the cap and stalk and reserve. Finely chop the others. Heat a little of the butter and the olive oil in a non-stick frying pan and fry the shallots for about 5 minutes until translucent, but not browned. Add the chopped ceps and a few thyme leaves, season and let soften. Add the chopped salsify and fry until tinged golden.

4 For the galettes, peel the potatoes and separately grate one of them. Heat a little of the oil in a large non-stick frying pan on a medium heat. Place 4 greased metal cutters in the pan and press a thin layer of grated potato into each one. Cook for about 5 minutes or until the bottoms are lightly browned. Remove the rings and flip over the potato galettes to cook on the other side. Repeat to make a further 4 galettes. Drain on kitchen paper.

5 Preheat the oven to 220°C (425°F/Gas 7). Cover the crowns with the lard strips or bacon and tie with string to secure.

6 Throw away the entrails, apart from the liver. Put the liver in a roasting tin together with the bones, rub lightly in olive oil and roast for about 20 minutes or until very well browned.

7 Heat a little olive oil in a non-stick, ovenproof frying pan. Season the breasts and legs, then sear the breasts well for a good few minutes on all sides. Add half the butter and, once it has melted, baste the birds and put in the oven. Baste every 5 minutes for 10–15 minutes until they are cooked to your liking. Remove from the oven and leave to rest

8 Meanwhile, pan-fry the seasoned legs in the remaining butter and 1 tbsp of the oil until cooked through.

9 To make the jus, pour the game stock into a saucepan and add the pre-roasted bones (but discard the liver) and the Armagnac, to taste. Bring to the boil, then lower the heat and reduce by half, skimming off any scum. Strain, then blend in a food processor with the prunes to thicken it slightly. You can add more prunes if you like, but watch it doesn't get too sweet. Check the seasoning.

10 To cook the remaining ceps, heat a little oil in a small, non-stick frying pan. Fry the halved ceps, cut sides down, until golden. Turn them over and cook on the other side. Add the large knob of butter and baste.

11 To assemble, cut the breasts off the birds and trim any ragged edges. Brush with a little melted butter. Arrange the breasts on plates along with the legs and crispy bacon. Sit a potato galette on each plate, top with some of the salsify and ceps mix, and then add another galette so you have a "sandwich", followed by some more salsify and ceps. Finally, balance a half mushroom on top. Strain the game jus into a sauceboat and serve alongside.

SALSIFY

Salsify is a member of the lettuce family and is also known as the oyster plant because of its flavour resemblance when cooked. These elongated taproots look like long, thin parsnips and become increasingly fibrous as they age. Go for smooth, firm roots, preferably with the green tops still on. A close relative and alternative ingredient is scorzonera, also known as black salsify. For this recipe, if you are unable to buy salsify, replace it with an additional 225g (8oz) wild mushrooms.

ROAST GROUSE WITH PARSNIP CRISPS AND A RICH RED WINE SAUCE

Peter Bayless ad creative turned author and 2006 champion

PREPARATION TIME
40 minutes

COOKING TIME
1 hour

SERVES 4

2 whole young oven-ready grouse,
  including giblets, about 425g
  (13oz) each
sea salt and freshly ground
  black pepper
2 large mushrooms, chopped
150g (5½oz) unsalted butter
4 fatty unsmoked streaky
  bacon rashers
1 square-section white loaf,
  preferably a day old
Dijon mustard, for seasoning
bunch of watercress
few redcurrants (optional)

FOR THE SAUCE
3 shallots, finely sliced
50g (1¾oz) unsalted butter
75cl bottle red Burgundy
100ml (3½fl oz) ruby port

FOR THE BOUQUET GARNI
1 carrot
1 celery stick
1 bay leaf
few sprigs of thyme
few sprigs of flat-leaf parsley
outer leaf of a leek

FOR THE PARSNIP CRISPS
1 litre (1¾ pints) sunflower oil
2 parsnips

1 Preheat the oven to 200°C (400°F/Gas 6). Undo the trussing string on the grouse and remove the giblets (and set aside) and the wishbone. Wipe the birds inside and out with kitchen paper. Then season inside the cavity with salt and pepper. Mix the mushrooms, a few leaves of thyme taken from the sprigs for the bouquet garni, and 50g (1¾oz) of the butter in a bowl and use to stuff both the grouse.

2 Wrap the bacon around the birds, being careful to cover the breasts and legs. Secure with string. Then place on a rack in a roasting tin and roast in the centre of the oven for 25–35 minutes, depending on the size of the birds.

3 Remove the bacon from the grouse for the last 5 minutes roasting time, but leave it in the oven to go really crispy. Remove the bird and bacon from the oven and allow to rest for 5–10 minutes.

4 Meanwhile, start making the sauce. Put all the giblets, except the liver, into another saucepan, cover with water, and season with salt and pepper. Add a bouquet garni made by tying the carrot, celery, bay leaf, thyme, and parsley into the outer leaf of a leek. Bring to the boil, reduce the heat and let the contents simmer at the back of the hob while preparing the rest of the sauce.

5 Sweat the shallots in the butter for about 5 minutes, until well softened. Add half the bottle of Burgundy and the port and let the

sauce reduce until it is thick enough to coat the back of a spoon. Strain the giblet stock and boil rapidly to reduce by about three-quarters. Add this to the wine reduction, strain again and keep warm at the back of the hob.

6 Cut 4 thick slices of bread (about 2cm (¾in) thick) and remove the crusts. Place on a baking tray and put in the oven for about 15 minutes until dry and well browned. Break up about 100g (3½oz) of the remaining bread and blend to breadcrumbs in a food processor. Fry the breadcrumbs in 50g (1¾oz) of the butter for about 6 minutes until golden brown, drain on kitchen paper and set aside.

7 To cook the parsnip crisps, heat the sunflower oil in a deep saucepan until it reaches the temperature when a small piece of bread will instantly begin to brown and have little bubbles all around it. Peel the parsnips and use a peeler to peel off strips lengthways. Fry these strips in the hot oil for about 10 minutes until crisp and golden brown. Drain on kitchen paper and set aside.

8 Fry the grouse liver in 25g (scant 1oz) of butter until well cooked. Pound the liver with the remaining butter to which you have added a touch of Dijon mustard. Spread this pâté onto the toasts.

9 When the grouse has rested, remove the string from the birds, and cut off the legs. If the thigh meat is too rare, you can return the legs to the oven for a few minutes while you assemble the rest of the dish. Carefully carve off the breasts, keeping them whole.

10 Place a toast on each serving plate, pâté side up. Cover with a little of the mushroom stuffing, then one breast and one leg of the grouse, topped with a bacon rasher. Place a small bunch of watercress alongside together with a small sprig of redcurrants, if using, and a stack of parsnip chips to the other side. Coat the grouse with the red wine sauce, sprinkle with fried breadcrumbs and serve immediately.

POT ROAST PHEASANT, PARSNIP FRITTER, AND BEER SAUCE

inspired by **Jamie Barnett** chef de partie and 2009 Professionals quarter-finalist

15g (½oz) salted butter
1 tbsp olive oil
2 pheasants, ready to cook
1 onion, finely chopped
2 garlic cloves, sliced
4 rashers smoked streaky
  bacon, chopped
2 dessert apples, peeled, cored,
  and sliced
1 bay leaf
1 tbsp sage leaves, chopped
200ml (7fl oz) beer
1 tsp light soft brown sugar
salt and freshly ground black pepper
100ml (3½fl oz) double cream

FOR THE FRITTERS
500g (1lb 2oz) parsnips, peeled
  and grated
1 egg, beaten
4 tbsp plain flour
½ tsp baking powder
15g (½oz) salted butter
1 tbsp olive oil

PREPARATION TIME
30 minutes

COOKING TIME
1 hour 30 minutes

SERVES 4

1 For the pot roast, melt the butter with the oil in a flame-proof casserole large enough to contain the pheasants – you will need to be able to put the lid on. Add the pheasants to the casserole and brown on all sides, then remove and set aside. Add the onion and garlic to the oil and butter and fry for a few minutes to soften, then add the bacon and brown slightly. Now toss in the apple slices and herbs, mix well and stir in the beer and sugar before placing the browned pheasants, breast-side down, back into the pan, nestling them down well. Season, then bring to the boil and place the lid on the pan. Turn the heat down to low and cook for about 1 hour, turning the pheasants the other way up halfway through cooking.

2 To make the fritters, put the parsnips in a mixing bowl and stir in the beaten egg, then the flour, baking powder, and some salt and pepper. Heat the butter and oil in a frying pan and fry tablespoons of the parsnip mixture for about 5 minutes before turning and cooking for a further 3 minutes on the other side, or until golden and crispy.

3 Now return to the pot-roast and finish off the sauce. Check that the pheasants are cooked through, and remove them to a warmed plate for carving. Stir the cream into the sauce and check the seasoning; simmer for about 2 minutes. Serve the pheasant slices on a bed of the apple and bacon, with the fritters on the side and the beer sauce spooned over the top.

TEA-INFUSED VENISON WITH PICKLED RED CABBAGE, ROAST POTATOES, AND A RICH PORT SAUCE

James Nathan barrister turned chef and 2008 champion

PREPARATION TIME
45 minutes, plus marinating time

COOKING TIME
1 hour 30 minutes

SERVES 4

4 venison steaks (see MasterTip, p.272), about 150g (5½oz) each
1 tbsp Lapsang Souchong tea leaves
finely grated zest of 1 navel orange
4 tbsp olive oil

FOR THE PICKLED RED CABBAGE
2 tbsp olive oil
500g (1lb 2oz) red cabbage, finely chopped
1 tbsp redcurrant jelly
3–4 tbsp red wine vinegar

FOR THE PORT SAUCE
3 tbsp olive oil
100g (3½oz) smoked streaky bacon, finely chopped

4 carrots, finely chopped
8 large banana shallots, finely chopped
1 tbsp redcurrant jelly
75cl bottle ruby port
1 tbsp finely chopped thyme
75cl bottle red Bordeaux
squeeze of lemon juice
2 tsp plain flour (optional)

FOR THE ROAST POTATOES
6 King Edward potatoes (see MasterTip, p.197), peeled and chopped
3 tbsp goose fat

1 Pound the tea leaves to a dust in a pestle and mortar. Add the orange zest and pour the oil over the mixture. Rub this into the meat, wrap in cling film and leave to marinate for 1–2 hours in the fridge.
2 Preheat the oven to 180°C (350°F/Gas 4). To make the pickled red cabbage, heat the oil in an ovenproof dish with a tight-fitting lid. Add the cabbage with the redcurrant jelly and fry until the sugars from the jelly start to catch. Then deglaze with the red wine vinegar, cover with a lid, and put in the oven to cook for about 30 minutes until the cabbage is tender. Remove from the oven and keep warm.
3 Meanwhile, for the port sauce, heat 2 tbsp of the oil in a large saucepan. Fry the bacon, carrots, and shallots for about 15 minutes or until golden brown. Add the redcurrant jelly, then deglaze the pan with the ruby port. Add the thyme and reduce until most of the liquid has evaporated, regularly removing any scum from the sauce.
4 Add the red wine and reduce to the same point again. Strain the sauce and return to a clean pan. Season with salt and pepper and the lemon juice to taste. The sauce should be thick enough to coat the back of a spoon. If it is not thick enough, make a thin paste with 2 tsp of plain flour and some olive oil, then stir this into the sauce with a whisk and boil again to thicken. Keep warm until required.

5 For the roast potatoes, turn the oven up to 200°C (400°F/Gas 6). Parboil the potatoes for 10 minutes, then drain and roughen the edges by shaking in a dry pan. Heat the goose fat in a roasting tin in the oven. Add the potatoes and spoon the fat over. Roast in the oven for 45 minutes until golden brown.

6 To cook the meat, remove the steaks from the cling film and wipe off as many of the tea leaves from the meat as possible. Heat an ovenproof pan on a high heat and sear the meat well all over. Transfer to the oven for 3–5 minutes until springy to the touch. Rest for 10 minutes before serving.

7 Serve the meat sliced on a bed of red cabbage with roast potatoes and the rich port sauce.

ROASTED RACK OF VENISON WITH GRAND VENEUR SAUCE AND ROOT VEGETABLES

Andi Peters presenter and producer and 2008 Celebrity finalist

PREPARATION TIME
20 minutes

COOKING TIME
50 minutes

SERVES 4

900g (2lb) 8-bone venison rack, French trimmed (see MasterTip, p.203), with the trimmings reserved
2 tbsp olive oil
25g (scant 1oz) stale white breadcrumbs
1 tbsp chopped thyme
1 tbsp chopped rosemary
1 tbsp Dijon mustard

FOR THE ROOT VEGETABLES
2 parsnips, peeled and finely diced
2 carrots, finely diced
150g (5½oz) celeriac, finely diced
2 small turnips, finely diced
2 tbsp olive oil
salt and freshly ground black pepper

FOR THE GRAND VENEUR SAUCE
25g (scant 1oz) butter
20g (¾oz) diced carrot
1 shallot, chopped
1 celery stick, finely chopped
20g (¾oz) chopped leek
sprig of thyme
1 bay leaf
8 black peppercorns
20g (¾oz) tomato purée
2 tbsp red wine vinegar
250ml (8fl oz) dry red wine
120ml (4fl oz) hot water
1 tbsp redcurrant jelly
1 tbsp double cream
1 tsp butter

1 Preheat the oven to 200°C (400°F/Gas 6). To roast the vegetables, place them in a roasting tin and pour over the oil, season well and toss to coat with oil. Roast in the oven for 45–50 minutes, turning over once or twice during cooking to ensure browning on all sides.
2 Season the venison rack and heat half the oil in a large frying pan. When hot, add the rack and sear for 3 minutes on each side. Transfer to a roasting tin, bone-side down, and cook in the oven for 10 minutes.
3 Meanwhile, toast the breadcrumbs in the oven for 5–7 minutes, turning once to ensure even browning. Then blend in a food processor with the thyme, rosemary, seasoning, and the remaining oil.
4 Remove the venison from the oven and brush with mustard, avoiding the bones. Then roll in the crumb mix, return to the oven and cook for 8 minutes for medium. Remove from the oven and let the meat rest.
5 To make the sauce, melt the butter in a casserole dish. Add the vegetables and leave to sweat for 5 minutes. Mix in the thyme, bay, peppercorns, and tomato purée and cook for 4 minutes. Deglaze the pan with the vinegar and reduce until almost dry. Add the wine and reduce by half. Then add the water and reduce again until the sauce coats the back of a spoon. Remove the herbs and strain the sauce. To finish, gently whisk in the redcurrant jelly, double cream, and butter.
6 To serve, carve the rack into 4 pieces. Arrange on a bed of the roasted root vegetables and finish by pouring over the sauce.

FALLOW VENISON, WITH ROAST SQUASH, POTATOES, AND BABY TURNIPS IN GRAVY

Harriet Jenkins food marketer and 2007 semi-finalist

PREPARATION TIME
15 minutes

COOKING TIME
30 minutes

SERVES 4

400–500g (14oz–1lb 2oz) venison loin
170ml (5½fl oz) vegetable oil
1 small butternut squash, peeled and
 diced into 5cm (2in) cubes
12 baby turnips, trimmed
2 sprigs of thyme
salt and freshly ground black pepper

4 large Desirée potatoes, peeled and
 chopped into 5cm (2in) cubes
knob of butter
salt and freshly ground black pepper
60ml (2fl oz) chicken or game stock
 (see MasterTips, p.21 and p.275)
60ml (2fl oz) red wine
2 tbsp rowanberry jelly

MASTER TIP

VENISON

Venison is very lean meat and needs to be hung for 3–10 days to tenderize and develop its gamey flavour. Look for dark red meat with a firm texture and fine grain. Venison is not marbled like beef and there should be some firm, white fat under the skin. Fallow venison is lighter in colour, finer in texture, and has a milder flavour than other types of venison. The most tender cuts are from the loin and haunch and are best served pink. Other cuts benefit from plenty of marinating and slow cooking.

1 Preheat the oven to 200°C (400°F/Gas 6). Put 60ml (2fl oz) of the vegetable oil in a roasting tin and heat in the oven until just below smoking point. Place the squash, turnips, and thyme in the tin, season and toss to coat with the oil. Roast in the oven for about 30 minutes, until crisp and tender.

2 Meanwhile, bring a pan of salted water to the boil, and add the potatoes. Parboil for 6–10 minutes until tender, but firm. Drain and add to the squash and turnips, tossing together to coat in oil. Roast for the remaining 15–20 minutes until crispy but holding their shape.

3 In a frying pan or skillet, heat 2 tbsp of the vegetable oil and the butter until just below smoking point. Season the venison with salt and pepper and add to the pan and sear for 1–2 minutes on all sides until sealed. Put the venison in a roasting tin and place in the oven for 15 minutes. When the loin is cooked to medium-rare it should be springy but not soft to the touch. Remove the venison from the oven and let it rest for at least 10 minutes. Meanwhile, transfer the pan juices to a frying pan.

4 Heat the juices in the frying pan, add the stock and wine and, using a balloon whisk, deglaze the pan and reduce the gravy by two-thirds. Whisk in the rowanberry jelly and continue to whisk until a thick sauce has developed. Remove from the heat.

5 To assemble the dish, slice the venison into 2.5cm (1in) thick slices (about 3 to 4 pieces per person). Reserve any juices and stir into the gravy. When crispy, remove the roasted vegetables from the oven. Using a slotted spoon, remove from the oil, drain briefly on kitchen paper and then arrange between 4 plates. Place 3 to 4 pieces of venison on each plate, slightly overlapping each other, and finish with a liberal amount of gravy. As a final flourish, you could garnish with a sprig of roasted thyme.

VENISON WITH A PINK PEPPERCORN SAUCE, CAVALO NERO, AND DAUPHINOISE POTATOES

Craig Revel Horwood choreographer and 2007 Celebrity finalist

4 thick venison steaks (see MasterTip, opposite), about 150g (5½oz) each
2 tbsp olive oil
150g (5½oz) onion, chopped
1 small carrot, chopped
1 celery stick, chopped
2 bay leaves
450ml (15fl oz) red wine
450ml (15fl oz) chicken or game stock (see MasterTips, p.21 and p.275)
2 tsp softened pink peppercorns
15g (½oz) unsalted butter

300g (10oz) cavalo nero, chopped
garlic and chilli oil, to serve (optional) (see MasterTip, right)

FOR THE DAUPHINOISE POTATOES
500ml (16fl oz) double cream
2 garlic cloves
2 bay leaves
500g (1lb 2oz) floury potatoes (see MasterTip, p.197), peeled
100g (3½oz) Gruyère cheese, grated
salt, freshly ground black pepper, and nutmeg

PREPARATION TIME
20 minutes

COOKING TIME
50 minutes

SERVES 4

1 Preheat the oven to 180°C (350°F/Gas 4). Butter a 23cm (9in) square ovenproof dish.

2 To make the Dauphinoise potatoes, put the cream, garlic, and bay leaves in a saucepan, bring to the boil and then remove from the heat and leave to cool slightly. Cut the potatoes into thin slices, about 3mm (⅛in) thick, and place in the buttered dish with 75g (2½oz) of the Gruyère cheese and season with salt, pepper, and nutmeg.

3 Remove the bay leaves and garlic from the cream and pour the cream over the potatoes. Sprinkle over the remaining cheese and bake for 50 minutes, until the potatoes are tender and golden brown.

4 Season the venison with salt and pepper and heat 1 tbsp of the olive oil in a frying pan. Cook the venison for 3–4 minutes on each side and then remove from the pan and leave to rest.

5 Heat the remaining olive oil in a medium-sized saucepan and fry the onion, carrot, and celery and cook for 5 minutes or until the onion is soft. Add the bay leaves and gradually add the red wine. Bring to the boil and simmer until it has reduced by half. Add the stock and continue to simmer for a further 10 minutes. Strain and then use to deglaze the frying pan. Finally, add the pink peppercorns and cook for 1 minute. Whisk in the butter until a smooth sauce is achieved.

6 Meanwhile, steam the cavalo nero for 5 minutes or until tender and then season with salt and pepper.

7 To serve, slice the venison and put on large plates with a portion of dauphinoise potatoes and steamed cavalo nero. Drizzle over the sauce and serve the chilli and garlic oil, if using, on the outside rim of the plate.

MASTER TIP

GARLIC AND CHILLI OIL

As a final flourish, drizzle some garlic and chilli oil around the assembled plates. To make, warm 2 garlic cloves and a green chilli in 4 tbsp olive oil in a small saucepan so the oil becomes infused with their flavours. Set the saucepan aside until needed.

VENISON LOIN WITH ROSTIS, WATERCRESS PURÉE, AND ROASTED BEETROOT

Steve Groves chef de partie and 2009 Professionals champion

PREPARATION TIME
1 hour

COOKING TIME
1 hour

SERVES 4

600g (1lb 5oz) piece of venison loin
 (see MasterTip, p.272)
3 tbsp olive oil
25g (scant 1oz) salted butter

FOR THE VENISON JUS
300g (10oz) venison trim
1 shallot, chopped
1 garlic clove, crushed
200ml (7fl oz) red wine
750ml (1¼ pints) game stock (see
 MasterTip, opposite)
1 bay leaf
2 sprigs of thyme

FOR THE POTATO ROSTIS
2 baking potatoes (see
 MasterTip, p.197)
25g (scant 1oz) salted butter

FOR THE WATERCRESS PURÉE
100g (3½oz) watercress leaves
2 tbsp chicken stock (see
 MasterTip, p.21)
salt and freshly ground
 black pepper

FOR THE BEETROOT
5 baby beetroot, peeled
3 tbsp balsamic vinegar
25g (scant 1oz) light soft brown sugar
knob of butter

FOR THE ROASTED ONIONS
25g (scant 1oz) salted butter, melted
pinch of salt
pinch of caster sugar
8 baby onions, skins left on and cut
 in half through the root

1 To make the venison jus, fry the venison trim in a saucepan for about 10 minutes until a deep brown. Remove from the pan, drain, and set aside. Then add the shallot and garlic to the pan and fry until golden, scraping the bottom of the pan to release the stuck-on venison flavour.
2 Deglaze the pan with the wine, then reduce until almost entirely evaporated. Add the stock, bay leaf, and thyme and return the venison trim. Simmer gently for around 1 hour, skimming regularly. Pass through muslin and, for the best results, chill overnight so it sets and any fat can be easily removed. Otherwise, return to a clean saucepan and reduce rapidly until it starts to become glossy and a deep flavour is achieved.
3 Preheat the oven to 180°C (350°F/Gas 4). To cook the venison, heat the oil in a roasting tin, add the venison and seal for 1–2 minutes on each side, and then add the butter. Baste and cook in the oven for 15 minutes for a medium-rare finish. Remove from the oven and rest for at least 5 minutes before carving. Keep the oven turned on for the roasted onions.
4 To make the potato rostis, parboil the potatoes in their skins for 10 minutes, allow to cool slightly, then peel and grate coarsely. Heat the butter in a large, non-stick frying pan and make 4 piles of the

grated potato in the pan. Flatten and cook for about 4 minutes on each side until the rostis are golden.

5 For the watercress purée, blanch the watercress in boiling water for 1 minute, then refresh in cold for 5 minutes. Transfer the watercress to a food processor and blend, adding the 2 tbsp of stock to make a relatively coarse purée that will hold its shape. Check the seasoning and keep warm.

6 To cook the beetroot, place the beetroot, vinegar, and sugar in a small saucepan and add enough water to cover the beetroot. Bring to the boil and then simmer for about 20 minutes until the beetroot are tender. Remove the beetroot and reduce the cooking liquor to a glaze with a consistency to coat the back of a wooden spoon. Whisk in the butter, then return the beetroot and check the seasoning.

7 For the roasted onions, take a small, ovenproof frying pan and, while cold, cover the bottom of the pan with about 1mm (1/16in) of the melted butter and sprinkle with salt and sugar. Place the onions, cut-side down, onto this, put on a medium-high heat and cook for 12–15 minutes, or until the onions are golden. Transfer to the oven for about 5 minutes until soft. Remove the onions from their skins before serving.

8 To serve, pool the plates with the sauce, and top with the rostis. Carve the venison and place on top of the rostis and position some onions and beetroot next to the venison. Finish with a spoonful of the watercress purée.

MASTER TIP
GAME STOCK

Making your own game stock is simple and adds to the flavour of dishes. Preheat the oven to 220°C (425°F/Gas 7) and roast 1kg (2¼lb) game bones and meat with 2 tbsp olive oil for 30 minutes. Remove from the oven, transfer to large saucepan and add 2 litres (3½ pints) water together with 1 carrot, 1 celery stick, 1 onion, 1 leek, and 2 garlic cloves, all chopped. Also add 5 juniper berries, 5 peppercorns, 1 bay leaf, and 1 sprig of thyme and flat-leaf parsley. Bring to the boil, remove any scum that rises to the top, then reduce the heat and let simmer for 3 hours, skimming regularly and adding more water as necessary. Strain into a bowl and remove any fat by blotting kitchen paper over the top. Store in a fridge for 2–3 days or freeze until ready to use.

SEARED SADDLE OF VENISON WITH A PORT AND BALSAMIC REDUCTION

Becky McCracken teacher and 2006 semi-finalist

PREPARATION TIME
15 minutes

COOKING TIME
35 minutes

SERVES 4

4 venison steaks from the saddle
  (see MasterTip, p.272), about 150g
  (5½oz) each
1 tbsp olive oil
50g (1¾oz) salted butter
2 tbsp port
1 tbsp balsamic vinegar
75ml (2½fl oz) chicken or game stock
  (see MasterTips, p.21 and p.275)
mixed salad leaves, to serve

FOR THE ROASTED BUTTERNUT SQUASH MASH
1 small butternut squash, peeled
  and cut into 5cm (2in) cubes
salt and freshly ground black pepper
2 tbsp olive oil
25g (scant 1oz) butter

1 Preheat the oven to 200°C (400°F/Gas 6). Place the butternut squash into a roasting tin, season with salt and pepper and coat with the olive oil. Roast in the oven for about 30 minutes, until crisp and tender. Then mash with the butter and keep warm.

2 To cook the venison, heat the olive oil and half of the butter in a frying pan. Sear the venison on each side and cook to taste as you would a fillet steak (about 3 minutes a side for medium rare). Set aside to rest.

3 Add the port, balsamic vinegar, and stock to the same frying pan, and reduce until the liquid is bubbling away and about half the volume. Take off the heat and stir in the remaining butter.

4 Put the venison steaks on serving plates and add a quenelle (see MasterTip, p.93) of roasted butternut squash mash and some mixed salad leaves. Drizzle the balsamic reduction around the edge.

ROAST SADDLE OF WILD VENISON, SAVOY CABBAGE, ROAST POTATOES, CELERIAC, AND A BEETROOT JUS

Derek Johnstone junior sous chef and 2008 Professionals champion

PREPARATION TIME
40 minutes

COOKING TIME
1 hour

SERVES 4

4 venison steaks from the saddle
(see MasterTip, p.272), about 200g
(7oz) each, boned and trimmed free
of any sinew
1 tbsp olive oil
salt and freshly ground black pepper
15g (½oz) salted butter

FOR THE ROAST POTATOES
4 Desirée potatoes, weighing about
200g (7oz) each, peeled
1 tbsp olive oil

FOR THE BEETROOT JUS
duck or other animal bones (optional)
1 tbsp olive oil
150g (5½oz) onions, finely chopped
75g (2½oz) carrots, finely chopped
75g (2½oz) celery, finely chopped
150ml (5fl oz) red wine

30g (1oz) redcurrant jelly
sprig of thyme
1 garlic clove, chopped
600ml (1 pint) game stock
(see MasterTip, p.275)
10g (¼oz) salted butter
2 cooked beetroot, finely diced

FOR THE CELERIAC
½ celeriac, weighing about 175g (6oz),
finely diced
25g (scant 1oz) butter

FOR THE SAVOY CABBAGE
50g (1¾oz) salted butter
½ Savoy cabbage, about 400g (14oz),
cored and finely shredded
20g (¾oz) pine nuts
20g (¾oz) sesame seeds
white pepper

1 Preheat the oven to 190°C (375°F/Gas 5). For the roast potatoes, halve each potato and cut each half into a 7-sided barrel shape. Parboil in a saucepan of salted water for 4–5 minutes, then drain. Place on a baking tray, drizzle with the oil, then cook in the oven for 25–30 minutes or until golden. Season and keep warm.

2 Meanwhile, start on the beetroot jus. Preheat a frying pan until hot then add the bones, if using, and oil and pan-fry for 3–4 minutes or until well browned. Then add the onions, carrots, and celery and cook over a high heat for 3–5 minutes or until softened.

3 Add the wine and redcurrant jelly and reduce to a sticky glaze. Add the thyme, garlic, and stock and boil for 8–10 minutes to reduce to a consistency that coats the back of a wooden spoon. Strain, return to the pan and heat for 1 minute. Then whisk in the butter to thicken slightly. Stir in the beetroot and heat for a further minute. Keep warm.

4 Meanwhile, place the celeriac in a saucepan, add just enough cold salted water to cover and add the butter. Cook for 8–10 minutes or until very tender and all of the water has evaporated. Set aside and keep warm.

5 Reduce the oven to 180°C (350°F/Gas 4). Oil and season the venison with salt and pepper. Heat an ovenproof frying pan until hot, then sear the venison for 2–3 minutes on each side or until well sealed and golden brown. Add the butter to baste the venison and cook in the oven for 6–10 minutes for a medium-rare finish. Remove from the oven and allow to rest.

6 For the Savoy cabbage, heat the butter in a frying pan, add the cabbage and sauté for 3–4 minutes over a high heat or until tender. Add the nuts and seeds, sauté for a further 1 minute and season with salt and white pepper.

7 To serve, slice the venison and put on serving plates with the roast potatoes, celeriac, and cabbage. Pour over the beetroot jus.

RABBIT SADDLE AND LANGOUSTINE MOUSSELINE WITH A CARROT, LEMONGRASS, AND GINGER PURÉE

Emily Ludolf 18-year-old student and 2008 finalist

PREPARATION TIME
45 minutes, plus chilling time

COOKING TIME
30 minutes

SERVES 4

1 small rabbit saddle, bones removed
1 tsp olive oil
1 tbsp unsalted butter

FOR THE LANGOUSTINE MOUSSELINE
10 jumbo raw langoustines, peeled
salt and freshly ground black pepper
1 egg white
100ml (3½fl oz) double cream
½ tsp Manzanilla sherry

FOR THE CARDAMOM BEURRE BLANC
8–10 green cardamom pods, split
1–2 tbsp boiling water
100ml (3½fl oz) double cream
100g (3½oz) unsalted butter

FOR THE PEAR SALAD
2 pears
squeeze of lemon juice
220g can water chestnuts, drained
 and chestnuts finely chopped
2 tsp rapeseed oil
few drops of verjus (see MasterTip, below)
handful of tatsoi leaves and mixed red
 and green microgreens (see MasterTip,
 opposite), or baby spinach leaves

FOR THE CARROT, LEMONGRASS, AND GINGER PURÉE
2 stalks lemongrass
400g (14oz) carrots, finely sliced
100ml (3½fl oz) double cream
100ml (3½fl oz) whole milk
60g (2oz) unsalted butter
2cm (¾in) piece fresh ginger root,
 finely grated

MASTER TIP
VERJUS

Verjus is a sour juice that was widely used in medieval European cookery and is still a mainstay of some French dishes. It is made from crushed and filtered young grapes or crab apples or other unripe fruit. This "green juice" (as its name translates) has a delicate aroma and can be used as an alternative to vinegar or lemon juice.

1 For the langoustine mousseline, blanch the langoustines for a couple of seconds in boiling, lightly salted water. Drain and place in a blender and process to a purée, adding a little salt and pepper. Spoon into a bowl and set aside, covered, to chill in the fridge.

2 Once chilled, spoon the purée back into the blender and blend again with the egg white. Leave to chill once more in the fridge. Return once more to the blender and combine with the cream and Manzanilla. Transfer to a bowl, cover, and chill overnight.

3 For the beurre blanc, place the cardamom in the boiling water and leave to infuse until cool. Strain into a pan, add the cream, bring to the boil and boil for 1–2 minutes or until reduced by about half. Beat in the butter, a bit at a time. Keep warm, but do not let it boil.

4 Fill a large bowl with ice cubes and then stand a smaller mixing bowl over the ice. Force the langoustine purée through a fine sieve into the bowl and incorporate enough of the cardamom beurre blanc, a little at a time, until the mousseline has a thick, silky, homogeneous texture. Spoon the mixture into a piping bag fitted with a plain nozzle.

5 For the pear and water chestnut salad, peel and finely chop the pears, squeeze over some lemon juice to prevent browning, and mix with the chopped water chestnuts in a bowl. Add the rapeseed oil and verjus. Add the tatsoi leaves and microgreens, or baby spinach leaves, to the bowl and mix until well coated.

6 For the carrot, lemongrass, and ginger purée, finely grate the lemongrass, but take care not to include the fibrous stalks. Place the carrots in a large shallow pan filled with the double cream and milk and half of the butter. Cover and simmer gently for 5–8 minutes or until the carrots are tender. Remove 8 of the most attractive carrot slices from the pan and set aside.

7 Using a hand-blender, blend the remainder of the carrots with the cream mixture that they were cooked in. Add the lemongrass and ginger and season with salt and pepper to taste. Blend again until very smooth. Keep warm. Heat the remaining butter in a frying pan, add the reserved carrot slices and pan-fry until lightly golden brown on all sides.

8 For the rabbit saddle, carefully pipe some of the langoustine mousseline (saving some for garnish) into the centre of the rabbit saddle, roll the saddle to enclose and tie into a cylinder with string.

9 Heat the olive oil and butter in a large frying pan until hot, add the rabbit, season with salt and pepper and fry for 3–5 minutes or until browned all over on a medium heat. Reduce the heat slightly and fry for a further 10 minutes or until cooked all the way through.

10 Remove the saddle from the pan, cover, and set aside to rest for 5 minutes. Place the pan back onto the heat and cook the juices until thickened slightly. Use these to glaze the resting rabbit saddle with a pastry brush. Let the rabbit rest for about another 10 minutes and then carefully remove the string and cut the saddle into thick slices.

11 To serve, use the back of a spoon to swirl the carrot purée onto 4 plates and scatter the salad over the top. Place the rabbit slices over the purée. Take the pan-fried carrot slices and trim to make long, even rectangles. Place on the plates around the rabbit and pipe the langoustine mousseline across the centre.

MASTER TIPS

TATSOI LEAVES AND MICROGREENS

Tatsoi leaves are one of the most popular of Oriental greens. They are related to bok choi and have thick, spoon-shaped leaves.

Microgreens are seedlings of various salad greens, herbs, edible flowers, and leafy vegetables that are harvested after they form their first true leaves. Sprouts (see MasterTip, p.102) are grown in water, but microgreens are grown in soil and their flavour is intense. They can also be very colourful, making them the perfect garnish or stand-alone salad. You can grow them at any time of year on your windowsill – they are available as kits or packets of seeds. The most popular microgreens are cress, purple and black radish, red and white cabbage, red kale, kohl rabi, and pak choi.

JOHN TORODE "I think the rabbit is great and the carrot is well seasoned and well done – and the herbs are fantastic. It is a seriously exciting dish."

STARTERS
VEGETABLES & FISH
POULTRY
MEAT
GAME
DESSERTS

CRANACHAN
Hardeep Singh Kohli comedian and broadcaster and 2006 Celebrity finalist

PREPARATION TIME
20 minutes

SERVES 4

225g (8oz) raspberries
90ml (3fl oz) peaty whisky such as Islay
100g (3½oz) demerara sugar
175g (6oz) medium oatmeal
 or porridge oats
200ml (8fl oz) double cream

1 Put the raspberries in a bowl, pour the whisky over them and leave to macerate for 30 minutes.
2 Put a large frying pan on a high heat and add the sugar and oatmeal or porridge oats. As the sugar melts, mix it in with the oats so that they are coated with soft, hot sugar that caramelizes. Take care with the heat – some oats will burn a little, but the rest should be a lovely, sweet, oaty mix. Turn this out onto a lightly greased tray and allow to cool.
3 Meanwhile, beat the double cream until it forms soft peaks. Once the oats have cooled, run a fork through them to break down any big lumps, but don't try to achieve a uniform size. Gently fold into the double cream, trying not to knock the air out of it – have patience waiting for the oats to cool as if they are hot they will warm the cream and make it lose its volume.
4 Place the whisky-flavoured raspberries in the bottom of a trifle bowl, reserving half a dozen or so. Now spoon the creamy, oaty, sugary mix on top and decorate with the reserved raspberries. Serve with a wee dram of whisky.

RASPBERRY AND POMEGRANATES WITH RASPBERRY SABAYON SAUCE

Mat Follas engineer turned chef patron and 2009 champion

1 pomegranate
200g (7oz) raspberries
1 tbsp basil, chopped
3 large egg yolks
100g (3½oz) golden caster sugar
3 tbsp crème de framboise

PREPARATION TIME
15 minutes

COOKING TIME
10 minutes

SERVES 4

1 First remove the pomegranate seeds. Cut the crown end off the pomegranate and discard. Lightly score the rind from top to bottom 5–6 times around the fruit, but don't cut all the way through. Soak the fruit in cold water upside down for 5 minutes. Holding the fruit under water in a bowl to prevent the juice from spattering, break the sections apart. The seeds will sink to the bottom of the bowl, while the rind and membrane will float. Strain off the rind and membrane using a slotted spoon. Drain the seeds and then pat dry. Crush them slightly in a bowl to release their juice.

2 Mix the raspberries, pomegranate seeds, and basil together and spoon into the base of 4 martini glasses.

3 To make the sauce, put the egg yolks and sugar in a large bowl and whisk until pale and thick, using a hand-held electric beater. Add the crème de framboise and place the bowl over a saucepan of gently simmering water, making sure the water does not touch the base of the bowl. Continue whisking for at least 10 minutes, until the mixture is pale, very foamy and the texture of thick custard. It should have increased in volume dramatically. Pour the sauce over the fruit and serve while warm.

MASTER TIP

CRÈME DE FRAMBOISE

One of a wide range of fruit liqueurs, crème de framboise is made by infusing or macerating raspberries in alcohol. In spite of the name, it contains no cream; "crème" signifies that it is a sweetened, thick liqueur with a rather syrupy consistency.

HAZELNUT AND RASPBERRY MERINGUE

Nadia Sawalha actress and presenter and 2007 Celebrity champion

PREPARATION TIME
20 minutes

COOKING TIME
40 minutes

SERVES 4

115g (4oz) whole shelled hazelnuts
4 large egg whites
250g (9oz) caster sugar
1 tsp vanilla extract
1 tbsp raspberry vinegar
300ml (10fl oz) double cream
200g (7oz) fresh raspberries
icing sugar, to dust

1 Preheat the oven to 160°C (325°F/Gas 3). Butter a 20cm (8in) sandwich tin and line with non-stick baking parchment.

2 Halve and dry fry the hazelnuts until lightly toasted, reserving a few.

3 Whisk the egg whites until stiff. Add the sugar 1 tbsp at a time and continue beating until the mixture is very stiff and stands in peaks. Whisk in the vanilla extract and vinegar, then fold in the hazelnuts.

4 Transfer to the sandwich tin. Alternatively, make individual portions by placing dollops of the meringue mix straight on to baking parchment, forming a slight hollow for the filling. Bake in the oven for 20–30 minutes, or until lightly browned and holding its shape. Leave to cool in the tin for 10 minutes then transfer to a serving dish.

5 Whip the cream and pile onto the centre of the meringue when it is completely cold. Place the raspberries. Finely chop the reserved hazelnuts and sprinkle over. Dust with icing sugar just before serving.

MASTER TIP

MAKING MERINGUES

The trick to making successful meringues is to ensure that the consistency of the egg whites is correct. Dip your fingertips in the whites; when you remove them, the whites should hang from your fingers in the hooked shape of a bird's beak.

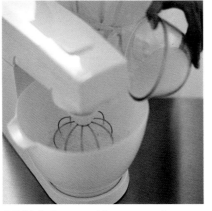

1 Whisk the egg whites on medium speed, adding sugar 1 tbsp at a time.

2 Whisk until the egg whites are firm, shiny and smooth.

SUMMER FRUIT COMPOTE WITH SCENTED CREAM

Helen Gilmour 2007 quarter-finalist

PREPARATION TIME
10 minutes

COOKING TIME
15 minutes

SERVES 4

1 punnet each of blueberries, raspberries, strawberries, blackberries, totalling about 675g (1½lb)
1–2 tbsp caster sugar
1½–2 tbsp rosewater
2 tbsp Greek-style yogurt
250g (9oz) mascarpone cheese

1 Preheat the oven to 190°C (350°F/Gas 6).

2 Place the berries in a baking dish. Sprinkle with caster sugar to taste and bake in the oven for 10 minutes, or 15 minutes if they are taken straight from the fridge – the berries should just be beginning to ooze their juice. Remove from the oven, chill the berries over iced water, and place in the fridge to cool.

3 In a small bowl, mix the rosewater and 2 tsp sugar to dissolve the sugar. In a separate bowl, mix the yogurt with the mascarpone. Mix the rosewater and sugar with the mascarpone, adding it slowly to avoid it splitting.

4 Serve the berries in large wine glasses, topped with a good spoonful of the scented cream.

SUMMER PUDDING KIR ROYALE

Hardeep Singh Kohli comedian and broadcaster and 2006 Celebrity finalist

750g (1lb 10oz) mixed summer berries, such as blackcurrants, strawberries (hulled), raspberries, blueberries, and blackberries
120ml (4fl oz) Champagne or prosecco
about 2 tbsp caster sugar

9 slices slightly stale sliced white bread, crusts removed

FOR THE GRANITA
300g (10oz) caster sugar
600ml (1 pint) Champagne or prosecco

PREPARATION TIME
30 minutes, plus setting time

SERVES 4

1 Heat the berries, Champagne, and sugar very gently in a pan – you need just enough heat to release the juice from the berries. Stir carefully, allowing a few berries to burst. Take off the heat and immediately strain, retaining both fruit and juice. Leave to cool.
2 Line a 1.2 litre (2 pint) pudding basin with bread dipped in juice (see MasterTip, below). Spoon in the berries and cover with more dipped bread to make a lid. Place a small plate on top and weigh down with a couple of cans of beans. Allow to set in the fridge for at least 8 hours.
3 To make the granita, heat 600ml (1 pint) water and the sugar in a pan and stir until the sugar has dissolved. Leave to cool. Stir in the Champagne, pour into a freezerproof container and place in the freezer. When starting to freeze break up any ice crystals that have formed with a whisk. Return to the freezer for another hour and whisk again until you have a soft, icy mixture.
4 To serve, turn out the pudding onto a plate. Serve portions of the pudding with a Champagne glass of granita on the side.

MASTER TIP

MAKING SUMMER PUDDING

A long-time favourite, summer pudding is easy to prepare. The bread absorbs the juices from the fruit, taking on their flavour completely and providing just enough texture and shape to contain the soft fruit. The version here gains some extra luxury from the inclusion of Champagne or prosecco.

1 Stir the berries with the sugar and Champagne or prosecco, taking care not to let the mixture boil.

2 Cut a circle of bread to fit the base of the bowl and triangles to line the sides. Dip both sides in the juice.

BLACK AND REDCURRANT FOOL WITH GINGER BISCUITS

Peter Thompson energy consultant and 2007 quarter-finalist

PREPARATION TIME
10 minutes

COOKING TIME
30 minutes

SERVES 4

FOR THE GINGER BISCUITS
100g (3½oz) plain flour
1 tsp baking powder
pinch of salt
½ tsp ground cinnamon
2 tsp ground ginger
½ tsp freshly grated nutmeg
50g (1¾oz) light soft brown sugar
50g (1¾oz) crystallized ginger,
  finely chopped
50g (1¾oz) unsalted butter, softened
1 tbsp milk

FOR THE FOOL
300g (10oz) redcurrants, plus extra
  to decorate
300g (10oz) blackcurrants
few drops of lemon juice
2 tbsp caster sugar
400ml (14fl oz) double cream, whipped
200g (7oz) Greek-style yogurt

1 Preheat the oven to 150°C (300°F/Gas 2). Grease 2 baking sheets.
2 To make the ginger biscuits, place all the ingredients except the butter and milk in a food processor and mix together. Add the butter and milk and work together to a smooth dough.
3 Roll the dough into a sausage and chill for 20 minutes before slicing into 5mm (¼in) thick biscuits (should make about 16 of them). Place on the baking sheets and bake in the oven for 20 minutes or until golden.
4 For the fool, lightly poach the fruit in separate pans with a little water and lemon juice and sugar (1 tbsp in each). Poach for 6–8 minutes. The fruit should remain recognisable and not a mush. It should also be reasonably sharp.
5 In a bowl, fold together the whipped cream and yogurt.
6 In each of 4 glasses, layer the black and redcurrants separately, intercut by the cream so that all 3 colours are visible. Serve with the reserved redcurrants and 2 biscuits per person, which should add the necessary sweetness. Store the remaining biscuits for a few days in an airtight container.

MARBLED WINTER FRUIT FOOL

Liz McClarnon singer and 2008 Celebrity champion

PREPARATION TIME
10 minutes, plus marinating time

COOKING TIME
10 minutes

SERVES 4

150g (5½oz) ready-to-eat dried peaches
150g (5½oz) ready-to-eat stoned prunes
2 tbsp brandy, plus extra to serve
300ml (10fl oz) orange juice
150ml (5fl oz) whipping cream
150g (5½oz) plain low-fat yogurt

1 Cut 30g (1oz) of the peaches and 30g (1oz) of the prunes into small diced shapes. Put into a bowl, pour over the brandy, and set aside to marinate for 30 minutes.

2 Place the remaining peaches and prunes in 2 separate saucepans and pour 100ml (3½fl oz) of the orange juice into each. Bring to the boil, then reduce the heat and simmer gently for 10 minutes, or until the fruit is tender.

3 Purée the peaches and prunes separately in a blender or food processor until smooth, adding half of the remaining orange juice to each of the purées.

4 Whip the cream in a mixing bowl until thick. Add the yogurt and whip to mix with the cream.

5 Layer alternate spoonfuls of the peach purée, prune purée, and cream mixture into 4 slim glasses, swirling slightly for a marbled effect. Squeeze the marinated fruit of excess alcohol and place on top of each dessert. Just before serving, spoon the smallest amount of the brandy on top.

STRAWBERRY MOUSSE WITH SHORTBREAD
Gary Heath ICT technician and 2007 quarter-finalist

200g (7oz) strawberries
2 gelatine leaves, soaked in water (see
    MasterTip, p.304)
100ml (3½fl oz) double cream
50g (1¾oz) caster sugar

FOR THE SHORTBREAD
85g (3oz) unsalted butter, chilled
125g (4½oz) flour

30g (1oz) caster sugar
1 pinch of salt
½ tsp vanilla extract

FOR THE COULIS
50g (1¾oz) strawberries, chopped
2 tsp clear honey
25g (scant 1oz) icing sugar

PREPARATION TIME
20 minutes

COOKING TIME
15 minutes

SERVES 4

1 Hull and chop the strawberries, then place them in a pan with the caster sugar and simmer for 5 minutes. Remove the strawberries from the heat and whizz in a blender, then leave to cool slightly. Add the gelatine and mix well, making sure it has dissolved completely.
2 Whisk the cream to form soft peaks and add to the cooled strawberries, folding it in with a whisk. Pour into 4 chilled ramekins then place in the fridge for 3 hours or the freezer for 45 minutes.
3 To make the shortbread, preheat the oven to 180°C (350°F/Gas 4). Dice the butter and put into a mixing bowl to soften a little. Sift the flour, caster sugar, and salt over it and add the vanilla extract. Rub together with your fingertips and form the mixture into a ball.
4 Lightly flour the work surface. Roll out the shortbread to about 5mm (¼in) thick and cut into 8 strips approximately 4cm (1¾in) wide and 10cm (4in) long. Lay on a greased baking sheet and prick the surfaces all over with a fork. Put in the fridge for 30 minutes. Sprinkle a little caster sugar over the shortbread then bake for 8–10 minutes, or until firm to the touch. Cool before removing from the baking sheet. Dust with caster sugar before serving with the mousse.
5 To make the coulis, put all the ingredients in a small pan and cook for about 5–10 minutes. Blend, then pour this over the mousse and shortbreads.

STRAWBERRIES WITH SABLÉ BISCUITS AND ORANGE AND LEMON SYLLABUB

James Nathan barrister turned chef and 2008 champion

PREPARATION TIME
40 minutes

COOKING TIME
8 minutes

SERVES 4

FOR THE SABLÉ BISCUITS
100g (3½oz) plain flour
75g (2½oz) unsalted butter
100g (3½oz) golden caster sugar
grated zest of 1 lemon
2 egg yolks

FOR THE SYLLABUB
50g (1¾oz) caster sugar
grated zest and juice of 1 orange
grated zest and juice of 1 lemon
300ml (10fl oz) double cream

FOR THE STRAWBERRY COULIS
350g (12oz) strawberries
  (English if possible)
50g (1¾oz) icing sugar
3 tbsp Grand Marnier

TO DECORATE
icing sugar, for sprinkling
mint leaves

1 Preheat the oven to 200°C (400°F/Gas 6). To make the biscuits, mix the flour, butter, sugar, lemon zest, and egg yolks together in a food processor until a soft ball of dough is formed. Rest in the refrigerator for about 30 minutes. Roll out thinly. Cut out 8 biscuits with a 7–8cm (2¾–3¼in) pastry cutter and bake in the oven on a greased baking tray until golden, about 6–8 minutes.

2 To make the coulis, hull 200g (7oz) of the strawberries. Purée with the icing sugar and Grand Marnier in a food processor. Check for sweetness and adjust if necessary. Pass through a fine sieve and chill the mixture until required.

3 For the syllabub, combine the sugar and zest and juice from the orange and lemon. Whisk the cream until it forms soft peaks. Add the citrus mixture and whisk to firm peaks. Chill until required.

4 To serve, put a swirl of the coulis on each plate. Set a biscuit alongside it. Put a few spoonfuls of syllabub in the centre of the biscuit and surround with the remaining strawberries, halved lengthways to make pillars. Top with another biscuit. Sprinkle with icing sugar and add some mint leaves to finish.

WHITE PEACHES WITH RASPBERRIES ENCASED IN A SPUN SUGAR BASKET

Roger Black Olympic sprinter and 2006 Celebrity finalist

PREPARATION TIME
1 hour, plus freezing time

COOKING TIME
30 minutes

SERVES 4

2 large white peaches
100g (3½oz) caster sugar

FOR THE RASPBERRY GRANITA
350g (12oz) fresh raspberries, plus
   extra for decoration
125g (4½oz) caster sugar
sprig of mint

FOR THE CIGARETTES RUSSES
60g (2oz) unsalted butter, softened
75g (2½oz) icing sugar
1 egg white
60g (2oz) plain flour

FOR THE CRÈME CHANTILLE
250ml (8fl oz) double cream
25g (scant 1oz) icing sugar
½ tsp vanilla extract

1 Put the peaches in warm water for 5 minutes, then peel off the skins and cut the flesh into 8 segments.

2 Next, make 4 sugar baskets. Heat the caster sugar gently in a heavy pan without stirring. When it starts to become liquid and golden, tilt the pan to blend together so it can dissolve properly. Allow to cool for 5 minutes, then take a greased ladle or small bowl and, using a spoon, crisscross the caramel in a trail across it, making a basket effect. Cool for 5 minutes then remove carefully.

3 To make the granita, blend the raspberries and sugar together or crush with a fork until you have a purée. Blend in 275ml (9fl oz) water and pour into a shallow freezerproof container. Freeze for 1 hour then stir the mixture with a fork, distributing the ice crystals evenly. Repeat 3–4 times until fully frozen.

4 Preheat the oven to 180°C (350°F/Gas 4). To make the *cigarettes russes*, beat together the butter and icing sugar. Add the egg white and mix well, then stir in the flour until you have a smooth, thick paste. Spread rounds 12cm (5in) in diameter on a non-stick baking sheet and bake in the oven for 7–8 minutes, working in batches of 3–4 as you need to handle them quickly when they are cooked. Once the mix is golden, remove from the baking tray as swiftly as you can and roll up into a cigarette shape. This quantity will make 8 "cigarettes".

5 To make the crème Chantille, whisk the double cream with the sugar and vanilla until it forms soft peaks.

6 To serve, place the caramel baskets on the plates and half-fill with the raspberry granita. Top with the peach wedges then decorate with the remaining raspberries and mint leaves. Place a spoonful of crème Chantille alongside and top with a *cigarette russe*.

PEACH PANACOTTA
AND PINK CHAMPAGNE SORBET

Hanna Payne junior sous chef and 2009 Professionals quarter-finalist

FOR THE PANACOTTA
300ml (10fl oz) double cream
300ml (10fl oz) whole milk
125g (4½oz) caster sugar
6g (scant ¼oz) gelatine leaves,
   pre-soaked (see MasterTip, p.304)
8 drops of peach flavouring (or orange
   flavouring if peach is not available)

FOR THE PINK CHAMPAGNE SORBET
180g (6oz) caster sugar
250ml (8fl oz) pink Champagne
   or sparkling rosé wine

FOR THE PEACH PURÉE
2 peaches
1 tbsp icing sugar

PREPARATION TIME
40 minutes, plus freezing time

COOKING TIME
20 minutes

SERVES 4

1 To make the panacotta, put all the ingredients into a saucepan, heat gently until the gelatine has dissolved and then bring to the boil. Pour into four 150ml (5fl oz) panacotta moulds. Stand them in a tray of cold water to cool quickly and then transfer to the fridge for about 3 hours, or until set.

2 For the sorbet, dissolve the sugar in 375ml (13fl oz) water in a saucepan on a medium heat. Increase the temperature and let the liquid boil gently for 5 minutes to thicken. Allow to cool a little before adding the pink Champagne or sparkling rosé wine.

3 Pour the syrup into an ice-cream maker and churn for about 20 minutes or until set. Transfer to a shallow freezerproof container and place in the freezer until ready to use. (If you don't have an ice-cream maker, see the MasterTip, p.347.)

4 To make the peach purée, plunge the peaches into boiling water for 2 minutes and then skin, de-stone and chop them up. Put the peach flesh and icing sugar in a blender and purée.

5 To serve, quickly dip the panacotta moulds into a bowl of very hot water and turn out onto chilled serving plates. Add 3 small scoops of sorbet to each dessert and drizzle the peach purée around the base of the panacotta.

PEARS BELLE HÉLÈNE
Steven Wallis creative director and 2007 champion

PREPARATION TIME
20 minutes, plus freezing time

COOKING TIME
20 minutes

SERVES 4

FOR THE PEARS
1 tbsp caster sugar
4 bay leaves
3 cardamom pods
2 vanilla pods
2 Comice pears, with stalks

FOR THE ICE CREAM
300ml (10fl oz) double cream
200ml (7fl oz) whole milk

2 vanilla pods, slit, seeds scraped
   out but reserved
4 egg yolks
85–100g (3–4oz) caster sugar

FOR THE CHOCOLATE SAUCE
1 tsp caster sugar
300ml (10fl oz) double cream
2 x 100g (3½oz) bars dark chocolate
   (70% cocoa – see MasterTip, p.351)

1 First make the ice cream. Pour the cream and milk into a saucepan. Add the vanilla pods and seeds to the pan and heat gently until steaming but not boiling. Leave to infuse for 5 minutes.
2 Whisk the egg yolks and sugar together until pale and foamy. Remove the vanilla pods and gradually whisk the warm cream into the egg yolk mixture. Return to the pan and cook, stirring, over a low heat until a custard thick enough to coat the back of a wooden spoon is formed. Transfer to an ice-cream maker and churn. (If you do not have one, see the MasterTip on p.347.)
3 To cook the pears, pour 300ml (10fl oz) boiling water into a saucepan, add the sugar and stir to dissolve. Add the bay leaves and cardamom and vanilla pods. Heat gently to boiling point. Peel and core the pears, leaving the stalk intact. Add to the syrup, cover with a lid and poach gently for 20 minutes or until tender.
4 For the chocolate sauce, put the sugar in a pan with 1 tbsp boiling water and stir until the sugar is dissolved. Set aside. Warm the cream in a heavy pan, add the chocolate piece by piece and stir very briefly to melt. Remove from the heat and stir in the sugar syrup. Keep warm.
5 To serve, slice the pears in half lengthways then make vertical cuts about 5mm (¼in) apart. For each diner, scoop out a ball of ice cream the size of a small orange and place in a chilled deep dessert bowl. Carefully lift the pear on top and mould it around the ice cream. Set the bowl on a plate and serve the chocolate sauce on the side.

GREGG WALLACE "It's probably one of the best chocolate sauces I've ever tasted – the whole thing is a creamy, melty, chocolatey delight."

MANGO AND PASSION FRUIT SUNDAE

Andy Oliver project manager turned chef and 2009 finalist

PREPARATION TIME
1 hour, plus freezing time

SERVES 4

FOR THE SORBET
2 mangoes
juice of 1 large lemon
250g (9oz) vanilla caster sugar
3 tbsp liquid glucose (see MasterTip)

FOR THE PASSION FRUIT SYRUP
10 ripe passion fruit
4 tbsp caster sugar
juice of 1 large orange

FOR THE SUNDAE CREAM
60ml (2fl oz) double cream
225ml (8fl oz) thick coconut milk
1 tbsp vanilla caster sugar

TO SERVE
1 mango, peeled and finely diced (see
  MasterTip, p.160)
45g (1½oz) fresh or desiccated coconut,
  lightly toasted

MASTER TIP
LIQUID GLUCOSE

Once only available from
chemists but now found on
supermarket shelves, liquid
glucose (sometimes called
glucose syrup) is a viscous
syrup derived from purified
corn starch.

1 To make the sorbet, first reserve 4 slices of mango for decoration. Cut the remaining flesh from the mangoes and blend in a food processor with the lemon juice and 3–4 tbsp water, until smooth. Transfer to a large bowl and put in the fridge.
2 To make a sugar syrup, put 200ml (7fl oz) water with the sugar and liquid glucose into a pan. Stir over a low heat until the sugar dissolves, then bring to the boil. Remove from the heat and allow to cool.
3 Stir the sugar syrup into the mango purée and then pour into an ice-cream machine and churn for about 30 minutes or until set. Transfer to a shallow freezer container and place in the freezer until ready to use. (If you don't have an ice-cream maker, see the MasterTip, p.347.)
4 To prepare the passion fruit syrup, halve the fruit and scoop the flesh into a blender. Process and then push through a sieve. Transfer the purée to a small saucepan and add the sugar and orange juice, bring to a simmer and reduce for about 5 minutes, or until a syrupy consistency. Put in a bowl in the fridge to cool.
5 To make the sundae cream, whisk the cream into soft peaks and then fold in the coconut milk together with the sugar and chill.
6 To serve, put scoops of the mango sorbet into 4 sundae glasses, top with some of the sundae cream mixture and then add mango cubes and a drizzle of syrup. Finish off with a slice of mango and a sprinkle of toasted coconut.

GREGG WALLACE "To keep all these flavours as natural as you can is the work of a talented man – pure heaven on the end of my spoon. It is a thing of absolute joy."

ELDERFLOWER SORBET WITH MARINATED BERRIES

James Shepherd horse groom turned caterer and 2007 quarter-finalist

FOR THE SORBET
150g (5½oz) caster sugar
360ml (12fl oz) elderflower cordial

FOR THE BERRIES
75ml (2½fl oz) Riesling
2 tbsp crème de cassis

juice of 1 lime
25g (scant 1oz) icing sugar
5 or 6 mint leaves, chopped
300g (10oz) mixed berries, such
as strawberries, raspberries,
and blueberries

PREPARATION TIME
20 minutes, plus freezing time

COOKING TIME
5 minutes

SERVES 4

1 To make the sorbet, dissolve the sugar in 360ml (12fl oz) water in a saucepan on a medium heat. Increase the temperature and let the syrup boil for 5 minutes to thicken. Add the elderflower cordial and remove from the heat and leave to cool.

2 Pour the syrup into an ice-cream machine and churn for about 20 minutes, or until set. Transfer to a shallow freezer container and place in the freezer until ready to use.)If you don't have an ice-cream maker, see the MasterTip, p.347.

3 For the berry marinade, combine the Riesling, crème de cassis, and lime juice in a bowl. Add the icing sugar, taste and add more if required – you are looking for a balance of sweet and sharp flavours. Add most of the mint leaves and set aside for the flavours to infuse.

4 To serve, wash the berries and drain them in a colander lined with kitchen paper to absorb excess water. Combine with the marinade and spoon into 4 glasses. Top with a quenelle of sorbet (see MasterTip, p.93) and decorate with the remaining mint leaves.

LAVENDER MOUSSE WITH HOKEY POKEY AND A BLACKBERRY SAUCE

Mat Follas engineer turned chef patron and 2009 champion

PREPARATION TIME
50 minutes

SERVES 4

FOR THE BLACKBERRY SAUCE
300g (10oz) blackberries
200g (7oz) golden caster sugar

FOR THE LAVENDER MOUSSE
13g (½oz) gelatine leaves, cut into
  pieces (see MasterTip, p.304)
500ml (16fl oz) whole milk
5 egg yolks

40g (1½oz) caster sugar
500ml (16fl oz) whipping cream
20g (¾oz) lavender flower heads
12 drops lavender essence

FOR THE HOKEY POKEY
75g (2½oz) caster sugar
2 tbsp golden syrup
1 tsp bicarbonate of soda

GREGG WALLACE

"You get a bit of fizz and you get deep blackberry. Then in comes this really mellow cream and it finishes with lavender. It is beautiful."

1 Set aside 12 blackberries of different sizes for decoration. Then put the remaining blackberries in a pan with the sugar and add 100ml (3½fl oz) cold water, stir and heat gently until the sugar has dissolved. Bring the sauce to the boil, reduce the heat and simmer for 5 minutes or until the sauce has reduced by half and thickened. Pass through a sieve, discard the blackberry pulp and leave to cool.

2 Transfer the sauce into a jug and pour a little into 4 freezerproof glasses, which the mousse will be served in. Put the glasses in the freezer and set the rest of the sauce aside in the fridge.

3 For the lavender mousse, put the gelatine in iced water for about 10 minutes to soften. Pour the milk into a saucepan and bring it to the boil. Place the egg yolks and sugar into a bowl and mix. Stir in the milk. Return to the pan, stirring and warming gently for 5 minutes or until the sauce coats the back of a spoon. Drain any excess water from the gelatine and add to the pan and stir until dissolved. Set aside to cool.

4 Whip the cream until stiff peaks are formed. Add the lavender heads and combine. Stir in the lavender essence, a drop at a time, until the flavour is to your taste. Gently fold in the cream.

5 Remove the glasses from the freezer and pour the crème anglaise over the frozen berry sauce. Return to the freezer for 20 minutes.

6 To make the hokey pokey, heat the sugar and golden syrup slowly in a saucepan, stirring constantly for 3 minutes or until the sugar is dissolved. Stir in the bicarbonate of soda and then pour onto a silicone sheet and leave to cool. Put into a plastic bag and gently smash it.

7 To serve, make a line of blackberry sauce on each plate and top with the reserved blackberries. Add the frozen mousses and put a piece of broken hokey pokey in the top of each one and add a small pile of hokey pokey crumbs alongside.

SPARKLING CRANBERRY JELLIES WITH ORANGE LANGUES DE CHAT BISCUITS

Caroline Brewester banker turned food writer and 2005 finalist

PREPARATION TIME
30 minutes, plus chilling time

COOKING TIME
10 minutes

SERVES 4

FOR THE JELLIES
360ml (12fl oz) cranberry juice, chilled
200g (7oz) cranberries
150g (5½oz) golden granulated sugar
8 gelatine leaves
375ml (12½fl oz) sparkling white wine
4 small sprigs of mint, to decorate

FOR THE BISCUITS
grated zest of 1 orange
60g (2oz) unsalted butter, softened
60g (2oz) caster sugar
2 egg whites, lightly beaten for about
  1 minute until foamy
60g (2oz) plain flour

1 Pour 300ml (10fl oz) of the cranberry juice into a saucepan and add the cranberries and sugar. Bring to the boil, reduce the heat and simmer for 5 minutes or until the cranberries are soft. Remove from the heat.
2 Meanwhile, soak the gelatine in the remaining cranberry juice for 5 minutes (see MasterTip, below).
3 Strain the cranberries and juice through a fine sieve into a large basin, pressing the cranberries with the back of a spoon. Measure the strained liquid – you should have about 500ml (16fl oz). Stir the soaked gelatine into the hot liquid until it has dissolved and then leave to cool.
4 Make the liquid up to 850ml (1½ pints) with the sparkling wine and stir to combine. Let the bubbles subside and pour into four 250ml (8fl oz) glasses. Skim off any foam and chill for 4 hours or overnight until set.

MASTER TIP
USING GELATINE

Gelatine comes in 2 forms, leaf and powder. Whichever you use, the principle is the same: the gelatine must be soaked in a little cold liquid for at least 10 minutes before being dissolved in warm, but not boiling, liquid. Gelatine is added to warm liquid so that it will melt and disperse evenly before setting.

1 Soak the required number of leaves of gelatine in cold water, or other liquid, to cover for at least 10 minutes. Squeeze out as much water as possible.

2 Warm some water or whatever liquid is specified in the method in a saucepan. Stir in the gelatine to dissolve and then leave to cool.

5 To make the *langues de chat* biscuits, preheat the oven to 200°C (400°F/Gas 6).

6 Put the orange zest and butter into a bowl and beat together until creamy. Add the sugar and whisk until pale and fluffy. Stir in the egg whites (the mixture will look slightly curdled). Beat in the flour, mixing to a fairly stiff cream.

7 Fit a piping bag with a 1cm (½in) plain nozzle and fill with the mixture (see MasterTip, p.340). Line a baking sheet with baking parchment and pipe about thirty 5cm (2in) thin strips of mixture. They spread dramatically, so leave a 5cm (2in) space between each biscuit.

8 Using a damp finger, press the peak of the mixture flat then bake for about 8 minutes until they are pale gold in the centre and darker at the edges. Transfer to a wire rack to cool.

9 Serve the set sparkling cranberry jellies with a sprig of mint and the biscuits.

APRICOT AND CARDAMOM TRIFLE
Jenny Shanks student turned chef and 2006 quarter-finalist

PREPARATION TIME
45 minutes, plus chilling time

COOKING TIME
50 minutes

SERVES 4

150g (5½oz) caster sugar
juice of ½ lemon
5 apricots, halved and stoned
4 trifle sponges
4 tbsp apricot conserve
100g (3½oz) amaretti biscuits
60ml (2fl oz) apricot brandy

1 tbsp toasted flaked almonds
150ml (5fl oz) double cream
100ml (3½fl oz) milk
3 cardamom pods, crushed
3 medium egg yolks
150ml (5fl oz) whipping cream
50g (1¾oz) pomegranate seeds
25g (scant 1oz) unsalted pistachio
   nuts, chopped

1 In a medium saucepan, heat 200ml (7fl oz) water with 100g (3½oz) of the caster sugar and the lemon juice. Bring to a simmer, then add the apricots and poach until just tender but still retaining their shape. Remove from the syrup and set aside to cool. Reduce the syrup by about two-thirds and set aside.

2 Split the trifle sponges horizontally and spread over the apricot conserve and sandwich together. Arrange the trifle sponges in the base of a glass trifle bowl, sandwiching them together with the apricot conserve, and then break up the amaretti biscuits over the top. Pour 3 tbsp of the brandy and 100ml (3½fl oz) of the reduced poaching liquor over them and scatter with the toasted almonds and then the cooled apricot halves. Cover and chill overnight.

3 To make the custard, pour the cream and milk into a small saucepan, add the cardamom pods and bring to just below boiling point. Remove from the heat and allow to infuse for 20–30 minutes, then remove the cardamom. Whisk the egg yolks with the remaining caster sugar then gradually pour into the infused cream and milk, whisking as you do so. Over a low heat, gradually cook the custard until it is thick, stirring frequently – make sure it does not boil or it will resemble scrambled eggs. Set aside to cool before pouring over the apricots.

4 Finally, whip the cream to soft peaks, gradually adding the remaining apricot brandy at the end, and spoon on top of the custard. Scatter with the pomegranate seeds and pistachio nuts to garnish.

SUMMER FRUIT TRIFLE
Sarah Whittle detective sergeant and 2008 semi-finalist

PREPARATION TIME
1 hour

COOKING TIME
25 minutes

SERVES 4

FOR THE CAKE
50g (1¾oz) unsalted butter, very soft
50g (1¾oz) self-raising flour
50g (1¾oz) caster sugar
1 large egg at room temperature
½ tbsp milk

FOR THE FRUIT LAYER
250g (9oz) strawberries,
  hulled and sliced
250g (9oz) raspberries
½ tbsp icing sugar
2½ tbsp sherry
  or orange liqueur (optional)

FOR THE CUSTARD
150ml (5fl oz) whole milk
150ml (5fl oz) double cream
½ vanilla pod, seeds only
3 large egg yolks
25g (scant 1oz) caster sugar
½ tbsp cornflour

FOR THE TOPPING
25g (scant 1oz) flaked almonds
150ml (5fl oz) whipping cream
1 tsp icing sugar

1 Preheat the oven to 180°C (350°F/Gas 4). Make 6 fairy cakes by putting all the cake ingredients into a food processor and blending until completely combined. Put the mix into greased non-stick fairy cake tins and bake in the oven for 12 minutes until risen and golden. Allow the cakes to cool.

2 Meanwhile, add the strawberries to the raspberries in a bowl and stir in the icing sugar. Macerate this for 30 minutes or so, then take half out and blend until smooth. Sieve the purée and add it back to the fruit. Set aside.

MASTER TIP
MAKING CUSTARD

Crème anglaise, or English egg custard, is a marvellous accompaniment to any number of desserts, hot or cold. The flavour will be best if you leave the vanilla to infuse in the milk overnight, but this is not essential. You can tell when custard is cooked to perfection by coating a wooden spoon and blowing on it; the custard should form a rosette shape.

1 With a sharp knife, split the vanilla pods lengthways. Scrape out the seeds with either your fingers or the tip of the knife blade.

2 Combine the milk and cream in a heavy pan. Add the vanilla pods and seeds. Bring to the boil then remove from the heat. Chill overnight.

3 To make the custard, heat the milk, cream, and vanilla seeds until barely simmering. Beat the egg yolks, sugar, and cornflour together in a bowl until the sugar is dissolved and the mix well combined. Slowly add the cream, vanilla, and milk mix, stirring well. Tip this back into the washed pan and cook gently, over medium heat, stirring all the time until the custard has thickened – take care not to let it boil or it will turn into sweet scrambled egg. Pour into a cold bowl, put cling film directly on top of the custard to stop a skin forming and leave it until completely cold. It will thicken as it cools, but just whisk it up again until it is smooth shortly before you assemble the trifle.

4 To make the topping, toast the almonds in a dry frying pan until golden (see MasterTip, p.40) and allow to cool. Lightly whip the sugar into the cream until it stands in peaks but is not stiff.

5 Assemble in 4 individual trifle bowls. Put in half the fruit mix, then crumble the fairy cakes into big chunks and place half on top of the fruit. Press down gently and add half the sherry or orange liqueur if using. Add the remaining fruit then top with more crumbled cake. Press down again. Add the remaining sherry or liqueur. Top with the custard and chill for an hour or so. Decorate with the cream and flaked almonds. This is best made 8 hours in advance of serving and kept in the refrigerator.

3 Discard the vanilla pods, bring the milk to the boil. Whisk egg yolks and sugar in a bowl, then pour in the milk in a thin stream, whisking as you go.

4 Pour the mixture back into the pan and continue to whisk over a medium heat until the temperature reaches 85°C (185°F).

CARIBBEAN TRIFLE GLORIES
inspired by **Mark Todd** ad man and 2005 finalist

PREPARATION TIME
30 minutes, plus freezing
and soaking time

SERVES 4

15g (½oz) desiccated coconut
1 Jamaican ginger cake
½ small pineapple
4 tbsp dark rum
1 small ripe mango
2 tbsp icing sugar
zest and juice of 1 lime

FOR THE COCONUT ICE CREAM
450ml (15fl oz) semi-skimmed milk
300ml (10fl oz) double cream
4 tbsp coconut cream powder
9 egg yolks
200g (7oz) caster sugar

1 To make the coconut ice cream, put the milk and cream in a saucepan and bring to the boil. Add the coconut cream powder, stirring to dissolve. Remove from the heat and leave to cool slightly. Meanwhile, in a bowl, whisk together the egg yolks and sugar and pour the hot liquid over them. Return the coconut cream to the pan and allow to thicken slowly over a gentle heat, stirring frequently until it coats the back of a spoon. Use a double cooker, if you have one, so that the mixture does not curdle.

2 Allow to cool and, when cold, transfer to an ice-cream maker and freeze according to the manufacturer's instructions. (If you do not have one, see the MasterTip, p.347.)

3 In a dry frying pan, toast the desiccated coconut until golden brown and allow to cool on a plate.

4 Cut the Jamaican ginger cake into 2.5cm (1in) slices and then into 2.5cm (1in) cubes. Cut the pineapple into similar-sized pieces. Divide the cake and pineapple chunks between 4 sundae glasses and pour 1 tbsp of rum into each glass. Allow this to soak in for at least 30 minutes and if possible a few hours.

5 In a food processor, blend together the flesh of the mango, the icing sugar, and the lime zest and juice. Spoon half of this coulis into the glasses on top of the rum-soaked cake and pineapple.

6 Add a few scoops of coconut ice cream to each glass, spooning the remaining coulis over the first 2 scoops and ending with ice cream. Finally, sprinkle with the toasted coconut to serve.

TIRAMISU
Hannah Miles lawyer turned cookbook author and 2007 finalist

60g (2oz) caster sugar
60g (2oz) unsalted butter
1 large egg
50g (1¾oz) self-raising flour
15g (½oz) cocoa powder,
  plus extra for dusting
100g bar of Toblerone,
  coarsely chopped

1 tbsp instant coffee powder
100ml (3½fl oz) boiling water
75ml (2½fl oz) amaretto
250g (9oz) mascarpone cheese
250ml (8fl oz) crème fraîche
1½ tbsp icing sugar, sifted

PREPARATION TIME
40 minutes, plus chilling time

COOKING TIME
20 minutes

SERVES 4

1 Preheat the oven to 180°C (350°F/Gas 4). In a mixing bowl, cream together the sugar and butter until light and creamy. Add the egg and whisk well. Sift in the flour and cocoa powder and fold gently with a spatula to incorporate.

2 Place 12 cupcake paper cases in a bun tin and half fill each with the cake mixture. Place a chunk of Toblerone in the centre of each and cover with a spoonful of the remaining cake batter. Bake in the oven for 15–20 minutes, until the cupcakes are firm to the touch and spring back when pressed with a finger. Leave aside to cool.

3 Dissolve the instant coffee in a jug with the boiling water. Pour in the amaretto liqueur and leave to cool.

4 Meanwhile, stir together the mascarpone cheese, crème fraîche, and icing sugar in a large mixing bowl.

5 Remove the cupcakes from their paper cases and soak them in the coffee mixture until they have absorbed some of it. Place half the cakes on the bottom of a small trifle dish, sprinkle over half the remaining Toblerone, and dust with sifted cocoa powder.

6 Spoon half the mascarpone mixture over the cupcake layer, dust with another layer of sifted cocoa and then repeat the layers again, ending with a cocoa-dusted layer on top of the mascarpone. Chill in the fridge overnight.

RAS MALAI
Daksha Mistry housewife turned caterer and 2006 finalist

PREPARATION TIME
10 minutes

COOKING TIME
1 hour 30 minutes

SERVES 4

FOR THE MILK SAUCE
850ml (24lf oz) whole milk
1 tsp rosewater
175g (6oz) caster sugar
200g can condensed milk
½ tsp cardamom powder
2–3 saffron strands

FOR THE CURDS
1.2 litres (2 pints) whole milk
4 tbsp lemon juice

FOR THE SYRUP
225g (8oz) caster sugar
2–3 saffron strands

TO SERVE
3 tbsp toasted flaked almonds
   (see MasterTip, p.40)
3 tbsp chopped pistachios

MASTER TIP

RAS MALAI

Ras malai is a Bangladeshi and Indian milk sweet made by curdling milk solids with heat and adding either lime juice or sour whey. It can also include flattened balls of paneer, a common south Asian acid-set, non-melting cheese. Malai is a south Asian word for cream, derived from its main ingredient, condensed milk, which is also used in kulfi, a flavoured frozen dessert popular in Asia and the Middle East.

1 To make the milk sauce, gently boil the milk in a heavy pan with the rest of the milk sauce ingredients for 1 hour, or until reduced by half and thickened slightly. Remove from the heat, leave to cool, and put in the fridge until needed.

2 For the curds, gently bring the milk to the boil and add the lemon juice. Let it boil, but do not stir, until you see curds forming. Then remove it from the heat. Stir gently and pass it through muslin. Gather the muslin together at the top and rinse the curds contained in the muslin under cold water to remove any sourness. Place the curds in their muslin in a colander over a bowl and leave to drain for up to 2 hours. Then once more gather together the muslin at the top and squeeze tightly to press out any excess water.

3 Tip the curds into a bowl and, with a damp hand, form the curds into a dough and knead for 3–4 minutes until it comes together into a ball. Pull off a small golf-ball sized piece and knead in the palms of your hands. Flatten it and shape into a disc. Make 12 discs and set aside.

4 To make the syrup, put 500ml (16fl oz) water together with the sugar and saffron into a wide saucepan and bring to the boil.

5 Put 4–5 curd discs into the syrup and cook for 5 minutes until set. Remove with a slotted spoon and drop them into the cooled milk sauce. Finish cooking the rest of the discs. Cover and chill the milk sauce for at least 4 hours.

6 To serve, spoon the pudding into shallow bowls and serve with the toasted almonds and a few pistachios scattered over.

LYCHEES AND TOFFEE APPLES WITH SESAME SEEDS

Mark Moraghan actor and 2008 Celebrity finalist

PREPARATION TIME
15 minutes

COOKING TIME
20 minutes

SERVES 4

2 cooking apples, about 450g (1lb) in total
50g (1¾oz) plain flour
1 egg, beaten
300ml (10fl oz) vegetable oil

2 tbsp sesame oil
175g (6oz) demerara sugar
1 tbsp sesame seeds
200g (7oz) peeled lychees

1 Peel and core the apple and cut into segments. Roll in 10g (¼oz) of the flour. Put 2 tbsp cold water with the egg and remaining flour into a food processor – or use a whisk – and blend to make a batter. Dip the apples in the batter to coat evenly.

2 Put the oil in a wok and heat until very hot: 190°C (375°F). Drop in the apple pieces and fry for 3 minutes or until lightly brown. Remove with a slotted spoon and drain on some kitchen paper.

3 Clean the wok and heat the sesame oil on a medium heat for 30 seconds until it is warmed through. Add the sugar and 75ml (2½fl oz) water and stir occasionally until the sugar dissolves (see MasterTip, below), then increase the heat and boil for 8–10 minutes until the sauce has caramelized. Remove from the heat (also see below) and then add the apples and sesame seeds and stir to coat in the syrup.

4 Remove the apples with a slotted spoon and dip in iced water or place on greaseproof paper to cool slightly. Serve with the lychees.

MASTER TIP
SUGAR SYRUPS

Sugar syrups form the basis of a range of delicious desserts, from exotic fruit salads, ice creams, and meringues to confectionery. The basic mixture of sugar and water is cooked to different temperatures to produce varying concentrations of sugar that make the syrup suitable for different pâtisseries, confectionery, and chocolate products. The recipe above uses a light caramel syrup and doesn't contain much water.

1 Use a wet pastry brush to wipe down the pan to stop grains of sugar becoming stuck, as this might make the syrup crystallize.

2 When the caramel is a golden colour and coats the back of a spoon, plunge the pan into a bowl filled with cold water and ice cubes to stop it cooking.

BAKED PEACHES AND RASPBERRIES WITH VANILLA MASCARPONE CREAM

Hayley Costa mother of three and 2007 quarter-finalist

4 ripe peaches, halved lengthways
  and stoned
4 tsp light soft brown sugar
250g (9oz) mascarpone cheese
seeds of 1 vanilla pod
1–2 tbsp icing sugar
300g (10oz) raspberries

PREPARATION TIME
15 minutes

COOKING TIME
35 minutes

SERVES 4

1   Preheat the oven to 180°C (350°F/Gas 4). Place the peaches in
an ovenproof dish, fitting quite snugly, cut side up. Sprinkle the sugar
over the top of the peaches and place in the oven for 20–30 minutes,
until a knife slides easily through them and they feel quite soft –
the timing depends upon their ripeness.

2   Meanwhile, mix the mascarpone with the vanilla pod seeds and the
icing sugar, using it to sweeten the mascarpone just a little – it should
not be too sweet as the peaches and raspberries are very sweet and
the mascarpone cream balances the flavours.

3   Once the peaches are cooked, add the raspberries over the top of
the peaches and place back in the oven for about 5–7 minutes until
they soften and start to make a sauce. Remove from the oven.

4   Serve the peaches, 2 halves per person, spooning the raspberries
and sauce over them. Add a large spoonful of the mascarpone cream.

POACHED PEAR WITH SAFFRON MASCARPONE

Matt James garden designer and 2007 Celebrity quarter-finalist

PREPARATION TIME
25 minutes

COOKING TIME
30 minutes

SERVES 4

4 large lemons
4 large oranges
3 cardamom pods, crushed
4 bay leaves
400ml (14fl oz) Beaumes de Venise
   dessert wine
about 3 tbsp acacia honey
4 ripe Comice or Conference pears
pinch of saffron threads
200g (7oz) mascarpone cheese,
   beaten until soft

MASTER TIP

SAFFRON

Crocus sativus, the plant from which saffron is derived, is sterile and requires human intervention to reproduce – hence the high cost of this spice, since the corms must be dug up, split and replanted to produce a new crop. It is thought to have been in use for medical and culinary purposes since the 7th century BCE.

1 Juice the lemons and oranges then add to a large shallow saucepan with the cardamom pods, bay leaves, and Beaumes de Venise. Gently warm on a medium heat for 20 minutes before stirring in honey to taste to soften the citrus tang. Continue to heat for about 5 minutes or until a thick sugary syrup is reached, but do not allow it to boil.

2 In the meantime, halve and peel the pears and, using a teaspoon, carefully scoop out the cores. Lay each half face down and make equal-width slices three-quarters of the way across – take care not to cut all the way through or the pear will not hold its shape while you cook it. Add the pears carefully to the saucepan and, continually spooning the syrup over the top, poach for 3–4 minutes, keeping the heat low.

3 Once the pears are soft, remove from the syrup and place on warmed plates face down. Finish cutting through each segment all the way. Overlap each slice for presentation. The syrup on the hob should now be thick and gooey; sieve out the cardamom and bay leaves then dribble it over the top. Finally mix a pinch of saffron into ice-cold mascarpone and serve on the side.

HONEY FIGS WITH MASCARPONE ICE CREAM
Caroline Brewester banker turned food writer and 2005 finalist

2 large eggs, separated
salt
250g (9oz) mascarpone
2 tbsp icing sugar
1 tsp vanilla extract
300ml (10fl oz) double cream
4 fresh figs, halved
1 tbsp mild-flavoured clear honey
  such as orange blossom, plus extra
  to serve

PREPARATION TIME
15 minutes, plus freezing time

COOKING TIME
2–3 minutes

SERVES 4

1 To make the ice cream, put the egg whites in a bowl with a pinch of salt and whisk to soft peaks. Put the mascarpone cheese in a bowl with the egg yolks, icing sugar, and vanilla extract and beat until just combined. Add the cream and beat again, until the mixture thickens slightly. Fold in the whisked egg white. Either transfer the mixture to a resealable container and freeze overnight, or tip the mixture into an ice-cream maker and churn, following the manufacturer's instructions. (If you do not have an ice-cream maker, see the MasterTip on p.347.)

2 Preheat the grill to medium. Put the figs cut side up on a foil-lined baking sheet. Drizzle a little honey on the cut side of the figs and place under the grill for about 2–3 minutes, or until the figs have warmed through.

3 Transfer the figs to serving plates and spoon over any fig juice that has collected on the foil. Add a generous scoop of ice cream to each plate and serve drizzled with a little extra honey.

Please note: This recipe contains raw eggs so is not suitable for pregnant women or those with a vulnerable immune system.

MASTER TIP
SELECTING FIGS

Fresh figs do not ripen well once picked, so avoid buying firm ones. Choose figs that are clean with smooth, unbroken skin. The fruit should be soft and yield to the touch. If figs smell slightly sour, they have begun to ferment. They should keep for about 3 days from the time of purchase, stored in a plastic bag in the coldest part of the fridge.

CRÊPES SUZETTE COYOACÁN STYLE

inspired by **Thomasina Miers** food writer turned chef and 2005 champion

PREPARATION TIME
10 minutes

COOKING TIME
15 minutes

SERVES 4

40g (1½oz) unsalted butter,
 plus extra for frying
200g (7oz) plain flour
pinch of salt
1 tbsp caster sugar
2 large eggs, beaten
450ml (15fl oz) whole milk
finely grated zest of 1 orange

FOR THE SAUCE
juice of about 2 large oranges,
 making 150ml (5fl oz)
150ml (5fl oz) *cajeta* or *dulce de leche*
4 tbsp Cointreau or Grand Marnier
 liqueur

1 For the pancakes, melt the butter and set aside to cool slightly. In a large mixing bowl, sift the flour and add the salt and sugar. Using an electric hand whisk, gradually incorporate the beaten eggs and then the milk, and finally stir in the orange zest and melted butter.
2 Melt a small amount of butter in a crêpe pan or frying pan, and wipe out any excess with kitchen paper. Fry the batter in ladlefuls (see MasterTip). Flip after 30–45 seconds, and cook the other side until golden brown. Wipe the pan with a butter-soaked piece of kitchen paper between each pancake, and stack them between sheets of baking paper, and keep warm in a low oven. Make at least 8 pancakes.
3 For the sauce, heat the orange juice in a small saucepan until it is simmering, and then add the *cajeta* or *dulce de leche* and the Cointreau or Grand Marnier liqueur.

MASTER TIP
MAKING PANCAKES

Pancakes can be thin and delicate, as in the recipe above, or fluffy and thick, made with less milk and more flour. The key to a well cooked crêpe is ensuring the surface sets before the underside turns too brown. This can be tricky to achieve the first few times and you may find you need to adjust the heat. If possible, leave the batter to rest in the fridge for 2 hours before using.

1 Ladle the batter into an oiled and heated frying pan and tip it quickly to cover the base of the pan. Cook the pancake for 30–45 seconds.

2 Use a metal spatula to peel the pancake loose and check it is brown. Then either turn it over by flipping in the air or use the spatula to do the job.

4 Let the sauce simmer until it is sticky, whisking to prevent it catching on the bottom.

5 Take each pancake, fold it in half and then half again to give a fan shape, and dip into the sauce. Transfer the sauced pancakes to a warm serving plate, fanning them out, and repeat until they are all done. Pour over any remaining sauce to serve.

SPICED SEMOLINA VERMICELLI
Daksha Mistry housewife turned caterer and 2006 finalist

3 tbsp ghee (see MasterTip, right)
300g pack of semolina vermicelli
few threads of saffron (see
  MasterTip, p.316)
300ml (10fl oz) whole milk, heated
3 tsp caster sugar

1 tsp cardamom powder
1 tbsp raisins
1 tbsp chopped pistachio nuts
1 tbsp almond flakes, toasted
  (see MasterTip, p.40)
chopped mixed nuts, to serve

PREPARATION TIME
15 minutes

COOKING TIME
15 minutes

SERVES 4

1 Melt the ghee in a saucepan and then sauté the vermicelli for 2–3 minutes until it is golden brown. Put the saffron into the hot milk and then add both to the vermicelli, a little at a time.

2 Add the sugar, cardamom, raisins, pistachios, and almond flakes and mix well.

3 Cover the pan and simmer for 5–8 minutes until all the liquid has been absorbed.

4 Serve the vermicelli in bowls and scatter over the mixed nuts.

MASTER TIP

GHEE

Ghee is widely used in Indian cooking and is made by simmering unsalted butter in a large saucepan until all the water has boiled off and protein has settled to the bottom of the pan. The clarified butter at the top is spooned off or drained through muslin and it is this that is used as ghee.

BAKED GINGER PEAR CRUMBLE
inspired by **Midge Ure** musician and 2007 Celebrity finalist

PREPARATION TIME
20 minutes

COOKING TIME
40 minutes

SERVES 4

500g (1lb 2oz) ripe pears, peeled,
  cored and quartered
100ml (3½fl oz) stem ginger syrup
3–4 pieces of stem ginger, chopped

FOR THE CRUMBLE
175g (6oz) plain flour
pinch of salt
125g (4½oz) cold butter, cubed
60g (2oz) porridge oats
125g (4½oz) demerara sugar
extra thick double cream, to serve

1 Preheat the oven to 180°C/350°F/Gas 4.
2 Place the pear quarters in a roasting tin and drizzle the ginger syrup over them, then roast in the oven for about 10–15 minutes. Transfer to an ovenproof baking dish and scatter with the chopped stem ginger.
3 To make the crumble, place the flour, salt, and butter in a food processor and pulse to a crumb consistency. Alternatively, rub the butter into the flour and salt with your fingertips until the mixture resembles breadcrumbs. Tip into a bowl and mix in the oats and sugar, then scatter this lightly over the top of the pears, but do not pack down. (See also MasterTip, p.322.)
4 Bake in the oven for 30–40 minutes, or until the top is golden and the fruit is bubbling through at the edges. Serve with extra thick double cream.

APPLE CRUMBLE AND CUSTARD
Christopher Bisson actor and 2007 Celebrity quarter-finalist

PREPARATION TIME
45 minutes

COOKING TIME
45 minutes

SERVES 4

6 nutty-flavoured apples such as
   Egremont Russet, peeled, cored
   and cut into wedges
75g (2½oz) unsalted butter
100g (3½oz) caster sugar
1 cinnamon stick, broken in half
1 vanilla pod, seeds only
icing sugar, for dusting

FOR THE CRUMBLE
125g (4½oz) plain flour
125g (4½oz) demerara sugar
100g (3½oz) unsalted butter

FOR THE CUSTARD
600ml (1 pint) milk
8 egg yolks
75g (2½oz) caster sugar
100ml (3½fl oz) double cream

MASTER TIP

PERFECT CRUMBLE

For the perfect crumble, the mixture should be the texture of coarse crumbs – a finer mix will be more like cake, losing the characteristic chunky topping that gives crumbles their charm. Use chilled butter and, if your hands are warm, cool them under cold running water before mixing. If need be, put the bowl of crumble into the fridge to chill before mixing further.

1 Place the apples in a pan with the butter, caster sugar, cinnamon stick, and half the seeds from the vanilla pod. Cook over a medium heat until the apple is soft and translucent but still holding its shape – about 15 minutes .

2 Preheat the oven to 190°C (375°F/Gas 5). Put the crumble ingredients in a bowl and rub in the butter until the mixture is the consistency of coarse breadcrumbs. Transfer to a baking dish and bake in the oven for 10 minutes until golden, breaking it up with a wooden spoon halfway through and stirring the crumble in the centre to the outer edges, and vice versa.

3 To make the custard, place the milk and remaining vanilla seeds in a pan and heat gently. Beat the egg yolks and caster sugar together in a bowl. Whisk the hot milk into the bowl, then return to the pan and place on a very low heat. Keep stirring until a custard consistency is reached, then add the double cream to loosen it a little. Remove from the heat and transfer to a cold bowl to halt cooking. (See also MasterTip, pp.308–9.)

4 Place the apples in 4 ramekins. Cover with crumble and put under a hot grill to turn the top golden brown. Dust with icing sugar. Pour the custard into individual jugs and serve together with the crumble.

VANILLA SOUFFLÉ WITH RASPBERRY AND PASSION FRUIT COULIS

Alix Carwood IT consultant and 2008 quarter-finalist

150ml (5fl oz) whole milk
1 vanilla pod
15g (½oz) unsalted butter
15g (½oz) plain flour
2 large eggs plus 1 large egg white
1 tsp vanilla extract
40g (1¼oz) caster sugar
40g (1¼oz) icing sugar

FOR THE COULIS
200g (7oz) raspberries
2 passion fruit, halved and seeds
  scraped out
4 tbsp icing sugar

PREPARATION TIME
30 minutes

COOKING TIME
15 minutes

SERVES 4

1 Put the milk in a pan, scrape out the seeds from the vanilla pod and add both seeds and pod to the milk. Bring to the boil, then take off the heat and leave to infuse.

2 Heat the oven to 200°C (400°F/Gas 6). Butter four 8cm (3¼in) ramekins and then place in the fridge.

3 Melt the butter in a saucepan, stir in the flour and cook the roux gently for 1 minute. Bring the milk back to the boil, strain, and pour slowly onto the roux, whisking continuously. Bring back to boil and simmer gently for 2–3 minutes. Remove from the heat and allow to cool slightly.

4 Separate the eggs, then beat the yolks into the sauce 1 at a time. Add the vanilla extract.

5 Whisk the 3 egg whites, then beat in the caster sugar until it forms soft peaks. Fold the egg whites into the sauce and then spoon into the ramekins. Using a palette knife, smooth the tops of the soufflés, then run a finger round the inside rim of each ramekin so that the soufflé rises evenly. Cook in the oven for about 10–15 minutes until risen and lightly brown on the top.

6 Meanwhile, make the coulis by whizzing the raspberries, passion fruit, and icing sugar in a blender. Pass the coulis through a sieve and into a jug. Just before serving, place the soufflés on small plates. Serve immediately or the soufflés will sink. Ask each guest to make a small hole in the centre of the soufflé with their spoon and pour a little coulis into the hole.

MASTER TIP
SOUFFLÉ SUCCESS

The two vital factors for soufflé success are the consistency of the base sauce and the correct cooking temperature. Whisk the egg whites to medium peak stage, and do not overfold when adding them to the sauce as you may lose volume in the mix. Put your baking sheet in the oven as it preheats to provide heat on the bottom when the soufflé goes in. At this point turn the oven up 1 setting to help the soufflé rise.

PEAR AND ROQUEFORT SOUFFLÉ

Ludovic Dieumegard head chef and 2009 Professionals semi-finalist

PREPARATION TIME
10 minutes

COOKING TIME
8 minutes

SERVES 4

15g (½oz) unsalted butter, softened
2 tbsp caster sugar
4 egg whites
40g (1½oz) caster sugar
50g (1¾oz) Roquefort
2 tbsp icing sugar, to dust

FOR THE SOUFFLÉ BASE
2 Packham pears, peeled,
  cored, and diced
juice of ½ lemon
50g (1¾oz) caster sugar
1 tbsp cornflour
2 tbsp poire William

1 Preheat the oven to 190°C (375°F/Gas 5). Butter four 150ml (5fl oz) soufflé ramekins and coat the insides with caster sugar, tipping out any excess.

2 To make the soufflé base, put the pears in a small saucepan over a medium heat with 4 tbsp of water, the lemon juice, and caster sugar. Simmer for 5 minutes, or until the pear is soft.

3 Soften the cornflour in the poire William in a small bowl.

4 Transfer the pears and their liquid into a food processor and blend until smooth. Return to the pan and, over a high heat, whisk in the dissolved cornflour. Set aside to cool.

5 Meanwhile, whisk the egg whites in a large bowl until frothy. Then add the caster sugar and continue whisking until firm.

6 Gently mix a third of the egg white with the soufflé base, then lightly fold in the rest of the egg white.

7 Half fill each of the ramekins with the mixture and crumble over the Roquefort, then cover with the rest of the egg mixture. Smooth the surface with a palette knife, place the ramekins in the oven and cook them for 7–8 minutes, or until the soufflés are risen and golden. (See also MasterTip, p.323.)

8 Serve immediately dusted with icing sugar.

MICHEL ROUX JR "I love the combination of pear and Roquefort."

TANGERINE SOUFFLÉ
Helen Cristofoli PR consultant and 2005 quarter-finalist

1 tbsp tangerine marmalade
2 tbsp fresh tangerine or orange juice
1 tbsp Cointreau

2 large egg whites
2 tbsp caster sugar
4 amaretti biscuits

PREPARATION TIME
20 minutes

COOKING TIME
13 minutes

SERVES 4

1 Preheat the oven to 180ºC (350ºF/Gas 4). Butter 4 individual soufflé or ramekin dishes and dust thoroughly with caster sugar.
2 Put the tangerine marmalade in a small saucepan with the tangerine juice and Cointreau. Bring to the boil. Remove from the heat and stir to break down and melt the marmalade. Transfer to a small saucer and leave to cool. Do not allow it to set.
3 Whisk the egg whites in a mixing bowl until stiff. Lightly fold in the caster sugar and the cooled tangerine mixture.
4 Spoon immediately into the soufflé dishes, piling it high like a pyramid, then run a finger round the inside rim of each one.
5 Put the soufflé dishes on a baking tray. Bake in the oven for 8–13 minutes until risen and golden brown on top. (See also MasterTip, p.323.)
6 Serve immediately on small plates with amaretti biscuits.

STICKY TOFFEE PUDDING

Wendi Peters actress and 2009 Celebrity finalist

85g (3oz) sugared, stoned
  chopped dates
85g (3oz) light soft brown sugar
45g (1½oz) unsalted butter, softened
1 egg
115g (4oz) plain flour
1 tsp bicarbonate of soda
1 tbsp vanilla extract

FOR THE TOFFEE SAUCE
150g (5½oz) demerara sugar
85g (3oz) unsalted butter, softened
4 tbsp double cream

PREPARATION TIME
20 minutes

COOKING TIME
35 minutes

SERVES 4

1 Preheat the oven to 180°C (350°F/Gas 4). Butter a 16 x 12cm
(6½ x 5in) ovenproof dish.
2 Put the dates into a bowl and pour over just enough boiling water
to cover them.
3 In a separate bowl, cream together the soft brown sugar and the
butter. Beat the egg into the creamed mixture with some of the flour
before adding the rest of the flour.
4 Add the bicarbonate of soda and vanilla extract to the dates and
then stir into the creamed mixture until well mixed. Pour into the
ovenproof dish and bake in the oven for 30–35 minutes or until well
risen and a cake skewer when inserted comes out clean.
5 Just before the pudding is cooked, make the toffee sauce. Preheat
the grill to hot. Put the demerara sugar, butter, and cream into a
saucepan and heat gently. Let simmer for 3 minutes. Remove the
pudding from the oven, pour over half the sauce and place under
the grill until it bubbles.
6 Serve the pudding while hot with the remaining sauce poured over
the top or alongside as an accompaniment.

JOHN TORODE "This is one seriously sexy pudding!
The butterscotch sauce is sweet and rich
and I love the taste of those dates! I've been
cooking for 25 years and you taught me how
to do a sticky toffee pudding properly. I thank
you very much for that."

BLUEBERRY SPONGE PUDDING WITH VANILLA ICE CREAM

Andi Peters presenter and producer and 2008 Celebrity finalist

PREPARATION TIME
40 minutes, plus freezing time

COOKING TIME
25 minutes

SERVES 4

FOR THE ICE CREAM
1 vanilla pod
300ml (10fl oz) double cream
300ml (10fl oz) whole milk
6 egg yolks
75g (2½oz) caster sugar

FOR THE SPONGE PUDDING
150g (5½oz) unsalted butter
150g (5½oz) icing sugar
150g (5½oz) ground almonds
30g (1oz) plain flour
3 eggs
50g (1¾oz) blueberries

1 For the ice cream, first make a custard (see MasterTip, pp.308–9). Split the vanilla pod down the centre with a sharp knife and scrape out the seeds. Place the cream, milk, and vanilla seeds into a saucepan and slowly bring to a simmer.

2 Whisk the egg yolks and sugar together in a large bowl. Then gradually add the hot cream and milk mixture to the eggs, whisking all the time.

3 Once all of the milk is incorporated, place the bowl over a pan of simmering water, ensuring the bowl is not touching the water. Stir continuously with a wooden spoon until the mixture thickens and coats the back of the spoon.

4 Remove the pan from the heat and allow the custard to cool. Then place in an ice-cream maker and churn until frozen. If you don't have an ice-cream maker, put the custard into a 900g (2lb) loaf tin and freeze for 1 hour. Take it out of the freezer and whisk to break up the ice crystals and re-freeze for 3–4 hours (see MasterTip, p.347).

5 For the sponge pudding, preheat the oven to 180°C (350°F/Gas 4). Grease four 7.5cm (3in) mini-pudding moulds with butter.

6 Using an electric mixer, beat the butter until it is pale and then add the icing sugar and beat again until pale. Continue to beat, adding the almonds and flour and then the eggs, one by one.

7 When all is mixed in, fold in the blueberries by hand and divide into the moulds. Transfer to the oven and bake the puddings for 20–25 minutes, until they are golden brown and the sponge feels springy to the touch.

8 Serve the puddings turned out onto plates and with a scoop of the vanilla ice cream alongside.

ROSE-SCENTED RICE PUDDING WITH RASPBERRY COULIS AND PISTACHIOS

Cassandra Williams food marketer and 2009 quarter-finalist

500ml (16fl oz) whole milk
2 tbsp caster sugar
grated zest of 1 orange
pinch of salt
85g (3oz) short-grain rice
120ml (4fl oz) double cream, whipped
1 tsp rosewater

60g (2oz) pistachio nuts, shelled and
   finely chopped
100g (3½oz) raspberries

FOR THE RASPBERRY COULIS
100g (3½oz) raspberries
30g (1oz) icing sugar
juice of ½ lemon

PREPARATION TIME
45 minutes, plus chilling time

COOKING TIME
40 minutes

SERVES 4

1 Put the milk, sugar, orange zest, and salt in a saucepan and bring to the boil. Add the rice and cook on a low heat for 30 minutes, stirring occasionally, until the rice is soft and the liquid absorbed.
2 Remove the pan from the heat and allow the rice to cool before stirring in the whipped cream and rosewater. Spoon into four 120ml (4fl oz) pudding moulds and place in the fridge for about 2 hours, or until set.
3 To make the raspberry coulis, blend the raspberries with the icing sugar and lemon juice in a food processor. Pass through a sieve.
4 When the rice puddings are cool, remove from the fridge and carefully unmould. Gently sprinkle the pistachio nuts onto the sides of the puddings and then place them on serving plates and top with up-turned raspberries. Drizzle the coulis around the puddings and serve immediately.

MASTER TIP
ROSEWATER

Rosewater is used throughout much of the Middle East and central Asia to flavour teas, drinks, jams, and sweets – it was originally an ingredient of marzipan. Rosewater is a by-product in the production of rose oil, which is used in perfume. It is available from Middle-Eastern stores and other speciality outlets.

CHOCOLATE CAPPUCCINO CUPS
Caroline Brewester banker turned food writer and 2005 finalist

PREPARATION TIME
20 minutes, plus chilling time

SERVES 4

100g (3½oz) dark chocolate (70% cocoa – see MasterTip, p.351), chopped into small pieces
300ml (10fl oz) double cream
2 tsp caster sugar
½ tsp instant coffee powder

1 tsp icing sugar
2–3 drops vanilla extract
2 tsp cocoa powder, to decorate
4 crisp biscuits, such as *cigarettes russes* (see p.296) or *langues de chat* (see p.304), to serve

1 Put the chocolate pieces into a large heatproof jug or a bowl with a pouring lip.

2 Pour 200ml (7fl oz) of the cream into a small saucepan together with the caster sugar and coffee and bring it slowly to the boil, stirring occasionally. Then pour the boiling cream onto the chocolate and stir the mixture until the chocolate has melted.

3 Pour the cappuccino mixture into 4 small espresso cups or small ramekins and put in the fridge for 2 hours, or overnight, until it has set.

4 To serve, put the remaining cream in a bowl with the icing sugar and vanilla extract and whip to soft peaks. Spoon the cream onto the top of the cappuccino cups and dust with cocoa powder. Put the cups on saucers and serve with biscuits on the side.

WHITE CHOCOLATE BRULÉE
Gary Heath ICT technician and 2007 quarter-finalist

PREPARATION TIME
5 minutes

COOKING TIME
25 minutes

SERVES 4

300ml (10fl oz) double cream
30g (1oz) white chocolate
3 egg yolks
30g (1oz) caster sugar, plus extra
  for sprinkling
1 tsp vanilla extract

1 Preheat the oven to 180°C (350°F/Gas 4). Put the chocolate and cream in a saucepan and heat gently until the chocolate has melted.
2 In a bowl, use a wooden spoon or electric whisk to beat together the egg yolks, sugar, and the vanilla extract until pale. Then, stirring continuously, add the chocolate cream and sieve into four 6cm (2½in) diameter and about 4cm (1½in) deep ramekins.
3 Place the ramekins in a roasting tin and fill half way up with boiling water. Bake in the oven for 18–20 minutes or until set. Transfer to the fridge and leave to chill for 1 hour.
4 To finish, preheat a grill to medium-hot. Sprinkle 1 tsp of caster sugar on top of each of the brulées and caramelize under the grill for 2–3 minutes. Leave to harden and serve.

CHOCOLATE AND AMARETTO TRUFFLE MOUSSE WITH A VANILLA CREAM

Jaye Wakelin interior designer and 2007 quarter-finalist

2 tsp cocoa power, for dusting
100g (3½oz) amaretti biscuits, crushed (see MasterTip, right), plus extra to decorate
225g (8oz) dark chocolate (70% cocoa – see MasterTip, p.351), broken into pieces

2½ tbsp liquid glucose (see MasterTip, p.300)
2½ tbsp amaretto
300ml (10fl oz) double cream

FOR THE VANILLA CREAM
150ml (5fl oz) double cream
½ tsp vanilla extract

PREPARATION TIME
25 minutes, plus chilling time

SERVES 4

1 With a piece of kitchen paper wipe the base and insides of a 14cm (5½in) round, loose-bottomed cake tin with vegetable or groundnut oil. Tip in the cocoa power and dust inside the tin. Tip out any excess.
2 Evenly sprinkle 75g (2½oz) of the amaretti biscuits over the bottom of the cake tin and put to one side.
3 Place the chocolate into a heat-resistant bowl that fits over a pan of lightly simmering water (make sure the bottom of the bowl doesn't sit in the water). Add the glucose and amaretto and leave to gently melt. Stir and put to one side to cool.
4 In a separate bowl, beat the cream until thick. Fold in half the cooled chocolate, then the rest of the chocolate. Mix gently until smooth and an even chocolatey colour. Spoon into the cake tin and give the tin a tap to remove air bubbles. Cover with cling film and chill for at least 2–3 hours, or overnight if possible.
5 To serve, whip up the cream for the vanilla cream, add the vanilla extract and mix well. With two dessertspoons, make the cream into quenelle shapes (see MasterTip, p.93). Remove the torte from the tin by loosening the edges and serve as wedges with 2 quenelles of cream and a little of the crushed amaretti biscuits sprinkled over the top.

MASTER TIP
CRUSHING BISCUITS

The easiest way to crush biscuits without creating an almighty mess is to put them in a plastic bag and then use a meat cleaver or rolling pin to break them up until they resemble fine breadcrumbs.

WHITE CHOCOLATE TOWER WITH DARK CHOCOLATE MOUSSE

Cheryl Avery purchasing manager and 2009 quarter-finalist

PREPARATION TIME
1 hour

SERVES 4

150g (5½oz) raspberries
1–2 tbsp Kirsch
200g (7oz) white chocolate
4 sprigs of mint leaves, to decorate

FOR THE DARK CHOCOLATE MOUSSE
125g (4½oz) caster sugar
2 large egg whites
250g (9oz) dark chocolate (70% cocoa
  – see MasterTip, p.351), broken
  into pieces
150ml (5fl oz) double cream
60ml (2fl oz) kirsch

JOHN TORODE "It's magical. The white chocolate melts away in your mouth. Then you think, 'I'm supposed to be tasting raspberry, but I'm tasting cherry.' Then the alcohol comes in the back of it. It's just beautiful."

1 To make an Italian meringue for the mousse, combine the caster sugar and 60ml (2fl oz) water in a heavy saucepan. Bring to the boil and then simmer gently for about 5 minutes or until the mixture is pale, thick and syrupy.

2 Whisk the egg whites with an electric mixer until stiff. Then, with the machine still running, gradually add the hot sugar syrup in a thin stream and continue to whisk until the meringue is cold. Cover and place in the fridge.

3 Put the raspberries in a small bowl, sprinkle with the kirsch, and set aside.

4 To make the chocolate mousse, melt the dark chocolate in a heatproof bowl placed over a pan of simmering water. Meanwhile, lightly whip the cream in a large bowl until it forms soft peaks. Fold in the melted chocolate, kirsch, and the Italian meringue. Cover and chill in the fridge for 10 minutes.

5 For the white chocolate tower, melt the white chocolate in a bowl placed over a pan of simmering water. Pour the melted chocolate over a slab of marble or some baking parchment, spread out to produce a thin sheet, and leave to set. Dip a 9cm (3½in) round cutter in hot water and use it to cut out 12 discs of chocolate.

6 To assemble, fill a piping bag (see MasterTip, p.340) with the chocolate mousse mixture. Place a white chocolate disc on each serving plate and pipe a layer of chocolate mousse on top. Add a layer of the reserved raspberries and repeat in layers, adding a final disc, topped with raspberries and a sprig of mint leaves. Spoon a few more kirsch-soaked raspberries alongside the tower and serve.

CHOCOLATE AND ORANGE ROULADE
James Nathan barrister turned chef and 2008 champion

PREPARATION TIME
1 hour 30 minutes

COOKING TIME
50 minutes

SERVES 4

6 medium eggs
125g (4½oz) caster sugar
200g (7oz) dark chocolate
  (70% cocoa – see MasterTip, p.351)
300ml (10fl oz) double cream

FOR THE ORANGE SAUCE
3 navel oranges
40g (1¼oz) caster sugar
175ml (6fl oz) Grand Marnier
1 tsp orange blossom water

FOR THE GANACHE
100ml (3½fl oz) double cream
100g (3½oz) dark chocolate
  (70% cocoa), chopped
cocoa powder, for dusting

FOR THE CHOCOLATE SAUCE
150g (5½oz) dark chocolate
  (70% cocoa)
150ml (5fl oz) double cream

1 Preheat the oven to 220°C (425°F/Gas 7). For the roulade sponge, line a Swiss roll tin with baking parchment. Snip the corners to fit the paper neatly into the tin. Separate 5 of the eggs and beat the yolks with the sugar until pale and foamy.

2 Melt 200g (7oz) of the chocolate in a bain marie or a bowl set over a pan of simmering water. Leave to cool for about 10 minutes before adding to the egg yolk mixture – if the chocolate is hot it will cook the eggs and make the mixture too stiff to incorporate the whites.

3 Whisk the egg whites until stiff but still moist. Gently cut and fold them into the egg yolk and chocolate, taking care not to lose too much air from the whites. Spoon gently into the prepared tin. Place in the

MASTER TIP
MAKING A GANACHE

A ganache is a rich, smooth mixture of chocolate and cream, thought to have originated in Switzerland or France in the 19th century. The proportions of cream to chocolate vary according to whether it is to be used as a filling, a shiny glaze, or a frosting, for example. The taste and quality will depend upon the type of chocolate you use – one with a high cocoa solids content will make a firmer ganache.

1 To chop the chocolate, place it on a work surface and use a knife with a serrated edge, pressing on the blade.

2 Incorporate the chocolate into the boiling cream, stirring with a wooden spoon and starting at the centre.

oven and bake for 12–14 minutes until just cooked – the top should spring back when gently pressed. Allow to cool.

4 To make the orange sauce, peel long strips of zest from the orange and set aside. Segment 2 oranges, removing all the pith and skin and holding them over a bowl as you do so to catch their juice. Put the orange segments in a small bowl and cover it. Sieve the orange juice into a small pan and add the juice of the third orange. Stir in the sugar and reduce to a syrupy consistency, then add the long strands of orange zest and the Grand Marnier and flame off the alcohol. Add the orange blossom water and reduce again to a syrup. Keep warm.

5 To make the ganache, bring the cream to the boil in a medium pan. Allow to cool for a few seconds then add the chopped chocolate. Cool, then refrigerate.

6 Whip 300ml (10fl oz) cream to a consistency that will sandwich the sponge together. Refrigerate until needed.

7 To make the chocolate sauce, melt the chocolate with the cream in a bain marie or in a bowl set over a pan of simmering water. Stir until the sauce is glossy.

8 To serve, cut 2 discs of about 6–7cm (2½–2¾in) diameter per person from the chocolate sponge. Spoon 1–2 tbsp chocolate sauce onto each plate. Place a disc of chocolate sponge on the chocolate sauce, spoon cream onto this then place a second disc on top. Make a quenelle (see MasterTip, p.93) of ganache and spoon this on top of the sponge. Dust with cocoa powder. Remove a strand of zest from the orange sauce and decorate the top of the sponge stack with it. Reheat the orange sauce and add the orange segments, taking care not to damage them. Spoon this to one side of the chocolate pudding.

CHOCOLATE AND PAPRIKA SORBET WITH MARSHMALLOWS, TRUFFLE AND PINE NUT SUGAR, AND PASSION FRUIT SYRUP

Emily Ludolf 18-year-old student and 2008 finalist

PREPARATION TIME
1 hour 30 minutes,
plus freezing time

COOKING TIME
15 minutes

SERVES 4

FOR THE SORBET
250ml (8fl oz) whole milk
225g (8oz) granulated sugar
½ tbsp liquid glucose (see
   MasterTip, p.300)
¼ tsp hot smoked paprika
200g (7oz) dark chocolate (70% cocoa
   – see MasterTip, p.351), chopped

FOR THE MARSHMALLOWS
500g (1lb 2oz) granulated sugar
2 tbsp liquid glucose
8 gelatine leaves
2 large egg whites
½ tsp vanilla extract
100g (3½oz) raspberries
icing sugar and cornflour, for dusting
   and coating

FOR THE PASSION FRUIT SYRUP
12 passion fruit, halved
300g (10oz) caster sugar
squeeze of lemon juice

FOR THE TRUFFLE AND PINE NUT SUGAR
1 black truffle (see MasterTip, p.231),
   finely sliced
25g (scant 1oz) pine nuts
2 tbsp golden caster sugar

TO SERVE
25g (scant 1oz) lemon basil
   cress (see MasterTip, p.281) (optional)
25g (scant 1oz) wood sorrel (optional)

MASTER TIP
SUGAR THERMOMETERS

A digital sugar thermometer is quicker and more accurate than coil-sprung "dial" versions. When you buy one, test it for accuracy by putting it in boiling water for 10 minutes and the reading should be 110°C (212°F). Don't let the thermometer touch the bottom of the pan, which will always be hotter than the sugar above. To prevent this from happening, use one that clips to the side of the pan or is surrounded by a thin metal cage.

1 For the plain chocolate and smoked paprika sorbet, place the milk, sugar, and glucose together with 100ml (3½fl oz) cold water into a large heavy saucepan over a medium heat and gradually bring to the boil, stirring continuously until the sugar has dissolved.

2 Remove the pan from the heat and add smoked paprika to taste. Then add the chocolate and stir until it has melted. Return the pan to the heat and bring to a gentle boil. Cook for 1–2 minutes and remove from the heat once more.

3 Let the syrup cool, stirring occasionally, so that a skin doesn't form. Transfer to an ice-cream maker and churn for 30 minutes or until the sorbet has formed and is firm and creamy in texture. Transfer to a freezer container and store in the freezer until required. (If you don't have an ice-cream maker, see the MasterTip, p.347.)

4 For the marshmallows, lightly oil a 30 x 20cm (12 x 8in) shallow baking tray and dust it with sieved icing sugar and cornflour. Place the sugar and glucose together with 200ml (7fl oz) water in a heavy pan. Bring to the boil and continue cooking over a high heat until it reaches 127°C (260°F) on a sugar thermometer (see MasterTip, left). Take care as the mixture will be very hot.

5 Put the gelatine leaves into a bowl and cover with 150ml (5fl oz) water and leave for about 10 minutes to soften (see MasterTip, p.304).

6 Place the egg whites in a large bowl and beat with an electric whisk until stiff peaks are formed when the whisk is removed.

7 When the syrup is up to temperature, remove from the heat and steadily pour in the softened gelatine sheets and the water they were in. Be careful of the syrup bubbling up.

8 Continue to beat the egg whites while gradually pouring in the hot syrup from the pan. The mixture will become shiny and start to thicken. Add the vanilla extract and whisk for 5–10 minutes, until the mixture is stiff and thick enough to hold its shape on the whisk.

9 Spoon half of the marshmallow mixture over the prepared baking tray and even it out with a wet spatula or palette knife.

10 Coat the raspberries with a mixture of icing sugar and cornflour, and lay over the marshmallow mixture. Cover with the remaining marshmallow mixture and smooth over the top with the wet palette knife. Leave for at least 1 hour to set.

11 Meanwhile, make the passion fruit syrup. Scoop the passion fruit seeds into a sieve and press the juice through to remove the pips. Bring the sugar and 300ml (10fl oz) water to the boil in a saucepan, along with the lemon juice. Reduce the heat and add the sieved passion fruit juice. Gently heat in the pan for about 10 minutes until it is reduced to a thick syrup with a gelatinous texture.

12 Dust a work surface with more icing sugar and cornflour. Loosen the marshmallow around the sides of the tray with a palette knife and turn it out onto the dusted surface. Cut into small squares and roll in sugar and cornflour. Leave to dry a little on a wire rack (it can be stored in an airtight container until ready to use).

13 Just before serving, dust the marshmallow with more icing sugar and, if you have a blow torch, caramelize and toast the outside. For the flavoured sugar, place the truffle, pine nuts, and sugar into a blender and process until all the ingredients are incorporated.

14 To serve, swirl the passion fruit syrup into a flame-like shape on each plate. Arrange the toasted marshmallows with the lemon basil cress and wood sorrel alongside, if using, and then place a scoop of the chocolate and smoked paprika sorbet onto each plate. Sprinkle with the truffle sugar and serve immediately.

JOHN TORODE "Your chocolate sorbet is absolutely delicious. And I think the idea of making your own marshmallow and toasting it is fantastic. It is so luscious, so well made."

MARBLED CHOCOLATE FONDANT WITH ORANGE AND MINT SYRUP

Adam Young junior sous chef and 2009 Professionals quarter-finalist

PREPARATION TIME
35 minutes

COOKING TIME
15 minutes

SERVES 4

75g (2½oz) white chocolate
75g (2½oz) dark chocolate (70% cocoa – see MasterTip, p.351)
100g (3½oz) unsalted butter, melted
2 egg whites

100g (3½oz) caster sugar, plus 2 tbsp
100g (3½oz) plain flour
grated zest and juice of 2 oranges, plus segments of 1 orange
handful of mint leaves, cut into fine shreds

1 Preheat the oven to 180°C (350°F/Gas 4). Grease four 7cm (2¾in) metal rings and line the sides with baking parchment. Put the rings on baking parchment on a baking sheet.

2 In separate bowls, melt the white and dark chocolates, each with 50g (1¾oz) butter over pans of simmering water. Remove from the heat. Whisk the egg whites and sugar until thick and creamy, then divide into 2 and fold into the chocolates with the flour.

3 Place each chocolate into separate piping bags (see below) and pipe both mixes together into the metal rings. Leave to rest in the fridge to solidify and then place in the oven for 12 minutes until the mixture shrinks away from sides of the rings. Remove from the oven.

4 For the syrup, put the juice and 2 tbsp sugar into a saucepan and slowly bring to the boil. Add the zest, mint, and orange segments and remove from the heat. Take each fondant from its ring and put on a plate. Drizzle around the syrup and serve with the orange segments.

MASTER TIP
FILLING A PIPING BAG

A bag and nozzle can be used to pipe more than just cream, including meringue, pastry, sorbet, and chocolate. Once the bag is three-quarters full, twist the top to clear it of any air pockets. The contents should be just visible in the tip of the nozzle. To pipe, hold the twisted end of the bag taut in one hand and use your other hand to gently press the filling to start a steady flow and direct the nozzle as desired.

1 Place the nozzle in the bag and twist it to seal and prevent leakage as you fill the bag with the chocolate.

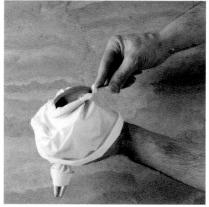

2 Hold the bag just above the nozzle, fold over the top to create a "collar", and spoon in the chocolate.

WARM CHOCOLATE FONDANT WITH PISTACHIO ICE CREAM

Daniel Graham sous chef and 2009 Professionals finalist

FOR THE PISTACHIO ICE CREAM
6 egg yolks
125g (4½oz) caster sugar
500ml (16fl oz) whole milk
30g (1oz) pistachio paste (see MasterTip, below)

FOR THE CHOCOLATE FONDANT
60g (2oz) dark chocolate (70% cocoa – see MasterTip, p.351), broken into pieces
60g (2oz) unsalted butter
2 eggs
2 egg yolks
45g (1½oz) caster sugar
2 tsp plain flour

PREPARATION TIME
30 minutes, plus freezing time

COOKING TIME
15 mins

SERVES 6

1 For the ice cream, whisk the egg yolks with half the sugar in a large bowl using an electric hand whisk for 2–3 minutes until very thick and creamy. Bring the milk and the remaining sugar to the boil. Remove from the heat, add the pistachio paste and stir to dissolve.
2 Gradually pour the hot milk into the yolk mixture and stir well. Return the mixture to the saucepan and cook over a low heat, continuously stirring, for 4–5 minutes or until it is thick enough to coat the back of a spoon. Resist the temptation to increase the heat otherwise the custard will curdle.
3 Chill, then strain the mix into an ice-cream maker and churn for about 20 minutes, or until frozen but not too stiff. (If you don't have an ice-cream maker, see the MasterTip, p.347.)
4 Preheat the oven to 180°C (350°F/Gas 4). Lightly butter and flour four 150ml (5fl oz) ramekins and place on a baking tray.
5 To make the fondant, put the chocolate and butter into a large bowl and place over a saucepan of barely simmering water, ensuring the bowl isn't touching the water. Heat for 5–6 minutes, stirring frequently, until the chocolate and butter are melted, well mixed, and smooth.
6 Meanwhile, place the eggs, egg yolks, and sugar in a bowl. Whisk using an electric hand whisk for 3–4 minutes or until the mixture has doubled in size and turned pale, almost white. Slowly fold in the flour. Then add the melted chocolate and butter and fold until fully incorporated. Pour the mixture into the ramekins and cook in the oven for 8–10 minutes or until well risen and just firm to the touch. They should not be cooked for longer otherwise you will not get the soft gooey inside to them.
7 Place the ramekins onto serving plates and serve immediately with a scoop of the pistachio ice cream to accompany.

MASTER TIP
PISTACHIO PASTE

Pistachio paste is not widely available, but you can make your own. Combine 100g (3½oz) finely ground blanched pistachio nuts and 30g (1oz) ground almonds with a drop of almond extract. In a small saucepan, heat 50g (1¾oz) caster sugar with 1 tbsp water until the sugar has dissolved. Then, using a sugar thermometer (see MasterTip, p.338), heat the mixture for 2–3 minutes until it reaches 120°C (248°F). Pour onto the nuts, stirring quickly. Add about 1 tbsp cold water, 1 tsp at a time, until you have a well mixed paste the consistency of marzipan. Knead lightly and cover with cling film until required. Freeze the remainder for future use.

CHOCOLATE SOUFFLÉ WITH WINTER BERRIES

inspired by **David Herbert** restaurateur and 2005 quarter-finalist

PREPARATION TIME
10 minutes, plus macerating time

COOKING TIME
11 minutes

SERVES 4

25g (scant 1oz) butter
60g (2oz) caster sugar, plus
  more for lining the ramekins
100g (3½oz) dark chocolate
  (70% cocoa – see Master Tip, p.351)
2 tsp dark rum
1 tsp vanilla extract
3 medium eggs, separated
icing sugar to dust

FOR THE WINTER BERRIES
100g (3½oz) blueberries
100g (3½oz) blackberries
4 tbsp crème de cassis

1 Begin by macerating the berries; allow at least 2 hours for this and preferably overnight. Combine the berries in a bowl, pour the cassis over them and allow to soak.

2 To make the soufflé (see MasterTip, p.323), preheat the oven to 180°C (350°F/Gas 4). Melt half the butter and brush it very liberally on the insides of 4 ramekins. Tip a little caster sugar inside and roll it round so it sticks to the butter, then tip out the excess.

3 In a bain marie or a bowl set over a pan of simmering water, melt the chocolate with the rum, vanilla extract, and remaining butter, then remove from the heat and beat in the egg yolks. In a clean bowl, whisk the egg whites to soft peak stage, then gradually add the caster sugar and continue whisking to stiff peaks. Stir a spoonful of the egg white and sugar mix into the chocolate to loosen, then fold in the rest in 2 or 3 stages.

4 Spoon the mix into the ramekins and level off the tops with a palette knife, then place on a baking tray in the oven for 11 minutes, when the soufflés should be well risen and set on top. Dust with icing sugar and serve immediately on 4 plates with the berries and their cassis juice to the side.

SOFT-CENTRED CHOCOLATE PUDDING WITH GREENGAGE COMPOTE

Peter Bayless ad creative turned author and 2006 champion

60g (2oz) dark chocolate (70% cocoa – see MasterTip, p.351)
60g (2oz) butter
1 egg
1 egg yolk
2 tbsp caster sugar
10g (¼oz) self-raising flour

FOR THE COMPOTE
juice and zest of 1 lemon
25g (scant 1oz) caster sugar
150g (5½oz) greengages or yellow plums, halved and stoned

PREPARATION TIME
1 hour

COOKING TIME
18 minutes

SERVES 4

1 Preheat the oven to 220°C (425°F/Gas 7). To make the chocolate puddings, begin by painting the inside of four 8cm (3¾in) ramekins with plenty of melted butter. Chill in the fridge before giving them a second coat, then dust them well with flour.

2 Break the chocolate into a bowl, add the butter and set the bowl over a saucepan of simmering water, making sure that the bottom of the bowl does not touch the water. When the chocolate and butter are melted together, remove the bowl from the heat.

3 Using an electric whisk, beat together the egg, egg yolk, and caster sugar to a thick and creamy consistency. Pour into the warm chocolate and sieve the flour into the mixture. Gently fold these ingredients together and spoon into the prepared ramekins. Place on a baking tray and bake in the oven for 9–10 minutes. Remove and allow them to cool a little before serving just warm.

4 To make the greengage compote, put the lemon juice, sugar, and 150ml (5fl oz) water in a saucepan and stir over low heat until the sugar has dissolved. Allow to simmer gently for a few minutes before adding the greengages. Simmer in the syrup for about 8 minutes until nicely cooked through. Allow this to cool a little before serving warm alongside the chocolate pudding, decorated with a little lemon zest.

HOT CHOCOLATE PUDDING WITH VANILLA ICE CREAM AND CARAMELIZED BANANA

Derek Johnstone junior sous chef and 2008 Professionals champion

PREPARATION TIME
1 hour 30 minutes, plus freezing time

COOKING TIME
20 minutes

SERVES 4

FOR THE VANILLA ICE CREAM
450ml (15fl oz) semi-skimmed milk
300ml (10fl oz) double cream
2 vanilla pods, split
9 egg yolks
200g (7oz) caster sugar

FOR THE HAZELNUT TUILES
2 large egg whites
85g (3oz) caster sugar
15g (½oz) strong plain flour
100g (3½oz) ground hazelnuts
4 tsp hazelnut oil

FOR THE HOT CHOCOLATE PUDDING
100g (3½oz) dark chocolate (70% cocoa
  – see MasterTip, p.351), broken
  into pieces
100g (3½oz) unsalted butter, diced
1 vanilla pod, broken in half
1 tbsp brandy
2 large eggs
2 egg yolks
60g (2oz) caster sugar
30g (1oz) plain flour
cocoa powder, for dusting

FOR THE CARAMELIZED BANANA
1 large banana
15g (½oz) caster sugar
2 tbsp maple syrup
2 tbsp clear honey

1 To make the vanilla ice cream, put the milk, cream, and vanilla pods in a saucepan and bring to the boil. Remove from the heat and leave to cool slightly. Meanwhile, in a bowl, whisk together the yolks and sugar and pour the hot liquid over them. Return the vanilla cream to the pan and allow to thicken slowly over a gentle heat, stirring frequently (see MasterTip, opposite). Use a double cooker, if you have one, so that the mixture does not curdle.

2 Transfer the mixture to a bowl to cool, then place in an ice-cream maker and churn for about 20 minutes, or until frozen. If you do not have an ice-cream maker, place in a freezerproof container and follow the instructions in the MasterTip, opposite.

3 For the hazelnut tuiles, preheat the oven to 150°C (300°F/Gas 2). Whisk the egg whites in a bowl until they are frothy and then whisk in the sugar until they are stiff. Lightly fold in the flour, hazelnuts, and hazelnut oil.

4 To shape the tuiles, create a template by cutting a 10cm (4in) diamond shape from a margarine tub lid. Place the template on a baking sheet lined with baking parchment. Then spread the tuile mixture very thinly over the template with a palette knife. Lift off the template, wipe it down and repeat to make 8 diamond tuiles.

Bake for 5–6 minutes until lightly coloured around the edges. Leave to cool slightly before lifting off the paper. Set aside.

5 Increase the oven temperature to 190°C (375°F/Gas 5). Butter four 150ml (5fl oz) dariole moulds and then swirl some cocoa powder around the insides, tipping out the excess.

6 For the hot chocolate pudding, put the chocolate, butter, vanilla pod halves, and brandy into a bowl and stand this over a saucepan of simmering water, ensuring it doesn't touch the bottom of the pan. Let the chocolate and butter melt.

7 In a large bowl, whisk the eggs, egg yolks, and sugar until they have trebled in size. Pour the melted chocolate mixture around the edge of the egg base. Then sieve in the flour and fold gently until all is incorporated. Fill the moulds three-quarters full, place on a baking sheet and bake for 8–10 minutes until firm, but not dry.

8 Meanwhile, caramelize the bananas. Cut them in half lenghways and then slice diagonally. Gently melt the caster sugar in a shallow heavy pan. When melted and beginning to caramelize, add the banana and cook until just turning golden on the cut surfaces. Then add the syrup and honey and heat gently until the bananas are glazed.

9 To serve, turn out the hot chocolate puddings onto plates, arrange 2 small scoops of ice cream on one side of each pudding and caramelized banana on the other. Place a tuile in each scoop of ice cream and trickle over the syrup from the bananas. Serve immediately.

MASTER TIP
MAKING ICE CREAM

If you don't have an ice-cream maker, place the mixture into shallow freezerproof container and freeze until mushy. Turn the mixture into a cold bowl and beat until the ice crystals are broken up. Return to the container and freeze again until mushy. Repeat the whisking and freeze one more. This method applies just as readily to a sorbet as it does to a cream-based recipe.

1 The basis of many ice creams is a crème anglaise or custard (see MasterTip, pp.308–9), which is then frozen and churned.

2 Ice-cream makers are the quickest way to make ice cream, churning and freezing the mixture in as little as 20 minutes, depending on its content.

CHOCOLATE TARTLET WITH SESAME SEED SNAP AND CRÈME FRAÎCHE

Chris Gates civil servant turned junior sous chef and 2009 finalist

PREPARATION TIME
15 minutes, plus chilling time

COOKING TIME
20 minutes

SERVES 4

100g (3½oz) cold butter
50g (1¾oz) icing sugar
175g (6oz) plain flour
2 egg yolks
crème fraîche, to serve

FOR THE FILLING
225ml (7½fl oz) double cream
1 tbsp caster sugar
1 tsp sea salt

150g (5½oz) dark chocolate
 (70% cocoa – see MasterTip, p.351),
 broken into pieces
3 tbsp whole milk
cocoa powder, to dust

FOR THE SESAME SEED SNAP
200g (7oz) caster sugar
25g (scant 1 oz) butter
handful of sesame seeds

1 To make the pastry, put the butter, icing sugar, plain flour, and egg yolks into a food processor and run it until everything comes together into a dough. Wrap in cling film and rest in the fridge for 1 hour.
2 Preheat the oven to 160°C (325°F/Gas 3). Butter four 10cm (4in) individual tart tins.
3 Roll out the pastry to a thickness of about 5mm (¼in) and line the tart tins. Prick the pastry and place the tins in the freezer for about 15 minutes. Then blind bake in the oven (see MasterTip, pp.368–9) for 12–15 minutes until the pastry is cooked through and slightly golden. Leave to cool.
4 To make the filling, put the cream, sugar, and salt in a saucepan and bring to the boil. Add the chocolate, remove the pan from the heat and mix until the chocolate has melted. Add the milk and mix well until smooth. Allow to cool slightly and then pour into the cooked tart cases. Leave to set, which will take about 2 hours at room temperature.
5 For the sesame seed snap, in a heavy pan, gently heat the sugar until it forms a golden caramel. Add the butter and sesame seeds and mix. Remove from the heat and pour onto a baking tray lined with baking parchment. Once slightly cooled, you will be able to cut the snap into whatever shape you like.
6 Remove the tartlets from their cases and serve on individual plates topped with a spoonful of crème fraîche and some broken sesame seed snap.

WHITE CHOCOLATE, BLUEBERRY, AND AMARETTO MASCARPONE CHEESECAKE

Becky McCracken teacher and 2006 semi-finalist

PREPARATION TIME
30 minutes, plus chilling time

SERVES 4

100g (3½oz) amaretti biscuits, crushed (see MasterTip, p.335)
50g (1¾oz) unsalted butter, melted
150g (5½oz) white chocolate, broken into pieces
500g (1lb 2oz) mascarpone cheese
25g (scant 1oz) icing sugar
200g (7oz) blueberries
2 tbsp amaretto

1 Mix the amaretti biscuits with the melted butter. Pack the biscuit mixture into four 8–10cm (3½–4in) ring moulds.

2 Tip the mascarpone into a large bowl. Melt the white chocolate in a bowl set over a pan of simmering water and then beat into the mascarpone cheese. Taste the mixture. It should be sweet, but not cloying. If necessary, add some sieved icing sugar to taste.

3 Put the cheese mixture on top of the biscuit bases and push some of the blueberries down into the mixture. Put in the fridge to chill for at least 1 hour.

4 To serve, gently heat a handful of blueberries in a pan with the amaretto liqueur until the blueberries just pop open. Remove the moulds (you may need to soften with a kitchen blow torch or a warmed knife if they are really cold) and transfer the cheesecakes onto individual plates. Spoon over the hot blueberry sauce and serve immediately.

DATE AND CHOCOLATE FILO SWEETS WITH VANILLA CRÈME FRAÎCHE

Perveen Nekoo wedding cake maker and 2006 quarter-finalist

25g (scant 1oz) dark chocolate (70% cocoa – see MasterTip, below), broken into pieces
6 dried medjool dates, stone removed
3 sheets filo pastry (see MasterTip, p.360)
30g (1oz) unsalted butter, melted

500ml (16fl oz) sunflower oil
300g tub crème fraîche
1 vanilla pod, seeds only
30g (1oz) icing sugar, plus extra for dusting

PREPARATION TIME
25 minutes

COOKING TIME
10 minutes

MAKES 6 SWEETS

1 Stuff pieces of the chocolate into the stoned dates.
2 Cut the filo pastry into 10cm (4in) squares and brush with the melted butter. Place each date diagonally onto a square of filo pastry and wrap it up, twisting the ends of the pastry to form a sweet wrapper shape.
3 Heat the oil in a small saucepan until it is sizzling – it needs to be hot enough so that the pastry does not go soggy. Put the "sweets" in the pan and fry for about 1 minute or until they are golden, occasionally turning (see MasterTip, p.101).
4 Mix the crème fraîche in a bowl with the vanilla seeds and the icing sugar.
5 Transfer 2 filo sweets to each of 3 serving plates and serve with a tablespoon of crème fraîche and a dusting of icing sugar.

MASTER TIP
COCOA SOLIDS

Chocolate is labelled to show its percentage of cocoa solids and butter. The higher this figure, the more intense the chocolate flavour will be – with the associated bitterness. For a good quality dark chocolate, the proportion of cocoa solids will be about 70%. Dark chocolate is made of cocoa solids, cocoa butter, and sugar, while milk chocolate has milk solids added.

HOT CHOCOLATE CAKE WITH WHISKY VANILLA CREAM AND CARAMEL SAUCE

inspired by **Andi Peters** presenter and producer and 2008 Celebrity finalist

PREPARATION TIME
45 minutes

COOKING TIME
30 minutes

MAKES 10–12 SLICES

150g (5½oz) dark chocolate
  (70% cocoa – see MasterTip, p.351)
150g (5½oz) butter
4 medium eggs
100g (3½oz) caster sugar
50g (1¾oz) light muscovado sugar
85g (3oz) plain flour
1 tsp baking powder
1 tbsp cocoa

FOR THE WHISKY VANILLA CREAM
250ml (8fl oz) double cream
2 tbsp icing sugar, sifted
1 vanilla pod, seeds only
2 tbsp crème fraîche
2 tbsp whisky

FOR THE CARAMEL SAUCE
100g (3½oz) light soft brown sugar
100g (3½oz) butter
100g (3½fl oz) double cream

1 Preheat the oven to 180°C (350°F/Gas 4). To make the cake, first melt the chocolate and butter in a bain marie or a bowl set over a pan of simmering water. In a separate bowl, whisk together the eggs and sugars until they are pale and frothy, and double their original volume.
2 Pour the melted chocolate and butter into the eggs and sugar and whisk in gently. Sift in the flour, baking powder, and cocoa and fold through. Pour into a 20cm (8in) base-lined and greased springform tin and bake for 25–30 minutes until a knife inserted in the centre comes out clean. Remove from the oven and cool slightly in the tin for about 10 minutes.

MASTER TIP

MAKING CARAMEL SAUCE

The basis of a caramel sauce is a simple sugar syrup (see MasterTip, p.314). Caramel sauce can be made with crème fraîche rather than cream, but expect the sauce to spatter more onto the sides of the pan. Wearing gloves is a good idea, since caramelized syrup is hotter than water; do not allow children near the pan until the syrup has cooled. Using a heavy pan lessens the chance of the syrup burning.

1 While the syrup is still warm, whisk in the butter and cream until the sauce is smooth. Bring gently to the boil.

2 A sugar thermometer is helpful. For caramel, remove the pan from the heat when the sauce reaches 103°C (217°F).

3 For the cream, whip the double cream with the icing sugar and vanilla seeds until it reaches soft peak stage, then whip in the crème fraîche and whisky.

4 For the caramel sauce, place the sugar and butter in a small saucepan over a low heat, stirring until the butter is melted and the sugar is dissolved. Add the cream and continue to heat until bubbling, stirring continuously to prevent burning. At this point the sauce is ready and can be removed from the heat until you are ready to serve.

5 Serve the cake while still very warm, cut into slices with the cream on top and the caramel sauce spooned around the sides.

JOHN TORODE "Well, it's delicious. It's chocolate, caramel, vanilla, and cream – of course it's delicious! And it's a fantastic pudding."

ST EMILION AU CHOCOLAT

William Leigh retail designer turned food writer and 2007 semi-finalist

100g (3½oz) dark chocolate (70% cocoa – see MasterTip, p.351), plus extra for decoration
100ml (3½fl oz) whole milk
50g (1¾oz) unsalted butter
50g (1¾oz) caster sugar

1 egg yolk
125g (4½oz) ratafia or amaretti biscuits, crushed (see MasterTip, p.333)
4 tsp brandy
double cream, to serve

PREPARATION TIME
10 minutes, plus chilling time

SERVES 4

1 Put the chocolate and milk in a saucepan and gently heat until the chocolate has melted.

2 Put the butter, sugar, and egg yolk in food processor and blend, and then pour into the chocolate mixture, continuously stirring.

3 With a piece of kitchen paper, wipe around four 7cm (2¾in) ring moulds with some softened butter, and place onto serving plates. Divide the crushed biscuits into the base of each of the rings. Sprinkle 1 tsp of the brandy over each of the bases and then carefully pour in the chocolate, dividing evenly between the 4 rings. Leave to chill in the fridge for 1 hour.

4 Remove the puddings from the rings and serve with double cream.

GOOEY CHOCOLATE CAKE WITH SPICED PLUM COULIS

Hannah Miles lawyer turned cookbook author and 2007 finalist

250g (9oz) dark chocolate
  (70% cocoa – see MasterTip, p.351)
100g (3½oz) salted butter
4 large eggs, separated
175g (6oz) icing sugar
1 tsp cocoa powder
1 tsp icing sugar
4 tbsp crème fraîche

FOR THE COULIS
10 ripe red plums, stoned
  and quartered

50g (1¾oz) caster sugar
1 tbsp amaretto
½ cinnamon stick

FOR THE TUILES
50g (1¾oz) plain flour
10g (¼oz) cocoa powder
60g (2oz) icing sugar
50g (1¾oz) salted butter, melted
2 egg whites

PREPARATION TIME
45 minutes

COOKING TIME
45 minutes

MAKES 6–8 SLICES

1 Preheat the oven to 180°C (350°F/Gas 4). Grease a 21cm (8½in) springform tin, or 4 individual-sized pudding basins or ramekins, and line the base with baking parchment.

2 Melt the chocolate and butter together in a microwave oven (about 3 minutes on High) or in a bain marie or a pan set over a pan of simmering water. In another bowl, beat the egg yolks with the icing sugar until creamy. Fold in the chocolate and butter mixture. Whisk the egg whites (not too stiffly) and fold in. Pour into the tin and bake in the oven for 30 minutes or until the mixture springs back when gently pressed; if making individual cakes they will need less time. Allow to cool slightly, then turn out of the tin or basins.

3 To make the plum coulis, simmer the plums with the caster sugar, amaretto, and cinnamon for about 15 minutes until soft. Purée in a food processor then put through a sieve.

4 For the tuiles, line a baking sheet with greaseproof paper. Place all the ingredients in a bowl and, using a spoon, mix them together. Spoon 8 mounds of the mixture onto the baking sheet and use a palette knife to smooth them into circles about 5cm (2in) in diameter. Place in the oven at the same heat for 6–7 minutes. Remove and, while they are still warm, lift them off with a palette knife and drape them over a rolling pin so that they set into a rounded shape. Lift off when cool. Any left uneaten can be stored in an airtight container.

5 To serve, pour 1 tbsp of the coulis onto each plate and sit the cake beside it. Dust with cocoa and icing sugar combined, place a spoonful of crème fraîche on top and set a tuile at an angle.

GRASS AND MUD PIE WITH RASPBERRIES

Emily Ludolf 18-year-old student and 2008 finalist

PREPARATION TIME
30 minutes, plus chilling time

COOKING TIME
45 minutes

SERVES 4

FOR THE SWEET PASTRY
130g (4¾oz) caster sugar
150g (5½oz) butter, softened
2 tsp vanilla extract
100g (3½oz) cocoa powder
20g (¾oz) dark chocolate
  (80% cocoa – see MasterTip,
  p.351), finely grated
250g (9oz) plain flour
½ tsp salt
1 egg, lightly beaten

FOR THE GANACHE
200g (7oz) dark chocolate (60% cocoa)
pinch of salt
100ml (3½fl oz) whole milk
100ml (3½fl oz) double cream
1 small bunch of thyme
1 tbsp clear honey

TO DECORATE
1 bunch of tarragon (whole leaves)
225g (8oz) caster sugar
175g (6oz) raspberries

1 Preheat the oven to 200°C (400°F/Gas 6).

2 To make the chocolate pastry, cream together the sugar, butter, and vanilla extract in a food processor until the mixture is light and fluffy. Add the cocoa powder and chocolate and mix until well blended. Spoon in the flour and salt and mix until well blended – you may find you need to add a few drops of water to help bring the dough together. Scrape out the pastry onto a sheet of cling film, wrap and refrigerate for 30 minutes.

3 On a floured work surface, carefully roll out the pastry to a thickness of 3mm (⅛in) and, using an 8cm (3¼in) cutter, cut out

---

MASTER TIP
MAKING SWEET PASTRY

You can make sweet pastry (pâte sucrée) in a food processor, with an electric mixer, or by hand. Many people enjoy the traditional way, and it also lessens the chance of over-processing. For making pastry by hand, it is best to use a wooden or marble pastry board. Knead the pastry as briefly as possible, then wrap in cling film and allow it to rest in the fridge before rolling it out.

1 Soften the butter in the mixing bowl, then add the sugar, salt, vanilla, eggs, and flour, in that order. Mix slowly, stopping as soon as a ball is formed.

2 When mixing by hand, sift the flour onto the work surface first, sprinkle with salt then rub in the butter. Mix in the other ingredients, eggs last.

8 pastry rounds. Place on a baking sheet lined with baking parchment and blind bake for 8 minutes (see MasterTip, pp.368–9).

4 Remove the beans and the baking parchment, then return to the oven for another 2–3 minutes until the pastry is cooked through.

5 While the pastry rounds are still hot, brush with the beaten egg and bake for another 1–2 minutes to seal the egg glaze. Remove and leave to cool while you prepare the ganache filling (see MasterTip, p.336).

6 Chop the chocolate and put into a large heatproof bowl. Add a tiny pinch of salt to the bowl.

7 Put the milk, cream, thyme, and honey into a saucepan and bring to a simmer, stirring well to blend in the honey. Bring to the boil then remove from the heat and leave to infuse for 1 hour. Pass through a sieve to remove the thyme sprigs then bring to the boil again and immediately pour the hot liquid onto the chocolate, whisking well until all the chocolate has melted and the combined mixture is smooth and silky. Allow to cool for 1 hour until the mixture is twice as thick as double cream.

8 Meanwhile, take the tarragon leaves and lay them on a sheet of foil. Place the caster sugar and 125ml (4¼fl oz) water in a saucepan and slowly bring to the boil to create a syrup. Use a sugar thermometer (see MasterTip, p.338) to check when it has reached "hard ball" stage, which occurs at 121–129°C (250–265°F). You can also test this by dropping a little syrup in cold water – it should form a firm ball that will not flatten when you take it out of the water, but remains malleable and will flatten when squeezed. Once the syrup is ready, use a pastry brush to brush it over the tarragon leaves to crystallize them.

9 To serve, place a pastry round on each plate and then top with a layer of the chocolate ganache. Place another pastry round on top and add another layer of ganache. Decorate with the crystallized tarragon leaves and raspberries.

MILLEFEUILLE OF RASPBERRIES AND BITTER CHOCOLATE WITH LAVENDER AND HONEY ICE CREAM

Steve Groves chef de partie and 2009 Professionals champion

PREPARATION TIME
45 minutes

COOKING TIME
45 minutes

SERVES 4

250g (9oz) ready-made puff pastry
  (or see MasterTip, p.365)
400g (14oz) raspberries
icing sugar for dusting

FOR THE ICE CREAM
500ml (16fl oz) double cream
6 heads of lavender
4 egg yolks
175g (6oz) clear honey

FOR THE CHOCOLATE MOUSSE
4 egg yolks
200g (7oz) caster sugar
100ml (3½fl oz) whole milk
150g (5½oz) dark chocolate
  (70% cocoa – see MasterTip,
  p.351), chopped
1 tsp salt
200ml (7fl oz) whipping cream

MICHEL ROUX JR

"This is a lovely millefeuille. It looks beautiful and the bitter chocolate still has enough sweetness to work perfectly with the raspberries."

1 To make the ice cream, bring the cream to the boil. Add 2 heads of lavender, remove from the heat, and allow to infuse for 10 minutes. Strain then return to near boiling point. Whisk the egg yolks and honey together then pour half of the cream onto them, whisking meanwhile. Return to the pan and heat to 80°C (176°F), then pass through a sieve. Chill and then put into an ice-cream maker and freeze according to the manufacturer's instructions. (If you do not have an ice-cream maker, see the MasterTip on p.347.)

2 Preheat the oven to 200°C (400°F/Gas 6). Roll the pastry out to around 3mm (⅛in) thick and cut into 12 rectangles measuring 3 x 6cm (1¼–2½in). Bake for 20–25 mins between 2 baking sheets, then remove the top baking sheet and return the pastry to the oven if needed to ensure it is golden throughout. Once cooled, trim the edges.

3 To make the chocolate mousse, whisk the egg yolks and sugar together until they are almost white. Bring the milk to the boil and then pour half onto the egg mixture while whisking. Once thoroughly mixed, return to the pan over a low to medium heat and heat to 80°C (176°F). Pour this mixture over the chocolate and stir until all the chocolate is melted and incorporated. Add the salt and allow to cool.

4 Whip the whipping cream to soft peaks and fold gently into the cooled chocolate mix. Put into a piping bag and chill.

5 To serve, arrange rows of raspberries on a layer of mousse on 8 pieces of pastry. Dust the flattest 4 pieces liberally with icing sugar and use a very hot metal skewer to make a crisscross pattern. Stack the layers up with the sugared one on top. Place on the serving plates with a scoop of ice cream garnished with a head of lavender.

RHUBARB MILLEFEUILLE

Helen Gilmour 2007 quarter-finalist

PREPARATION TIME
40 minutes, plus chilling time

COOKING TIME
5 minutes

SERVES 4

2 sheets filo pastry (see MasterTip, below), each measuring 50 x 25cm (20 x 10in)
30g (1oz) unsalted butter, melted
225g (8oz) caster sugar
8 sticks young rhubarb, cut into 4cm (1½in) pieces
icing sugar, to decorate

FOR THE PASTRY CREAM
200ml (7fl oz) whole milk
1 vanilla pod
1 large egg, plus 1 egg yolk
25g (scant 1oz) caster sugar
20g (¾oz) plain flour, sifted

MASTER TIP

FILO PASTRY

Filo pastry comprises paper-thin sheets of pastry that are used in layers in Greek, Eastern European, and Middle-Eastern sweet and savoury dishes. When laying it out you must work quickly otherwise it dries out. Keep it brushed with oil or melted butter, or cover it with cling film. Filo pastry is likely to tear when stretched, but this usually doesn't show once the dish is made up.

1 Preheat the oven to 180°C (350°F/Gas 4) and grease 2 baking sheets. Brush a sheet of filo with melted butter and lay another on top. Cut out 12 rectangles of the filo, each measuring 10 x 4cm (4 x 1½in). Transfer to the baking sheets and bake for 5 minutes, until golden. Remove from the oven and leave to cool.

2 To make the pastry cream, gently warm the milk and vanilla pod. In a separate bowl, whisk the eggs and sugar until thick and creamy. Then add the flour and whisk again. Remove the vanilla pod from the warm milk and whisk the milk into the egg mixture.

3 Put the bowl over a gently simmering saucepan of water and cook until the cream becomes thick. This needs continuous whisking with a balloon whisk as the mixture can easily catch on the bottom. Cover the pastry cream with cling film and leave it to go cold.

4 Make a sugar syrup by dissolving the caster sugar in 300ml (10fl oz) water and let it simmer gently for about 15 minutes until slightly thickened. Add the pieces of rhubarb and continue to simmer for about 10 minutes until tender, but make sure the rhubarb keeps its shape and some bite. Use a slotted spoon to remove the rhubarb from the syrup and set the rhubarb aside to cool.

5 Increase the heat beneath the sugar syrup and let it reduce to a thick syrup.

6 To assemble, layer a piece of filo, spread it with some of the vanilla custard and top with poached rhubarb. Place another layer of filo on top and repeat. Then place a final layer of filo on top and sprinkle with icing sugar. Drizzle the plates with the reduced rhubarb syrup.

PINEAPPLE TARTE TATIN WITH COCONUT CARAMEL

James Nathan barrister turned chef and 2008 champion

4 x 1cm (½in) thick slices of pineapple
250g (9oz) ready-made puff pastry (or
  see MasterTip, p.365)
25g (scant 1oz) unsalted butter
1 tbsp golden syrup
25g (scant 1oz) caster sugar

FOR THE COCONUT CARAMEL
3 tbsp desiccated coconut
2 tbsp golden syrup
1 tbsp caster sugar
100ml (3½fl oz) double cream

PREPARATION TIME
20 minutes

COOKING TIME
40 minutes

SERVES 4

1 Preheat the oven to 180°C (350°F/Gas 4) and grease 2 baking sheets. Skin the pineapple slices and cut a small circle out of the centre of each to remove the tough core.

2 Roll out the puff pastry to about 5mm (¼in) thick and cut 4 circles that are 4cm (1½in) wider than the pineapple slices. Put on one of the baking sheets, cover with cling film and put in the fridge.

3 Put a non-stick frying pan over a medium heat and heat the butter until it is gently foaming. Add the syrup and sugar and increase the heat to high. Lay the pineapple slices in the pan and cook for 1–2 minutes until the sugar starts to caramelize. Reduce the heat to medium and cook the pineapple for about 7 minutes until they are browned and caramelized. Occasionally lift each slice and trap bubbling sugar and syrup underneath to aid the caramelization.

4 Turn the slices over and repeat the process. Make sure the slices of pineapple don't start to break up; you want them to stay whole. Remove each slice and put on the second baking sheet. Spoon over any caramel still left in the pan and leave for 15 minutes or so to cool.

5 Cover each pineapple slice with a pastry circle, tucking it under each slice. Put into the oven and cook for 15–20 minutes until the pastry is golden and well risen. Remove from the oven, turn over so the pineapple is facing upwards and keep warm.

6 Meanwhile, make the coconut caramel. Heat a non-stick saucepan over a moderate heat. Add the desiccated coconut and dry-fry it, stirring continuously, until it turns golden brown. Add the golden syrup and sugar and fry for another 3–4 minutes until the coconut is coated in the sugar and syrup. Then add the cream and cook for a further 1–2 minutes, stirring continuously, until you have a glossy, well combined sauce (see also MasterTip, p352).

7 To serve, place the pineapple tarts on plates and spoon the sauce over the top and into the holes where the core was removed.

RHUBARB TARTE TATIN SERVED WITH MASCARPONE

Marianne Lumb private chef and 2009 Professionals finalist

PREPARATION TIME
15 minutes

COOKING TIME
30 minutes

SERVES 4

200g (7oz) ready-made puff pastry
  (or see MasterTip, p.365)
6 sticks rhubarb
150g (5½oz) unsalted butter, softened
125g (4½oz) granulated sugar
grated zest of 1 orange
2 vanilla pods, each split and cut into
  4 pieces
200g (7oz) mascarpone cheese

MASTER TIP

BLINI PANS

Blini pans are small heavy frying pans that have many uses in addition to making blinis (see MasterTip, p.34), such as pancakes and fritters. They have a diameter of 12cm (5in) and triple blini pans, joined together with just one handle, are also available. For this recipe, you might prefer to follow the cooking method given for Fig tarte Tatin on page 364, using a baking tray with portion-sized shallow indents, such as a Yorkshire pudding tin, in place of the blini pans.

1 Preheat the oven to 190°C (375°F/Gas 5) and get out 4 heatproof blini pans. Roll the puff pastry to about 3mm (⅛in) thick and cut into 4 discs with a diameter slightly larger than the pans. Prick each disc and leave to chill in the fridge.

2 Choose the thicker pieces of rhubarb and cut to fit the 4 pans perfectly in 2 layers. Cover the base of each pan with the butter and then sprinkle over the sugar, orange zest, and a piece of vanilla pod, and then add the rhubarb pieces.

3 Cook the rhubarb on a very high heat on the hob for about 10 minutes to reach a good, bitter caramelization (see MasterTip, p.237). Check by carefully lifting up the rhubarb with a palette knife, but do not be tempted to stir the rhubarb.

4 Cover each pan carefully with a disc of puff pastry, allowing the pastry to tuck just inside the pans. Place the pans on a baking sheet and cook for 20–30 minutes, or until the puff pastry is perfectly cooked and the tartes have a good caramelization. Remove from the oven and allow to rest for a few minutes.

5 Carefully invert each pan onto a plate, letting the tarte drop gently down. Serve immediately, each topped with a scoop of mascarpone cheese and a remaining piece of vanilla pod, to decorate.

FIG TARTE TATIN WITH CLOTTED CREAM AND PISTACHIOS

Gillian Wylie property developer turned chef and 2007 quarter-finalist

PREPARATION TIME
25 minutes

COOKING TIME
25 minutes

SERVES 4

100g (3½oz) caster sugar
100g (3½oz) unsalted butter
4 ripe figs, cut into segments
375g (13oz) ready-made puff pastry
  (or see MasterTip, opposite)
115ml (3¾fl oz) clotted cream
1 tbsp pistachio nuts, roughly chopped

1 Preheat the oven to 180°C (350°F/Gas 4). To make individual tartes Tatin, you will need a baking tray with portion-sized shallow indents, such as one designed for Yorkshire puddings.
2 Sprinkle the sugar into a non-stick frying pan. Slice the butter, lay it on top of the sugar and slowly let them melt together over a medium-low heat until a caramel forms. Resist the urge to stir until the sugar has melted – you need to be patient, as this will take at least 15 minutes.
3 Arrange the figs in a spiral in the base of 4 of the baking tray's indents and put 1 tbsp caramel into each. Roll out some puff pastry on a floured surface and cut out 4 discs the same diameter as the indents in the tray. Place the discs over the figs and tuck in the edges a little.
4 Cook in the oven for 20–25 minutes until the pastry is golden and risen. Remove and allow to rest for a few minutes before inverting onto a board – be careful, as the caramel will be hot.
5 To serve, transfer the tartes Tatin onto serving plates, place a quenelle (see MasterTip, p.93) of clotted cream in the centre of each, swirl some extra caramel around the plates and finish with a sprinkling of chopped pistachio nuts.

1 Roll out your dough to a long rectangle on a cool floured surface.

2 Add the butter, turn the parcel over and roll out from the centre.

3 Fold both ends of the dough inwards to meet in the centre.

4 Fold the dough in half at the centre, flatten slightly and chill for 30 minutes.

5 Roll out to a rectangle again, then fold and chill as before. Repeat once.

6 Roll into a rectangle then fold one end to the middle and the other over it.

MASTER TIP

PUFF PASTRY

In puff pastry, a dough called the *détrempe* is made from flour, salt, water, and a small amount of butter. The main butter content is then rolled into the dough.

First roll out your dough to a rectangle on a sheet of baking parchment. Prepare softened butter half the weight of the dough by rolling it out between 2 sheets of cling film to a rectangle about half the size of your dough. Take off 1 sheet of cling film, lay the butter in the centre of the dough and remove the second sheet. Fold the dough over it, pinching the edges together, then roll and fold as shown. If you are making the pastry ahead of time, leave the last step until you are about to use the pastry, allowing 30 minutes chilling time afterwards.

PEAR, APPLE, AND PISTACHIO TART WITH CLOTTED CREAM ICE CREAM

Alix Carwood IT consultant and 2008 quarter-finalist

PREPARATION TIME
45 minutes

COOKING TIME
40 minutes

SERVES 4

250g (9oz) ready-made puff pastry
  (or see MasterTip, p.365)
1 egg yolk
50g (1¾oz) pistachio nuts
30g (1oz) ground almonds
30g (1oz) softened unsalted butter
30g (1oz) caster sugar
½ tsp vanilla extract
1 sweet, juicy pear, such as Williams
1 aromatic apple, such as Cox's
10g (¼oz) unsalted butter, melted
2 tbsp clear honey

FOR THE ICE CREAM
200ml (7fl oz) whole milk
1 vanilla pod
2 egg yolks
50g (scant 1oz) caster sugar
175g (6oz) clotted cream
4 tbsp double cream

1 To make the ice cream, pour the milk into a non-stick saucepan. Cut open the vanilla pod and scrape out the seeds into the milk, then add the pod. Bring the milk to the boil, then take off the heat and allow to cool. When cool, remove the vanilla pod.

2 Whisk the egg yolks together with the sugar in a large bowl. Pour in the cooled milk mix and whisk together. Return this custard mixture to the saucepan and heat gently, stirring, until it has thickened, taking care not to let it boil. Remove from the heat and allow to cool a little.

3 In a large bowl, mix the clotted cream and double cream together to loosen the consistency of the clotted cream. Add the cooled custard mixture and stir to combine.

4 Pour the mixture into an ice-cream maker and freeze according to the manufacturer's instructions. (If you do not have an ice-cream maker, see the MasterTip, p.347.)

5 To make the tarts, preheat the oven to 200°C (400°F/Gas 6). Roll out the puff pastry until it is approximately 5mm (¼in) thick. Cut out four 12cm (5in) circles. With a sharp knife, score a smaller circle within each circle of pastry, taking care not to cut through it. Prick some holes in the centre of the pastry, using a fork. Brush the pastry circles with beaten egg yolk.

6 Put the pistachio nuts in a freezer bag and crush them, then place 30g (1oz) of them in a large mixing bowl, reserving the remainder for decorating the top of the tart and the ice cream. Add the ground almonds, softened butter, caster sugar, and vanilla extract. Mix together so it forms a paste. Spread the paste on the puff pastry bases in the inner circle.

7 Peel the apple and pear and cut into fine slices. Arrange on top of the pistachio paste and then brush with the melted butter. Sprinkle half the remaining crushed pistachios on top of the tart and place in the oven for 15 minutes. Remove from the oven, drizzle some honey over the top and then replace in the oven for a further 10–15 minutes.
8 To serve, place the tart on a plate with a good scoop of the ice cream. Sprinkle the remaining pistachio nuts over the ice cream.

APPLE AND PEAR TORTE

inspired by **Jayne Middlemiss** presenter and 2009 Celebrity champion

115g (4oz) butter
60g (2oz) light soft brown sugar
125g (4½oz) plain flour
250g (9oz) cream cheese
115g (4oz) caster sugar
1 egg

½ tsp vanilla extract
3 apples, peeled, cored, and sliced
3 pears, peeled, cored, and sliced
½ tsp ground cinnamon
25g (scant 1oz) pine nuts

PREPARATION TIME
25 minutes

COOKING TIME
1 hour

MAKES 10 SLICES

1 Preheat the oven to 230°C (450°F/Gas 8). Butter a 23cm (9in) round, springform tin.
2 Cream together the butter, light soft brown sugar, and flour and press into the base of the tin.
3 Blend the cream cheese with half of the caster sugar, then add the egg and vanilla extract and mix well before spreading over the base.
4 Combine the apples and pears with the remaining caster sugar and ground cinnamon and scatter over the cream cheese mixture.
5 Bake for about 10 minutes before reducing the oven temperature to 200°C (400°F/Gas 6) and baking for a further 35–40 minutes until golden brown on top and slightly set when tipped.
6 Scatter over the pine nuts and bake for another 10–15 minutes until they are browned. Remove from the oven and let the torte cool completely in the tin before serving.

PEAR AND ORANGE FRANGIPANE TART WITH GRAND MARNIER SYRUP

Fiona Marshall teacher and 2006 quarter-finalist

PREPARATION TIME
45 minutes, plus chilling time

COOKING TIME
30 minutes

SERVES 4

FOR THE PASTRY
125g (4½oz) plain flour
85g (3oz) "00" pasta flour
   (see MasterTip, p.52)
100g (3½oz) unsalted butter
25g (scant 1oz) caster sugar
1 large egg, beaten

FOR THE TART FILLING
75g (2½oz) unsalted butter
75g (2½oz) caster sugar
75g (2½oz) ground almonds

grated zest of 1 large orange,
   plus the juice, for the syrup
1 large egg, beaten
1 tbsp plain flour
4 pears

FOR THE SYRUP
100ml (3½fl oz) Grand Marnier
   or Cointreau

TO SERVE
small tub of mascarpone cheese

1   To make the pastry, place both flours, butter, and sugar in a food processor and pulse until combined. Add the beaten egg to bind. On a floured work surface, knead lightly until smooth and then wrap in cling film and leave to rest in the fridge for 20 minutes.
2   Preheat the oven to 180°C (350°F/Gas 4) and butter four 12cm (5in) diameter tart tins.
3   Remove the chilled pastry from the fridge, roll it out to 5mm (¼in) thick and line the tart tins. Blind bake for 10 minutes (see, below).

MASTER TIP

BLIND BAKING

Blind baking means baking a pastry shell without a filling. Pastry cases are often pre-cooked either partially or fully, depending on the filling to be used. If a moist filling, such as custard, is to be cooked in the tart, the case is partially cooked to prevent the moist filling from making it soggy. The pastry has to be weighted down with ceramic baking beans or dried beans to prevent it from losing its shape during the baking process.

1 Cut a circle of baking parchment slightly larger than the tart ring or tin. Fold the disc in half several times, then clip the outer edge with scissors.

2 Cover the base and sides of the pastry with the parchment, taking the paper above the dies of the ring. Fill with dried beans or baking beans.

4 To make the frangipane filling, place the butter, sugar, almonds, orange zest, and egg in a food processor and combine until smooth. Then fold in the plain flour.

5 Peel, core, and slice the pears and divide between the 4 tart tins. Pipe or spoon the frangipane mixture around the pears, allowing room for it to rise and so the pears peep out from the middle. Bake in the oven for 15–20 minutes until the frangipane is golden and feels springy to the touch.

6 For the syrup, place the orange juice and Grand Marnier (or Cointreau) in a pan, bring to the boil and then gently reduce for about 10 minutes until syrupy. Keep an eye on the saucepan, as the sauce can quickly go too sticky.

7 To serve, remove each tart from its tin and transfer to a serving plate. Carefully pour the syrup around the edge of each tart and add a scoop of mascarpone cheese.

3 Place the shell in the oven and bake according to recipe instructions. For a fully baked case, remove the beans and paper, then return the shell to the oven.

4 Cool the pastry case on a wire rack. Lift off the flan ring (or remove from the tart tin) before or after filling, according to the recipe directions.

PEAR AND BUTTERSCOTCH FRANGIPANE TART
Susie Carter administrator turned food writer and 2006 quarter-finalist

PREPARATION TIME
45 minutes

COOKING TIME
40 minutes

SERVES 4

50g (1¾oz) caster sugar
clotted cream, to serve

FOR THE BUTTERSCOTCH SAUCE
50g (1¾oz) unsalted butter
50g (1¾oz) light muscovado sugar
2 tbsp golden syrup
2 tbsp double cream

FOR THE PASTRY
200g (7oz) plain flour
100g (3½oz) butter
1 egg, beaten

FOR THE TART FILLING
50g (1¾oz) ground almonds
50g (1¾oz) caster sugar
50g (1¾oz) butter
1 egg
few drops of almond extract
2 pears, with stalks, to serve

1 To make the butterscotch sauce, put the butter, sugar, and golden syrup into a small saucepan and bring slowly to the boil, stirring. Reduce the heat and simmer for 3 minutes or until thick. Stir in the cream, then remove from the heat and set aside to cool.

2 Make the pastry by rubbing the butter into the flour, then adding enough cold water to bind into a pliable dough. Rest in the fridge for 30 minutes, then roll out on a floured surface and use to line 4 tartlet cases about 10cm (4in) in diameter. Trim the excess with scissors, allowing a little to overhang, and prick all over the base with a fork.

3 Preheat the oven to 180°C (350°F/Gas 4). Line each pastry case with baking parchment and blind bake (see MasterTip, p.368) for 10 minutes. Remove the baking parchment and beans, brush the pastry with beaten egg and return to the oven for 5–10 minutes or until crisp.

4 Spoon 2 tbsp butterscotch sauce into each pastry case and reserve the rest to serve with the finished tarts. To make the frangipane, whisk together all the tart filling ingredients except the pears until light and spoon into the pastry cases to come halfway up the sides.

5 Peel the pears and cut in half through the stalk. Carefully remove the core, then slice along the length like a fan, without cutting all the way through at the stalk end. Use half a pear to top each tartlet, snuggling it down. Bake for 20 minutes or until the pear and frangipane are both cooked. Leave to cool a little.

6 Heat the caster sugar in a small pan, shaking occasionally until it has liquefied and turned light brown. Pour onto a non-stick baking mat in a thin layer and leave to cool for a few minutes. When set, break into shards. Serve the tartlets with a pool of butterscotch sauce, a quenelle (see MasterTip, p.93) of clotted cream and a caramel shard.

PEAR AND ALMOND TART WITH CINNAMON AND MASCARPONE ICE CREAM

Matt Dawson professional rugby player and 2006 Celebrity champion

PREPARATION TIME
40 minutes, plus freezing time

COOKING TIME
50 minutes

SERVES 4

FOR THE ICE CREAM
30g (1oz) caster sugar
2 eggs, separated
½ tsp ground cinnamon
2 tsp vanilla extract
300ml (10fl oz) double cream
250g (9oz) mascarpone cheese, beaten
  until smooth

FOR THE PASTRY
200g (7oz) plain flour
pinch of salt

100g (3½oz) cold butter
30g (1oz) caster sugar
1 egg yolk

FOR THE TART FILLING
150g (5½oz) caster sugar
150g (5½oz) butter, softened
3 eggs, beaten
½ tsp almond extract
150g (5½oz) ground almonds
50g (1¾oz) plain flour
2 ripe pears, peeled, cored,
  quartered then sliced
a little lemon juice for brushing

1 For the ice cream, whisk the sugar and egg yolks together until thick then whisk in the cinnamon, vanilla, and cream. Gradually beat into the mascarpone in a separate bowl until smooth. Whisk the egg whites to soft peaks then fold into the mascarpone mixture. Transfer to an ice-cream maker and churn following the manufacturer's instructions. (If you do not have one, see the MasterTip, p.347.)

2 Preheat the oven to 180°C (350°F/Gas 4). To make the pastry, add the flour, salt, and butter to a food processor and pulse to breadcrumb consistency. Stir in the sugar, egg yolk, and cold water to bind to a soft but not sticky dough. Wrap in cling film and chill for 30 minutes.

3 Roll out the pastry on a floured surface. Use to line the base and sides of a 23cm (9in) round flan dish, trimming off any excess. Bake blind (see MasterTip, pp.368–9) for 12 minutes. Remove the baking beans and cook for a further 3–5 minutes. Leave to cool slightly while you make the filling. Reduce the oven to 160°C (325°F/Gas 3).

4 For the filling, cream the sugar and butter together until fluffy and smooth. Add the eggs and almond extract and beat well then stir in the ground almonds and flour. Spoon into the pastry-lined dish.

5 Carefully arrange the pears on top of the frangipane mixture in a pretty pattern, pressing them into the mixture slightly. Brush the exposed parts of the pear with a little lemon juice to help prevent discolouration then place in the oven and cook for 30–35 minutes or until well risen and golden brown and the filling has set. Leave the tart to cool for about 5 minutes before cutting into slices and serving with the ice cream.

CITRUS TART WITH CUCUMBER SORBET
David Henry sous chef and 2009 Professionals semi-finalist

FOR THE SORBET
1 cucumber
250g (9oz) caster sugar

FOR THE PASTRY
85g (3oz) unsalted butter
50g (1¾oz) icing sugar
2 egg yolks
175g (6oz) plain flour

FOR THE CURD FILLING
3 eggs
75g (2½oz) caster sugar
grated zest and juice of 1 lemon
grated zest and juice of 1 lime
100ml (3½floz) double cream

PREPARATION TIME
20 minutes

COOKING TIME
40 minutes

SERVES 4

1 To make the cucumber sorbet, peel the cucumber, remove the seeds, and cut into chunks. Put into a bowl and use a hand blender to purée the flesh. Pass the mixture through a sieve and set aside.

2 Meanwhile, dissolve the sugar in 250ml (8fl oz) water in a saucepan on a medium heat. Increase the temperature and let the syrup boil for 5 minutes to thicken. Add the cucumber purée and remove from the heat and leave to cool.

3 Pour the cucumber syrup into an ice-cream maker and churn following the manufacturer's instructions. (If you do not have one, see the MasterTip, p.347.)

4 Preheat the oven to 200°C (400°F/Gas 6). Lightly grease an 18cm (7in) round, loose-bottomed, fluted flan tin.

5 To make the pastry, put the butter and icing sugar in a food processor and mix for 30 seconds. Slowly add the egg yolks and continue to mix for about 10 seconds or until the egg is blended in. Slowly add the flour, until combined. Wrap the pastry in cling film and leave to chill for 30 minutes.

6 Unwrap the pastry, roll out to a thickness of 5mm (¼in) and line the flan tin. Prick the base and sides of the pastry with a fork and blind bake (see MasterTip, pp.368–9) for 15 minutes, or until golden.

7 Remove the flan from the oven and reduce the temperature to 140°C (275°F/Gas 1).

8 For the curd filling, put all the ingredients in a heavy saucepan and gently simmer, whisking constantly until the mixture begins to thicken. Pour the citrus curd filling into the tart case, return to the oven and bake for 25 minutes or until the filling is firm and the pastry is golden. Leave to chill for 1 hour.

9 Serve a portion of the citrus tart on a large round plate with a scoop of sorbet on the side.

BAKED LIME CHEESECAKE WITH RUM CREAM

Dennice Russell manager turned food writer and 2009 semi-finalist

PREPARATION TIME
25 minutes

COOKING TIME
25 minutes

SERVES 4

8 digestive biscuits, crushed
  (see MasterTip, p.333)
50g (1¾oz) unsalted butter, melted
300g (10oz) mascarpone cheese
100g (3½oz) ricotta cheese
1 tbsp plain flour
100g (3½oz) golden caster sugar
40g (1½oz) desiccated coconut
grated zest and juice of 3 limes, plus
  strands of lime zest, to decorate
2 eggs
1 vanilla pod, scraped

FOR THE RUM CREAM
200ml (7fl oz) double cream
1 tbsp icing sugar
4 tbsp dark rum

1 Preheat the oven to 180°C (350°F/Gas 4). Mix the biscuits into the melted butter. Place four 10cm (4in) chef's rings on a baking sheet and press in the biscuit mix.
2 Put the cheeses, flour, sugar, coconut, lime juice and zest, eggs, and the seeds of the vanilla pod into a bowl and whisk until blended.
3 Pour onto the biscuit base and bake for 20 minutes, until golden. It should be slightly wobbly in the centre when ready. Leave to cool in the oven.
4 To make the rum cream, put the cream, icing sugar, and rum into a bowl and whisk to form soft peaks.
5 Put the cooled cheesecakes onto serving plates and top with quenelles of rum cream (see MasterTip, p.93) and strands of lime.

GREGG WALLACE "Cleansing lime, going into deeper coconut, going into hints of rum. This is the taste of the Caribbean in a cheesecake. The flavour combinations are simply superb."

MASCARPONE CHEESECAKE WITH RASPBERRY COULIS

Julia Paterson client service advisor and 2007 quarter-finalist

PREPARATION TIME
30 minutes

COOKING TIME
45 minutes

SERVES 6–8

150g (5½oz) ginger biscuits, crushed
 (see MasterTip, p.333)
50g (1¾oz) unsalted butter, melted
25g (scant 1oz) candied ginger, chopped
500g (1lb 2oz) mascarpone cheese
100g (3½oz) caster sugar

2 large eggs, separated
grated zest and juice of 2 lemons

FOR THE RASPBERRY COULIS
200g (7oz) raspberries
60g (2oz) icing sugar
juice of 1 lemon

1 Preheat the oven to 180°C (350°F/Gas 4). Grease and line the base of a 20cm (8in) springform cake tin (see MasterTip). Mix the crushed biscuits with the melted butter and candied ginger. Press evenly across the base of the tin and leave to cool (also see MasterTip).

2 In a bowl, beat together the mascarpone, sugar, egg yolks, and lemon zest and juice. In a separate bowl, whisk the egg whites until they are stiff and fold them into the cheese mixture. Spoon on top of the biscuit base and bake for 30 minutes.

3 Reduce the temperature to 160°C (325°F/Gas 3) and cook for 15 minutes more, or until the mixture is set and starting to shrink from the side of the tin. Remove from the oven and cool slightly, then place in the fridge to cool completely before turning out onto a serving dish.

4 To make the coulis, blend the raspberries with the icing sugar and lemon juice. Pass through a sieve and serve with the cheesecake.

MASTER TIP
CHEESECAKES

Cheesecakes are traditionally baked from fresh soft cheeses, cream, eggs, sugar, and spices on a pastry, sponge, or crushed biscuit base. There are also unbaked versions that set by chilling them in the fridge.

1 To line the tin, place a large piece of baking parchment on the base, clip on the outside ring and trim the paper.

2 The best way to spread the biscuit and butter mixture across the tin is with a flexible metal spatula.

RHUBARB AND ORANGE CAKE WITH FLAKED ALMONDS

Rachel Thompson mother of three and 2009 quarter-finalist

400g (14oz) English rhubarb, trimmed and cut into 2cm (¾in) pieces
200g (7oz) golden caster sugar
150g (5½oz) unsalted butter, softened
2 eggs, lightly beaten
75g (2½oz) self-raising flour

½ tsp baking powder
100g (3½oz) ground almonds
grated zest and 2 tbsp juice of 1 small orange
25g (scant 1oz) flaked almonds

PREPARATION TIME
15 minutes, plus standing time

COOKING TIME
45 minutes

MAKES 8–10 SLICES

1 Preheat the oven to 190°C (375°F/Gas 5). Grease and line the base of a 23cm (9in) springform cake tin (see MasterTip, opposite).
2 Place the rhubarb in a bowl and cover with 50g (2½oz) of the sugar. Leave for 30 minutes while you prepare the rest of the cake.
3 With an electric whisk, beat together the remaining sugar and the butter in a bowl, then whisk in the eggs. Using a metal spoon, gently fold in the flour, baking powder, and ground almonds, then stir in the orange zest and juice.
4 Stir the rhubarb and its sugary juices into the cake mixture and spoon into the prepared tin. Place on a baking tray, sprinkle over the flaked almonds, and bake for 25 minutes. Reduce the temperature to 180°C (350°F/Gas 4) and cook for a further 20–25 minutes, or until firm. Allow to cool in the tin for 10 minutes.
5 Serve warm or cold, with softly whipped cream or custard.

RHUBARB AND SHORTBREAD WITH ELDERFLOWER CREAM

Gillian Wylie property developer turned chef and 2007 quarter-finalist

PREPARATION TIME
40 minutes, plus chilling time

COOKING TIME
20 minutes

SERVES 4

4 sticks rhubarb, as pink as possible
200ml (7fl oz) sweet rosé wine
1 vanilla pod, split lengthways
60g (2oz) caster sugar
1 orange

FOR THE SHORTBREAD
125g (4½oz) plain flour
pinch of finely ground sea salt
125g (4½oz) unsalted butter,
  at room temperature

2 tsp vanilla extract
60g (2oz) caster sugar
2 tsp crème fraîche
1 large egg yolk

FOR THE ELDERFLOWER CREAM
150ml (5fl oz) whipping cream
2 tbsp icing sugar
1 tbsp elderflower cordial

1 To make the shortbread, sieve the flour and salt together onto a large board. Cube the butter and put in a mixing bowl with 1 tsp of the vanilla extract, the caster sugar, the crème fraîche, and the egg yolk. Stir briefly until just combined, then make a well in the flour and tip the contents of the mixing bowl into it. With the tips of your fingers, start to draw in the dry flour and continue until the dough has been brought together and the cubes of butter have broken down. Immediately wrap the dough in cling film and put it in the freezer for 30 minutes.

2 Preheat the oven to 180°C (350°F/Gas 4). Line a baking sheet with greaseproof paper and flour the work surface and your rolling pin. Remove the dough from the freezer and, working quickly, roll it out until it is less than 5mm (¼in) thick. You will be using small ramekin dishes to serve this dessert, so choose a pastry cutter the same diameter and cut out as many discs as you can from the dough. Place them on the prepared baking sheet, allowing enough space for them to spread, and put in the oven for 15–20 minutes until light golden brown.

3 Leave to harden up a little on the sheet when you take them out of the oven, then transfer to a wire rack to cool – they will be very fragile, so handle them carefully. When they are cool, sprinkle them with caster sugar.

4 Grease 4 ramekins with butter. Reserve a quarter of 1 rhubarb stick and cut the rest into lengths the same height as the ramekin dishes. Bring the wine to a simmer in a small saucepan and add the split vanilla pod, caster sugar, a strip of orange peel, and a squeeze of orange juice. Stir until the sugar has dissolved. Add the rhubarb and cook for 4–5 minutes or until it is just soft but still holding its shape. Leave to cool a little then stack the stalks vertically into the ramekins, packing them tightly.

5 To make the elderflower cream, place the cream in a mixing bowl, add the icing sugar and elderflower cordial to taste and whip until it is just stiff.

6 Preheat the grill to hot. Slice off 8 strips of the remaining rhubarb stick using a mandolin, sprinkle with caster sugar and caramelize under the grill. Test that the rhubarb in the ramekins is still warm – if not, heat in the oven for a few minutes.

7 To serve, invert your dessert plates onto the ramekin dishes one at a time and turn out the rhubarb so that the sticks stand vertically on the plate. Place a disc of shortbread on top and dress with a quenelle (see MasterTip, p.93) of elderflower cream and a strip of caramelized rhubarb.

ALMOND SHORTBREAD WITH A LAVENDER CREAM AND BALSAMIC STRAWBERRIES, SERVED WITH A STRAWBERRY SAUCE

Angela Kenny administrator turned chef and 2009 semi-finalist

PREPARATION TIME
40 minutes

COOKING TIME
15 minutes

SERVES 4

400g (14oz) strawberries, hulled
  and halved
3 tbsp fresh orange juice
1 tbsp icing sugar
2 tbsp balsamic vinegar
200ml (7fl oz) double cream
1 tbsp lavender sugar

FOR THE SHORTBREAD
200g (7oz) plain flour
175g (6oz) unsalted butter, softened
75g (2½oz) ground almonds
50g (1¾oz) caster sugar
grated zest of 1 lemon

1 Preheat the oven to 160°C (325°F/Gas 3). To make the shortbread, rub the flour, butter, ground almonds, and sugar together until the mixture resembles breadcrumbs in consistency. Add the lemon zest, bring the mixture together into a dough and leave in the fridge for 10–15 minutes.

2 Meanwhile, put the strawberries in a bowl and add the orange juice, icing sugar, and balsamic vinegar. Set aside.

3 Remove the shortbread dough from the fridge and roll out in batches as thinly as possible without it breaking. Cut out circles with an 8cm (3¼in) pastry cutter, place on a greased baking tray, and put in the oven for 10–15 minutes until very lightly golden. Remove and transfer to a wire rack to cool. You should have about 20 biscuits – plenty to put aside in an airtight tin for another day.

4 Whip the double cream with the lavender sugar until it reaches stiff peaks. Remove three-quarters of the strawberries for decoration and blend the rest along with the liquid with a hand blender. Pass through a sieve to remove any pips. Add more balsamic vinegar if needed to taste.

5 Pool the sauce on each serving plate. Lay a shortbread on the plate, top with strawberries then cream and top with another shortbread. Dust with icing sugar to serve.

ANISEED TUILE BISCUITS WITH ROSEWATER ICE CREAM

Nadia Sawalha actress and presenter and 2007 Celebrity champion

150ml (5fl oz) whole milk
150ml (5fl oz) double cream
60g (2oz) blanched ground pistachio nuts (see MasterTip, right)
4 cardamom pods, seeds removed and very finely ground
2 egg yolks
85g (3oz) caster sugar
2 tbsp rosewater
drop of red food colouring (optional)
rose petals, to decorate (optional)

FOR THE ANISEED TUILE BISCUITS
50g (1¾oz) butter, softened
50g (1¾oz) icing sugar, sifted
1 egg, beaten
50g (1¾oz) plain flour
a pinch of fennel seeds, crushed to a fine powder
10g (¼oz) flaked almonds

PREPARATION TIME
30 minutes, plus freezing time

COOKING TIME
10 minutes

SERVES 4

1 Pour the milk, cream, pistachio nuts, and ground cardamom seeds into a saucepan. Bring to just below the boil then set aside to cool slightly.
2 In a mixing bowl, beat the egg yolks and sugar until they are pale, then beat in the boiled cream and milk. Now put it all back into the saucepan and, over a really low heat and stirring constantly, heat for a further 5–6 minutes until it is the consistency of custard. Do not be tempted to increase the heat or the custard will split.
3 Sieve the custard mixture, pressing it through the sieve to extract all the pistachio green colour. Now add the rosewater and food colouring, if using, and put it all into your ice-cream maker and churn until thick and creamy, following the manufacturer's instructions. (If you do not have an ice-cream maker, see the MasterTip, p.347.)
4 To make the aniseed tuile biscuits, cream the butter and sugar together until smooth then beat in the egg and fold in the flour and crushed fennel seeds. Line a baking tray with greaseproof paper and, using a palette knife, carefully spread thin layers of the mixture onto the tray in the rounded tuile shape. Sprinkle with flaked almonds and bake in the oven for 4–5 minutes or until just golden. Remove from the oven and leave the biscuits to cool and firm up a little before transferring to a wire rack to cool completely. Repeat with the remaining mixture to make about 16 biscuits.
5 To serve, scoop the ice cream into serving glasses and serve accompanied by the tuile biscuits and a scattering of rose petals, if using, for decoration.

MASTER TIP

BLANCHED PISTACHIOS

Blanched pistachio nuts have had their shells and outer husk removed and are thus bright green in colour. They can be bought from ethnic supermarkets or some health food shops. If you are using shelled pistachio nuts with their husks on, these need to be removed by soaking in hot water and rubbing off before grinding the nuts to a smooth powder in a small food processor.

INDEX

Page numbers in *italics* indicate MasterTips.

Contributing chefs

Recipes on the following pages were written by Amy Carter, based on the original dishes from the show: 19, 31, 39, 46, 58–60, 62, 74, 88, 94,100, 118, 153, 166, 198–9, 238, 254–5, 267, 270306, 310, 318–19, 320, 352–3, 367

Judges' biographies

John Torode

John Torode is widely known as the straight talking co-presenter and judge of BBC's MasterChef, Celebrity MasterChef and most recently the Junior MasterChef series.

Australian by birth, John is credited as being one of the main players in introducing Australasian food to the UK in the mid-1990s. He opened his popular and well-established restaurant Smiths of Smithfields in 2000 and in 2009 launched The LUXE in Spitalfields Market.

John is also the author of a number of successful cookbooks.

Gregg Wallace

Gregg Wallace is the country's highest profile greengrocer. He is best known for co-presenting and judging MasterChef, MasterChef: The Professionals and Celebrity MasterChef.

Gregg was born in Peckham and began his career selling vegetables at a stand in Covent Garden. He now supplies London restaurants with fresh fruit and vegetables from Secretts Farm in Surrey. His latest business, Wallace & Co., is a café retail project which opens in 2010 in South West London.

Michel Roux Jr

Michel Roux Jr took over the helm at the world famous Michelin-starred Le Gavroche in 1991. Since then, Michel has won numerous awards for his cuisine and has continued to set the standard for classical French fine dining in London.

Prior to Le Gavroche, Michel honed his skills working for master chefs in Paris, Lyon, Hong Kong, and London, spending two years with Alain Chapel and cooking at the Elysée Palace for President Mitterand. He is the presenter and judge of MasterChef: The Professionals.

Monica Galetti

Monica has worked with Michel Roux Jr for six years. She trained in New Zealand and whilst travelling throughout Europe, sent her CV to Le Gavroche. Michel employed her in 2000 and since then she has worked her way up through the kitchen and set up Le Gavroche des Tropiques in Mauritius.

Monica now juggles her time as Senior Sous Chef at Le Gavroche in London with her role in MasterChef: The Professionals and being a mum.

DK Penguin Random House

Senior Editor Alastair Laing
Senior Art Editor Sara Robin
Senior Jacket Creative Nicola Powling
Senior Production Editor Jennifer Murray
Production Editor Ben Marcus
Senior Production Controller Man Fai Lau
Creative Technical Support Sonia Charbonnier
Art Director Peter Luff

Editors Emma Callery, Diana Vowles
Designer Jim Smith

Recipe photography William Reavell
Photography art direction Nicky Collings, Luis Peral
Food stylists Fergal Connolly, Jane Lawrie
Judges' photography Peter Kindersley
Retouching Steve Crozier at Butterfly Creative Services

Cover photography
Front: main image © Jason Ingram; recipes: William Reavell
Back: top left © Jane Sebire; all other images Peter Kindersley

NOTE: The authors and publisher advocate sustainable food choices, and every effort has been made to include only sustainable foods in this book. Food sustainability is, however, a shifting landscape, and so we encourage readers to keep up to date with advice on this subject, so that they are equipped to make their own ethical choices.

First published in Great Britain in 2010
by Dorling Kindersley Limited
80 Strand, London, WC2R 0RL

This paperback edition published in 2015

ISBN 978-0-2411-8708-1
Colour reproduction by AltaImage
Printed and bound in Slovakia

All images © Dorling Kindersley Limited
For further information see:
www.dkimages.com
A WORLD OF IDEAS:
SEE ALL THERE IS TO KNOW

Acknowledgments

Shine would like to thank
David Ambler, Laura Biggs, Angela Braid, Martin Buckett, Amy Carter, Beverly Comboy, Liz Cooney, Laura Edwards, Simone Foots, John Gilbert, Jessica Hannan, Fiona McDonald, Jamie Munro, Linsey Nathan, Claire Nosworthy, David Oudot, Louise Plank, Lyndsey Posner, Franc Roddam, Karen Ross, Gurvinder Singh, and Alan Williams.

A massive thank you must go to all the creative and production teams who have worked on the 12 series of MasterChef that these recipes have been selected from. Without your exceptional talents none of this would have been possible.

...and finally to the hundreds of contestants who have shared their skill, their passion, their ambition, and their cooking dreams with us – you have been an inspiration! Thank you.

Dorling Kindersley would like to thank
Stephanie Jackson for her deal-making; food consultant Jane Milton at Not Just Food and recipe testers Lesley Ball, Helen Barlow, Julie Board, Diane van Bueren, Sue Davie, Maureen Gyles, Jill Joynson, Sarah King, Gill Marczak, Deirdre Taylor, Jill Weatherburn, Amanda Wright, and Sue Wrigley; Amy Carter for recipe writing and advice; Sarah Fassnidge for tireless screengrabbing and quote-noting; Sue Morony for proofreading; Susan Bosanko for indexing; Victoria Allen for props styling; make-up artist Katie Reedman at www.slap.uk.com; stylist Boo Attwood; and Adam Brackenbury for his technical expertise on the jacket.